Managing the Wet Garden

Managing the Wet Garden

Plants That Flourish in Problem Places

JOHN SIMMONS

TIMBER PRESS
Portland · London

All photographs are by the author.
Frontispiece: A natural, clay-lined pond in the author's
garden showing the vigour of *Iris pseudacorus*

Published in 2008 by Timber Press, Inc.

The Haseltine Building   2 The Quadrant
133 S.W. Second Avenue, Suite 450   135 Salusbury Road
Portland, Oregon 97204-3527   London NW6 6RJ
www.timberpress.com   www.timberpress.co.uk

Printed in China
Designed by Susan Applegate

Library of Congress Cataloging-in-Publication Data

Simmons, John, 1937–
    Managing the wet garden: plants that flourish in problem places/John
Simmons.
      p. cm.
    Includes bibliographical references and index.
    ISBN-13: 978-0-88192-900-3
    1. Damp gardens. 2. Aquatic plants. I. Title.
    SB423.3.S56 2008
    635.9'55—dc22

                                    2008002927

A catalog record for this book is also available from the British Library.

CONTENTS

PREFACE & ACKNOWLEDGEMENTS

Water is essential to the survival of all cellular creatures, plants and animals, and for humans it also has a great visual appeal; there is a premium on waterside homes, and rare is the large garden that does not have a water feature. Seemingly for all humans, a raised site, with a view across grass to water, meets our fundamental and inherited habitat expectations. Notwithstanding the appeal of such a landscape, many home gardeners now find themselves with too much water on heavy or low-lying soils, as climate change brings more extreme weather.

In both dry and wet gardens, the pleasures and pangs of gardening are amplified, but my enduring love of water and wetland plants has become a particular enthusiasm over the last twenty-two years as I have enjoyed the challenges presented by my own wet garden. However, in the frequent presentations by the media of gardens and gardening, little is mentioned of the difficulties a naturally wet soil presents. Certainly after decades of gardening on a warm, acid, sandy soil, wet gardening came as a steep learning curve.

A richness of form and flower characterises wet gardens. Whether in the tropics itself, or in a tropical conservatory, the rapid growth of large sculpturally formed leaves and exotic blossoms and scents have always excited my senses. And I still find in my own cool temperate garden a swelling pleasure in a plant growing luxuriantly, be it gunnera, rheum, or lysichiton, or flowering extravagantly, as with the cardiocrinums or Japanese water iris. Water is also a magnet for wildlife.

Wet gardens by their nature will invariably possess water areas, but because so many books detail every aspect of water gardens—from pool construction to fish care and waterlilies—I have focused

OPPOSITE A seventeenth-century *tsukubai* (stone washbasin) at the Ryoan-ji Temple, Kyoto, inscribed "I learn only to be contented"

this work on plants for wet soil. I have also taken a fairly catholic gardener's view of the definition of a wet soil for, even in a small area, changes of level and drainage can greatly modify the amount of available soil moisture. Thus, while keeping wet soil as my central theme, I have also briefly included water and bog plants and, in the other direction, mentioned plants for moist soils, particularly moist woodland. Inevitably there are many more plants that can grow on wet soils than can be considered here. The range of wet woodland plants has therefore been limited, and carnivorous and many tender plants had to be left out. I have, however, assumed that owners and managers of wet gardens will wish to grow a good range of plants and will thus require to know what will require greater attention on a wet soil as well as what grows easily.

My work with botanical collections has imbued me with the constant wish of finding ways to extend the range of plants grown in a garden, either by modifying the given microclimate or through learning about any particular plant's habitat tolerance. Fortunately for gardeners, many plants have considerable environmental flexibility and can withstand both wet and dry soils, and with climate change many more plants once considered tender are now appearing in cool temperate gardens. The hardiness notebooks of my earlier gardening years have had to be discarded: it really is now the case of trying out new plants to see how they fare, rather than following old rules.

Where hardiness in general is mentioned for any particular species, this relates to USDA Zone 8 (and corresponding regions of Britain, including my own garden; see Huxley 1992), where average minimum winter temperatures are −12 to −7°C (10 to 20°F). Where specific hardiness zones are given, this indicates the lowest temperatures at which the plant should thrive. These zone definitions are very broad-brush, and I err on the side of caution: so many factors are involved, from natural genotypic variation in a species, to latitude and levels of exposure to infrared and ultraviolet light, which can increase hardiness of tissue.

In compiling this book I first reviewed the plants by family, since related plants frequently have needs in common. Systematic studies ever advance the understanding of plant relationships, and taxonomic changes are frequent; I have thus worked from the accepted, if conservative, definitions (Brummitt 1992; Stace 1997). In particular, I am very grateful to James Cullen, whose advice and help, as well as his superbly edited book, guided my approach to genera and plant families (Cullen 2001). For a considered consensus view of current taxonomy and nomenclature, I have followed the excellent and widely available *RHS Plant Finder*, compiled annually by the Royal Horticultural Society (see the bibliography for these and other helpful general sources).

Molecular systematic studies are currently having a profound effect on the understanding of plant relationships, and usually with such advances, the perspective of time and more research will crystallise a new understanding (for some of the earlier findings related to garden plants, see Phillips and Rix 2002). I am very conscious that the given geographic range for any species is just a rough guide because, other than with restricted endemics, a plant's known range is frequently extended or otherwise changed following field work, and the conclusion of systematic studies also often requires a redefinition of range for a revised taxon.

The photographs in this book are my own; many were taken in my own garden, others in gardens I have worked in or visited. I am grateful to the many with whom I have worked for their enduring association and help, and I am also ever appreciative of those many committed people who open their gardens to the admiring gaze of visitors. I am very grateful for Allen Patterson's general advice and John Woodhams's advice on ferns. My particular thanks go to my wife, Valerie, for her patience and help in this book's overall preparation.

My hope is that this book will at least bring some wider enlightenment to its subject, transforming what might otherwise be seen as problem sites and soils into rewarding gardens.

CHAPTER 1

The wet garden environment

THE BALANCED GARDEN

The term "wet soil" is open to wide definition. For this book it means "damp" most of the time, and "very wet" on occasion—never "saturated." Few plants can survive saturated soil, where standing water occurs at surface level for long periods; bog plants or raised beds are the only options for planting such a site.

All gardening is a challenge: the wish to create, to impose a form and structure within which desired plants may be grown. However, and despite all the extra demands, I will always choose a wet garden over a dry—for the lushness of growth and range of plants, cool green lawns in summer, the reflective appeal of water and the wildlife it attracts. But bear in mind: the overall maintenance requirement of a dry garden is far less than for an equivalent area of wet garden.

Accepting that wet gardens are a commitment, their successful management needs a degree of self-discipline. As a garden owner and manager I am acutely aware of the amounts of labour, materials, and machine time needed to properly care for any garden and its features; indeed, this tends to constrain me, since I never wish to develop something that cannot be maintained. Those with grand visions often, and perhaps necessarily, have a low regard for the maintenance consequences of their creations, but the average home gardener must address the scale of commitment. The greater the aspiration, the greater the maintenance challenges!

Great personal commitment to a garden rarely survives for more than one generation; most often it recedes with the passing of the inspired manager or owner, and a garden's decline can be rapid.

OPPOSITE The immaculate waterside plantings at Longstock Park in Hampshire

11

Sometimes the creation proves too much for the creator during their lifetime, necessitating a move away from the created burden. Achieving the right balance between creation and maintenance is thus all the more critical for a wet garden.

At the outset one has to have a concept of how much personal time and resources are needed to maintain a garden to an individual's standard, remembering that even a small vegetable or alpine garden, maintained intensively, can be very time demanding. Also these days, with many private gardens opening to visitors for charitable or other purposes, visitor expectation can put intense pressure on the garden owner, leading to a frenzy of planting and tidying.

For a public garden there is always the unspoken expectation for it to be as good as possible, but for the private garden I usually advise owners that it must first give them pleasure, secondly reflect their interests, and thirdly be developed only to the extent and standard that they can resource without stress.

There is little doubt that the well-balanced garden can offer its owners great satisfaction and provide the ingredients that contribute to a long and healthy life. Working with the living world is therapeutic, calming, satisfying, and provides natural exercise that can be age-adjusted. And then there is the delight of wildlife, from birds to butterflies, and the opportunity to express latent artistic skills, in colour or form of planting and sculpture—a garden can develop all manner of interests and talents.

To maintain a high standard, a mixed garden of one hectare (just over two acres) which has water, bog, herbaceous beds, trees, and mown grass is going to require the almost full-time commitment of one person.

Lawn grass on wet soil requires a weekly cut for much of the year, and herbaceous beds need more staking and a fortnightly weed through the growing season. On a dry soil this can be left to a monthly check, and also on a dry soil a hoe can be used with the weeds left to dry and shrivel, whereas on a wet soil they must be raked off, or otherwise removed, to prevent their recovery. In just two weeks in summer on wet soil, hitherto small, unnoticed weed seedlings of fast-growing species such as annual epilobiums and sow-thistles can rapidly extend their growth, to flower and start to seed. Trees and shrubs too need more pruning, and all this extra growth results in more green matter recycling; however, obvious gains include greener lawns and much less need for watering.

Other factors may weigh in, such as the possibility of an occasional flood and the need for drainage, and on a light soil, rare is the day when some garden work cannot be undertaken. Wet weather is also more limiting on wet soils in winter. Thus with wet gardens there is a much greater need to consider the area to be maintained in relation to the labour and other resources available.

Large-scale lakes, if created naturally on an impervious subsoil, can (other than the occasional but considerable expense of removing the accumulated silt) be reasonably economically maintained. Much time, however, can be diverted into managing fish stocks, wild fowl, or waterlilies, and marginal plantings that present control problems. Similarly, bankside plantings need regular care. The rampant summer growth of water and bog plants means that failure to balance maintenance requirements with resources is quickly noticed; such gardens can get out of control in just a few weeks, and they usually need attention every week.

Thus when developing any feature its scale has to be considered in relation to maintenance. However with large and deep lakes, where depth prevents marginal plants spreading across the lake, an increase of water area does not proportionately increase labour commitment.

INDICATORS OF A WET SITE

Native flora

The natural floristic composition of any site has long been used as a guide to its underlying soil, and those searching in remote regions for valuable minerals are often guided by floral surveys. For gardens, the occurrence of plants known to grow on wet soil is similarly useful, and for most parts of the world, identifying plants growing on a potential garden site gives a good indication of its nature. To help further in this, many floras usefully add the ecological preferences of plants (but remember that a winter-wet site might be very dry at other times).

Long years back, my colleague and respected mentor George Brown, then an assistant curator of the arboretum at the Royal Botanic Gardens, Kew, in London, caused me to look more carefully at the flora as an indicator of soil conditions. We were looking to increase natural wildlife in the Queen's Cottage Grounds there and had concluded that a small pond would be a valuable addition. Kew is

formed on some 20 m (67 ft.) depth of sand and gravel resultant from river changes and deposits during the glacial periods. More impervious silt layers occur where the adjacent river Thames has historically changed the course of its meanderings, and natural indicators of this underlying, moister layer, such as hemp agrimony (*Eupatorium cannabinum*), guided our decision to add a pond.

For each country, certain plants indicate wetland. For example, in both Britain and the United States, marsh marigold (*Caltha palustris*) and cuckooflower (*Cardamine pratensis*) are wetland indicator species.

Garden flora

A look around other gardens in the neighbourhood also helps indicate what might grow well in the garden under consideration; however, looking for indicator plants is more difficult because of the wide environmental tolerance of many garden plants. A preponderance of ferns and primulas suggests moist conditions, as does the presence of mosses, and the luxuriant growth of plants (*Brunnera macrophylla*, for example) that flag on dry soils. On seeing a garden for the first time, I take in the range of plants grown, noting what is growing well and what poorly. From this I learn more about the requirements of different plants. But while the comparative size and vigour of plants gives a clue to the wetness or dryness of soils, they are not, as this book describes, the only factors affecting performance.

Garden weeds can give even better clues; giant hogweed (*Heracleum mantegazzianum*) or butterburs (*Petasites*), for example, can be seen spreading along riparian areas. Horsetails (*Equisetum*) are very good indicators of wet soil; the worry for gardeners, of course, is their invasiveness, and their tough resistance to any form of control. In wet areas, horsetails can spread readily from their fine airborne spores, or come unseen from their underground rhizome-like stems.

GARDEN MICROCLIMATES

Light and shade

By their situation, surface aquatics are normally exposed to very high light levels, with optimal, direct and reflected solar energy. Add to this all the water they could require, often supplemented by a plentiful nutrient supply, and their growth can be exponential. Most owners of pools will be familiar with the summer growth explosion of aquatic plants, and algal blooms.

The wet garden too has similar "advantages" in warm conditions. While winter wet can be devastating to many plants, warmth and moisture in summer will cause rapid growth of both garden plants and weeds.

For many shade-requiring plants, extra moisture is an advantage, because it is then possible to grow such plants in moist but more open sites. Shade is a relative concept, and judging the right level of shade is a complex evaluation. When using living systems, such as woodland, to create shade, this judgement becomes quite difficult because the trees are dynamic and ever changing. Too much shade, and growth and flowering is suppressed; too little, and delicate woodland plants shrivel and weeds compete. On wet soils, this drying by tree roots offers some advantage to plants that expect a summer rest (bulbous iris, cyclamen, snowdrops), but others (vinca, geraniums, hellebores, violas, primroses, cowslips) can also prosper.

For woodland gardens the type of tree used to form the main canopy is important. In Britain, among deciduous trees, *Quercus robur* (pedunculate oak) is the preferred species; its roots are not too competitive, and it allows in a reasonable level of light for such plants as rhododendrons, whereas, for example, denser-canopied, surface-rooted trees limit what can be grown beneath them.

OPPOSITE TOP *Eupatorium cannabinum*
OPPOSITE BOTTOM *Caltha palustris*
BELOW Azaleas under oaks, Ray Wood, Yorkshire

The ash *Fraxinus excelsior* is not too competitive and fairly wet-soil-tolerant, but produces an abundance of seedlings; sweet chestnut (*Castanea sativa*) is really too competitive for plants like rhododendron. *Fagus sylvatica* can grow on heavy soil, although it too is fairly competitive: precious little grows well underneath a mature beech, with the exception of snowdrops, bluebells, and other such bulbs.

Crown density must be considered as well as tree type; it is necessary to check shade trees each year to see if their crowns need lifting, or individual trees need removing. A traditional approach in creating a woodland garden has been to plant birch (*Betula pendula*), to give quick shade and a light woodland appearance, but also to interplant these with oak for long-term cover. This assumes some regular thinning, first of the birch (after about twenty-five years), and then the oaks, as they increase in size and girth. Many betulas are unstable on wet soils, however; *B. alleghaniensis* is a possibility, and though more densely foliaged, some of the quick-growing wet-soil-tolerant maples such as *Acer rubrum* can be useful as starters.

Evergreens are often added to act as windscreens for tender plants within a deciduous wood. If flowering trees are to be included in woodland, it will be necessary to create open glades, with clear sky overhead, for the trees to grow and flower properly. How often does

THE WET GARDEN ENVIRONMENT

one see a tree growing out at forty-five degrees from beneath the canopy of a larger tree, in its attempt to reach light?

Many dark-leaved, tropical and subtropical evergreens are adapted to the low light conditions within a moist forest, in part because at lower latitudes, with naturally higher light levels, more light penetrates. Given very light shade, moisture, and deep leaf mould, the range of plants that can be grown is extensive. My favourites are the yellow shuttlecock-flowered *Kirengeshoma palmata*, an herbaceous perennial from northeastern Asia; the shorter-lived Himalayan and Sino-Himalayan meconopsis (*Meconopsis horridula*, or the challenging golden *M. integrifolia*); and smaller trees and shrubs that need shelter in temperate regions, such as the fiery-flowered *Embothrium coccineum* from Chile.

Screens

Screen trees are often planted to hide unsightly views or to give privacy, and in large gardens they are of importance as windbreaks. As they develop over years, they offer additional benefits: the microclimate they create allows sheltered plants to grow better, and the range grown to be increased.

In towns, buildings provide warmth and shelter (that is, excepting tall buildings, which create their own vortex winds), but few town gardens can accommodate large trees. Within a country garden, the warmth and shelter given by surrounding trees and hedges not only makes the garden more comfortable for its owner, but even plants such as roses and bracteate poppies respond by being more vigorous and producing more and larger flowers.

Where room allows, a mixed screen of native deciduous trees and shrubs can prove useful from many viewpoints. Such plants establish quickly, benefit wildlife, and integrate an area into the surrounding countryside. The screen mix for a moist soil might include cherries, wild apple, field or hedge maple (*Acer campestre*), alder, and some common whitebeam (*Sorbus aria*), with a few larger forest trees such as oak and an edging of fruiting plants such as the shrubby guelder-rose (*Viburnum opulus*), the dogwood *Cornus sanguinea*, and the spindle *Euonymus europaeus*. Most of these small trees can cope with wet soil; a more saturated soil might reduce the list to alder, guelder-rose, dogwood, and oak. Many trees are not wind secure on a wet soil, but such a screen can start to become effective within a decade.

Trees on wet soil grow more quickly but are susceptible to disease problems, particularly after pruning. Thus I should not plant pop-

Viburnum opulus in fruit

lar (*Populus*) and willow (*Salix*), but use alder (*Alnus*) where larger, quick-growing trees are required. Alder buckthorn (*Rhamnus frangula*) can be a useful smaller tree on wet soils, but for shrubby screens in gardens on wet soil, sorbaria grows well and needs minimal care. The only problem is in having to cut back and remove its suckers if it spreads too far.

Where denser screening is required, as say to protect tender plants, a matrix of evergreens can be added within the deciduous tree plantings. These can be large-growing conifers, such as cryptomerias, or smaller-growing yews and hollies; bamboos are also much used.

On an open site, a solid line of evergreens may cause the wind to just hop over the top, and quickly resume its previous velocity, but a mixed planting, including deciduous trees, tends to filter and slow the wind.

A close initial planting for a screen (2 × 3 m, 6.6 × 10 ft.) is frequently used, and closer for any added shrubs, to achieve the quick effect required, with the assumption of progressive thinning. The depth of the screen will depend upon the space available and the area to be screened. For a large arboretum, a 30–50 m (100–164 ft.) wide screen might be used if, as in the northern hemisphere, it is necessary to protect plants from cold northerly winds. For smaller gardens, screen trees must be carefully selected for their likely spread and effect.

Hedges

Regularly clipped hedges are similarly valued, not only for screening and shelter but, most importantly, to give structure to formal garden areas. Sadly, "frequently used, often abused" is the common fate of hedges, for while they are so intrinsic to the design and function of a garden, they sometimes receive little thought or care. Often, and particularly for boundaries, easy to propagate, quick-growing plants are chosen, and these then go on to cause problems for both owner and neighbour. The ubiquitous Leyland cypress (×*Cupressocyparis leylandii*), which makes an excessively large hedge, has sparked many conflicts between neighbours—though its cut tops can make useful Christmas trees! It has a use in the short term but needs frequent clipping and soon exceeds its purpose; not much else can grow close to its competitive roots. Similarly the evergreen Lawson's cypress (*Chamaecyparis lawsoniana*) grows rapidly on moist soils, and ultimately becomes a very large tree.

Among other evergreens, thujas grow well on wet soils and make

THE WET GARDEN ENVIRONMENT

good hedge plants. Generally, though, it is better to select a slow-growing, more durable plant that needs only an annual clip. For this, *Taxus baccata* is undoubtedly the best subject since it is very tolerant of clipping and pruning, and yew hedges can last for two to three centuries. Though slow at first, young nursery plants can form a 1.2–1.5 m (4–5 ft.) hedge within ten years, and yew grows well on my wet soil. Waterlogging does cause problems with yew hedges, however; where it occurs, and individual plants die, this can permanently spoil the uniform appearance of the hedge. With yews, an early sign of waterlogged roots is the bronzing of foliage, from which the plant may recover (or, if the soil stays saturated, die).

For a smaller formal evergreen hedge, the widely used *Buxus sempervirens* has much to commend it, and certainly box survives well on my wet soil, but several diseases, including box blight, are becoming widespread problems. Escallonias form larger evergreen hedges on moist to wet soil; and of the quicker-growing deciduous plants, beech and hornbeam are very useful, particularly as their clipped shoots hold their brown autumn leaves over winter.

Regular clipping has a bonsai-like effect on trees and shrubs. With yew hedges, the main stems of plants are noticeably of a small diameter for their age. Spacing in the rows will vary with plant size: 45–65 cm (18–24 in.) for most subjects, 15–30 cm (6–12 in.) for small-growing plants, such as box.

For boundary hedges in the countryside, mixed native small trees and shrubs benefit wildlife. On wet soil, emphasis can be given to dogwoods (*Cornus alba*, *C. sanguinea*) and guelder-rose (*Viburnum opulus*); if not too wet, field maple, spindle, and hawthorn will grow well.

Walls

In colder climates, walls offer shelter and, collecting the sun's heat through the day, act as heat storage radiators at night. Each aspect—north, south, east, or west—offers a different microclimate for plants, and a heated wall can be used to good effect for tender plants. The following comments on aspect relate to the northern hemisphere; these, of course, are reversed in the southern hemisphere.

Over many years I have found that north sides of walls or buildings, contrary to expectation, often provide better sites for tender plants. This is because low-angled winter sun does not directly reach anything planted there, and thus when plants are frozen, thawing is a more gentle, less damaging process; for example, *Hydrangea quercifolia*, which has a southern distribution in eastern North America, can make a large, vigorous, free-flowering shrub if set against a north wall. For another north-wall example, on heavy wet soil, I have been encouraged to watch the leaves of the Canary Island *Euphorbia mellifera*, drooping at −10°C (14°F) in winter, recovering without damage after several such frosts.

A south-facing wall on a moist soil creates a greenhouse-like effect. The warmth and moisture produce abundant growth. Roses, for example, will grow and flower magnificently, though they will be a little more susceptible to disease. Such a site is also perfect for large tender bulbs, such as *Crinum ×powellii*.

In contrast, beds against north walls create wonderful locations for ferns of every description. For climbers, obvious candidates such as *Hydrangea anomala* subsp. *petiolaris* and parthenocissuses do well, as (less expectedly) does *Jasminum officinale*, which ranges from the Caucasus through the Himalayas to China (just mentionably, *J. nudiflorum* seems to flower best on an east wall). Camellias are very shade tolerant, and, against a north wall, their slightly later flowering reduces frost damage to their blossoms. For ground cover, hostas and primulas are obvious choices, but almost any moist woodland plant will grow well.

East and west faces on wet soils seem a compromise between the interest that can be created on both north and south faces. There are some of the south wall's advantages but, comparatively, growth rate and flowering are reduced. Roses grow but are not so floriferous; bamboos do well, as do other large grasses such as miscanthus. Hellebores are happy in such situations, as are astilbes and the large ligularias.

Frost hollows

Like water, cold air runs down slopes, accumulating in valley bottoms or where its flow is blocked by a hedge or wall. Thus, the upper part of a north-facing hillside offers great advantage for otherwise tender plants.

For young trees, late spring frosts are much more damaging than winter's cold, and since wet gardens are often in frost hollows, this is a concern. My own garden is no exception; I sometimes grow trees in containers for three or four years before planting, until they have a sufficiently woody stem. Late frost damage can adversely affect many common tree seedlings, such as cherry, davidia, magnolia, and cercidiphyllum. As I prefer to plant out young trees, I have been caught out many times with young seedlings.

Soil temperature

Heavy wet soils warm up more slowly in spring. An apocryphal tale suggests that, in the past, farm workers lowered their trousers and sat on the soil to check if it was warm enough to sow seed. A bare elbow might have worked as well with less discomfort, but the point is that on wet soils, in cold damp conditions, early sown seed—be it of grass, or vegetables, or summer flowers—will rot and fail to germinate. Sowing should wait until the soil has warmed.

In shaded, colder parts of the wet garden, summer may be well advanced before natural germination commences, and then—whether weeds or self-sown garden plants—all come in a rush. Plants that will survive wet soils in warm conditions are often susceptible to damage by cold wet conditions.

Seasonally dry conditions and summer wilt

When droughts occur, moisture-loving plants are quick to show stress. Nothing is sadder than seeing a drooping gunnera whose giant leaf stems are no longer rigid enough to hold up its great green umbrellas. The amount of permanent damage done to plants relates to many variables and particularly to season. If dry in spring, new growth is slowed and young shoots may be damaged. Autumn is less damaging in that plants can close down earlier; trees can shed leaves prematurely, and herbaceous stems dry off. High summer drought is the most damaging, but some useful lessons can be learned when drought strikes in this season. In particular, drought at this time allows a gardener to analyse a wet site: the whereabouts of the driest and wettest parts of the garden are clear. There is invariably a surprising variation in the rate of drying, even in a small area, depending on the nature of the underlying soils. Impeded drainage, through compaction or impervious layers, will give a site that appears very wet in winter but will be the first place to dry out in summer. With a good deep soil, some shade, shelter, and mulch, plants can happily live through extended dry periods.

The most vulnerable plants are those in their first year or sometimes second year of growth following planting or transplanting. There is a marked difference between plants that have been in their site for a full year and those that are in their first summer: the latter are the ones to target for watering. Quick-growing herbaceous subjects will soon develop sufficiently extensive root systems to cope with dry periods, but young trees and shrubs, particularly if they were previously pot grown, are the most vulnerable.

The very early-season leaves of *Sorbus caloneura*, from Guizhou, western China, are hardy in the author's frost hollow.

I tend to the view that, once started, summer watering has to continue. Watering seems to encourage surface rooting, rather than allowing the roots to search deep for moisture. Thus I do not water other than for new plantings. The exception is where plants are in the root zone of mature trees. Most plants growing within a large tree's root zone quickly wilt in a drought; it is hardly worth troubling to set plants like philadelphus or hydrangea in such situations.

Mulching obviously helps the retention of soil moisture, and, while this practise has everything to recommend its use on a dry soil, some caution is needed on a wet soil. That is, unless the bed is raised, mulch will keep the soil too wet at times other than when there is a drought.

In contrast, excessive rain in summer that fully saturates the soil for long periods can be just as damaging to roots, with the plants behaving as when affected by drought (yellowing leaves, premature leaf fall). Further, if the damaged roots have allowed fungal entry, wilting and death may ensue.

Soil acidity and alkalinity

Using wet soil tolerance as the primary definition for this book tends inevitably to mask many of the other factors involved in planting successes or failures, not least soil pH. Many published guides address what does well and what badly in a soil of either extreme, but, when faced with gardens on wet acid or alkaline soils—both of which in themselves are very variable, their effects on plants changing with soil type and climate—finding what succeeds or fails from a wide palette of plants becomes a challenge. The annual field poppy (*Papaver rhoeas*), for example, is noted for its abundant display on chalky soils but fails on wet soil, whereas the perennial *P. bracteatum* grows well on heavy soils. Both the field and the bracteate poppies grow better on warm soil, and both can also cope with light acid soils; however, while the latter will grow reasonably well on alkaline soils, its growth rate and spread are curtailed. Lime-loving genera (*Alchemilla*, *Geranium*), which can prosper on a very moist soil, regenerate more abundantly on an alkaline soil, and others (*Aquilegia*, *Helianthus*) behave similarly.

Among shrubs, the red and white dogwoods, elders, roses, and viburnums can cope with both wet and drier alkaline soils; and though using raised planting beds allows clematis to be grown on wet soils, their growth and flowering are considerably more prolific on a drier alkaline soil.

With such a complex situation, the sensible approach must be to try out new introductions and then, after making a judgement on their performance, either accept, and possibly increase their number, or write off any particular plant. Monitor pH regularly and make any necessary adjustments with annual dressings (lime raises pH, flowers of sulphur lowers pH).

WATER SOURCES

Water supply and quality

Natural watersheds that retain their covering of forest release water slowly; cleared areas and hard surfaces quickly cause floods and soil erosion. And sadly in our environmentally degraded world, extreme weather patterns—and consequent flood or drought—are becoming more frequent.

When looking at stream-fed water features, it is easy to forget how quickly a small, seemingly benign stream can become a damaging torrent after heavy rain. Provision for the occasional, excessive water flow or flood needs careful consideration. Flooding invariably carries debris that can quickly block overflows and drainage pipes.

Where stream-fed, large water areas can be kept at a constant level, but, and depending on the area of catchment, surface drainage ponds can dry out. Such "seasonal" ponds are useful for amphibians (predatory fish and waterfowl do not become established); dry periods also offer the opportunity to clear out the pond. A good, deep pond, by contrast, can usefully supply water for irrigation; however, the water may need to be kept aerated, and the pump inlet filters arranged so that the pump does not suck in too much filter-blocking debris.

Where water runs off from an area of raised or sloping land, it can be channelled to the pool via ditches. At first thought, ditches are unattractive features but they are very functional, easy to keep clear, and can work well, particularly in naturally landscaped areas, and the ditch sides can be gently sloped for mowing rather than sheer. For those who are averse to ditches, drainage pipes work just as well.

Other factors affecting natural water supplies for large water areas include the increase in fertiliser and other chemical residue in runoff from agricultural land or suburban lawns that leads to abundant algal growth. Perversely, in the case of my own large pond, most field runoff comes via a road that has its own contaminants, including winter salt, the effect of which is to kill off any fish. There is thus an advantage to first running such water through a reed bed to help remove sediments and contaminants.

Though only minimal irrigation is required for wet gardens, watering newly planted stock, in times of summer drought, and container plants creates a demand. In very wet areas, wells are worth considering, and certainly water from roofs should be caught. A large tank is often a good investment. Not many years ago, all of Kew's greenhouses, even small propagation houses, had large linked underground tanks, though this originally stemmed from a requirement for soft water for the irrigation of most tropical and subtropical plants.

Rainwater is naturally mildly acidic through the absorption of atmospheric carbon dioxide, but regular measuring shows that the pH of rainwater varies considerably and becomes more acid through the absorption of atmospheric pollutants. Hard water from chalk or limestone sources has to be used with caution and may be treated by either deionisation or acid injection. Orchids, ferns, and carnivorous plants generally are very sensitive to water with a high pH, though some have a wide tolerance. Most aquatic plants are adapted to acid water, fewer to alkaline water. With water features, the need to shift pH usually relates to algal control: a high or low pH tends to inhibit algae.

Whatever else comes of climate change, moderation has been lost, and we are having, and will have, more frequent extremes of weather, be it rain, sun, drought, snow, or wind. Other changes have particularly affected the rural landscape. Over centuries, ditches were cleared each winter and drainage carefully maintained. On wet land, permanent field drains made of clay tiles laid in herringbone fashion fed the ditches and the ditches fed streams, and there was a general awareness of the need to care for water flow. Sadly this understanding has often been lost, along with the maintenance of drains and ditches, and flooding is a common consequence.

Of course, rainfall frequency varies significantly. Where I garden, I have been aware of very wet winters occurring at least once every fifteen years. Between the extreme years—and although I should know better—I am lulled into a false sense of security, becoming more adventurous with planting, only to be frustrated by the occasional very wet year that kills off newly acquired treasures.

Drainage

On a heavy soil, water will collect in any hollow. It pays to be observant of the natural gradients within a garden; the surface flow of water is greatly assisted by grading and levelling (or just filling and smoothing out) shallow hollows, so that heavy rain flows away naturally. For difficult sites, piping or ditching may be the only solution, though the permeability of the topsoil may also need attention.

In my own garden I have learned to pay particular attention to drainage and water flow. For the past century or more it was pastureland for carriage ponies, and buried within are aged earthenware land drains, which I have restored to use. I am uncertain of their age, but in the infill debris above the drains I have found shards of seventeenth-century Bellarmine jars. I have supplemented this system by using slit-sided flexible pipes to drain particular hollows; this piping, 80 mm (3.15 in.) in diameter, comes in lengths of 30 m (100 ft.), is reasonably effective, and easy to install.

Impeded lawn drainage

Pipes can silt up quickly, so where large piped flows are involved it is sensible to form access points as inspection chambers or manholes, particularly where the pipe direction, connection, or gradient changes, so that pipes can be cleaned with rods or by jetting. The pipes are laid in a herringbone fashion, but on a wet soil the catchment ditch, or culvert, needs to be of a good size. A ditch on heavy land may need to be 1.2 m (4 ft.) deep or more, depending on the length of run.

The need for drainage relates to the underlying geology, but an impervious layer of clay may be sought when a natural pool is required, and inevitably clay soils give rise to most wet gardens. Where loams are formed from fine glacial loess, any surface depression can soon fill with rain.

Hard pans need to be broken if plants are to be grown. Compacted pans can occur on many soils, not least just below the plough depth on regularly ploughed fields. This latter can usually be remedied by deeper ploughing with a mole plough. In part of my garden, quite close to the surface, I have a 20 cm (8 in.) deep plate of impervious gravel bound by ferrous deposits. It is tougher than concrete and can only be broken up by powerful machines or explosives! Where it has been broken, springs arise. Trees planted above it are unstable because roots have to stay on the surface, and while the soil above this plate stays very wet in winter, it is equally fast drying in summer.

CHAPTER 2

Forming a wet garden

ELEMENTS OF A WET GARDEN

Design considerations

When presented with any garden project, a designer will want to know what the customer's aims are, and the balance of plantings to hard landscape required, as well as the available budget. With a large budget, much is possible, but I often find that with a wet garden, ideas can quickly become shredded by the thought of ongoing maintenance costs.

For most a garden is a sanctuary. Any views out should be to something that is pleasing and relaxing to the eye. Town and urban gardeners may need to green-clad ugly buildings with climbers, and selectively enclose or focus views using small trees or shrubby evergreens. Hard landscape surfaces have gained favour in urban gardens, and I suppose with the work involved in mowing and weeding, this is understandable. Certainly in wet gardens, hard all-weather surfaces have significant advantages.

Designers and plants people have very different approaches to the selection of plants. With both groups their gardens are invariably as idiosyncratic and individual as their owners. For the plant enthusiast, every square foot of the garden appears as a place for another plant, while for many designers, less is generally more.

For small gardens much can be learned from Japanese gardens. In Japan, where private urban gardens are very small and a window box sometimes has to suffice, the maximum use is made of small spaces. Gardens are uncluttered, and their deceptively simple appearance and appeal comes from an underlying, complex, artistic thought and historical tradition.

The palette of plants used in classic Japanese gardens is, by European standards, somewhat restricted. Conifers, particularly pines and cryptomerias, are frequently featured and regularly pruned or clipped to achieve specific effects. I was once fascinated to watch neatly uniformed imperial garden gardeners using wire-noose-tipped bamboo canes to remove all the new season's young upright shoots from the branches of large pines, so as to retain the trees tabular form; the white-gloved gardeners placed the removed shoots on a small canvas stretcher and carefully carried the load of clippings out of the garden. This memorable image is for me very suggestive of the time and diligent care needed to properly maintain Japanese gardens.

Many plants, particularly azaleas, are tightly clipped and their form then gives emphasis to a free-flowering cherry or sasanqua camellia. The natural spirits of the garden extend to rock and water, and mosses and ground cover are skilfully used. Water is often used in Japanese gardens, frequently in the form of calm mirrored pools.

I find the gardens of artists invariably of interest for their original ideas and interpretation. William Morris (1834–1896) had a theme for gardens that echoed his fabric designs: floral abundance within formal bounds. Gertrude Jekyll (1843–1932) had an artist's way with colour and a vital concern to ensure the "joins" between formal and informal were well made. The impressive Parque del Este, in Caracas, Venezuela, landscaped by Roberto Burle Marx (1909–1994), appeals

Tabuliform pines enhance the tranquil beauty of the garden of the Katsura Imperial Villa, Japan.

to me as a symphony in the use of native South American plants; my lasting memory of my visit there is of the renowned designer's vision in using plants as architectural elements. More recently, in the small London garden of a botanical artist, each plant was carefully placed with the artist's connecting links to its source, be it person, place, or painting; yet the whole garden had a pleasing harmony. In so many subtle ways, every garden reflects something of the character of its creator.

The challenge of wet gardens is in harmonising the strong architectural character of often large-leaved herbs, and the summer vigour of plants in what can be an ethereal chorus of green tones.

Increasing planting options

When presented with a wet soil, while a rethink of the normal practises used on well-drained sites is necessary, it is rarely an absolute rethink. Even the smallest site will usually possess changes of level, however slight, which will make some parts drier than others. Soil level changes can be subtle and are often masked by plants or long grass, only showing after heavy rain that leaves pools of surface water.

Where a wider range than just bog plants is required, the following actions may be considered.

- Study the site carefully over the first full year, looking for and noting high and low points, and how surface water flows or holds. Remember too that extremely wet and extremely dry years will occur—more frequently now, with climate change.
- Use the soil from any excavations, such as when making paths, bogs, or ponds, to fill and grade small hollows, and or to raise levels in other areas.
- For very wet areas consider the use of drainage pipes or ditches to remove excess water. Also planting such trees as alders or taxodiums will dry out the soil.
- For smaller plants and bulbs needing good drainage, form raised beds or plant within the root zone of established trees where drier summer conditions will prevail.
- Use temporary plantings, such as summer bedding, to add colour and interest. Many more plants tolerate wet soils given warm conditions.
- Grow in containers any favourite plants that need drier conditions.

Paths

Keeping paths walkable in wet areas takes extra effort, and, for very wet areas and bogs, one option is a raised boardwalk. However, such raised walks are expensive, as they need to be made from very durable timber, and are time consuming to make. On wet ground, I have found that for light traffic (that is, foot, mower, or wheelbarrow traffic), it is possible to form a stable footpath by just lying in hardcore and stone to a depth of about 25 cm (10 in.) and binding the surface with gravel or chippings. The path needs a camber and to be slightly (2.5–3 cm, 1–1.2 in.) above the surrounding soil. Wood chippings or gravel on their own simply become trodden into the boggy soil and have no benefit. Also, wood chippings and bark break down quickly on wet soil, within one to two years, and then absorb more water, making matters worse.

Mown paths through long grass

Wet soils move—they expand when wet and shrink when dry—so be prepared for any solid paving to move and break its sealed joints, allowing the entry of weeds. For load-bearing paths on wet sites, full foundations and drainage are essential. Where a path crosses a slope, catchment points or a ditch will be needed, with pipes to carry the flow on under the path, so as to prevent the path washing away in heavy rain.

Most private gardens will use grass paths or rides. For these, the grass path is mown shorter than the surrounding herbage. Ideally such paths should be slightly raised by the addition of sand and gravel as a top dressing on heavy soils, through which the grass can grow and establish. For light use it may be sufficient just to level out the hollows with sand, or, less desirably, garden soil. A wet path, particularly if shaded, can take very little foot traffic without showing signs of wear; the grass soon dies, and the path becomes a boggy mess. This is always worse where feet are channelled by the bottle-necking of a path, often where shrubs or trees grow over the path, so concentrating foot traffic into a reduced width.

Over time, even if slightly wet, access will improve in areas that are laid to trees and grass, as the trees dry out the soil; and in open areas, rhizomatous grasses form a tightly bound turf that will take considerable wear.

Water features

The vision of a fine classical building seen across water is eternally appealing. Thus the positioning and design of even the simplest building is important. I like the Chinese classical ideas of having a

place to sit and observe the moon across water, or to sit and listen to nightingales! More prosaically, having an arbour positioned to watch sunsets is very appealing. Many books treat garden buildings and water features; the main focus of this book is plants. One slight indulgence, though—bridges, because these are so often needed in a wet garden to cross ditches, streams, or water inlets.

Bridges

Bridges very easily make or mar a garden, and, for the small garden, simplicity seems to be the key. One has only to think of the famous bridge over a waterlily pool in Monet's garden in France to realise that a well-designed bridge can be a focal piece of art that creates views to it and from it, and walking over water is normally a joyful human experience and an aid to contemplation.

ABOVE Monet's bridge, Giverny
RIGHT Bridges at the Katsura
Imperial Villa, Kyoto

FORMING A WET GARDEN

Siting is critical, as the bridge must also be functional—taking you where you wish to go, allowing the crossing of a stream or inlet to reach something of interest (an island, for instance). In home gardens most will be footbridges, but sometimes there is a need for bridges to carry machines; and, of course, in larger gardens, grander and road-bearing bridges are often used. Monet was much inspired by Japanese art, and I find delight in the elegantly simple bridges of classical Japanese gardens.

With small bridges over still water, foundations need only be sufficient to cope with the weight of the structure and wet soil. Be cautious where flowing water is involved, because foundations then need to cope with erosion and flood.

Lakes

When working on the scale of a lake, test boring, to check the underlying geology of the site, is critical and with any luck a clay deposit may be found. It is also important to check at an early planning stage with the local government and/or water board to meet with any legislative requirements. Historically, the almost standard way of forming a lake in a garden was by damming a stream valley; but all dams need to be well engineered as their collapse, with the release of the contents of the lake, can be disastrous. More often, simple earth dams are eroded by overflows or burrowing animals and the water slowly leaks away.

Lapping surface water, driven by wind, can be eroding, as can the overflow from heavy rain. With heavy water flow, gabions (stones in heavy galvanised iron cages) are used to consolidate eroded streambanks. Overflow points need to be well constructed, with permanent pipes for normal flow and some form of sluicing to cover heavy flows.

Plants can consolidate the earth banks of large ponds or lakes; tree roots make firm mats, and water margin plants such as iris prevent erosion. Where wildfowl are kept, a hard edge may be a requirement.

Desilting a lake is a task for a well-equipped contractor with experience of the procedure. For more information, see "Pool Cleaning" later in this chapter.

Ponds

I made my first pond when about nine, using the "sunk in the ground" concrete base of the family's Second World War outdoor bomb shelter. Lined and part-filled with clay, it soon accommodated a collection of plants and amphibians gathered from local ponds at a time when almost every farm field on grazing land contained a pond. Each seemed to have accumulated its own set of flora and fauna. One old pollard-willow-edged pond had tiny freshwater bivalves, smooth newts, and water-plantain (*Alisma plantago-aquatica*); another had great crested newts; and yet another had *Ranunculus aquatilis* (white water-crowfoot). As I grew older, I fished in larger waters and added tench and *Nuphar lutea* (yellow waterlily)—and then quickly learned about the problems of putting large plants into small ponds.

In almost all my gardens, private and public, I have had pools. In my personal gardens, for reasons of safety, they were banned for a while when my children were young, but, as life and the family moved along, sitting by a pool, even if just for a coffee-break, always gave pleasure and brought calmness, for there is ever interest in the natural movement of wildlife in and around a garden pond. In one sunny spot the goldfish bred so well, that later in winter, I did not begrudge the passing kingfisher a meal.

A small pond of just a few square metres, with a depth of a few centimetres at its edge, and perhaps half a metre at its deepest, can make a good contribution to a small garden and be used to grow an array of plants. For the home garden, ponds can be fed with rainwater from nearby roofs. Remember however that a lot of water will come from even a small roof such as a shed, so provide an overflow, and always make provision for draining and clearing the pond and having temporary tanks (or an attached but separate pool) to hold plants and fish while this occurs. Where a permanent body of water is required, then the pool needs an impervious lining and a source of topping up, be it borehole, springs, or rainwater from hard surfaces. The rising cost of mains or municipal water and constraints on its supply pretty much limit its use to very small garden pools. More simply, if varying water levels can be tolerated, excavating a pool to a greater depth to increase its capacity does help to retain water over summer.

Clay was long the favoured material for waterproofing, but a good seal is essential. Clay is a variable commodity and can fail to seal if it contains a sand fraction. The simple test for this is to shake up a sample of the clay in a bottle of water until it disperses. Left to stand it will slowly settle out, with any sand forming a separate band. The best clays for sealing ponds are those used for making bricks. Preformed plastic and concrete have also been much used for small pools.

Many ponds, large and small, are now formed with butyl rubber liners, which are both flexible and very durable. The main concern

in their use is of puncturing by lying the liner over a poorly prepared base containing sharp stones or other such objects. Liners
can be repaired, but emptying the pool for this purpose is a chore.
Thus much care is needed in site preparation, with the hollow for the
pool or pond being finely finished with sand to give a smooth surface, free from anything which might cut the liner when the weight
of water presses. Another possible problem is of seasonal springs, or
impeded drainage beneath the liner that will cause it to rise. Such
problems need consideration early on in the project. When calculat-
ing the area of liner, in addition to the surface area, an allowance
must be made to cover the depth and a good overlap of the edge. The
edge is normally buried and covered with paving, rocks or plantings,
according to need. For large areas, sheets will have to be profession-
ally welded together.

Fitting sluices to control water levels and overflow, along with the
need to be able to drain and clean the pond on occasion, needs more
thought when using a flexible liner. Also when selecting a liner, ensure
it is intended for pools and will not release any noxious chemicals.

There is much published work on the construction of ponds, large
and small, and their maintenance. This is especially so for ponds
intended primarily for fish. The good management of koi, for example, is testing and far beyond the scope of this book.

Settling pools

Water-absorbing land surfaces—woods, meadows, winter stub-
ble fields—have often been replaced by chemically cleared pan-sur-
faced crop soils. These increase the runoff, and silt is carried with
it. Thus the amount of silt now deposited by just a tiny stream is
remarkable. Though I have a very imperfect settling scheme for my
own large pond, which is fed by a small ditch, it accumulates on average one or two large barrow-loads of sand and silt each week. Thus
the construction of some form of small settling pool just upstream
of any water feature can be of great benefit. The need is for a pool of
water, which slows the flow, and allows suspended silt to be deposited. Such a pool should be hard bottomed, and have a hard access
way, so that machines can be used to clear and cart away the constant
accumulation.

Again, a reed bed at the head of a pond not only can slow water
but also catches the finer suspended silt particles in all but storm
conditions, though a heavy machine may be needed to clear reeds
when silted. Wet silted soil and plant growth is very heavy to lift.

The removed silt can be usefully employed in the garden but (depending on its age and source) can be loaded with weed seeds. Thus I bury my sand and silt beneath the top spit of beds or other planting sites that need raising. If the silt has a high sand fraction, it is tempting to use it to level small hollows or unevenness in lawns; just remember that there will be a need, next season, to control the resultant introduced weed seedlings.

Bog beds

Liners are successfully used to form bog beds on a porous soil. The process is much the same as when forming a pool except that the liner, when laid at a depth of 30–45 cm (12–18 in.), will be back-filled with soil. While this can work well, it is vital to remember that if sited where there is no natural inflow of water, in dry weather the hitherto wet soil can dry quickly, to the point where plants collapse. Thus it is usual to bury a perforated hose in the bed so that the bed can be topped up when dry; and, equally, holes may be made in the sides of the sheet to drain off surplus water.

Buried under soil, polythene sheet of 500 gauge is often used and should persist for many years, whereas in a pool, where it is exposed to sunlight around the rim, it can quickly degrade. Also, as it goes brittle, terrapins and other animals can more easily damage it. Most plastics similarly degrade; reinforced PVC is sometimes employed, but butyl rubber forms a much more durable liner and is readily available for this purpose. Remember that the depth of the bog garden adds to the required area of sheeting, and allow a good edge

overlap, which can then be buried and covered with soil or stone (see also the earlier section, "On Forming Ponds").

On naturally wet sites, there may be boggy areas that can advantageously used to form a bog bed or garden. If possible, it helps to leave the bed fallow for a while before planting, to ensure any remaining perennial weeds can be cleared, and annual weeds reduced.

Waterside plantings

Harmony is important in gardens, and water, with its calm reflective quality, contributes much to this, amplifying colour and form. Grass too provides a uniting harmony in gardens, but its impact is not as strong as that of water, which mirrors the sky's ever changing light and pattern. Combining the two—grass to the water's edge—is even more satisfying. For the architecturally inspired garden, a crisp clear edge to the grass is often required and keeping it tidy probably means the use of a hard, flat edging, such as stone. But where plants are used to edge a pool, part of their beauty is their spilling over into the water. Water levels in pools will vary naturally with the prevailing weather; in dry conditions, there is often a muddy gap between bank edge and water that can be masked by plants.

Wet soil gives rise to a superabundance of vigorous weeds; and,

OPPOSITE The bog garden, Hillier Gardens, Hampshire
BELOW Another view of the densely planted watersides at Longstock Park

Iris ensata cultivars behaving nicely in the lake at the Heian Shrine, Kyoto

when visiting gardens, one often sees very weedy waterside beds. In such cases, water reflections then amplify the presence of weeds, so doubly spoiling the scene. For a wildlife pond, an abundance of plant life may be required, but the invasiveness of bog and aquatic plants and the devastation caused by waterfowl means taking an early decision on the aims of the garden. Still, well-managed poolside planting drifts can be an absolute delight. Winter mulching helps enormously with the control of summer weeds, but this work must have the gardener's hope that waterside beds will not be flooded, especially if bark is used! There is nothing more irritating than seeing an expensive mulch of bark chippings floating off a bed.

It is important to select plant material not prone to prodigious increase; for example, while *Iris ensata* or even *I. sibirica* cultivars provide an easy-to-manage display from slowly expanding clumps, *I. pseudacorus* (yellow flag) soon becomes aggressively vigorous. A single plant of this last species can, over a few years, grow to become a clump 2–3 m (6.6–10 ft.) wide; further, each flower produces a large fat pod of viable floating seed—a combination of growth and seeding that can soon convert even a largish pond into a flag fen.

The choice of plantings for watersides is extensive, so it is wise to keep size and spread in mind. For a large pond, a waterside clump of a sweet-scented deciduous azalea can add tranquillity and reflected beauty. Architectural plants are often favoured for their summer effect. A clump of *Gunnera manicata* makes a strong statement, but as summer progresses its large long-petioled leaves will lower to the pool and cover any surrounding plants. The deep-rooted lysichiton, another popular choice, forms a large clump of its soft aroidaceous leaves but can also spread by seeding, particularly along narrow water gullies.

Water gardens show what is possible with highly maintained waterside plantings. Some favour smaller herbaceous plants; astilbes, filipendulas, hemerocallis, mimulas, and polygonums are reasonably easy to manage. Much depends upon the frequency with which economics allows regular replanting—that is, lifting, dividing, and re-soiling where needed. Some plants will need annual attention; others can stay and flower well for several years.

Containers

Almost any plant can be grown in a container, and because pots can be moved to shelter in winter, cabbage palms and many other otherwise slightly tender wet garden plants can be enjoyed. Hardier plants such as hostas and Japanese maples form excellent long-lived pot plants. Bog and water plants, such as the sacred lotus, can be grown in decorative watertight containers. Containers also give the option of growing plants that will not tolerate wet soil; near the house, thyme, rosemary, sage, and other herbs may fit the bill.

With so many containers now available, it is easy to choose a style that complements house and garden, but potting-on a large container plant can be testing physically. I usually lay the plant and container on its side on a lawn so that it can be slid out. It is possible to set smallish plants, such as bulbs or palms, in a large container and to leave them to grow on for years; but, if not regularly divided, some can burst a large pot when no room is left for their heavy root systems. Drainage is rarely a problem, but for those needing good drainage, some coarse gravel can be included in the base of the container. For all container plants, it is sensible to incorporate coarse sand or stone chippings in the compost.

The biggest daily chore is watering in summer. A simple irrigation system, such as a flexible line of drip nozzles, will help, as will incorporating water-absorbing gel crystals into the compost.

A potted cabbage palm, *Cordyline australis* 'Torbay Dazzler'

SELECTING PLANTS FOR WET SOIL

I am still surprised by the consequences of abundant moisture. Instead of languishing for its first two seasons, as it might in dry soil, a young ornamental rhubarb (*Rheum palmatum*) set in a moist garden can develop, in the same period, into a great clump of handsome leaves, topped by a magnificent 3 m (10 ft.) flower spike. *Matteuccia struthiopteris* (ostrich fern) struggles to survive a dry summer on sandy soils; but on the shaded north side of a wall, on heavy soil, it soon produces its admired young, spring-green, shuttlecock fronds—and runners too, in abundance, forming additional rosettes whose summer fronds can crowd out adjacent plants. Worse, in that sense, the dry-site demure *Blechnum chilense* can become aggressive, and, given the same shade and moisture, its densely packed rhizomes and large pinnate leaves, can completely oust any smaller surrounding plants. But the dense growth of the Chilean blechnum makes it a good ground cover plant for a moist site under trees, where its strong, dark green leaves can give a tropical effect. Under trees, it will be a little more inhibited but still suppressive of weeds. For most gardens plant selection is a matter of picking the winners, and then increasing on success.

Because of the combined diversities of site and plant, the selection of suitable plants for almost any garden involves much trial and error, but in wet gardens poor selection is very quickly marked by failure. General horticultural reference literature always plays safe with comments like "suitable for a moist but free-drained soil" (for "does poorly" in dry soils, read "dies quickly"). Thus where a wider range than "bog plants" is required, it is (and has been for me) a very extended case of trial and error.

When looking to introduce new plants, I invariably start with relatives of plants that are already proving their worth on wet soils; through their anatomical and physiological design, some plants are better able to withstand climate extremes than others, and such characteristics are usually shared within families. Checking on the selected plant's natural habitat follows, but I confess, I often only remember to do this later, after I have noticed a new plant coping well. Invariably I find that the plant in question may be found growing naturally on wet soils, but this does not always follow. Many factors come into play. Following the logic of using garden plants whose progenitors are adapted to wet soils is a useful guide, but, with many such plants from subtropical and warm temperate regions, a wet soil in cooler climes, particularly in winter, can be lethal. Even some cool temperate species, such as the widely grown *Physostegia virginiana*, which includes wet ditches in its natural habitat, will not tolerate wet soils in cold winters.

It is always wise to look for ideas in other gardens, both locally and further away, where conditions have some parallels. Also in a new garden the progress of any initial plantings should be closely observed since their performance will greatly assist with the choice of subsequent plantings. Generally it seems the view of what will or will not grow on a wet soil is influenced by people's experience of a plant on well-drained soils. The natural world is, however, all about diversity—the need for uniformity seeming to be more of a human condition. Thus the degree of adaptability that is inherent in an individual plant's genes invariably offers greater scope than didactic gardeners allow.

I do not have the almost ruthless confidence expressed by such as my colleague, garden designer James Russell, who would plant fearlessly in quantity, accepting that many plants would be lost, but knowing that those that succeeded would never have been planted by a more cautious rule follower. My caution comes from hating to lose the plants I have put effort into collecting and growing. But, having had to look after James Russell's late life collections in North Yorkshire for the last decade or more, I am constantly surprised and delighted by those of his plantings that have survived in both wet woodland and heavy, sometimes boggy, meadow soils.

Finally, for now-well-publicised reasons, many plants are under threat worldwide, including several of those mentioned in this book. It is thus important when acting on your selection only to acquire scarce plants from *bona-fide* sources that have ensured their production in cultivation.

Trees

As with so many other plants, trees on wet soils will either languish or grow embarrassingly large, making it difficult to achieve the right balance. It is also most important to appreciate that fungi thrive in wet gardens and, as a consequence, the trees therein are more subject to disease. Saturated soil can quickly cause roots to die and become more susceptible to entry by damaging fungi. Trees with decayed roots, or butt decay, are more likely to be blown over by wind on a wet site.

Disease spreads rapidly. Bacterial canker on apples can, for example, advance quickly; and on young (9–12 m, 30–40 ft.) balsam poplar, I noted dieback so severe that almost all the branches were dead, and the tree had to be removed within three to four years of its first becoming infected.

Growth is also more rapid, but—and there always is a "but"—the wood of fast-growing trees has wider annual rings and is thus weaker. Branches are particularly vulnerable to high winds especially at that point in late summer where growth for the year has extended branches, but strong wood tissue has not yet been laid down. In such circumstances, a high wind can literally tear a tree to pieces. It is important not to place a forest tree anywhere near a house on heavy soil because of these risks, not to mention the more certain soil shrinkage as the tree grows and dries heavy soil, which causes subsidence and foundation damage.

Of all the worries in a garden, it is probably tree removal that causes garden owners the greatest concern. Trees, like all other living creatures, are very competitive, and the successfully dominant plant suppresses all plant growth beneath. However removing very large trees from an established garden is expensive and difficult since they have to be brought down in sections to avoid damage to other plantings. It always best to take out unwanted or badly sited

Shrubs in spectacular winter colour
at Anglesey Abbey, Cambridgeshire

trees when they are young. When up to ten years old, they are still relatively easy to remove with a handsaw; thereafter, their removal quickly becomes a task for a tree surgeon with all the equipment, safety aspects, and cost that involves.

Specimen trees are invariably planted too close to each other. A 5–6 m (16–20 ft.) spacing looks distant when plants are small, but will be seen as too close within a decade, when 10–15 m (33–60 ft.) might be seen as more appropriate for the long term. Certainly on a wet soil there is a higher risk of loss, but so few people think about thinning out young garden trees. As a guide for individual trees, think of their ultimate height, and that the width of a spreading tree can almost equal its height. For columnar trees or intentional group plantings, spacing can of course be reduced.

Guidance points
- Choose wet tolerant species.
- Plant on raised (10–20 cm, 4–8 in.) planting mounds.
- Remember trees on wet soils grow faster, become larger, and are structurally weaker and more susceptible to decay.
- Site trees carefully and do not plant large-growing species near buildings.
- Do not cover the tree's root area with hard impervious surfaces, such as concrete, which will trap water below.

Shrubs and climbers

For shrubs, as with trees, there seems little compromise on wet soils. It is either feast or famine—that is, plants growing extremely well or poorly. Given a good moist soil the growth of shrubs can be double that of similar plants on a poor dry soil. For all shrubs, even those that relish wet soil, I prefer to raise their planting bed a few centimetres above the general soil level. This particularly suits plants like deutzias, roses, viburnums, and weigelas and is a requirement for rhododendrons and other fine-rooted plants. Certainly where raised beds are provided, a fairly wide range can be grown; however, cistuses and cytisuses suffer and will die in wet winter cold, and the latter is particularly susceptible to wind rock on wet soils.

By their nature—growing among the roots of the plants they climb on—climbers are invariably in soil that is drier than that surrounding, and by using raised planting mounds, the limited range of climbers for wet gardens is extended to roses, clematis, and honeysuckles (see chapter 5). These can be run up trees or trained against a house wall. Warm sunny walls keep climbers active, and thus more able to cope with wet soil; a shaded wall is more limiting.

Autumn colour

In theory wet sites offer great potential for the formation of autumn colour because of the extra moisture that is available, but this does not always follow. The spectacular fall colour seen in eastern North America is well known, and its enduring images have inspired the deliberate planting of good autumn foliage plants in European gardens. Clones that colour well, from genera like *Acer* and *Liquidambar*, have been extensively propagated and are widely available. *Hydrangea anomala* subsp. *petiolaris* and the parthenocissuses also colour well in wet soil.

For good autumn colour on trees growing on a wet site, ensure frost drainage and shelter from drying winds. Shelter is relatively easily provided and important: not only do leaves need to stay on the trees, but drying winds will shrivel up leaves before they can colour. Also, since damp sites are invariably frost hollows, hard frosts can remove all the autumn leaves from mulberries, magnolias, and much else. In regions with a drier atmosphere, select plants carefully; some (*Aronia melanocarpa, Liquidambar, Nyssa*) dependably deliver both red and yellow tints even in areas with drying winds.

The National Collection of Japanese maples at the National Arboretum, Westonbirt, Gloucestershire

Cladrastis kentukea in autumn

With shelter and a moist atmosphere many others perform well, including ash, cercidiphyllum, cornus, ginkgo, hamamelis, oaks, parrotia, and viburnum. For the sensitively aware, there is pleasure in all the changes of autumn. Many grasses and other herbaceous plants offer subtle end-of-season attire, and now with warmer summers I enjoy the calmer *Cladrastis kentukea* (Kentucky yellowwood) from the mideastern United States, a relatively slow-growing medium-sized tree that is rare in the wild but widely cultivated.

Herbaceous beds and borders

Where wet soils and warmth combine to yield abundant growth, gardening approaches need to be adjusted. Conventionally a new herbaceous bed or border will need renewal (division of plants and soil improvement) every three or four years, whereas wet soil beds can get out of hand in two seasons. Herbs on wet soils may fail, and it is harder to manage flowerbeds on wet soil. On well-drained soils, plants are more "obedient" in the sense that they will stay longer in their planned groups. Those who garden on wet soil are likely to have a preference for tufted or tightly clumped plants that are not invasive!

Wet soil affects the spacing used when setting out plants and increases the need for staking. Generally plants grown in wet soil are laxer, taller, and susceptible to wind damage; without staking, everything flops over. Staking such plants as heleniums and herbaceous peonies will contribute to a fine display. Rudbeckias and other spreading plants can quickly crowd out weaker companions. Thus to get the desired planting composition, wet beds need additional annual attention, dividing and increasing, or lifting and reducing. Flowering can diminish as the size of clumps increases, and some beds may require a two-year cycle of division and replanting.

There are, I suppose, two main routes to sanity when managing beds and borders on wet soil. One is to use beds that are raised above the general soil level, by adding sand, gravel, and organic matter, so that a more conventional gardening approach can be used. The other is to accept the consequences of boggy conditions, and plant tough-growing plants (lysichitons, ligularias), and then doing little more than selective weeding, and in winter clipping down the previous summer's growth.

As a general strategy for dealing with herbaceous plants in wet beds I suggest banning the aggressive colonisers (symphytums and some lysimachias, for example), using them instead as ground cover in rough areas, or setting them in long grass areas where they can

Piet Oudolf's herbaceous perennial plantings feature many wet-soil-tolerant plants, as here at Pensthorpe, Norfolk.

spread naturally and be contained by mowing. The weaker plants then need to be separated out and grown together. I have lost many choice plants by simply forgetting exactly where they were located only to find them choked out by a vigorous neighbour. Through years of care for large collections, that are physically being gardened by others, I have often found that there seems to be a reduced "responsibility of care" that is proportionate to the distance a plant is set from the natural centre of a garden's activities—usually the house. So rare or choice plants that need regular attention are best grown near at hand, where they can be seen and monitored.

This leaves the bulk of more ordinary herbaceous candidates—astilbes, hellebores, hostas, geraniums, heleniums, hemerocallis, iris, peonies, thalictrums—to be grouped and arranged according to season, colour, form, and taste. Most silver- and grey-leafed herbaceous plants grow poorly on a wet soil, the exceptions being *Anthemis punctata* subsp. *cupaniana*, *Lychnis coronaria*, and, in summer only, *Helichrysum italicum* subsp. *serotinum* (curry plant; Z8).

Bulbs

Bulbs are such an appealing group of plants that they are planted in most gardens and seemingly on an ever-increasing scale, with large

TOP *Tigridia pavonia*
ABOVE *Nicandra physalodes*

drifts being frequently added. The horticultural term "bulb" covers a wide range of perennating organs but almost all bulbs are mono-cotyledons. As a consequence, with their parallel veins and symmetrical form, they fit easily into both formal and informal gardens.

Fortunately many bulbs, even some of the garden favourites (daffodils, hyacinths, tulips), are able to grow on wet soil, but winter soil temperature must be considered: many common bulbs are native to regions with Mediterranean climates. Such bulbs are often adapted to hot and dry resting conditions, and in cultivation, where the required out-of-ground dry rest period can be made coincidental with cold winter conditions; this has greatly extended the range grown. It can be a little more complicated than that, however. For example, bulbs from summer-rain areas respond differently to those from winter-rain regions.

As a general point, since heavy wet soils can be colder and slower to warm than light soils, growing slightly tender species in a bed set by a house or greenhouse will be advantageous. Another approach is to make use of the shelter and root zone drying effect of trees and shrubs.

Many bulbs, particularly those that naturally flower early in the growing season in deciduous woodland, can be grown advantageously among trees and shrubs in gardens. The sumptuous tigridias have surprised though: not only have the bulbs of *Tigridia pavonia* from Mexico survived in my cold wet soil over several winters, they have produced an abundance of overwintering seedlings.

Annuals and biennials

The advantage of annuals on cold wet sites is that dormant seed allows the plant to avoid the cold and wet of winter, and thus many can be grown in summer, even in a wet garden. However, they also germinate later, and too wet and cold a year can cause many seeds to succumb to fungi, whereas a sunny warm year can cause excessive growth of seedlings.

In temperate climates these points relate especially to subtropical species. So, again, when cold in spring, it is best to delay sowing until the soil warms. For example, the blue-flowered *Nicandra physalodes* (apple of Peru), from the tomato family, might grow 25–30 cm (10–12 in.) high and wide on a dry soil, but if warm and moist, it can quickly become a plant 1 m (3.3 ft.) high and wide, even within just two to three months of a summer sowing. In contrast *Nigella damascena* (love-in-the-mist) may grow only to 25 cm (10 in.) on wet soil but double that in drier conditions. It is thus difficult to plan a display. More usefully, the delightful annual *Limnanthes douglasii* (poached-egg flower) occurs naturally in marshy areas in California and southern Oregon and is thus well suited to a wet temperate garden in summer.

Biennials like the common foxglove (*Digitalis purpurea*) will grow well and overwinter on a just slightly raised site. Unexpectedly however, seedlings of the evening primrose *Oenothera glazioviana* will sit and overwinter in somewhat wet conditions. For those who enjoy the open growth of *Verbena bonariensis*, I have found the similarly sized and very wet-soil-tolerant North American *V. hastata* f. *rosea* equally attractive in late summer. It seeds heavily; and often, in boggy conditions, the abundant seedlings may behave as overwintering biennials or annuals, though the plants are not long-lived.

The mixed border

For most home gardens a bed or border containing a mix of shrubs, herbs, and bulbs that gives interest throughout the year is almost inevitably the border of choice. Certainly, in wet gardens such a border has particular value, as it is more accommodating of the greater amplitudes of the success or failure of border plants. However, the choice of shrubs needs careful consideration because of those able to grow on wet soil most, as already indicated, will grow larger, necessitating regular pruning if not eventual removal. This applies to roses as well and, since they are very likely to be included, a careful choice of variety has to be made. Many of the vigorous shrub roses and hybrid teas will grow too large, whereas among shrub roses many cultivars of *Rosa* ×*odorata* can be kept to a height of not much more than 1 m (3.3 ft.) on a damp but well-drained soil. The lovely large pale-pink-flowered *R*. 'Fru Dagmar Hastrup', which has fat red hips in autumn, grows to a similar size on a light damp soil, but it will need regular pruning on a heavy wet soil.

When planted around a house on a wet site, shrubs will need far more pruning than those on a dry soil, just to keep the windows clear! For mixed borders formed by or near a house, winter-flowering shrubs give a special value. Of these I find witch hazels most accommodating, particularly slow-growing cultivars such as the primrose-yellow *Hamamelis* ×*intermedia* 'Pallida', which can also be regularly pruned. Of winter-flowering honeysuckles, as another example, it might be better to choose say *Lonicera standishii* rather than its more vigorous hybrid *L*. ×*purpusii* (*L. fragrantissima* × *L. standishii*). Some

TOP *Verbena hastata* f. *rosea*
ABOVE *Rosa* 'Fru Dagmar Hastrup'

evergreen shrubs can be similarly useful, such as the late winter-flowering sarcococcas, but even these, and as another example, the *Camellia* ×*williamsii* hybrids, can express almost too much vigour after a few years' growth, though the latter can be a fine sight in full early blossom.

Spring bulbs can be easily worked in among shrubs, particularly where the foliage of later-growing herbs can cover their dying foliage. Also these bulbs complete their growth cycle before the deciduous shrubs are in full leaf and growth. Snowdrops, the smaller crocuses, scillas, and chionodoxas work well. The bulbous iris form large leaves and need more vigorous herbs (rudbeckias, *Geranium* 'Ann Folkard' or other creeping geranium) to cover their summer fading leaves. Setting larger bulbs, like *Fritillaria imperialis* or camassias, away from the front of the border helps mask their dying foliage.

Summer bulbs need more light, and where there is space between shrubs, summer-flowering bulbs (crocosmias, crinums) can boldly fill the gap.

To some extent shrubs can limit the vigour and spread of perennials, but it is best to avoid vigorous spreading plants like the Shasta daisies or lysimachias. Much hinges on the rate of spread; for wilder parts of the garden, annuals or biennials like red campion (*Silene dioica*) and foxglove (*Digitalis purpurea*) will produce a dense mat of seedlings if grown in a bed among shrubs. They can look pretty impressive when in flower, the foxglove following on when the campion finishes; however, when they have died off, by high summer, such a bed cannot help but look tatty, and the growth of these early-season herbaceous plants invariably masks the growth of weeds. A missed removal of old flowering stems can be a real seeding and then weeding worry with many plants, including alchemillas, senecios, and crocosmias.

On wet soils, more than other soils, it is a matter of experiment to find satisfying combinations and sequences. I find the seasonal flowering sequence of peonies, herbaceous poppies, astilbes, rudbeckias, and Japanese anemones pleasing. Over time I have come to settle on a four-season mix of winter-flowering shrubs with camassias and other spring bulbs; followed by summer bulbs and a few summer roses; and then rudbeckias and helianthus, ending the season with perennial asters and schizostylis.

Ground cover

A dense cover of plants restricts seed germination by reducing available moisture and the amount of light that can fall on the soil. Wet soil invariably holds a great reserve of seeds, and where beds are newly formed (as from rough grass), weeding may be required fortnightly throughout the growing season for up to seven years before the store is significantly reduced. Mulches, particularly of bark, can help, but good ground cover has a much longer-term benefit. However the range of ground cover plants suitable for wet soils is limited.

Woodland gardens on wet soil enjoy the widest choice of ground cover plants, whose task of weed suppression is made easier by the physiological effects of the canopy trees and leaf litter. In light open woodland, the hardy *Geranium macrorrhizum* and its selections give both good ground cover and flower. With increased tree cover, the several forms of the western North American *Dicentra formosa* provide a delicate-leaved spreading ground cover, as do the evergreen pachysandras and the wood rush *Luzula sylvatica*.

Euphorbia amygdaloides, *E. amygdaloides* var. *robbiae*, and other spurges give good ground cover, but the former may be short-lived. Others such as the much-used *E. sikkimensis* can take some years to form stands, and even then they will not be dense or effective. Also, most woodland euphorbias need reasonable drainage.

Ferns are more useful. In light but very wet woodland, *Onoclea sensibilis* makes dense stands. With a more complete tree cover, both the larger *Blechnum chilense* and the more diminutive but equally aggressively spreading *B. penna-marina* form dense, long-lasting mats.

In light woodland, *Convallaria majalis* (lily-of-the-valley) and the related *Maianthemum bifolium* can also form densely matted sheets. Other useful if aggressive plants include dwarf bamboos, ferns, and wood grasses. Of the latter I find *Milium effusum* (wood millet) both attractive and effective. The persistent symphytums will establish around the base of specimen trees, even where branches are low, which greatly simplifies maintenance.

In open situations, the vigour of ground cover plants presents difficulties. Such plants are best excluded from herbaceous beds and borders, which are better grown densely to provide their own ground cover. In shrub beds, more options arise. *Alchemilla mollis* is excellently dense and competitive but may need renewal after a few years; also it seeds extensively—that is, unless the faded blossom stems are removed each year before seed is shed. Bistorts are more durable; *Persicaria bistorta* can form dense clumps that rarely need weeding. Similarly, though needing good light, *P. affinis* 'Superba' forms prostrate mats and has an extended flowering period, the flower spikes retaining their deep red colour long after the flowers have faded.

In a bog garden, *Iris sibirica* and other iris can produce reasonably tight, weed-free clumps and combine well with any of The Pearl Group of *Achillea ptarmica*, which can form a dense mat. Lysimachias, inulas, and filipendulas can compete well with grasses.

Establishing ground cover normally means starting with a clean site that is free from perennial weeds, and then planting densely. The time and cost involved in raising large numbers of plants thus favours the use of naturally spreading plants that can be divided into many pieces and planted *in situ*.

In sun or shade, ivy (*Hedera*) is a mixed blessing as a ground cover. It is evergreen and provides a dense cover within which little else, other than the odd bramble or common elder (*Sambucus nigra*) seedling may arise, and it can also be clipped. Its spread does however have to be constrained, most easily in borders by cutting annually to 15 cm (6 in.) downward with a sharp spade along the boundary defined for its spread, or by tight mowing to stop its spread into lawns. Since it will also ascend into specimen shrubs and trees, such growth must be cut away annually. It is considered a noxious weed in some U.S. states.

Other ground cover plants need less attention, and deciduous plants just need a winter clip of the previous season's flowering shoots. Once established they will function well for a good many years. The quickly spreading creeping-Jenny (*Lysimachia nummularia*) makes a low attractive flowering cover, but grows so well on wet soil that it is difficult to remove and will swamp other herbaceous plants; nor is it good at suppressing weeds. *Lysimachia punctata* and *L. ciliata* can form dense weed-suppressing clumps, but they too are best confined to wilder parts.

Succession is nature's way. Renewal of ground cover is a perennial requirement, though some are more durable than others. In an open wet site I had a large drift of *Pulicaria dysenterica* (common fleabane), and the plants were dominant and free-flowering for about fifteen years. Gradually, however, the old centres of growth weakened, and docks (*Rumex*) and other perennial weeds increasingly appeared. Its renewal or replanting on a new site then had to be considered. Others last longer; some lysimachias and persicarias can hold well for two decades or more.

In shaded conditions, such as under trees and shrubs, more stable ground cover is possible, but even then circumstances frequently change. For each garden careful observation of its plantings will give a guide to any particular plant's competitiveness, ability to exclude weeds, and ease of propagation, thus allowing a personal selection of ground cover best adapted to any garden. In my own garden this process has led me to use swirling, winter-bright, self-seeding clumps of *Carex comans* 'Frosted Curls' (hardy to −9°C, 16°F) on open wet sites. And whereas great wood-rush (*Luzula sylvatica*) seeds around too much on open wet soil, it forms a good dense cover under trees on wet soil. Both, however, need renewal after three or four years.

Pulicaria dysenterica, covering ground at water's edge

GARDENING FOR WILDLIFE

Wet gardens, if managed sensibly, can be great havens for wildlife, with all the pleasure and interest that brings. If you are lucky, as I have been, this extends to small mammals, such as water vole, water shrew, and many bats, as well as frogs, toads, and newts, a great variety of birds, and fascinating insects such as the jewelled dragon and damson flies. There was a time when I only cautiously promoted the value of gardens for wildlife, but with the unceasing decline of natural habitats, gardens have become even more important refuges.

Habitat diversity—which is, after all, nature's way—is key. Provide

Moorhen and young on
Nymphaea 'Escarboucle'

a mix of trees, shrubs, herbs, and climbers, short and long grasses, eco-heaps of decaying wood and other vegetation, rock and stone piles—and don't be too tidy. A wide mix of plants helps to provide an extended year of leaf, flower, berries, and dry seed, and native plants will either already be present or able to be blended in with most themes.

Water is a great attraction to many creatures, and long grasses and herbs provide shelter for frogs and voles. In my own garden, the latter are hunted by barn owls, but the owls are very fussy about their hunting area. They seek open grassland: as soon as trees are planted—albeit they are still small and the grass with its rodents remains—the owls will hunt elsewhere. Long grass is also a food source for many brown butterflies, and a good population can soon develop; ringlets (*Aphantopus hyperantus*) seek out damp places to lay their eggs. Having long vegetation close to ponds is valuable for emerging dragonflies and young amphibians, as well as water shrews and water voles.

Sadly many insect-eating, summer migrant bird populations are in decline worldwide. Two or more decades back, colleagues in North America attributed their losses to habitat destruction in Central and South America. For European birds that migrate to Africa, feeding

FORMING A WET GARDEN

stops on their long journeys, as well as overwintering habitats, have all degraded. In wet gardens, and especially by water, many biting insects occur in summer, but because their normal control, from birds such as flycatchers, martins, and swallows, as well as bats and dragonflies, is reduced, such insects may become a greater nuisance.

The case is often made for having native plants for native animals, and while this can be vital for endemic species on a world scale, it does not have to become extreme advice. Britain, for example, shares most of its native flora and fauna with continental Europe, and many species are circumboreal. From casual observation, the seeds of, say, a Caucasian alder are just as useful to a redwing for winter sustenance, as would be those of a native alder, and even though all but a few evergreen trees and shrubs in Britain are not native, garden evergreens nevertheless provide useful shelter and nest sites. I was amused recently to find wood mice making cosy nests from an abundant supply of the plumed seeds of a Tibetan clematis, and I have also noticed that both snipe and water rail prefer to probe mown grass, not long grass, for food in hard weather.

Decaying trees present a conflict: they provide food and essential environments for wildlife, but are hazardous for people. One solution is to lop off any large branches, leaving the more stable trunk to decay standing, and then stacking the cut branches nearby, at the base of a hedge, for example. Where a tree has a disease such as honey fungus, however, it is best removed and if possible burnt.

In brief: increase the diversity of plants, incorporate native species, use minimal or zero biocides (see the next chapter), do not be too tidy, allow areas where wood and other vegetation can decay, and be observant. And remember that as much as anything else, available food determines population size for most creatures.

CHAPTER 3
Operations

MANAGING GRASS ON WET SOIL

Green lawns have long been an important feature of traditional gardens, but, as with all else, their care on a wet soil is a little more exacting. The small fine grasses that are used in quality turf, as prepared for games such as croquet, need good drainage, whereas wet soils tend to support coarser grasses.

Mowing

On wet soils lawn grass has to be cut frequently, but the gain is that lawns are green in summer, when elsewhere the grass may be shrivelled brown by drought. When it is warm and wet in summer, grass may require cutting every three days; though once a week should suffice for most of the summer growing season and, with a roller mower, an immaculate and impressively lined finish can be achieved. Latitude can make a difference: North Yorkshire is not many miles north of my own garden in Norfolk, but its slightly longer summer and shorter winter days mean that grass growth is slower at the start and end of the summer season, and it seems to almost race away in early summer, as flowering stalks extend their growth. Thus higher latitudes shorten but intensify the growing season.

Ideally wet soil lawns should be cut when the grass is dry, but the demands of large grass areas are such that mowing is often undertaken when the grass is wet with dew or rain. This puts a greater strain on the mower; it is best therefore to have an adequately powered and robust machine. To reduce winter damage, when grass is growing slowly, it is all the more important on wet lawns to set the mower blades higher, leaving more leaf on the grass to aid recovery from wear.

Machines for large-scale mowing are now as expensive as a luxury car, while machines for the domestic market have become relatively

52

more affordable, so much so that it is generally cheaper to replace a damaged domestic machine than to have it serviced or repaired. The rotary cutters on most domestic machines are simple to maintain; the once popular cylinder mower is now used only on fine turf. Rotary cutters also offer rollers, mulching decks, twin blades (to cut the grass more finely), and grass collectors. Roller mowers are useful where flowerbeds are set in lawns, as they can mow over the edge of beds.

Collecting grass clippings helps to keep a lawn in good condition, but the practicality of collecting clippings from large areas tends to limit this practise to fine lawns. If cuttings are not to be collected, then with less frequent cutting the faster growth of grass on wet soil can result in a large amount of clippings, which if left on the surface will, in damp weather, soon start to decay, spoiling the grass beneath. These clippings will also stay on the grass until the next cutting, so adding to the problem. More frequent cutting reduces the amount of clippings, which will then mulch in. The solution to such conundrums is to determine which areas are to be the fine lawns, and to mow these frequently (once a week in temperate summers); and for the less frequently cut grass to set the cutting blade higher (7.5–10 cm, 3–4 in.), so that the clippings can be left. Where grass grows vigorously this may mean a fortnightly cut in the height of summer, but otherwise monthly. Intervals longer than a month may necessitate raking.

On newly sown areas, if the soil is particularly wet, native small sedges may germinate in abundance ahead of the sown grass. These are harder for mowers to cut (they take the edge off steel blades), though over time they become replaced by grass, as they do not recover well from regular mowing.

Where wet sites attract water birds, these will graze heavily on waterside lawns, keeping the grass well shorn and well fertilised by their droppings; but, as a consequence, they do seem to introduce more lawn weeds! Mosses too are a damp-lawn problem. Mosses may be intentionally encouraged, particularly in woodland areas, but if a fine grass lawn is wanted, the soil must be well drained.

For quality lawns, all the rituals of good grass care apply: the use of fine-leaved grasses, scarifying, slit-tining, and top dressing, with drainage and levelling being at the top of the list. A warning: over time, no matter what seed is sown, lawns tend to become dominated by locally native species of grasses, but observing this progressive transition has its own fascination! While there is pleasure in mown grass, concern to reduce carbon consumption and give a wildlife gain is a contributive incentive in the conversion of mown to long grass.

Managing the mead

Though on wetland the natural seed bank springs eternal, once covered by grass, little then germinates save where a mole or other creature turns up fresh soil. Some plants (*Anthriscus sylvestris, Heracleum sphondylium, Urtica dioica*) can seed in, and jays will bring in oak acorns. Bulbs and perennials are best established early in the development of a meadow and planted according to the effect required and the intended mowing regime.

For spring bulbs, a first cut (of their faded foliage) and grass removal in mid-summer followed by an early autumn cut, leaving the mowings *in situ*, is ideal. For summer bulbs, a late summer cut may be appropriate. Mowing in late autumn reduces the summer's growth of brambles and unwanted tree seedlings.

If you enjoy the flowering of grasses, and also the delight of autumn dew or winter's haw frosts gleaming on their remaining flower stalks, then an early winter cut might appeal. A mid-winter cut, or a little earlier if there are bulbs, which have started into growth, will readily shorten the sward in preparation for the bulbs to emerge and stand in flower above the turf. Winter cutting makes much less of a power demand on mowers. On frozen ground, the machine does not bog down, and since the grass stems are aged and partly decayed or perhaps brittle with frost, they cut easily and chop to fine iced mulch that does not need to be raked off. Where bulbs are naturalised, be warned that the new season's shoots may emerge before the shortest day. For *Anemone nemorosa* (wood anemone), I like to lightly cut over the area in early March so that when the flowers open they can stand free in the grass; however before mowing I check carefully, for their flowering shoots can extend rapidly in early spring as temperatures rise.

Reducing the vigour of grass

Because long grass on wet soils is so vigorous and thus competitive of other plants, the concept of the "flowering mead" has to be modified somewhat. The usual advice of taking a hay crop for seven years, so reducing nutrient levels, may work on a light soil, but (and almost by definition) wet soils are often heavy, nutrient-rich soils, and alternative techniques must be considered. Also hay-cutting machines need a free run at long grass, and where gardens are crowded with trees and beds, smaller machines have to be used.

One currently fashionable option is to use a semi-parasite, such as *Rhinanthus minor* (yellow-rattle), to reduce grass vigour. Again this works well on light soils, but rhinanthus is less happy on heavy wet soils. *Rhinanthus minor* subsp. *stenophyllus* is tolerant of moister soils, and several hemi-parasites, such as louseworts (*Pedicularis*), grow naturally on wetter soils and might be worth a trial.

Trees are very effective in reducing grass vigour. As they grow they create ecological changes in the surrounding flora, progressively suppressing vigorous meadow grasses and allowing other woodland species to colonise. Also, in cool temperate regions, the light penetrating through the tree canopy can be so reduced and the soil made so dry in summer, that few, other than woodland adapted species, will survive.

Grasses alone can be a great delight, and the natural variety of grasses that will arise on any site is invariably appealing. The composition of the meadow evolves as new species arise and colonise, but generally over years, coarser grasses tend to dominate.

Bulbs in grass

In cold temperate regions, daffodils are perhaps the easiest bulbs to naturalise on heavy soils. They form dense root mats, often below

Daffodils naturalised in an orchard

TOP *Camassia cusickii* growing in grassland
ABOVE *Filipendula ulmaria*
OPPOSITE TOP *Filipendula rubra* 'Venusta'
OPPOSITE CENTER *Iris pseudacorus*
OPPOSITE BOTTOM *Crocosmia* 'Lucifer'

the main area of grass roots, and produce their leaves in late winter and spring, before the grass extends its summer growth. The familiar pale corolla and yellow trumpeted *Narcissus pseudonarcissus* subsp. *pseudonarcissus* and its countless hybrids can thrive in heavy grassland, increasing year on year from seed, most readily on light soils.

The stately camassias can compete well with long grass but are particular as to the degree of wetness in the soil. If too wet, they die out (and if too shady, they do not flower). *Camassia leichtlinii* and its forms produce the most reliable flowering displays.

Fritillaria meleagris is well adapted to moist meadows, but to be frank it will grow better and increase more in a bed of organic soil or even under the light shade of a tree, where there is less competition from grasses. *Triteleia laxa* is worth a gamble because it competes reasonably well and extends the season with its early summer flowers. Alliums too, particularly taller-growing species such as *Allium hollandicum*, can add interest. A further option is to treat bulbs as expendable bedding, accepting their possibly short-lived existence in a meadow and adding new ones each autumn.

The success of individual plants in meadows will vary according to the meadow's underlying soil, as well as aspect and other conditions. Where bulbs multiply quickly, there will be a need to divide and increase the planting—or, if not wanted, sell or give away the surplus bulbs. The challenge is to accurately locate dormant bulbs in grass. Marking clumps with canes before the leaves die down is an option, but one that is invariably forgotten. My own approach is to wait until the bulb noses show above ground and then lift and divide. Since the soil is normally moist at this time (from late November onward in my garden), this proves a relatively easy process and if planted promptly divided clumps of bulbs should go on to flower without a check.

In warmer climates, many other bulbs can be grown in grass on wet soils; some of these are mentioned in chapter 6.

Herbaceous plants in grass

Unless the meadow is already established it is best to start with "clean" soil by means of cultivating, grading, levelling, and removing any large stones, ready for future mowing. Then locally sourced meadow seed, or a suitable wildflower seed mix, can be sown. In the early days of the meadow's establishment, unwanted perennial weeds can be either hand-dug or, if preferred, spot-treated with a herbicide.

Many gardeners will wish to leave their wet meadows to what arises naturally, and there is great delight to be had from what will then be a mainly grass-based succession evolving over many years. Some will wish to introduce native species, and on a heavy soil this can be achieved by planting out young plants on prepared sites. Where more exotic mead is required, introduced plants are best established initially as large clumps.

My comments here apply particularly to northern temperate conditions, but, even then, every site will vary and only trial and error will determine which plants can look after themselves in competitive grass. Such plants are usually vigorous and well adapted to heavy soils. *Filipendula ulmaria* (meadowsweet) is well adapted to wet soils, tolerating a summer mow, and even recovering after premature decapitation by mowing to flower again later in summer; and *F. rubra* 'Venusta' can also be naturalised in heavy grass. *Iris sibirica* and other clump-forming irises have grown well for me in grass for twenty years, but, again, beware *I. pseudacorus* (yellow flag), which takes over all around, brooking no challenge, and is hard work to remove.

Inulas do well, as does the related *Pulicaria dysenterica* (common fleabane). Some lysimachias (*Lysimachia punctata*, *L. ciliata* 'Firecracker') can also outcompete grass, and the vigorous *Crocosmia* 'Lucifer' seems to delight in open damp grassland.

Many buttercups occur naturally in wet meadows, but in heavy grass they tend to be sparsely spaced, though their flowers still fleck the mead with gold. *Ranunculus repens* (creeping buttercup) can form very dense patches either on fresh soil, for the year or two after the grass has been turned in by cultivation, or where animals disturb grass. Meadow cranesbill (*Geranium pratense*), with pale blue flowers, also copes with grass and can be found growing naturally in damp sites, to 60 cm (2 ft.) or more.

Happily, *Primula vulgaris* (primrose), *P. veris* (cowslip), and their hybrids grow in wet grassland. So do members of the dock family; common sorrel (*Rumex acetosa*) and common bistort (*Persicaria bistorta*) are particularly successful. Some of the more popular and vigorous cultivated grasses (cortaderia, miscanthus) can be planted as large clumps in rough grass; however, from an aesthetic viewpoint, these need careful positioning and will have to be cut down in late winter.

Centaurea nigra (knapweed) survives well, and its flowers are attractive to butterflies and day-flying, summer-migrant silver Y

This false oxlip (a hybrid between a cowslip and a primrose) can, like its parents, compete in wet grassland.

moths (*Autographa gamma*). For me a most unexpected success arrived unaided when native wood anemones appeared and increased, by both seed and rhizome, in competitive wet grass, where they now form large clumps. *Saxifraga granulata* (meadow saxifrage) has also increased, but under the shade of trees.

SAFE USE OF CHEMICALS

Biocides, however termed—be it herbicide, fungicide, insecticide, acaricide, molluscicide—are chemicals that can act toxically on living cells of both plants and animals; they must be treated with caution. Legislation has greatly reduced the range of biocides available to the home gardener; check with local authorities or extension agents for current specifics. What cannot be outdated is that thought must be given to the potential hazards even approved substances might bring. It goes without saying that the safety and usage instructions that come with the biocide must be read and followed. Even if there are no written instructions advising on particular care, it is sensible always to use rubber gloves and goggles at the minimum, particularly when handling concentrates or spraying, and ideally to further cover up with overalls and rubber boots. In commercial practice much more is known and legislated for—requirements involving risk assessments, full safety clothing, and facilities such as emergency showers, washing down areas, safe disposal of containers, safe storage of materials, warning notices, closure to the public of sprayed areas, and above all, certified training.

So even though legislation will vary from country to country, for all use of biocides, safety must be the paramount consideration, and for wet gardens particularly, avoid contaminating any areas near water.

WEEDS

For good weed control, the guiding principle is to remove weeds when young, which means weeding little but often, and never letting a weed distribute its seeds. Remember too that pernicious weeds can easily be imported in untreated soil.

A great many native plants, from buttercups to grasses and sedges, are able to produce seed that can keep for years under the anaerobic conditions of wet soil. The fact that fern spores survive well in these conditions may be useful from a conservation standpoint in

58

the recovery of lost plants, but for the gardener the amount and frequency of weed germination is sometimes amazing.

For herbaceous beds, there are few options to regular hand-weeding and bark mulches. But again, when hoed off on wet soils, young weeds shrivel only in very dry conditions; most often, they will reroot and recover. Nevertheless, I always minimise the use of weed-killers. And certainly with watersheds that feed river systems used for water extraction, water authorities rightly exercise strict control and licensing over any waterside use of chemicals.

When I do resort to an herbicide, I use a small (10 cm, 4 in.) sprinkler bar on a watering can, which gives both economy and control, to apply a narrow band only along the grass edge of beds. This inhibits weeds, stops the incursion of perennial grasses, and reduces to a minimum the otherwise frequent need for edging the grass. Weed germination slows after the longest day, but expect another germination and growth blip in autumn, especially if the weather is warm and moist.

Sometimes it is convenient to treat tree planting rings early in the year, in late March, and although much slower to act in cold temperatures, the translocated herbicide glyphosate (marketed under several trade names) still works. Also when the trees are dormant it is less likely to be damaging, particularly to plants like cornus and magnolias, which seem very sensitive, particularly when buds are opening. However since annuals will then germinate on the then-bare soil in summer, nonsusceptible trees are best treated later in spring. Keeping the planting ring clear for about five years encourages growth; thereafter, trees can usually outcompete grasses. Weed-killing around the base of young trees in grass also helps to avoid damage to trees by mowers: where grass grows close to trees, one is encouraged to mow closer to them, which in turn increases the chance of mechanical damage. Such wounds can allow the entry of decay organisms and are often the cause of death for young trees.

Gravel and paved areas

Weeding gravel paths and other areas is yet another concern in wet gardens. A membrane beneath the gravel greatly reduces perennial weed growth; but again, gravel over a moist substrate provides perfect conditions for the germination of seedlings. This is useful in some respects. I find I can take a regular supply of seedlings from gravel, because almost every garden plant that borders it produces seedlings (*Schizostylis* and other bulbs, in abundance); I notice now a ring of freely flowering muscari seedlings in the gravel around the raised bed in which their parent bulbs no longer survive.

Inevitably weed seeds germinate with equal vigour. Early in the year I hand-weed, thinking robotically, "I will control," but as the season warms I am usually defeated in this battle unless prepared to give it time weekly. Proprietary path and drive weedkillers remain available to the public, but some of the more persistent have now been banned. When treating gravel or paved areas, remember that tree roots may well be running underneath; and rain, soon after application, can wash off some herbicides onto adjacent areas. Because I tend to spot-treat only heavy infestations, a curious effect of this has been the selective adaptation of annual meadow-grass, *Poa annua*. Normally light green, in very Darwinian fashion, a superbly camouflaged form with red leaves occurred in the gravel. I missed it as a young plant, and now have a great hand-weeding battle against the maroon progeny of this hard-to-spot strain.

Even given a good foundation, wet soil contracting or expanding beneath paving, as it dries or saturates, causes its joints to move and crack. These fill with soil from ants and worms beneath and dust above, and weeds then colonise the cracks. On the plus side, this also allows desirable plants to grow and soften the effect of the paving. I use the Sicilian silver-leaved daisy *Anthemis punctata* subsp. *cupaniana* for this purpose, in a warm spot, among paving and gravel on a wet soil, where it provides a mat of silver foliage throughout the year; lasting for about two years, it regenerates freely from its copiously produced seed. But the cracks also require the regular cleaning off of such plants as procumbent pearlwort (*Sagina procumbens*) and grasses.

Pernicious weeds

Every region of the world has its problem weeds. Many are persistent annuals and biennial weeds of open ground, such as the bittercresses (*Cardamine*) with their explosively distributed seed. A few on wet soil are problematic, once seeded, but most are easily controlled. For grass areas and woodland gardens I should mention cleavers (*Galium aparine*); its small hooked fruits cling, like those of burdock, meaning mammals can readily spread it, and its seeds germinate all year long. The soft thin-stemmed seedlings will succumb to herbicides or hand hoes, or even rakes for plants in long grass or among shrubs, but all must be removed before seed is set and ripe. Hand-pulling small colonies can be effective; any missed plants can be mown out, if in grass, or carefully weed-killed if among herbs in a woodland garden. Ideally it is desirable to have it under control by May. Some people's skin is sensitive to the clinging stems of the mature plant and, when still green, its seeds can stain clothing.

The airborne seeds of annual and perennial epilobiums, goat willows, fleabanes, and sow-thistles can germinate all over a wet garden. The annuals are relatively easily controlled by conventional means; it is the perennial weeds, thriving among the roots of herbaceous garden plants, that are most difficult to control.

Umbellifers include some of the worst weeds, notably *Aegopodium podagraria* (ground elder), which has persistent spreading underground parts; these require at least two applications of a systemic herbicide, a forking out of the remnants in the dormant season, and probably further forking out of any surviving pieces the following summer. On heavy soil, big umbellifers like cow parsley (*Anthriscus sylvestris*), along with docks and nettles, can be controlled on a small scale by hand-digging. It is this or nothing for hogweed (*Heracleum sphondylium*): hogweeds "laugh" at the regular passage of a mower or the use of selective lawn herbicides. Once seeded, new seedlings will arise year after year and because they are so difficult to control, and deep rooted, they are best removed as soon as seen. In the Castle Howard arboretum, hogweeds happily dominate the heavy grassland among trees, and they are, in a rugged way, an attractive and useful addition for wildlife.

The perennial *Urtica dioica* (stinging nettle) spreads by new shoots arising from runners that are close to the surface, and in long grass also from the stems of last year's growth that fall and lie on the soil surface over winter. If these are in their second year, they are likely to be shallow rooted and can be skimmed off from grass with the turf in which they are embedded. Also, to some extent, they can be mown out, but lawn herbicides also give good control.

Bindweed (*Calystegia sepium*) can be a problem once established among other plants, leading desperate gardeners to train its growth onto canes, which are then treated with a translocated herbicide in the hope of killing its thin, deep set, brittle, white rhizomes. Creeping thistle (*Cirsium arvense*) is certainly very pernicious and defeats any attempt to dig it out; it can take over a garden, producing offsets as much as 3 m (10 ft.) away from the main plant. Any translocated weedkiller used to control this species will be more effective if it is used in an oil-based suspension that can adhere to the foliage.

Attractive as they are in flower and leaf, it is not wise to introduce

Aegopodium podagraria (ground elder)

Blanket weed can be raked out of small ponds.

any butterbur (*Petasites*) to a wet garden, for they will soon dominate large areas, and they are also very difficult to remove. Their spreading rhizomes go deep, and they can recover from many herbicide treatments and mowing. Even more impossible to control are horsetails (*Equisetum*). The roots of these very successful, very tough survivors (their ancestors helped form the coal measures) go deep, and their water-shedding stem surfaces resist herbicides (from some species, these silica-coated shoots were once used as pan scourers). The aboveground shoots can be killed easily enough, but not the underground stems; and the wetter the soil, the more equisetums can spread. Reducing the spore-bearing cones, which are produced on separate short stalks in spring before the new season's shoots emerge, might help reduce new colonies. Mowing scarcely affects it: it can travel under 2 m (6.6 ft.) of tightly mown grass. The oft-recommended crushing of the leaves, in the hope they will absorb enough translocated herbicide to kill the underground parts, is in my experience a faint hope, so it is best not to let it get started! Be warned.

As for pernicious weeds of bog and water, blanket weeds, which are formed from filamentous algae, become a problem where their long, ever-extending chains of cells fill ponds. In summer heat, they float up to the surface in yellowy green masses. This is notably a concern in new ponds with high nutrient levels, where the natural balance of aquatic animals and plants has yet to be achieved.

On a small scale, surplus algae can be raked out or their long threads removed by twirling them, like candyfloss, onto a stick. Be sure to protect any creatures caught up in its mass of fine strands; newts lay their eggs in filamentous algae, and it also provides shelter for the aquatic stages of several other amphibians. Various algicides are now available including slow-release formulations; barley straw has been used to good effect in small ponds, as has tannic acid; and I have seen large ponds treated with lime, though not very successfully.

Unicellular algae can turn the water green; this often occurs after a pool is refilled, or in spring as the water warms, simply because the algae can respond by quickly increasing to take up the winter's accumulation of nutrients. This abundance of algae is usually short-lived where there are higher plants that can take up the nutrients by their growth, and their leaves will also shade out the algae. Organic dyes are sometimes used to darken water and reduce light transmission, but where the water has naturally become too dark or milky,

OPERATIONS

this may indicate rotting vegetation that needs removal. Autumn leaves, too, darken water (and are grazed by the tadpoles of frogs and toads in spring); even a gentle trickle of water into a pool will allow an overflow that will at least keep the surface clear.

Many introduced water plants have become invasive weeds with excessive growth that can block waterways and fill ponds, so devastating local waterlife. This is especially true in tropical regions. As a general guide, be very careful when disposing of nonnative plants from garden ponds; ideally they should be composted and not given the chance to escape into local waterways.

Conservation bodies worldwide are targeting introduced species. The New World *Azolla filiculoides* (Z7), for example, has established in some Old World ponds; this small tropical American floating water-fern can quickly cover water surfaces. Others include the North American *Hydrocotyle ranunculoides* (floating pennywort), which is spreading rapidly in Britain, though it was first recorded as an established alien only in 1990. It is slightly similar to, but larger than, the peltate-leaved *H. vulgaris* (marsh pennywort), native in Britain. *Lagarosiphon major* (curly waterweed) from South Africa is a well-known and long-established concern, and seemingly *Ludwigia grandiflora* (water-primrose) is also now a worry. The South American *Myriophyllum aquaticum* (parrot's-feather), which is often grown in aquaria for its attractive foliage, is a concern for its likely disposal into drains, by which means it could reach waterways; it can persist as a terrestrial on wet soil and is naturalised widely in North America, where it is considered noxious, and in scattered locations in Britain. The Eurasian *M. spicatum* is an aggressive waterweed in North America.

It is easy to accidentally introduce aquatic weeds when bringing in new plants for a pool. Wet soil presents similar worries; of particular concern must be *Crassula helmsii*, a pigmyweed from Australia, Tasmania, and New Zealand. I have been "less than amused" by the tenacity of this now notoriously noxious perennial. Not content with being an amazingly successful aquatic plant, it also thrives well out of water on damp soil. It can readily colonise plant beds, is immune to any method of control, and is almost impossible to remove once established.

There are of course invasive weeds for all habitats, but for wet soil others that come to mind are the eastern Asian knotweeds *Fallopia japonica* and *F. sachalinensis* and their hybrid, which are aggressive

Lythrum salicaria (purple loosestrife), a Eurasian weed of American wetlands

Eichhornia crassipes (water-hyacinth) covering a lake in Honduras

spreaders and very difficult to eradicate, and the Eurasian *Lythrum salicaria* (purple loosestrife), an unwelcome invader of North American wetlands. (In Britain these plants, the "long purples" of William Morris's description of his Thames-side flora, are relatively well behaved, but will grow rankly in warm wet conditions and will seed around.) Many aquatic plants are naturally invasive. Cattails (*Typha*), for example, are aggressive colonisers of shallow water and lake margins; and even if containerized, their seed disperses in the wind. *Eichhornia crassipes* (water-hyacinth) from South America can quickly increase to form a floating mass on the surface of warm water; killed by frost, it can just survive through summer on pools in temperate regions.

Control by animals

Ducks have their pros and cons in gardens, but an ability they have in their favour is the control of waterweeds. Against this, their droppings increase nitrogen levels and encourage algal blooms. Once, a cleared part of my large natural pond was quickly and extensively colonised by a potamogeton, most of which are persistent, spreading weeds. But the mallards thought it a good addition to their diet, and it was soon completely removed and did not recur. Mallards will also eat large quantities of blanket weed. Tadpoles and toads graze on algae, as do koi and many other fish.

Many commonly used herbicides and insecticides (particularly, with the latter, the pyrethroids or their analogues) do great damage to fish and other wildlife. So at least water birds have a useful role in this respect. They will, if numbers increase, even control *Crassula helmsii*, but they will take all other plants as well, save for the very vigorous.

Mulching

Because of the considerable weed growth on heavy soils, mulching (especially with shredded bark) to suppress weeds is a useful practice, but some repeated words of caution. Heavy organic mulches and synthetic materials, particularly black plastic sheet, will keep an already wet soil very wet. This may cause the decay of mulched plants in winter. This general caution to avoid heavy mulches on wet soils extends to other organic mulches, such as weed-free garden compost.

Bark that has been stacked for a year can be used among herbaceous plants but may need perhaps three applications over a period of three to four years to build up a good weed-suppressing layer. Unfortunately, and frequently, blackbirds and other garden birds will literally throw the bark off the bed within a few days. Over a year or two, the bark breaks down to a peat-like substance that is particularly conducive to the growth of woodland plants.

With wet beds, sand or gravel can also be added to good effect. Curiously I find that these materials can be very inhibitive of underlying grass and weed seeds but can encourage more fresh seed germination, though weed seedlings are easily pulled from sand. As ever, mulching is more effective where the plant bed is slightly raised above the general soil level; also, when drier, the mulch will break down more slowly.

DISEASES AND PESTS

The mass movement of people, plants, and materials has greatly facilitated the spread of pathogens as well as weeds. Plant introductions new to a country are normally established without their naturally occurring diseases and pests, but as the stock of each new plant is increased, it represents a waiting food source. Sooner or later a pest or disease will arise to exploit this resource and then spread rapidly. Most such problems are then carried to gardens on newly acquired plants, so some isolation of new introductions to any garden is worthwhile until they are shown to be healthy.

Plants in wet gardens are more vulnerable to disease: notice the rate at which fence posts, whether treated or not, turn to dust on a wet soil under attack from both insects and fungi, such that concrete posts become the preferred choice. From leaf blight on potatoes and tomatoes; to black spot on roses, which attacks small stems as well as leaves; to mildews—all seem more damaging on wet soils. Waterlogging, too, can cause root decay, and by weakening and killing roots, will allow disease entry. Trees can be attacked by a range of fungi, from the more obvious honey fungus (*Armillaria mellea*) to similarly lethal phytophthoras.

For most gardens it is generally uneconomic to undertake large-scale spraying, but it can be worthwhile when using newer systemic fungicides against diseases on roses and other prized ornamentals; bud blight on rhododendrons, for instance, is controlled by spraying an insecticide in July to control leafhoppers.

Rosa 'Maiden's Blush'

Guidance points
- Select disease-resistant varieties and rootstocks. For example, the shrub rose *Rosa* 'Maiden's Blush' grows on its own roots and is resistant to most rose diseases, including black spot.
- Remember good hygiene, especially when propagating: use pasteurised compost and clean pots for seedlings, and select disease-free cutting material. Remember, too, that fungi can be carried in the water of storage tanks.
- Keep the crown of susceptible plants above any waterlogging when planting.
- Avoid pruning trees and shrubs that have poor wound-healing ability.
- Remove and burn (where allowed) all diseased shoots and wood.
- Allow for the free flow of air around vulnerable plants where feasible.
- Use chemicals safely.

Curiously, it is often larger animals, not insects, that cause intractable problems in gardens. Deer are a real worry; nature lovers adore having them visit their gardens but for those who love their specimen plants, especially trees, an expensive perimeter deer fence is the only effective defence. Similarly, badgers can be amazingly destructive of lawns, if populated by chafers or other grubs, and they can damagingly root up a woodland garden. They can also excavate deeply and quickly beneath a fence to gain entry, but low electric fencing can help keep them out. Fortunately for the wet garden, they prefer light well-drained soils

Similarly, if rabbits and hares gain access to a garden, all young trees, roses, and choice herbaceous plants are at risk, though some azaleas are sufficiently toxic to be avoided by their incisors. Even smaller mammals such as field voles will take small seedling trees and will even debark fig trees, but not terminally. Since I like voles more than figs, I live happily with them (they tend to favour life in uncut vegetation).

Certainly a wildlife-friendly garden has its concerns, not least of which, in my case, is the endless damage caused by wild ducks. One of the most significant factors in bank soil erosion is the bill of a duck! Unchecked a flock of mallard ducks can expand the radial area of a large pond by a metre a year.

Within a garden, a good balance of amphibians and other wildlife usually keeps invertebrate pests within bounds. Though I rarely need to use biocides, I am pleased to see a molluscicide based on the relatively safe ferric phosphate now being marketed: wet gardens are renowned for slugs and snails. Allowing garden insects open access to my greenhouse in summer provides full natural biological control of aphids, red spider mites, and whitefly on the normally vulnerable cucumbers and tomatoes, and it is always home to the odd frog and toad.

As long as it is not carrying a damaging disease, decaying wood is also an important habitat for many beneficial hover flies, which are equally encouraged by sweet-smelling flowers. Many people (even those who do not suffer a dangerous allergy to wasp stings) take fright on seeing a wasp nest and seek its destruction. I usually have two or three common wasp nests and the occasional tree wasp nest in my garden; I warn children to avoid the immediate nest areas and leave the wasps to usefully control flies and other insect pests.

Happily biological control agents can now be purchased for use against an increasing range of pests, and the encouragement of the garden's natural control agents—from beetles to parasitic wasps—is increasingly recognised as effective. And for both healthier plant growth and increased disease resistance, the supplementary use of mycorrhizal fungi has become common practise in commercial plant production.

Iris sibirica shows where the pond bank was before erosion by ducks.

MANAGING PLANTS ON WET SOIL

Planting

Freshly dug soil slowly sinks, sometimes reducing by about twenty percent of its volume. Thus planting level with the surrounding soil will, as the soil compacts, leave the new plant in a waterlogged sump. Keeping the crown of the tree or shrub—the point where stem and roots meet—above any possible standing water, greatly helps survival. Except of course if, perversely, a dry spell follows, and one has to resort to watering. But the bonus of wet soils is that planting can take place in almost any month of the year, normally without the need for watering. Early autumn is the best time to plant trees and shrubs, but it is preferable to divide and plant herbaceous plants in spring.

Small trees will be subject to wind rock; a light wind can loosen birch or liquidambar when in full leaf on a wet soil, even two years after planting, and wind rock tends to be progressive, being worsened by subsequent winds. Part of the problem is in the greater amount of shoot growth and correspondingly weaker roots shown by plants being established on wet soils. Accepting this, I sometimes find it necessary to securely stake young trees with short (75 cm, 30 in.) diagonally set stakes during their first few years. Raised beds can help, and trees grown under the competitive effects of long grass are invariably more secure.

Pruning

Many well-known pruning guides tell how to keep popular garden shrubs—deutzias, philadelphuses, shrub roses, weigelas—within the bounds of their chosen site and in good flower. On a wet soil, in smaller gardens, the need for such pruning increases because of the generally more vigorous growth. This shows particularly with soft fruits, such as red and white currants, and only to a slightly lesser extent with black currants: unless these are hard-pruned annually, it is not long before a saw will be needed to more dramatically constrain their expansion.

This extra vigour is also more noticeable on wall climbers. With the warmth and protection afforded by walls on moist soils, climbing roses, for example, will need both winter and summer pruning—and sometimes twice in summer. Shadier walls are more manageable, but even then, climbers will produce a mass of new growth. With parthenocissuses, if the abundant summer growth is not a concern, pruning can be left until after leaf fall so as first to enjoy its autumn colour. But more often, on house walls, the growth of shoots over windows and roofs demands summer pruning.

Because of the higher risk of disease in wet areas, it is best to prune only when essential. This applies particularly to snake-bark maples and other plants that do not wound-heal very well. With slow wound-healers, such as magnolias, I tend to undertake any pruning required in mid-summer so that they have the rest of the growing season to form callus. With such trees, it is also sensible to carry out any formative pruning at an early stage because the cuts made when removing small branches heal more successfully. Such pruning might be to give a clear bole or to eliminate split leads; over time, as the weight of the branches increase, the point where the branches narrowly diverge becomes stressed and can split in strong wind.

Pruning can be undertaken at most times of the year, but avoid pruning in spring when sap is rising and, where flowering is important, prune after flowering. Some trees, such as birch and tulip trees, may grow too fast on wet soils and carry too much leafy growth on stems that can snap or tear off in light wind. Pruning is thus necessary to reduce the sail effect of wind on their foliage; not only will they lose branches, but they can rock and become insecure.

Labelling

People assume they will remember the name and details of the plants they acquire for their gardens, but as the years pass and acquisitions increase, few are the owners who can recall all that they possess. It is a good discipline to keep a garden book, noting all new plants or packets of seed, with (if possible) any notes about the plant. Also, with such accessible online guides as the Royal Horticultural Society's database (http://www.rhs.org.uk/databases/summary. asp), the correct spelling and form of name can be checked at the start; all too often plants are sold with superseded or incorrectly spelled names.

Though fiddly and needing careful use, etching zinc or zinc-coated labels with an acid "ink" gives a very durable label; alternatively, aluminium-coated labels, on which pencil and certain types of ink can bond chemically, last for twenty years or more. When attaching labels by wire, a pliable wire is easier to manipulate and reattach, as will be needed from time to time; the wire should be plastic-coated because metal labels often suffer corrosion by electrolysis when a different metal is used for the attaching wire.

Labels can be lost with herbaceous plants when they are buried by burgeoning growth or, if small, removed by birds, or, on trees and shrubs, if they have been attached to lower branches that die and drop off. Labels on woody plants need checking at least annually. Where they are attached to trees, the label's attachment wires can quickly strangle an expanding branch or main stem. I can recall a young, 4 m (13 ft.) liquidambar, which in autumn showed the presence of a stem-constricting tie by having bright red leaves above the tie and green below. Also if such wires are eventually subsumed into the growing tree, they form a weak point that may later fail.

Labelling is a demanding task, but it is the key to learning about plants—especially as one embarks on the trials and errors of plant selection for the wet garden.

CHAPTER 4
Ferns and conifers

FERNS

Perhaps because they are so different from higher plants, ferns are often thought of as difficult or demanding. In fact, they are an easy way to bring a green and tranquil grace to gardens, and many are adapted to moist soils.

Ferns have a cosmopolitan distribution; they are abundant in moist tropical forests, where many grow as epiphytes. Their dust-like spores germinate on moist surfaces to form a small, delicate, disk or peg-like, sometimes liverwort-like, prothallus. Some form separate male and female prothalli, but many are bisexual, and critically they need a moist film in which the motile male gametes can swim to fertilise the female gamete. The fertilised egg germinates on the prothallus to form the sporophyte, which is the more recognisable fern. The types of spore case, or the arrangement of sori on a frond, are important guides to fern identification.

Of the wealth of ferns, somewhere between 10,000 and 12,000 species from 230 or more genera, only a small proportion have become familiar garden plants.

Cultivation

Ferns vary in their tolerance to a very wet soil. Most aquatic ferns are easy to grow (indeed, many have become weeds); a few of these are considered a little further in chapter 7. Some streambank ferns can cope with regular flooding, and for cool temperate gardens the rhizomatous *Onoclea sensibilis* (sensitive fern) spreads well on wet soil and will even stray into the water of a pool. Though sensitive fern is often seen, osmundas are perhaps the most popular ferns for waterside plantings in temperate gardens.

With habitat loss and change, many ferns are now scarce in nature. As a matter of principle, then, it is best for gardeners to use only plants that have been raised in nurseries; a good range, in both form and beauty, is normally available. With many of those considered here, raised beds can greatly extend the range of species grown on a wet soil. In recent years the Victorian stumpery has recovered some appeal, and carefully arranged cut stumps and gnarled branches can be used to support raised beds, using plenty of leaf mould, thus providing ideal conditions for many ferns.

Some of the more popularly grown garden ferns, such as the hardy polystichums, can be accommodated in normal flower beds, particularly if partly shaded, such as by a north wall. Most ferns, however, are more usually grown in shaded woodland areas. For me, one of the pleasures of a wet garden is in creating sites where ferns can prosper, rather than shrivel, which is often the case on summer-dry light soils.

Fortunately, hardy ferns are little troubled by pests and diseases. Where scale insects or other pests arise, remember ferns are often far more sensitive than higher plants to insecticides, so the dilution rate may need to be halved. Where feasible, the use of biological control agents is now preferred.

Young fronds under glass are sensitive to sun, particularly in spring; shading can prevent damage. The red colour of young fronds, as seen in blechnums, is there to help protect against sun scorch in warm regions.

Most ferns require neutral to acid soils, in the range of pH 6.0–6.5, though some (*Asplenium scolopendrium*, *Polystichum setiferum*) tolerate a higher pH. Similarly, watering with soft water (rainwater, for example, where it can be collected and stored) is required.

TOP *Onoclea sensibilis*
ABOVE *Polystichum setiferum*
Divisilobum Group

Propagation

Generally fern spores can be collected once the sori have fully developed. The fertile frond is then cut and held dry in a well-sealed paper envelope, wherein spores will quickly be shed naturally. Those with green spores may ripen in summer (as with *Osmunda*), or in winter (as with *Onoclea*); such spores tend to be short-lived. In all cases, it is better to sow fresh spores.

Because they are so fine and readily airborne, care has to be taken and an isolated place is needed for sowing spores, with only one species being dealt with at a time. They are usually sown into small (7.5 cm, 3 in.) pots filled with acid organic compost. The pot is surface "sterilised" with boiling water, spores sown, and the pot then covered with a glass lid and stood in a tray of clean water in a shady place (or the whole pot can be sealed in a polythene bag). Sometimes spores will germinate naturally in gardens, given constant moisture.

After a month or so, a fine green film indicates the germination of the spores and the initial growth of prothalli. At a later stage prothalli, with emergent sporophytes, may be patched off into larger pans or, if several plants are required, left until the sporophytes are large enough to pot individually.

Division of rhizomes or splitting of clumps is fairly straightforward, and for hardy ferns can be undertaken in late autumn or early spring, though recovery can be slow and they need to be kept moist and shaded during this period. Many produce bulbils or gemmae, as often suggested by their names (*Polystichum proliferum*, *Woodwardia unigemmata*). More unusually, with the hardy *Asplenium scolopendrium*, the basal part of the leaf may be used as a cutting.

From the multitude of ferns a few, mostly temperate, are considered here (arranged by family), but for the fern enthusiast with a wet garden, a great many more can be grown.

BLECHNACEAE

CHAIN FERN FAMILY

A family of cosmopolitan terrestrial ferns, with the blechnums mostly from the southern and woodwardias from the northern hemisphere. Some blechnums have upright, stem-like rhizomes; others are creeping, and all are fairly robust. The evergreen *Blechnum spicant* (hard fern), native in Britain, tolerates both wet soil and dry periods. The large (1.2 m, 4 ft.) southern South American *B. chilense* (Z7) and smaller (30 cm, 12 in.) sprawling surface-rooting *B. penna-marina* from Australia, New Zealand, and southern South America, occur by streams and swamps and are very tolerant of wet soil. *Blechnum penna-marina* has an alpine form that is hardy in Zone 5; it is particular in its requirements, and not easy to establish in some sites, as it needs a moist well-shaded north slope. Once established, however, it is capable of forming a dense, dark green, weed-excluding spreading mat of many square metres in area, making it a valuable ground cover among large shrubs. Similarly, *B. minus*, *B. wattsii*, and several other subtropical and tropical species occur on wet soil.

Woodwardias (chain ferns) provide some attractive garden ferns; most tolerate wet sites and some are hardy. *Woodwardia areolata* (60 cm, 24 in.) and *W. virginica* (1.2 m, 4 ft.) from eastern North America occur in wet acid places; another to try is the wide-ranging, western North American *W. fimbriata* (1.2 m, 4 ft., or more; Z8). Some Asian species are also grown, but hardiness is a question, as it is with the European chain fern *W. radicans*, which has an Atlantic distribution in southwestern Europe (Z9) and is often found by streams. Given warm conditions, its fronds can grow to 2 m (6.6 ft.) but −5°C (23°F) sets its limit; in mild gardens, 75 cm (30 in.) might be a more reasonable expectation.

The spreading, rhizomatous blechnums can be readily divided, but recovery is slow. *Woodwardia radicans* and some other chain ferns will produce plantlets (gemmae) where their fronds touch the ground.

CYATHEACEAE

TREE-FERN FAMILY

Looking up into the crown of a mature cyathea, as sunlight filters through, is a magical experience. *Cyathea* is a large genus of tree-ferns, often occurring on moist mountains, from the tropics and subtropics. Individual fronds, which are evergreen, may be 2–4 m (6.6–13 ft.) long; and in temperate gardens, the trunk-like caudices of *C. australis* from eastern Australia and *C. smithii* from New Zealand can grow to 3 m (10 ft.) or more (they reach several times that height in their native environment). Another New Zealand cyathea—and one of the most sought-after, for the beautiful silvered reverse on its fronds (3 × 1 m, 10 × 3.3 ft.)—is *C. dealbata*. All require a moist atmosphere and moist soil with good drainage, and winter protection: they are on the edge of hardiness, being often restricted to moist, mild coastal regions (Z9/10). Mature "trunks" (the tough central caudex that carries the conductive vessels) are more frequently imported now, and while these have to be kept moist, especially when being reestablished, some, such as *C. australis*, are proving hardier than expected, and *C. dealbata* regenerates naturally from spores in southwest Ireland.

DICKSONIACEAE

SOFT TREE-FERN FAMILY

In the 1980s, the out-of-doors cultivation of tree-ferns was more or less confined to mild coastal gardens in Zone 9, but the considerable importation of their large trunk-like caudices has made dicksonias compulsory for the make-over garden in Zone 8. Most are the very easily grown Australian *Dicksonia antarctica*, which soft tree-

Blechnum chilense

Polystichum polyblepharum

fern is evergreen and can reach 15 m (50 ft.) in moist forest, often by streams; in temperate gardens, it grows a caudex up to 3 m (10 ft.) with fronds of 1.5–2.5 m (5–8 ft.). Without crown protection, small plants are more vulnerable to winter damage, becoming deciduous; though usefully, they are tolerant of the occasional watering with hard water. *Dicksonia fibrosa* from New Zealand and *D. sellowiana* from tropical America will grow outdoors if sheltered, although they are not as tolerant of cold wet winters as *D. antarctica*.

While enjoying moist conditions, most soft tree-ferns require reasonable drainage. Plants can be readily raised from spores.

DRYOPTERIDACEAE

WOOD FERN FAMILY

The evergreen holly ferns of the small genus *Cyrtomium* have short erect rhizomes and simple shiny pinnate leaves. The genus is familiar to gardeners through two temperate species, *C. falcatum* (30–50 cm, 12–20 in.), which is often grown as a houseplant, and the smaller, narrower-fronded *C. fortunei* from eastern Asia. They tolerate both slightly acid or alkaline soils and sun and shade. *Cyrtomium falcatum*, which has a wider Asian distribution, is set back and loses its leaves around −8°C (18°F). *Cyrtomium fortunei* (Z8) is hardier. Both require a moist but reasonably drained soil.

Dryopteris (buckler-fern) is a very large genus that includes many tough, hardy, and mostly deciduous garden ferns. The habitat requirement of buckler-ferns varies from dry rocks to bog, though I find those of wet woods as well as the "bog" species grow well on my wet soil, where, once established, some even survive dry periods. The easily grown European *D. dilatata* (broad buckler-fern; Z4) has streamsides and water meadows in its habitat range, and the hardier *D. cristata* (Z3), which occurs both in Europe and North America, grows on wet acid marshy ground. Though native in southern Britain, *D. cristata* is scarce and endangered; its fertile fronds are upright and up to 1 m (3.3 ft.) in length, twice the size of its sterile fronds.

The robust *Dryopteris filix-mas* (male fern; Z4) from Eurasia and North America is a tough garden plant, often occurring naturally or naturalising in gardens. In my own Zone 8 garden, it has been spreading by spores for some years along a wet ditch, but it can be weak-growing if heavily overshadowed by trees. Its fronds will grow to 1.2 m (4 ft.).

Of the many buckler-ferns in gardens I have a soft spot for *Dryopteris erythrosora* (Japanese shield-fern; Z6) from eastern Asia with its red under-frond sori and bronze-red young fronds. A modest plant, 30–60 cm (12–24 in.) for me, it offers a permanent association with the hillsides of Kyoto. It is partly deciduous in cold conditions.

The cosmopolitan polystichums are very popular garden plants, not least the many hardy garden forms of *Polystichum setiferum* (soft shield-fern; Z5) from Europe. The finely divided foliage is a dark shining green, and the fairly evergreen fronds reach 30–120 cm (12–48 in.). Good drainage is recommended, but it grows well on permanently wet heavy soil, as do several other shield-ferns. *Polystichum aculeatum* (Z4), with a similar range, is sometimes confused with this species, though the pinnules of *P. aculeatum* are attached acutely.

The evergreen *Polystichum polyblepharum* (60 cm, 24 in.; Z6) from eastern China, Japan, and Korea, and *P. tsussimense* (30 cm, 12 in.; Z7), which ranges more widely in northeast and eastern Asia, are commonly available and are very tolerant of wet soil, as it seems are most shield-ferns.

HYMENOPHYLLACEAE

FILMY-FERN FAMILY

The delicate cosmopolitan filmy-ferns are cautiously mentioned here: several are rare and protected, and for those in cultivation, special care is needed. Their translucent leaves are mostly just a single cell's thickness, and they require constantly damp, shaded conditions but good drainage. They can be grown in closed cases and terraria but on very rare occasions may occur naturally in gardens, as does *Hymenophyllum tunbrigense* (Tunbridge filmy-fern; Z8) at Wakehurst.

Many spread by fine rhizomes to form clumps, but the roots of filmy-ferns are reduced and delicate, and sometimes absent (with tiny hairs then taking on their task). For many years Kew had a greenhouse within a greenhouse for these ferns, deeply shaded and set on the north side of the Orangery; the ferns were grown on tufa limestone in constant humidity. Such conditions suit another member of this family, *Trichomanes reniforme* (kidney-fern) from New Zealand. Most are propagated by division.

MARATTIACEAE

VESSEL FERN FAMILY

These are impressively large, tropical and subtropical evergreen ferns for the tropical garden. *Angiopteris evecta* from tropical Asia,

Hymenophyllum tunbrigense growing on moist sandstone under trees in deep shade at Wakehurst

Osmunda regalis with spores borne on the upper part of summer fronds

Polynesia, New Guinea, and Queensland, has long been cultivated for its massive arm-thick stipes on fronds that can reach 6 m (20 ft.).

Several marattias are in cultivation. In nature they occur in deep, moist and shaded forest gullies, often near streams in the tropics and subtropics in the Far East extending to New Zealand, Australia, and the New World. Though not as large as angiopteris, *Marattia excavata* from Mexico and Central and South America grows 2–5 m (6.6–16 ft.) and *M. salicina* from tropical Asia, Queensland, New Zealand, and South Pacific islands, to 4 m (13 ft.). They too have long succulent stipes, and their bi- and tripinnate fronds with glossy leaflets are distinct.

Angiopteris and marattias are relatively easy to grow given warmth moisture and an acid soil, though need good drainage to survive winters in a heated greenhouse. They both produce offsets, and angiopteris has thick roots from around the leaf bases, but both are difficult from spores. Their prothalli have fungal associations and will sometimes regenerate naturally around parent plants.

OSMUNDACEAE

ROYAL FERN FAMILY

This family includes some of the most desirable and beautiful ferns for wet gardens; however, they tend to be slow growing and have short-lived green spores. *Leptopteris superba* (Prince of Wales's fern) from New Zealand has gorgeous but delicately thin, evergreen fronds with a lustrous sheen, and a short stipe. Not only is it slow growing, but it has a need for constant moisture, though eventually it forms a small trunk, which can reach 1 m (3.3 ft.) on mature plants. Thus like filmy-ferns, while it needs humid conditions and soft water, it also needs good drainage. Several old specimens of the similar *L. hymenophylloides* were cultivated for more than fifty years in Kew's onetime cool but frost-free filmy-fern house.

The more familiar osmundas, of which there are ten or more species, vary in their tolerance of wet soil. The very hardy *Osmunda regalis* (royal fern; Z2) and its forms have a cosmopolitan range in Eurasia, Africa, and the Americas, and it is an ideal pondside plant, being very tolerant of wet soils. Over time it builds a large branched rhizome, and the deciduous fronds can be from 30 cm (1 ft.) in their early years to 3 m (10 ft.) in ideal warm, moist conditions. The fertile fronds are more erect, and bear sporangia on reduced pinnae on their upper part. Other osmundas may bear them part way down the frond, as in *O. claytoniana*, which is also very hardy and grows naturally in damp woodland in eastern Asia and North America, or have fully spore-bearing fronds without normal pinnae as in the hardy *O. cinnamomea* (cinnamon fern), which grows in swamps. Increase by spores or division.

PTERIDACEAE
BRAKE FERN FAMILY
Both the evergreen *Acrostichum speciosum* (mangrove fern; 60–200 cm, 2–6.6 ft.) from tropical Asia and Australia and the larger (1–3 m, 3.3–10 ft.) pan-tropical *A. aureum* from tidal mud flats grow in brackish water. They are relatively easy to grow in bright conditions on the margins of tropical pools. Increase by division or spores.

SCHIZAEACEAE
CLIMBING FERN FAMILY
A mainly tropical family of delicate-looking but tough climbing ferns. Several of the approximately forty species in *Lygodium* are grown. They have persistent rhizomes, and the climbing stems of the temperate (minimum 5°C, 40°F) Asian *Lygodium japonicum* are deciduous. Most, like *L. palmatum* (Hartford fern; to 1.2 m, 4 ft., or more) from eastern North America, which is reasonably hardy to –5°C (23°F), occur on moist acid soil, in swamps and on stream-banks. Spores are green and found on pinnules, usually toward the top of stems. Increase by spores or division.

THELYPTERIDACEAE
MARSH FERN FAMILY
Several members of this family of terrestrial ferns are of value in wet gardens. The European *Oreopteris limbosperma* (lemon-scented fern; 60–120 cm, 24–48 in.) is occasionally cultivated; in nature it is found on acid sand, often in mountains and sometimes by streams. *Phegopteris connectilis* (beech fern; Z2) from Eurasia and North America occurs in damp shady places, often by streams; its decidu-ous fronds can be 15–50 cm (6–20 in.), depending upon conditions, and it spreads slowly. Both species need a cool, moist acid soil with reasonable drainage. The former can be increased from spores, the latter also by division.

For wetter soil, the cosmopolitan *Thelypteris palustris* (marsh fern; Z4), as its common name indicates, occurs in fens and marshes in Eurasia, North Africa, and North America, with a restricted distri-bution in Britain. It has black rhizomes; its sterile fronds (15–60 cm,

Athyrium niponicum var. *pictum*

6–24 in.) are shorter than its fertile fronds (30–100 cm, 1.0–3.3 ft., or more). *Thelypteris simulata* (Z4) from North America occurs on moist soils, but it is not a bog dweller. Increase by spores or division.

Other tropical and subtropical ferns from this family that grow on wet soil are *Ampelopteris prolifera*, *Cyclosorus interruptus*, and *Pneumatopteris pennigera* (Jones 1987).

WOODSIACEAE

LADY FERN FAMILY

A very valuable family of ferns, particularly for wet temperate gardens. Most temperate species are deciduous, are easily raised from spores, and have either multiple crowns or rhizomes. The deciduous *Athyrium filix-femina* (lady fern; Z4) grows naturally in part-shaded sites on wet, neutral to acid soils and ranges through Eurasia and the Americas. Frond size is about 1 m (3.3 ft.)—more in good conditions, less (45–60 cm, 18–24 in.) when poorer. Its several cultivars offer a variety of delicately fronded forms for garden use.

Many athyriums grow well on permanently moist soil. In fact, the attractive *Athyrium niponicum* var. *pictum* (Japanese picture fern; Z6 or lower) from eastern Asia grows poorly, if at all, on soil that dries in summer. Some hybrids of this small coloured-frond fern (the silver-foliaged *A*. 'Ghost', for example) are increasingly popular in gardens.

Many of the more vigorous tropical and subtropical evergreen diplaziums grow well on wet soil. The rhizomatous *Gymnocarpium dryopteris* (oak fern; Z3), which occurs in Eurasia and eastern North America, also grows naturally on wet acid soils, to 22.5–30 cm (9–12 in.). Its spreading nature makes it a useful ground cover under woody plants.

The popular *Matteuccia struthiopteris* (ostrich fern; Z3 or lower), noted for its spring-green shuttlecocks of new fronds produced from a small erect caudex, becomes vigorous and colonising on a wet soil, even on a cold wet clay, and will soon produce new plants from the tips of stolons that run just below the soil surface. Its deciduous sterile fronds are 75–100 cm (30–40 in.) in length, but can grow half as much again; its fertile fronds, which stand upright and brown over winter, are about half this height. Spores are green and short-lived. This species occurs in central Europe, eastern Asia, and eastern North America, though the North American form is sometimes treated as a separate species, *M. pensylvanica*. All in this small genus, including *M. orientalis* (Z7) from the Himalayas and eastern Asia, grow well on wet soils.

Onoclea sensibilis (Z2) from northern Asia and North America is distinct; notably, its pale green fronds have netted veins. These fronds are upright and of two types: the shorter fertile fronds grow to around 80 cm (31 in.), the sterile fronds to around 1 m (3.3 ft.). It grows well on cold wet soil, its spreading rhizomes forming dense clumps, and can be invasive, though it may take a year or two for young divisions to establish and grow away. It is sensitive to drought, but its epithet is a reference to its summer leaves' sensible habit of dying down after the first frost of autumn.

All those mentioned can be increased by spores or division.

FERN ALLIES

EQUISETACEAE

HORSETAIL FAMILY

When it comes to growing horsetails, I am reminded that one man's weed is another man's treasure! In any case these distinctive plants—with unbranched main stems and whorls of very filiform, photosynthesising branches radiating from nodes—are supremely well adapted to wet soils. Leaves are much reduced and sheath-like, and the annual stems connect to persistent, spreading, sympodial rhizomes that, with many, penetrate deeply into the soil. The stems and branches are characteristically fluted and have added silica particles on their surfaces. They are widely distributed but do not occur naturally in Australia and New Zealand, where their importation is prohibited: several are troublesome weeds.

Some grow in shallow water, and many grow in neutral wet soils, but they are not much cultivated, albeit there is a privately held NCCPG collection. I once regretted introducing to a conservatory the tall (to 3 m, 10 ft.) *Equisetum giganteum* from Central and South America and the West Indies, for despite requests to keep it in a container it soon "escaped." On wet soil, equisetums spread unstoppably, and though their aboveground stems may be regularly mown or weed-killed, their rootstock has great powers of regeneration.

They can be attractive. I find pleasure in the white and dark green-banded deciduous stems, to 1.5 m (5 ft.), of *Equisetum telmateia* (great horsetail; Z4); I regularly pass this widespread (Eurasia, North Africa, and North America) species when walking my dog near my home, and I look especially in spring for the emergence of its sturdy spore-bearing strobili borne on short, branchless, pale stalks.

Equisetum telmateia

SELAGINELLACEAE

LESSER CLUBMOSS FAMILY

A large genus, mostly tropical in origin, of small-leaved herbaceous evergreens with a creeping rhizome and scale-like leaves. They are heterosporous, with both mega- and microprothalli. Sporophylls form at the tips of shoots. Most selaginellas occur in shady moist conditions, often growing in dense patches on the forest floor, or over rocks, though some are drought-adapted.

Many are cultivated, often under glass, but one or two, such as the African *Selaginella kraussiana* are hardier, and this latter has naturalised in parts of North America and Britain. They are relatively tough, easily grown plants, given constant moisture and good drainage. The Mexican *S. martensii* is hardy to 10°C (50°F) and grows to 30 cm (1 ft.).

Some are low-growing, only 2.5–5 cm (1–2 in.) high. Others are scandent, growing to 1 m (3.3 ft.) or more; these sometimes occur naturally on drier sites. Stem cuttings of scandent forms or division of clumps are reasonably easy to establish.

GYMNOSPERMS

Gymnosperms, a major division of seed-bearing plants, are distinguished by their ovules not being enclosed in an ovary (and their seed's endosperm is formed before fertilisation). They are ordered taxonomically into seventeen families, and among these it is from those more popularly known as conifers that several useful wet tolerant trees occur. Some members of these families are adapted to dry conditions and others to wet forest, but here I have restricted the entries to conifers and *Ginkgo*.

Conifers occupy a variety of habitats; many exhibit both adaptability to wet and dry soils and environmental flexibility, having extensive latitude and altitude ranges. Often derided, conifers nevertheless offer a wealth of differing forms, many of great beauty. They can be important specimens in their own right in gardens; cedars and redwoods, for example, form instantly recognisable monuments to the magnificent presence of trees. Many are long-lived trees: *Cryptomeria japonica* from Japan, *Lagarostrobos franklinii* from Tasmania, and *Sequoia sempervirens* from coastal California and Oregon can all live for 2000 years; *Sequoiadendron giganteum*, also Californian but montane, 3500 years. A specimen of *Pinus longaeva* in eastern California has lived for 4600 years, and some conifers are thought to be older still.

All but five genera are evergreen, which makes conifers particularly useful for shelter and visual screens. They also form the dark canvas against which we can better enjoy the seasonal colours of a garden—the spring blossom of magnolias, or autumn maples. Equally they have colour of their own; the pale green spring foliage of the northern Chinese *Larix gmelinii* var. *principis-rupprechtii* is simply stunning, as are the spring flowers of the spruces, which are often bright red, as in the female flowering cones of *Picea likiangensis* from western China.

Most conifers produce separate male and female flower cones, the latter then forming the more familiar seed cone. Some, such as *Araucaria*, have male and female flowers on different plants, but most are monoecious.

One strong word of warning (especially to those with smaller gardens): many of the conifers mentioned grow to become large plants requiring large gardens, and growth is particularly rapid in warm, moist conditions. The nursery industry has responded by offering many dwarf cultivars but, as is well known, some of these clones do not remain dwarf. An aunt once kindly gave me a "dwarf prostrate cedar" for my birthday; it soon outgrew any pretence of prostrate dwarfness and is now a fine young pendulous deodar cedar (*Cedrus deodara*), 8 m (26 ft.) high and heading for the sky. Fortunately, by sheer chance, its site has accommodated its growth.

Larix gmelinii var. *principis-rupprechtii* with leaves emerging in spring

Cultivation

Conifers generally tolerate heavy soils and grow well where there is good rainfall and high humidity, as can be seen by the presence of many champion trees at Castlewellan in Northern Ireland, or the range and dimensions of native conifers on the west coast of North America. But not all require constant moisture; a number (the eastern Mediterranean *Cupressus sempervirens*, for instance) grow on sparse, dry, sun-scorched hillsides. And even conifers from moist forest can succumb to a saturated soil—as I found to my cost with a cryptomeria.

A point to watch: although some spruces (*Picea*) and *Thuja occidentalis* will grow well on wet soil, they are more susceptible to wind blow. Overall a great many conifers are successful on a heavy soil *provided it is not waterlogged*; however, swamp cypresses (*Taxodium*)

Fitzroya cupressoides

and the related *Glyptostrobus pensilis* are adapted to grow in shallow water or bogs, even coping with occasional inundation.

Propagation

Most conifers are seed raised. Large seeds (those of araucaria, for example) do not store well unless held in controlled conditions of low moisture and temperature; and in general, conifer seed does not retain its viability for long without special treatment. Most seed is stored cool (5°C, 41°F) in winter for spring sowing or is stratified. Yews need moist postharvest ripening at 20°C (68°F) for three months prior to cool storage; otherwise they may not germinate until their second spring.

Cuttings can be used for several. Chamaecyparis, junipers, and yews root readily; tsugas are harder to root; and ginkgos are difficult. Many selected forms are grafted. When selecting scions or cuttings, it is important to take upright shoots, as those that grow horizontally may stay that way.

ARAUCARIACEAE

ARAUCARIA FAMILY

Araucaria araucana (Z7) from southern South America grows well on my heavy wet soil, but mowing around its low branches with their hard, sharp-tipped leaves is a painful experience. Araucarias are tough plants, tolerant of a wide range of soils; they grow mostly on well-drained soils, some coping with volcanic peaks.

CEPHALOTAXACEAE

PLUM-YEW FAMILY

These yew-like conifers (*Cephalotaxus* spp.) from the Himalayas and eastern Asia are slow growing and often little more than shrubs in cultivation. They occur as understorey plants in moist forest, in Zone 7 or warmer, but need reasonable drainage.

CUPRESSACEAE

CYPRESS FAMILY

Most members of this family are plants of moist forest. To name just a few, *Austrocedrus chilensis* (Z8) from southern South America; *Calocedrus* (incense cedar) from western North America and eastern Asia; *Fitzroya cupressoides* (Patagonian cypress; Z7/8) from southern South America; *Fokienia hodginsii* (Z7/8) from southeastern China and northern Laos and Vietnam; *Libocedrus* species from New Caledonia and New Zealand; the shrubby decumbent *Microbiota decussata* (Z2) from the Russian Far East; *Thujopsis dolabrata* (Z5) from Japan—all seem to cope well with heavy moist soil, but they require reasonable drainage. Cypresses (*Cupressus*) have similar drainage requirements, though some are well adapted to seasonally dry conditions that would, for example, kill an austrocedrus.

The shrubby, montane Tasmanian *Diselma archeri* (Z8) grows naturally in wet places; similarly, *Pilgerodendron uviferum* (Z7), from southern South America, grows slowly on wet soils, forming a small tree.

I find the tall thujas grow well on wet soils, particularly the northeastern North American *Thuja occidentalis* (Z2) and its many forms and the western North American *T. plicata* (Z5); some of their slower-growing forms also make good hedging plants. *Chamaecyparis* too responds well on wet soil, particularly the very common *C. lawsoniana* (Lawson's cypress; Z6), which originates from western North America. It can grow on acid sands or limestone soils, regenerating naturally on both, to the extent that it can become a weed. It will form a large tree, to 60 m (197 ft.) in its native state, so it is best not planted unless a dark, quick-growing screen is required. For gardens, chamaecyparis and thujas offer a wide range of selected garden forms, some of which are slower growing.

GINKGOACEAE

GINKGO FAMILY

Often included with conifers, *Ginkgo biloba* (Z4) has some characters in common with both cycads and conifers. It is a tree that can grow on both dry sands and heavy wet clay, and for an ancient plant, it is very environmentally tolerant, with the ability to withstand even polluted town atmospheres. It is tolerant too of the cold of a continental winter; in Holland, an original introduction has survived well into its third century. The oldest specimen I know of, with some 1700 years of documented history, grows in the middle of a village and partly incorporates a temple in the Dadu Valley of western Sichuan.

Grown for its attractive foliage, which turns butter yellow in autumn, most cultivated trees tend to be male (the propagation and planting of females was discouraged because of the strong sour-milk-like smell of the outer flesh of their seeds). Cleaned of this flesh, the inner seed is edible and sold freely in local markets in China. In gardens it forms a slow-growing but structurally strong tree, rarely damaged by high winds or troubled by decay.

The 2000-year-old *Ginkgo biloba*, in the Dadu Valley, western China

PINACEAE

PINE FAMILY

Pinaceae is a predominantly northern hemisphere family, all members of which grow well on moist soils; some, such as the piceas, can cope with slightly wet soils, though they generally grow better with good drainage.

Silver firs (*Abies*), mostly montane in origin, grow well in cool, moist soil, and their upright mature cones offer a welcome range of colours. They can be sensitive to air pollution, but firs are relatively easy to grow and quick growing once past their establishment years, responding well to fertile soils. Many from warm montane regions, such as Mexico or southwestern Spain, are surprisingly hardy. Some such as the popular blue-green *A. concolor* from the western United States are hardy to Zone 3; but the occasional really cold winter in Zone 8 can, for example, cause bark split in the Californian *A. bracteata*.

Larix gmelinii (Z2) from northeastern Asia and *L. laricina* (Z1) from northern North America are tolerant of wet soil and though very hardy can be damaged when young by being induced into growth too soon by variable early-season climates. Losses are high, for example, when trying to establish *L. gmelinii* var. *principis-rupprechtii* (Z5) in Zone 8.

True cedars (*Cedrus*; Z6/7) grow much more quickly—almost twice as fast, to judge from growth rings—on a constantly moist as opposed to dry soil, but their wood then has less structural strength.

Spruces (*Picea*) have a mostly northern temperate distribution, and where they occur with abies on mountains they usually occupy a separate altitudinal zone. They are probably the most tolerant in this family to wet soil; however (and as ever with such generalisations), there are exceptions, in that, for example, while moist conditions favour the graceful weeping curtains of growth from the western North American *P. breweriana* (Brewer's spruce; Z5), the similarly weeping *P. smithiana* (Z6) occurs in dry valleys in the Himalayas and grows well on dry acid sand hills with low rainfall (yet, happily, I find it also grows well on my wet soil).

Among pines, the slow-growing *Pinus palustris* (southern pitch or longleaf pine; Z7) from the southeastern United States grows naturally on seasonally wet, swampy soil. Other American pines that grow well on heavy soils include the hardy *P. contorta* (lodgepole pine; Z5), *P. ponderosa* (ponderosa pine; Z4), and the very large-coned *P. coulteri* (Z8).

Pseudolarix amabilis (golden larch; Z4) is so beautiful in autumn, and also in flower in spring, that its slow growth, particularly on dry soils, is a disappointment. Here again it can gain from moist conditions, as in eastern China, Jiangxi Province, on low, cloud-mist mountains, where it reaches 50 m (164 ft.).

PODOCARPACEAE
PODOCARPUS FAMILY

Many podocarps occur in tropical regions and, originating in Gondwana, it is not surprising to find that half the eighteen genera are restricted to the southern hemisphere. Risking another generalisation, given reasonable drainage, almost all respond well to very moist conditions. *Dacrycarpus*, with nine species from Myanmar to China, Fiji, and New Zealand, does not give any hardy plants, but for warm temperate gardens *D. dacrydioides* (kahikatea) from New Zealand, which makes a graceful tree, occurs naturally on both dry and swampy sites.

Unfortunately the dacrydiums, many of which make attractive trees, are hardy only in favoured temperate gardens. To complicate the situation, the genus has been split, thus the following generic names may be less familiar. Several grow well on damp sites, including (and still within the genus) *Dacrydium cupressinum* (rimu; Z8/9) from New Zealand. The small-growing (to 3.5 m, 11.5 ft.) *Halocarpus bidwillii*, also in New Zealand, can grow on both dry and wet soils, while the similarly small, shrubby *Lepidothamnus fonkii* from southern South America occurs in bogs. Both are as tolerably hardy as the rimu.

Lagarostrobos franklinii (Huon pine) from Tasmania is a slow-growing plant of damp forests, attractive with its scale-like leaves. At one time in the same genus (and earlier in *Dacrydium*), *Manoao colensoi* occurs in the same habitat in New Zealand; both need sheltered (Z8/9) gardens.

The shrubby, often prostrate *Microcachrys tetragona*, a Tasmanian endemic, grows naturally in a cool, moist montane climate, and the related *Microstrobos*, also shrubby with one species in Tasmania and the other in the Blue Mountains of southeastern Australia, similarly occupies wet habitats. Both need Zone 9 temperatures.

Podocarpus itself is a large genus. Several species are cultivated, but only a few (*P. macrophyllus* from China and Japan; the low spreading alpine totara, *P. nivalis*, from New Zealand) are hardy in Zone 8. Most species grow well in a moist climate, as does *Saxegothaea con-*

spicua (Prince Albert's yew; Z7), from the rain forests of southern Chile.

TAXACEAE

YEW FAMILY

Amentotaxus, from east and southeastern Asia, and *Torreya*, with species in California, Florida, China, and Japan, form understorey shrubs or small trees in moist forests in Zones 7–9. Rare in cultivation, some species are now scarce in the wild.

Of all the conifers, yews must be the most widespread in temperate gardens. Slow growing and darkly evergreen, *Taxus baccata* (Z6) has the greatest of uses—whether as hedging, topiary, or specimen tree—and it grows well on wet soils, given reasonable drainage. It has a good environmental tolerance, surviving dry acid and alkaline soils, and recovers well from pruning.

TAXODIACEAE

REDWOOD FAMILY

Farjon (2001) and many other authorities now include this family with Cupressaceae. The King Billy pines (*Athrotaxis*) from Tasmania are medium-sized, slow-growing columnar trees. *Cryptomeria japonica* (Z5/6) is a large redwood-like tree from the forests of Japan, known for its tolerance of pruning and many cultivars; I was once impressed by a large specimen of the Chinese form (var. *sinensis*) in the eastern Chinese province of Jiangxi said to be 500 years old. *Cunninghamia lanceolata* is the distinctively leaved Chinese fir. All these—along with *Sequoia* and *Sequoiadendron* from western North America and *Taiwania cryptomerioides* from Taiwan—can grow on fairly moist, if reasonably drained soils. Of these only *Cunninghamia* (Z8) and *Taiwania* (Z8/9) have any hardiness problems; however, *Sequoia sempervirens* (coastal redwood) from Oregon and California can be blown over by gales, particularly if on a wet soil, in contrast to *Sequoiadendron giganteum* (giant redwood), which is wind resistant.

The unusual *Sciadopitys verticillata* (umbrella pine) from Japan, with its twin-fused needles, is considered slow growing but speeds up its rate of growth when cultivated, for example, on Long Island, New York.

The deciduous genera *Metasequoia*, *Glyptostrobus*, and *Taxodium* (swamp cypress) offer the best conifers for wet soils. Swamp cypresses, which occur from the southeastern United States to Mexico and Guatemala, are well known for their pneumatophores (descriptively,

Taxodium mucronatum, the great tree of Tule in Mexico

"knees"), the breathing roots that enable these trees to grow in shallow water (though all taxodiums can grow on drier soils if there is water within reach of their roots). Often seen as a riverside tree in Mexico, there are some very large specimens of *T. mucronatum* (Z8) in Oaxaca. I was pleased to finally visit the great tree of Tule in the churchyard of Santa María Asuncíon, for I had long carried a memory of it from a picture in my school botany book! In 2005, it had a girth of 36.2 m (119 ft.) and was 35.4 m (116 ft.) tall; some consider it to be three fused trunks.

Glyptostrobus pensilis (Z9/10) from southern China and North Vietnam is the Asian counterpart of *Taxodium*; it grows in river deltas and can cope with shallow water but is not as hardy as *T. distichum* (Z6). It can however be grafted onto taxodium rootstock, which should make it hardier.

The western Chinese *Metasequoia glyptostroboides* (dawn redwood; Z5) is also able to grow in very wet soils, but in a cold site its early growth is slowed if on saturated soil.

CHAPTER 5
Trees, shrubs, and climbers

ACACIA
WATTLE
LEGUMINOSAE

Acacia is a large genus occurring in the tropics and subtropics, and, given moist warm conditions, acacias can grow very quickly. They are very attractive trees, but their free seeding habits and rapid growth have led to their becoming pernicious weeds, particularly in areas of the world with a Mediterranean climate.

Some of the Australian wattles occur naturally on wet soil. The lovely weeping and bushy (3–6 m, 10–20 ft.) *Acacia riceana* from Tasmania grows in damp, shady, but usually well-drained places. *Acacia pataczekii*, a rarer endemic from northeastern Tasmania, has recently spread in cultivation because it is self-fertile and produces viable seed; it is hardy to at least −8°C (18°F) and tolerant of permanently moist heavy soils, forming a compact, relatively slow-growing small tree that is readily accommodated in a garden.

Other species that occur in both Tasmania and southeastern mainland Australia—the popular *Acacia dealbata* (silver wattle), the shrubby *A. verniciflua*, and the taller (to 30 m, 100 ft., or more) *A. melanoxylon*—are also tolerant of moist soils but are only hardy in climatically favoured Zone 8 locations. With *A. dealbata*, which has finely divided, glaucous blue-green foliage and sprays of yellow mimosa flowers, this is not completely limiting, for it can easily be raised from seed and grown against a sunny wall of a heated building, where it will make an impressive display for a few years—until it is killed by the odd colder-than-average Zone 8 winter. Where only light frosts occur, it can eventually reach 25–30 m (82–100 ft.), which makes it then entirely unsuited to planting close to a house. It also suckers. For propagation, see Leguminosae.

ACER

MAPLE

ACERACEAE

There is much variation to wet soil tolerance in this large genus, and happily several, such as *Acer campestre* (field or hedge maple; Z4) from Europe and the Near East, grow well on both light and heavy soil. Japanese maples (*A. palmatum*; Z5) prosper in damp but well-drained woodland; the wonderful specimens of the National Collection of Japanese maples at the National Arboretum, Westonbirt, Gloucestershire, benefit on that site from wind shelter given by good-sized oaks and pines, and moisture from a heavy soil with springs. The foliage of these small trees frequently shrivels in dry summer heat, but given shade and some wind shelter they can hold their leaves through the season to achieve glowing autumn tints. The selections 'Bloodgood' and 'Sango-kaku' are justifiably popular as being among the few Japanese maples that can grow well in drier conditions. When young, Japanese maples are susceptible to frost damage, which points up another advantage of having the protection of a high oak canopy.

Maples occur around the northern temperate zone and vary in stature from plants of 2–3 m (6.6–10 ft.) to large trees. Most are deciduous and are especially noted for their autumn colours; a few slightly tender species are semi-evergreen. They tend to produce their small flower chains early in the season, some before, others after leafing; and their seeds form, often by mid-summer, in chains of paired keys, each nutlet having a wing on one side. They are, in general, fast growing, especially on wet soils.

The very hardy *Acer negundo* (box elder; Z2), a medium-sized tree of floodplain forests, also grows well on dry soil. I used to wonder why an old *A. negundo* I knew had such a mass of pollard-like stems arising from its short trunk, but I now find my own plant beginning to take on a similar form. The cause appears to be the soft structural nature of rapidly growing branches in Zone 8, which on young trees break off easily in summer winds. From each broken stub, a multitude of replacement shoots arises, and a tree may regrow its branches several times before the branches gain sufficient girth and strength to withstand wind. The species is widely distributed in North America with several selections or varieties in cultivation, including the variegated *A. negundo* 'Flamingo' and the lovely *A. negundo* var. *violaceum*, the reddish violet flowers of which stand out from afar.

The attractive Chinese *Acer grosseri* var. *hersii* (Z6) is one of the approximately twenty species of snake-barks. Most of these medium-sized trees occur in the Himalayas, China, and Japan, in lower altitude mountain forests, and all grow best in sheltered moist woodland. In Guizhou, western China, I noted large specimens of *A. davidii* (Z7/8) arching over riversides at only 1000 m (3300 ft.) altitude; and similarly I have seen the hardier North American representative, *A. pensylvanicum* (striped maple; Z3), in the Smoky Mountains of Tennessee in riverine forest at c. 500–600 m (1600–2000 ft.). Snake-bark maples do, however, need good drainage; they suffer in saturated soil, and their soft stems seem particularly vulnerable to stem-decaying fungi entering through wounds caused by damage from sun scorch or frost, or wind-broken branches.

Interestingly, *Acer rubrum* (Z3) grows well both on light soil and in occasionally inundated sites in its eastern North American home. Its fiery selection 'October Glory' is equally tolerant of heavy wetland, growing well, albeit slowly, when young. Several maples prosper in one of the wettest soil areas of Castle Howard's arboretum (Z8), particularly the large North American *A. saccharinum* (Z3), which occurs naturally in hardwood swamps. Another in this damp area is the Chinese *A. longipes* subsp. *amplum* (Z7); however, where it is very wet, growth can be much slower than on a better soil. An exception is the Mediterranean *A. opalus* (Z6), which, though growing well on dry soils, also looks good on this heavy, very wet soil. *Acer cappadocicum* also grows well on heavy land, and some established clones are very hardy; one I collected with a colleague, Hans Fliegner, from 1300 m (3600 ft.) in the Alborz Mountains of northern Iran, proved susceptible to winter cold on a low wet site at Kew, though it recovered after being cut to the ground. Similarly the western Chinese form of this species can be frost tender when young, yet plants from northern Pakistan are hardy in Zone 8.

Seed viability varies. Maples are mainly monoecious and, with the slow-growing, chestnut-barked *Acer griseum* (Z4) for example, it is said that seed taken from trees growing in groups germinates more readily (perhaps because it is cross-pollinated) than that taken from single trees. Selected forms are side-grafted onto seedling stocks of their own or closely related species. Several can be propagated from semi-ripe cuttings set in a mist propagation unit.

AESCULUS

HORSE CHESTNUT, BUCKEYE
HIPPOCASTANACEAE

Aesculus flava

Horse chestnuts are readily recognised year-round, by their large resinous winter buds; long-stalked summer palmate leaves with five to seven leaflets and often spectacular flower "candles" (terminal panicles); and autumnal conker fruits in a thick-shelled capsule. They form a small genus of trees and shrubs mainly from the northern hemisphere—temperate North America, southern Europe, and temperate Asia—and most, other than where mentioned, form substantial trees.

Accepting that most aesculus can grow well on dry soils, it is fortunate that some of these magnificent flowering trees can also cope with heavy soils, though all should have reasonable drainage. Certainly plants from the section that includes *Aesculus indica* (Z7) and *A. chinensis* (Z6) tolerate heavy soil, as does *A. hippocastanum* (Z3). Some of the American buckeyes (section *Pavia*), which are mostly rated Zone 5, occur naturally on wet soils. The shrubby (1–1.5 m, 3.3–5 ft.) *A. sylvatica* (Georgia buckeye; Z6) is a plant of moist woodland and also occurs on streambanks; *A. pavia* (red buckeye) and *A. glabra* var. *arguta* (Ohio buckeye; to 6 m, 20 ft.) are also moist woodland plants. *Aesculus flava* (sweet buckeye) is a large tree of deep bottomlands, and I have been delighted with my own young trees of this species, which are growing in very wet soil. Sweet buckeye is a tolerant plant in other respects as it may, for example, be found growing naturally over a range of altitudes (274–1920 m, 900–6300 ft.) in the Great Smoky Mountains.

Horse chestnuts tend to establish slowly, and do not respond well to transplanting from open ground, sometimes taking many years to recover. They are better planted out from containers. Most are tolerably hardy, though young plants of some, such as *Aesculus assamica* (Z8), can be vulnerable to cold damage (and remember, many wet sites are frost pockets). Also, new shoots can be weak and vulnerable to wind break; and older trees on wet sites seem more susceptible to fungal attack of roots and butt. Horse chestnuts do, however, offer a range of sizes. Several are even suited to small gardens; for example, the slow-growing *A.* ×*neglecta* 'Erythroblastos' (a hardy hybrid of *A. flava* and *A. sylvatica*) produces carmine-red new shoots and makes a lovely small tree.

If kept cool and moist over winter, the large seeds germinate readily in spring. *Aesculus flava* seedlings produce a long carrot-like primary root, which grows perhaps to some 30 cm (1 ft.) deep on a seedling that is little taller, and this is easily accidentally snapped off when transplanting. Side-grafting or budding onto seedling stock of a related species is used to propagate *A.* 'Dallimorei' and other selected cultivars and hybrids. The suckering, clump-forming (to 10 × 4 m, 33 × 13 ft., wide and high) *A. parviflora* (Z4) can be increased by dividing off suckers.

ALNUS
ALDER
BETULACEAE

Alders are well known for their adaptation to very wet soils (yielding the alder carr), and they have nitrogen-fixing bacteria (actinomycetes) in their roots. Where they are planted around ponds, their shade (along with the tannins that accumulate in the pond from their shed and decaying leaves) produces the bonus of clear dark water in which golden orfe, for example, can thrive. On wet sites alders grow remarkably quickly, forming a useful screen, and their dark green leaves hold on the tree until early wind and cold remove them. As they develop, they cast a dense shade, but they can usefully dry out wet sites.

Alders are mainly northern temperate in distribution, with some forms occurring in the Andes down as far as Argentina. In cultivation they vary from shrubby trees to 40 m (130 ft.) tall trees and also vary in their cold tolerance. For example, the Turkish form of *Alnus orientalis* (Z9) is slightly frost hardier than those coming from the mountains of Cyprus, while *A. acuminata* (Andean alder) is not hardy in most cool temperate regions, tolerating only light frosts. I have an attachment to the large-leaved *A. subcordata* (Caucasian alder). Many years ago I was impressed by its speed of growth, under irrigation, in the dry and warm National Botanic Garden of Iran, near Tehran; I was further impressed by the height of 45 m (148 ft.) achieved by these trees, where they grow naturally higher up along river valleys in the Alborz Mountains there. Plants with this northern Iranian provenance grow well here in Zone 8, though I had it on authority that they would not succeed. Admittedly as young plants they are sensitive to late frosts or salt winds, but they recover damaged young spring growth from secondary buds. Once established on a moist site, they can reach 15–17 m (50–56 ft.) in under

Winter catkins of *Alnus subcordata*

TREES, SHRUBS, AND CLIMBERS

twenty years—useful for giving the perception of maturity to new gardens.

Unfortunately alders have the habit of frequently shedding small dead branchlets, and this can either be seen as a gift of useful kindling or just a nuisance to the tidy gardener. Alders seem to wound heal well, with any fresh cuts quickly stained by the tree itself to a bright orange-brown.

Flowers are unisexual; both occur on the same plant, with the male flowers formed in catkins. The catkins of most open in late winter or early spring to shed their wind-blown pollen before leaves emerge. The seeds are carried in persistent woody cone-like strobili, and the small seed, which has a papery disk, is shed naturally over winter and in early spring. Seed raising is fairly easy from spring-sown seed that has been held over winter in a cold store. Seedlings should be pricked out at an early stage and then potted on regularly throughout the growing season as they grow quickly. Selected forms are grafted.

AMELANCHIER

SERVICEBERRY
ROSACEAE

Slightly stemmed, mostly very hardy, small trees and shrubs, with attractive white blossom in early spring, and good autumn leaf colour, serviceberries are very garden-worthy. Most of the approximately ten species occur in North America, a few in Eurasia; several are very hardy. Habitat requirements vary. While most will grow on light free-drained soils, *Amelanchier laevis* (Allegheny serviceberry) and *A. arborea* (both Z4) also grow in alluvial forests in eastern North America; and *A. canadensis* (Z3) and a few others will grow on wet soils, often on swampy land. On visits to the United States, I have been delighted by the sight of their billowing white clouds of blossom held out over water from small bankside trees. In early spring, while the woodland is still dark, the contrast of this blossom endorses their promise of warmer days.

Most are easy to grow, notably *Amelanchier lamarckii* (Z4), which prefers better-drained soils and is locally naturalised in Britain. The identity of this and other North American species has been confused in Europe; seedlings may be variable. Some, such as *A. canadensis* will sucker, but semi-ripe cuttings are difficult even with good facilities.

Amelanchier canadensis flowering by a creek in Maryland

ANDROMEDA
BOG-ROSEMARY
ERICACEAE

Pink-flowered *Andromeda polifolia* (Z2/3), which occurs from north-ern Europe across Asia to Japan, and its equally hardy northern North American counterpart, *A. glaucophylla*, are small (to 10–35 cm, 4–14 in.) attractively flowered shrublets. All bog-dwelling erica-ceous plants are obviously candidates for the wet garden, but even in a bog, they often sit on slightly raised mounds of moss, so my instinct is always to give a slightly raised planting site when on wet soil. For propagation, see Ericaceae.

ARALIACEAE
ARALIA FAMILY

This family includes some hardy trees, shrubs, and herbs. Most ara-liads tolerate very moist, shady woodland, and as a group they are relatively easy to cultivate, coping with low light levels and exces-sive dryness or moisture—hence their popularity as houseplants. Almost all possess dark green, shade-tolerant leaves, a good propor-tion of which are very ornamental. Their wood tends to be soft, and the leaves of several are dimorphic (that is, their juvenile leaves have a distinctly different form compared to their adult leaves). Their flowers are small but often formed as large inflorescences, which can be a feature with some aralias and fatsia.

Schefflera has its own entry (which see). Other genera for moist but well-drained soils include *Eleutherococcus* (Z6), a large Asian genus of small trees, and the hardy *Kalopanax septemlobus* (Z5), a 30 m (100 ft.) tree. The large, glossy-leaved *Fatsia japonica* (Z8) grows slowly to about 2 m (6.6 ft.) in moist shade with good drainage; its cultivars include the popular 'Variegata' and also ×*Fatshedera lizei* (Z7), a cross between *F. japonica* 'Moseri' (female) and the very wet-soil-tolerant *Hedera helix* subsp. *hibernica*, of which bigeneric hybrid there are also several cultivars.

The shrubby (1–2 m, 3.3–6.6 ft.) *Oplopanax horridus* (devil's club; Z4) from northern North America occurs in wet places. The lovely *Tetrapanax papyrifer* (rice-paper plant) from southern China and Tai-wan is on the edge of hardiness, withstanding only light (−5°C, 23°F) frost; nevertheless, increasingly it appears in temperate gardens, where it makes a very attractive small tree with a white reverse to its large leaves.

Seed germinates readily. With access to mist propagation, most woody araliads can be propagated from semi-ripe cuttings formed from juvenile wood. Some such as eleutherococcus and tetrapanax produce suckers that can be removed as propagules when small (25–50 cm, 10–20 in.) and grown on; this implies that root cuttings, taken in winter, may be another option. Deciduous herbaceous aralias can be divided.

ARONIA

CHOKEBERRY
ROSACEAE

A small genus of hardy (Z4) deciduous shrubs (to 4 m, 13 ft.), native to eastern North America, which are popularly grown for their attractive fruits and good autumn foliage. The stalked leaves are simple, alternate, with toothed margins, and the white, sometimes pink, five-petalled flowers are borne in small corymbs.

Aronia arbutifolia (red chokeberry; to 3 m, 10 ft.) grows naturally in a range of habitats that includes wet woods and swamps; it has red and bluish black fruited forms. Similarly but at half the height, the black-fruited *A. melanocarpa* can be found in bogs. Several cultivars are available. A frequently grown hybrid of the two species, *A. ×prunifolia*, has dark purple fruit; it grows, but not quickly, to 4 m (13 ft.) and is happiest on a heavy moist soil. Plants may be seed raised (stratified), layered, or increased from semi-ripe cuttings.

Aronia ×prunifolia, with leaves just turning to autumn colour and ripening fruit

BAMBOO

GRAMINEAE

Bamboos attract many enthusiasts, and more and more bamboos are available to gardeners. The quiet background role they play in gardens means they are sometimes overlooked, but they are wonderful, architecturally pleasing plants. A colleague once told me he liked to have them by buildings because their leaves brought light down to shaded areas. Usefully, too, most bamboos will grow on wet soil, though they may be on the verge of hardiness in temperate gardens, perhaps reaching only one-third to one-half the height they would if grown in the southeastern United States, southern China, or some other warmer and moister region. Bamboos are very adaptable, many also coping well with drier soils, but overall it is worth trying out any bamboo on a wet soil, particularly if it is also a warm and sheltered site.

Bamboos make fine feature plants, and, as visual screens and shelter under woodland, their green foil enhances the delicate flowering of woodland plants. Light deciduous oak woodland suits them well, whereas the light levels provided by dense competitive woodland with evergreens significantly slows their growth. If grown as a collection in open grassland, clumps can be mown around to keep them separate, but where plants are required to be in close proximity, separation can be achieved only by sinking a tough impervious, nondegradable sheet to a depth of at least 60 cm (2 ft.) between clumps.

Few pests and diseases affect bamboos, but because the young culms are edible they are vulnerable to rodent damage; grey squirrels, for example, favour young chusquea shoots. Flowering is variable; there tends to be a set frequency (sometimes annually, but mostly at longer interludes running into decades) when there may be some gregarious flowering in a species. Some species flower regularly without dying back; it is often the case with arundinarias, for example, that the odd naturally regenerated seedling will arise. Other species can regrow after dying back.

Because of possible poor recovery in colder climates, bamboo divisions are often potted and established in a cool greenhouse. It is certainly easier to split up a young bamboo rather than having to hack into an established clump. Some bamboos conveniently produce shallow underground runners, which form young canes with a small ball of roots after a season's growth; these can be detached with a spade. Watering in dry periods, to aid establishment, is important for the first year, and tall stems need cutting back to avoid wind rock. A few bamboos will also regenerate from short stem sections laid on their sides in a moist soil trench.

Bamboo genera with separate entries are *Chusquea*, *Phyllostachys*, *Pleioblastus*, *Sasa*, and *Sasaella*.

BERBERIS

BERBERIDACEAE

Berberis often occur naturally on woodland margins, in open, grazed scrub and in hedges, and need good light to flower well. Flowers are small, 0.3–2.5 cm (0.12–1 in.), and have motile stamens, which spring up when touched. Most species have bright yellow or orange flowers; some have green flowers. Many, such as *Berberis wilsoniae* (Z6) from western China, have attractive fruit; a few, such as *B. thunbergii* (Z4) from Japan, have fine autumn colour. Often relegated to the back of the border, many berberis can nevertheless serve as feature plants, with their attractive flowers, foliage, and fruits, and both the southern South American *B. darwinii* (Z7) and its hybrid *B. ×stenophylla* (Z5) can make spectacular dense flowering evergreen hedges.

Most berberis grow well on heavy, rather moist soils while being able to cope with dry soils. Certainly the Asian species are often seen in damp mountain meadows, and the North American *Berberis canadensis* (Z5) grows naturally along streamsides. There are some 600 species of *Berberis*, of which about one-sixth are cultivated, along with their many hybrids and selections. All are spiny shrubs, some erect, others arching, with the largest growing to 5 m (16 ft.). Their spines may be on the leaves, as in the evergreen *B. darwinii*, or on the stems, as in the large Chinese *B. julianae* (Z5) and most other deciduous species; spines are formed in groups of three.

Berberis darwinii

In China, the seed is ground to make a pepper-like condiment; the wood is bright yellow, as are the many pills made from berberis or mahonia that are used in quelling upset tummies there: I have seen mahonias collected by the lorry-load for use in traditional Chinese medicine. Also because berberis are the alternate host of wheat rust (*Puccinia graminis*), wild berberis have often been cleared from wheat-growing regions.

Seed should be cleaned before sowing, and seedlings of *Berberis darwinii* and other species will regenerate naturally in wet gardens. They do hybridise freely, so seed may not come true. Berberis cultivars may be propagated by heeled stem cuttings in summer, or autumn hardwood cuttings protected over winter in a cold frame.

RELATED GENERA

Several other genera in Berberidaceae, such as the very popular epimediums, are useful in damp woodland. Among rhizomatous herbaceous perennials, *Caulophyllum thalictroides* (blue cohosh; Z7) from eastern North America, *Diphylleia cymosa* from the Appalachian Mountains, *D. grayi* from Japan, and *D. sinensis* from Yunnan (although some regard this Asian pair as just geographical variants of *D. cymosa*, all Z7), and the more delicate *Jeffersonia diphylla* from eastern North America and *J. dubia* (Z5) from northeastern Asia are all well suited to moist organic soils.

Betula alleghaniensis

BETULA

BIRCH

BETULACEAE

Birches occur naturally around the northern temperate zone and are variable in their tolerance of wet soils. Some, like *Betula nigra* (river birch; Z4) from central and eastern North America, grow naturally by riversides. River birch can make a large tree with very dark bark; 'Heritage' is its lighter-barked clone. In western North America, *B. occidentalis* (water birch) likewise occupies riparian areas, but it is smaller growing. Others, such as the upright-catkined polyploids, *B. medwedewii* from the Transcaucasus and *B. insignis* (both Z7) from western China, grow in damp forest; and *B. alleghaniensis* (yellow birch; Z3/4) can be found in hardwood swamps in North America and grows well on heavy moist soil.

Birches vary from shrubs to 30 m (100 ft.) trees, and most are fairly hardy, though some, like the Japanese *Betula ermanii* forms, can be vulnerable as seedlings to winter cold in northern climes. Lighter-barked trees, such as *B. utilis* var. *jacquemontii* (Z7) from northern India and Pakistan, or the European native *B. pendula* (Z2) seem better adapted to hot dry soils, and though just about tolerant of heavier soils, can be vulnerable both to wind blow and fungal root decay on wet soils. Birches are popular garden subjects for their lightness and grace of form, which is enhanced by bright coloured barks, golden autumn leaves, and often in late winter, as on *B. pendula*, a haze of plumy-red branchlets when seen from afar.

Birches are susceptible to fungal entry through cuts, which do not heal well. The rise of spring sap in birch is so strong that it is difficult to staunch an early-season wound, and any pruning of birch is better delayed until later in the season. When a good trunk is required, it pays to prune off side branches from seedlings at a very early stage in their life.

Birches are dioecious. Male flowers are formed in catkins, and seed forms in cones, which shatter when ripe in late summer or early autumn. Seed can be shed in great quantity. A papery disk surrounds these small, light seeds and helps their distribution. If kept in a cold store over winter, seed usually germinates freely in spring. Seedlings grow quickly, but very young seedlings can be susceptible to root damage by mushroom flies. These are more frequent where the composts used are rich in organic materials, as opposed to loam-based. Control can be through the use of a systemic or soil-acting insecti-

TREES, SHRUBS, AND CLIMBERS

cide. Grafting onto seedling stocks is the usual method of propagating selected forms.

BUXUS

BOX, BOXWOOD
BUXACEAE

Though seemingly dull, with insignificant unisexual flowers, boxwood endears itself to most gardeners. Its crisp, simple, evergreen leaves, slow growth, and ability to withstand clipping make it an excellent subject for topiary and ideal for dwarf hedges for potagers or to set around formal herbaceous beds. The extent of its popularity is endorsed by their being over 50 cultivars of the common European boxwood *Buxus sempervirens* (Z5), and a good many too of *B. microphylla* (Z6). Many of the seventy or so species of *Buxus*, from western Europe to Asia, Africa, and Central America, are perfectly hardy in cold temperate zones—even *B. balearica*, from the Balearics and southern Spain into North Africa, has survived as a small tree for many decades out of doors at Kew.

First thoughts on the natural habitat of box in Spain or on the dry chalk hills of Surrey may suggest that it is not a likely candidate for this book. However I have seen *Buxus hyrcana* (Z6) growing naturally in wet forest, and find box survives well on my own wet soil. It is a very undemanding plant.

Box roots readily from spring or summer cuttings given a mist propagation unit or propagating frame, and also roots well from woody 10–20 cm (4–8 in.) stem cuttings set in open ground. Also, where there are mature plants, seedlings of *Buxus sempervirens* will regenerate naturally.

CALLISTEMON

BOTTLEBRUSH
MYRTACEAE

The Australian callistemons are rightly popular plants, grown throughout the subtropical world for their attractive bracelets of bright long-stamened flowers. Several hardy species and cultivars are now grown in temperate gardens; many years ago I was very surprised by the hardiness of *Callistemon subulatus* (1–1.5 m, 3.3–5 ft.) from New South Wales, on a sandy soil. Subsequently I have been even more impressed by a naturally regenerated seedling from this plant which, for two decades, has grown and flowered abundantly on

Callistemon subulatus seedling

Camellia granthamiana

my heavy wet soil and has formed a much bushier plant than its parent. *Callistemon subulatus* and *C. viminalis* grow naturally by streams; others, such as *C. acuminatus*, *C. pallidus*, *C. pinifolius*, and *C. rigidus*, also grow on moist soils; and *C. salignus* occurs on low-lying river flats. *Callistemon citrinus* occurs naturally on swampy ground and is hardy to at least –10°C (14°F), as is *C. viridiflorus*, which also copes with wet soils. For propagation, see Myrtaceae.

CAMELLIA

THEACEAE

Unsurprisingly, camellias are one of the few plants able to withstand having the cold contents of tea pots regularly tipped over their roots! (This tannin-rich mulch is most useful on alkaline soils—but tea bags have somewhat spoiled the party.) In some parts of eastern China, on misty mountains where tea plants (*Camellia sinensis* cultivars) are grown, winters can be severe, with three months of ice and snow; what's more, all the tea plantations in Sichuan are on the wetter, eastern side of mountains. In cultivation, camellias fall on both sides of the hardiness line and can grow on heavy wet soil, but a raised bed will be needed on saturated soil.

The blossoms of the dark evergreen *Camellia japonica* (Z8/9) and its countless cultivars vary in their susceptibility to frost. The pink-flowered *C.* 'Mrs D. W. Davis', for example, is always browned, even with low rather than freezing temperatures, but others are much hardier. Hardiest of all are the *C.* ×*williamsii* hybrids (crosses between *C. japonica* and *C. saluenensis*), and if their first blossoms are caught by frost, undamaged buds will soon open to provide a replacement display. As expected of hybrids, cultivars of *C.* ×*williamsii* grow reasonably quickly. A shaded site, on the northern side of a wall (in the northern hemisphere) or light woodland, suits them well, with acid soils preferred. *Camellia japonica* is able to grow and flower well in deep shade.

The large-flowered *Camellia reticulata* cultivars, *C. pitardii* from Yunnan, and *C. granthamiana* from Hong Kong, with its poached-egg-like flowers, are encountered in very favoured mild (Z9) localities. Similarly *C. oleifera*, a small white-flowered camellia, which is still grown in parts of China for its oil-rich seeds, also needs frost protection or a very favoured site. The many cultivars of the autumn-flowering *C. sasanqua* (Z7) are often seen enlivening the small gardens of traditional houses in southern Japan; however, the plants and their blossoms can be damaged in winter.

Camellia fruit capsules are woody, and the seeds tend to be on the large side with an oily endosperm. Such seeds are not noted for their longevity and are best sown when fresh—that is, sown in autumn and kept cool and moist until spring or cool-stored similarly over winter, with the germination temperature raised to 18°C (65°F) in spring. Seedlings need careful handling, ensuring the seed, with its remaining food store, is not detached from the young seedling. Semi-ripe stem cuttings are used, but there are clonal differences, with some rooting more easily than others. *Camellia reticulata* cultivars, which are very difficult to propagate from cuttings, are usually grafted.

RELATED GENERA

Cleyera, *Eurya*, and *Ternstroemia*, with fruits that are more like berries, are sometimes cultivated in Zone 9, as is the tender but attractive *Tutcheria spectabilis*. *Eurya*, some species of which can also be found by woodland streams, is less popular, not least *E. japonica* (Z8), whose hard-to-spot small flowers pervade the surrounding air with a rather unpleasant smell. All require similar conditions to camellia.

CARPINUS

HORNBEAM

CORYLACEAE

Some of the twenty-six or so species of *Carpinus*, which are spread over the northern temperate zone, are slightly tender when young. *Carpinus betulus* (European hornbeam; Z4/5) was the coppiced, or sometimes pollarded, understorey species of the oak woods of my youthful playground; its hard wood was once extensively used for making tools, butcher's blocks, and much else. Later in life I gained greater appreciation for the beauty of the mature hornbeam, a tree that often grows to 20 m (67 ft.) and can reach 30 m (100 ft.). Its simple, double-toothed margined leaves are not as coppery as the beech in autumn; nevertheless, it displays deliciously subtle shades of gold over a sculptured trunk and is often hung with masses of the clustered leafy bracts that enclose its small hard seeds.

Hornbeams grow on a range of soils, from dry to wet, but young plants are slow to establish on heavy soils, and they do need good drainage. They make useful hedge plants, as they hold their autumn leaves over winter, like beech. They can be pleached and were also used in formal seventeenth-century gardens to form stilt hedges (that is, clipped hedges on 2 m, 6.6 ft., clear stems). Hornbeams are monoecious, and propagation is from stratified seed or grafting for selected forms.

CARYA
HICKORY
JUGLANDACEAE

Though they occur in eastern and southeastern Asia and also in the Mexican highlands, it is mainly the very hardy (Z4) North American species of *Carya* that are cultivated. *Carya cordiformis* (bitternut hickory) and *C. ovata* (shagbark hickory) can be spectacular when autumn turns their leaves to gold. Several caryas, including these two, occur on bottomlands; for wetter soils, *C. aquatica* (water hickory; Z6) is in cultivation.

As a generality, these large deciduous and monoecious trees are not easy to establish in temperate regions and are slow growing on heavy wet soils, particularly in more northern climes, where they fruit only during a warm summer. They also have to be given good drainage. Pecan cultivars may be grafted in winter, and fresh seed may be sown after stratification.

CEPHALANTHUS
BUTTONBUSH
RUBIACEAE

Of the several *Cephalanthus*, *C. occidentalis*, from eastern North America and extending to Mexico and Cuba, is sometimes cultivated. This straggly, untidy-looking shrub can occur in taxodium swamps. It grows up to 3 m (10 ft.) tall, but regular trimming will make it more compact, and it is attractive when in flower. Relatively easy to grow, and fairly hardy, to Zone 7 or lower. It can be increased by seed or stem cuttings.

CERCIDIPHYLLUM
KATSURA-TREE
CERCIDIPHYLLACEAE

As a young student I was enamoured of the butter-yellow autumn colour and burnt-sugar smell of the cercidiphyllums in the Westonbirt Arboretum, Gloucestershire, and even more impressed later by a lovely waterside tree in the Morris Arboretum, Pennsylvania. All the more so because Thames-side sand was just too dry for this tree, with no specimen lasting more than a few years before it succumbed to the occasional very dry summer. They do require a moist heavy soil to grow well.

In the dripping-wet temperate forests of western Sichuan, on the eastern side of the high mountains around Gongga Shan, there are some very large old trees of the Chinese form (var. *sinense* to some authorities) of *Cercidiphyllum japonicum* (Z4). They occur naturally in such wet forests, at relatively low altitude, around 2000 m (6562 ft.); in cultivation, young plants are susceptible to frosts, particularly in wet hollows where late frosts can occur. There is in Japan a higher montane form with larger leaves (considered by some to be a separate species, *C. magnificum*), but I find this plant just as susceptible to frost. In spring, when light frost damages the young leaves, they emit their lovely burnt-sugar smell, which is no compensation for the frost damage. Given a slope to drain off cold air, and some shelter, *C. japonicum* can grow well in temperate gardenss.

Cercidiphyllums are so distinct as to merit their own family. Their lineage is ancient and, though frequent in cultivation, they are rare in the wild and regarded as endangered in China. They form large deciduous trees (to 30 m, 100 ft., or so) with spirally twisted bark, and broadly ovate leaves with scalloped edges. They are dioecious; their small unisexual flowers, which are borne in early spring, are subtly attractive. The emergence of their small, round, bright-green leaves in early spring is a delight, particularly when viewed through low-angled sunlight. More reddish leaved seedlings do occur, particularly with the Chinese plants, and a dark red-leaved cultivar is now becoming popular in gardens.

Propagation is normally by seed, which usually germinates well if fresh, and seedlings are easily grown on in pots (ideally for three or four years, until the stem becomes woody). With the use of auxins and a good propagation unit, it is possible to root early-season cuttings. Because of their frost susceptibility, planting should be delayed until any danger of frost is past. If late-planted in a moist site, there is less of a need to water for establishment.

CHUSQUEA
ANDEAN BAMBOO
GRAMINEAE

The Chilean *Chusquea culeou* (Z7/8) seems very happy to grow 3–4 m (10–13 ft.) on a poorly drained, permanently wet heavy soil—though preferably in a warm spot. It is an attractive small-leaved bamboo with solid stems, and dense whorls of twiggy shoots at each

TOP *Cercidiphyllum japonicum* in the Morris Arboretum, Pennsylvania
ABOVE A *Cercidiphyllum japonicum* seedling with red autumn foliage

Chusquea culeou, new sheathed cane and an older cane with its characteristic clusters of nodal branchlets

node. Several other hardy Chilean species from this large Andean genus are now available, including the similarly sized *C. montana* and slightly smaller *C. quila*. For propagation, see bamboo.

CLEMATIS

RANUNCULACEAE

Clematis are among the most popular garden climbers for temperate gardens, but many of the large-flowered hybrids are not, I fear, for the wet garden. However, the small-flowered *Clematis virginiana* (Z4) grows on wet soils in the Great Lakes region, and I was pleased to see it growing by forest margins in Tennessee. The almost herbaceous *C. integrifolia* (Z3) with its thin deciduous stems grows reasonably well in wet but well-drained soil; I have had some limited success with several of its hybrids using mound planting. A further option for clematophiles is to plant at the base of young trees, where tree roots keep the ground drier and the clematis can be trained up into the tree. *Clematis tangutica* (Z5) and others in the Orientalis Group persist and grow well in fairly damp soil. The gorgeous, evergreen Chinese *C. armandii* (Z7/8) and *C. viticella* (Z6) from southern Europe also seem more tolerant of moist soils. *Clematis montana* (Z6) romps away on both acid and alkaline soils, but dies in waterlogged soil.

Herbaceous forms can be divided, with care, and the species can be readily raised from seed, but the processes of rooting internodal stem cuttings of the climbers or grafting require good propagation facilities. The weaker hybrids are sometimes produced commercially by grafting onto more vigorous rootstock, such as that of *Clematis vitalba* (traveller's-joy; Z4), but this species (native here and introduced on the west coast of the United States) prefers a free-drained chalky soil and is not too happy on wet soil.

CORDYLINE

CABBAGE PALM
AGAVACEAE

In my early horticultural years, I thought of *Cordyline australis* (cabbage palm) as only being hardy in milder (Z9) maritime areas that bore some comparison to its home climate in New Zealand, where it can reach 20 m (66 ft.). But climate change and availability have seen cordylines much more widely and dependably grown in temperate regions. They can occur naturally on riverbanks and at the edge of swamps; *C. indivisa* (mountain cabbage tree) is found in wet mountain forest, and *C. australis* is very tolerant of my wet soil.

In addition to *Cordyline australis*, other New Zealand cordylines—*C. banksii* (to 4 m, 13 ft.) and *C. indivisa* (to 8 m, 26 ft.)—have been proven reasonably hardy, and several coloured-foliage selections of these plants are now in commerce. *Cordyline australis* 'Albertii' has attractive leaves with cream stripes, pink margins, and a red midrib; it has affinities with *C. australis* 'Torbay Dazzler', a striking light variegated form. The red-foliage forms, too, are popular, and seedlings that regenerate naturally in gardens may be very variable. "Architectural" is an often-applied descriptive term for these small trees, and they associate well with the built landscape.

Cordyline australis sets viable seed in a good summer, with the myriad small white fruits ripening and falling by mid-winter. Each contains three to four black seeds. Plants are also propagated from stem cuttings and suckers.

CORNUS

DOGWOOD
CORNACEAE

The genus *Cornus* includes woody herbs, shrubs, and small trees, and the curving main veins of their simple leaves make them instantly recognisable. Flowers are small (often in corymbs or rounded heads) but made more obvious in some by their large floral bracts. Dogwoods occur around the world's northern temperate zone. The European *C. sanguinea* (to 3 m, 10 ft.; Z4/5) can be found on limestone or base rich clays, and the eastern North American *C. florida* (to 6 m, 20 ft.; Z5) occurs on acid and limestone soils. The latter's western North American counterpart, *C. nuttallii* (to 12 m, 40 ft.; Z7) grows here in woodland on acid sands, as do the floriferous hybrids between these two species. The North American *C. stolonifera* (to 2 m, 6.6 ft.; Z2) and *C. obliqua* (Z4) grow by streamsides or in swamps; and for wet woodland ground cover, the diminutive, creeping *C. canadensis* (Z2) is a gem, beloved for its attractive white-bracted flower heads and red fruit. The equally hardy rare dwarf *C. suecica* (Lapland cornel) grows on peat soils in damp forests in northern Europe, and other boreal areas.

On the limit, *Cornus controversa* (Z5), a beautifully tabular-form small tree from temperate Asia, will wilt and die back during hot summers on dry soils, but—and along with *C. mas* (cornelian cherry; Z5) from Europe and west Asia—likewise fails if the soil is overwet in winter. However, almost all grow well where there is adequate moisture year-round.

Cordyline australis in flower

Cornus kousa 'Heart Throb'
in Eugene, Oregon

Dogwoods are valued in gardens. Forms of *Cornus alba* (Tartarian dogwood; Z3) bring brilliant winter bark. Others—*C. mas* and similar *C. officinalis* (7 m, 23 ft.; Z6), for example—have early spring flowers on bare branches. Some—notably *C. kousa* (Z5), from China, Japan, and Korea, and *C. nuttallii*—offer large-bracted summer flowers. Late summer fruit and autumn colour are other features of many. Those mentioned are hardy, but the evergreens are tender, and late frosts can be very damaging to young cornus. Some are also very sensitive to the use of herbicides around their base. All transplant and establish readily when young.

Fruits may be formed as an aggregate, as in *Cornus kousa*, and with this species along with some others (the more cherry-like *C. mas*), they are edible. Seeds of hardy species should be stratified before sowing. Softwood cuttings can be rooted in summer, and many taxa root readily from stem cuttings, even in a jar of water. Given a damp site, stems of plants such as *C. alba* 'Elegantissima' can be rooted *in situ*; stems should be 60–90 cm (2–3 ft.) in length and 1–2 cm (0.4–0.8 in.) wide. Many will layer naturally where lower branches rest on moist soil, and some form suckering clumps. Suckers or layers can be removed in late winter or early spring and set in their permanent sites. Rooted pieces of *C. canadensis* should be removed with particular care, holding onto any fine roots with soil, since they are slow to reestablish; in dry situations, they are best put into pans of leafy compost and kept cool and moist over summer while they reestablish for planting in autumn.

CORYLUS

HAZEL

CORYLACEAE

Because when cut back it readily forms a suckering clump, *Corylus avellana* from western Europe is commonly seen as a hedge plant and more frequently as woodland coppice, its strong, flexible young shoots used to make hurdles, brooms, and water-divining rods. Uncut it may grow 6–10 m (20–33 ft.). It is most easily spotted in early spring, when its male catkins hang golden on bare winter twigs, and their flowers open to release clouds of pollen. The separate female flowers are less conspicuous but marked by their crimson stigmas. Its fruit is the well-known hazelnut, of which there are many selected varieties. The fruit of *C. maxima* is known as the filbert, though both are sometimes called cobnuts. 'Purpurea', a purple-leaved form of the latter species, was once a popular choice for shrub borders.

The fifteen or so species of *Corylus* occur mainly in northern temperate zones, and all seem able to grow on moist heavy soil. *Corylus colurna* (Turkish hazel) makes a tall (to 30 m, 100 ft.) and showy, light scaly-barked tree with large catkins, but most smaller hazels grow as understorey or forest-edge plants. *Corylus tibetica* (Tibetan hazel) encloses its nuts in a chestnut-like spiny case; seed is difficult to extricate from the case with fingers, and once removed, its viability is sometimes frustratingly low. Most corylus are frost hardy to Zone 4/5, but *C. heterophylla* (at least the form from low-altitude Guizhou, in western China) and the Himalayan *C. ferox* struggle to grow well in areas with heavy winter frosts (below –10°C, 14°F).

As is generally understood from eating hazelnuts in winter, seed quickly shrivels if poorly stored. Those buried by rodents as soon as ripe germinate best! So keep fresh seed cool and moist, either sown and held in a cold frame over winter or stored stratified in a refrigerator before sowing in spring. Named forms are usually propagated from suckers, or layers.

COTONEASTER

ROSACEAE

A large genus of shrubs, some small-tree size, from Asia and Europe, extending to North Africa, with the greatest diversity in the Himalayas and western China. There are both deciduous and evergreen species. All have bisexual flowers and fruit heavily; their small pomes are a good autumn and winter food source for birds, which leads to seedlings arising randomly, often at a distance from the parent plant, and not surprisingly, many have naturalised. Some are apomicts (in confirmation of this, the seedlings of several are very uniform); and many hybrids have been raised. There has also been selection for the most colourful and heavily fruited forms.

Many of the deciduous species produce fine coloured autumn foliage, and they are hardier in comparison to some of the evergreen species, which can be damaged by winter cold. Cotoneasters fill many garden niches. At one extreme is the tiny-leaved (1 cm, 0.4 in.), procumbent to arching *Cotoneaster integrifolius* from the Himalayas to western China, which is where the frequently grown *C. horizontalis* (both Z4) also originates. With training, the herringbone-like stems of the latter can be used to cover low (1 m, 3.3 ft.) paling or brick

Crataegus monogyna

fences, or can be grown to trail down steep banks. In nature this species can be found on mountains, spreading bonsai-like on rocks; it can also be kept dwarfed as a small pot plant. There are many 2–3 m (6.6–10 ft.) shrubby red- or yellow-fruited cotoneasters from which to choose; for large gardens, there is the bright red-fruited *C. frigidus* (5–6 m, 16–20 ft.; Z7) and its popular Exbury-raised selection 'Cornubia' (6 m, 20 ft.). Most can withstand pruning and, though a little lax, some can be used as hedging plants. All are pretty tolerant of heavy wet soils, but very wet soils can constrain growth. Increase species by seed (stratified) or semi-ripe cuttings.

CRATAEGUS

HAWTHORN

ROSACEAE

A familiar genus of mainly hardy small trees and shrubs, perhaps known best as field hedge plants but also enjoyed as freestanding trees when in flower or when covered in their small pomes, or haws. Most grow well on heavy soils, although some variation is to be expected among the roughly 100 wild species in North America and the equal number spread across Europe and Asia.

Only two of the several species cultivated here are native to Britain, and both have a more extensive Eurasian range. One of these, *Crataegus monogyna* (Z5), with single-seeded haws, is widely known as a fruiting hedgerow plant, especially in the English countryside where it was planted in bulk at the time of the enclosure movement. It has a very tough wood that can withstand the severe treatment of hedge laying, and it has the power to regenerate a mass of strong thorny shoots from cut stems, making it greatly valued for stock hedging. It is less often seen as a specimen tree, yet it can be a feature when in massed flower, or heavily adorned with shining dark red haws, though birds and other wildlife quickly remove these. The closely related and less common *C. laevigata* (Midland hawthorn; Z5) has given rise to several cultivars, including a red double-flowered form, and in hedgerows, forms of this species often show pinkish flowers. It has two seeds in each pome. The blossom of *C. monogyna* has a pungent, not entirely pleasant scent; an old tree stood by the garden door of my family home, and my mother banned the use of its flowers indoors, not so much for the smell but because it was said to bring bad luck. *Crataegus monogyna* grows well on cold wet clays and regenerates freely in my wet garden; and while *C. laevigata* is better adapted to light soil, it is reasonably tolerant of wet soil.

TREES, SHRUBS, AND CLIMBERS

In the Near East, larger-fruited species occur. *Crataegus orientalis* from southeastern Europe and southwestern Asia has downy lacini-ate leaves and large orange haws; the thornless *C. tanacetifolia* (both Z6) has downy leaves, large yellowish haws, and, for the garden, is usefully slow growing. The American thorns are also often grown. Generally their leaves are less parted than the Eurasian species, and the fruits are larger but less abundantly produced. The most popular of these, *C. persimilis* 'Prunifolia' (Z5), is planted for its fine autumn foliage and large red haws. Many seem reasonably tolerant of wet soils, and notably too, some of the American species, such as *C. doug-lasii* (Z5), occur naturally on wet soils and along streamsides.

Seed may take two years to germinate and needs stratifying; selected forms are budded or grafted.

CRINODENDRON

CHILEAN LANTERN TREE
ELAEOCARPACEAE

Crinodendrons, from temperate South America, are small trees with simple leathery leaves, growing 3–4 m (10–13 ft.) in cultiva-tion. They are greatly cherished for their attractive, pendent, fleshy-petalled flowers. The larger deep red flowers of *Crinodendron hooke-rianum* are particularly appealing, but it is a little more difficult to establish than the scented, white-flowered *C. patagua*, which seems a tougher plant. Crinodendrons prefer moist but well-drained soils, and interestingly *C. patagua* grows in central Chile, along riversides, where it can reach 15 m (50 ft.). In cultivation, however, it tolerates drier conditions than *C. hookerianum*. Both grow well in my moist soil, hardy to –10°C (14°F), but are happier in moister milder mari-time regions.

Fresh seed, when available, germinates without special care (and self-sown seedlings of *Crinodendron patagua* can arise in southern Britain). Semi-ripe summer, or earlier summer greenwood cuttings may be taken, but these require a bottom-heated frame or a mist propagation facility.

Crinodendron hookerianum

DAVIDIA

DOVE TREE
CORNACEAE

The sight of the myriad white fluttering bracts of a davidia in full flower, whether on a remote Chinese mountain or a woodland gar-den, is very special. The small flowers of this famous tree are formed

in stalked, cherry-sized clusters, and each cluster is held within a sumptuous pair of large, but unevenly sized white bracts. *Davidia involucrata* (Z5/6) is quick growing on a moist soil, reaching 25 m (82 ft.) or more in good conditions. It occurs in mixed wet forest, though I have seen it by riversides as well, between 1000–2000 m (3281–6562 ft.); in the wild, davidia is restricted to western China (Hubei, Guizhou, and Sichuan).

Complete germination takes two years. The fruit is usually a drupe (a woody ridged seed within a fleshy coat); and because these plum-sized seeds (seemingly, and from only a small range of samples, round on trees from Hubei, elliptic in west Sichuan, and intermediate between these two for Guizhou provenance trees) are attractive to rodents, it is important to keep them cool and moist in a cold frame that is secured against pests.

Notwithstanding their hardiness rating, davidias are very sensitive to frosts when small. Consequently I prefer to keep them in a container for three or four years so that they can be brought into shelter over winter. While they need a good level of soil moisture, and the shelter of woodland, they also need light and air all around to flower well, especially on their lower branches. Once established, they need only minimal attention.

DRIMYS

WINTERACEAE

Drimys are evergreens with very fragrant leaves and bark. *Drimys winteri* (Winter's bark, canelo) from southern South America, extending down to Cape Horn in the southern half of Chile, has abundantly produced loose umbels of large (to 2 cm, 0.8 in.) fragrant, bisexual flowers and shares with magnolia a simple spiral arrangement of its floral parts; its leaves have an attractive bluish glaucous reverse. It can grow to 15 m (50 ft.) in favoured temperate sites, reaching 30 m (100 ft.) with a trunk 1 m (3.3 ft.) in diameter in its native home. A dwarfed form, *D. winteri* var. *andina*, is useful for small gardens.

There are three other species of *Drimys* in southeastern Australia and Tasmania, and of these *D. lanceolata* (mountain pepper) is of smaller stature than *D. winteri*. Particularly in its Tasmanian alpine form, it is often cultivated and has proved to be hardy over two decades in northern England. Like *D. winteri* its berries have a blackish hue and, with unisexual flowers, these are freely set where a small group of plants, including males and females, is grown.

These are forest to moist montane plants that are invariably associated with moist climates and soils, but not bog, as they require good drainage (though a short drought is sufficient to kill established plants of *Drimys lanceolata*). Apart from droughts they are easily grown, fairly trouble-free plants; however, they are on the edge of hardiness in Zone 8.

Fresh seed, stratified over winter, normally gives good spring germination at 18°C (65°F) minimum, and seedlings grow readily. Summer stem cuttings can be rooted, given good propagation facilities, including bottom heat (that is, a warmed substrate). Layering is also possible with multi-stemmed plants.

EPACRIS

SOUTHERN HEATH
EPACRIDACEAE

Richea scoparia

More and more often, evergreen winter-flowering southern heaths are cultivated where the winter temperature stays above –7°C (19°F). Most grow to a height of 1–2 m (3.3–6.6 ft.). Several of the thirty or so species in southeast Australia and Tasmania grow on wet heaths, such as *Epacris obtusifolia*, *E. gunnii* (coral heath), and *E. paludosa* (swamp heath). Others—mostly forms of the southeast Australian *E. longiflora*, with tubular flowers up to 4 cm (1.6 in.) long, and *E. impressa* (Z9)—absolutely require a raised bed on wet ground: their fine, erica-like root systems need constant moisture but excellent drainage.

Seed is difficult to germinate; storage in the dark has been recommended to overcome germination blocks. Most epacris can be rooted from softwood cuttings in summer using either a mist propagation unit or frame with bottom heat.

RELATED GENERA

The Australian *Sprengelia incarnata* (pink swamp heath) is able to grow on constantly moist soils in a warm temperate climate. The bushy richeas, though slow growing, can live for many years; these epacrids have distinct leaf-scarred stems and attractive, spiky terminal inflorescences. *Richea scoparia*, a Tasmanian endemic, offers various flower colour forms, from white to pink and orange to deep red; it reaches only 1 m (3.3 ft.) or so in cultivation. A slightly raised bed of organic compost set over a cool, moist substrate makes a good planting site, though *R. gunnii* may be found on wet peaty heaths in Tasmania. *Richea scoparia* is hardy to –15°C (5°F); *R. gunnii* seems to need more shelter. All richeas are difficult to root from cuttings.

ERICACEAE

HEATH FAMILY

This family of approximately 3250 species in 116 genera is significant for the great number that are grown in gardens, especially cool, moist gardens where just one genus, *Rhododendron* (which see), is dominant. In nature, ericoids are widely distributed through moist temperate and subtropical and tropical montane regions. Most are shrubby, though there are some trees and scramblers. Leaves are generally petiolate, simple, mainly evergreen, and lack stipules. Flowers have a persistent calyx and usually five corolla lobes; they are bisexual and may be in racemes or solitary.

Most members of this family grow well in cool, moist atmospheric conditions with their roots in moist, well-aerated but not saturated, acid organic soil, with partial shade, though a number grow in bogs. There are some exceptions, such as *Arbutus*, which is tolerant of drier soils with a higher pH. Roots are mostly fibrous, and they have well-documented endotrophic mycorrhizal associations. Given adequate moisture, the smaller-growing species need a reasonable level of light and tend to die back if overshaded by trees or larger shrubs. Gardening in drier climates is constraining on the cultivation of Ericaceae, though this can sometimes be overcome in more maritime (Z9) regions, where sea mists frequently occur, or further north, where atmospheric moisture levels increase; a north-facing slope then offers the opportunity to grow many species.

Fibrous root systems make these plants amenable to cultivation in pots—a convenience for those enthusiasts who live on an alkaline soil but wish to grow them. They are extensively grown as tender pot plants in the temperate northern hemisphere, particularly the winter-flowering Cape heaths (ericas from South Africa) and evergreen azaleas.

Seed is small, as initially are the seedlings, which are also slow growing, and need particular care in pricking-out and potting-on to avoid damping-off. These slow-growing plants may need to be kept in pots for two to three years before planting in a bed to grow on to final planting size. Usually the bed is raised and composed of an organic medium with some coarse sand added.

The rooting of ericoid cuttings is also an art; timing being critical for many, with cuttings taken when the summer season's shoots begin to stiffen as woody tissue is laid down. The use of acid substrates, soft (low pH) water, and rooting auxins are critical requirements, and mist propagation is a helpful aid. Previously, grafting was much practised, particularly for rhododendrons, using stocks such as the invasive *Rhododendron ponticum*, which sometimes sprouted below the graft union. Side or saddle grafting were the main techniques.

On a small scale, with large plants, layering of low branches is a simple way of increasing one's own plants. This also happens naturally: when growing on a moist peaty soil, *Gaultheria mucronata* (Z6) from Chile spreads by means of stems that grow horizontally, just below the surface; new roots and shoots develop from nodes on these stems, and a thicket is soon formed.

With an immense range of forms, including many coloured-foliage cultivars from which to choose, it is worth noting that the wide-ranging common and hardy heather itself, *Calluna vulgaris*, may be found on both wet and dry heaths. The even more diverse hardy ericas offer species varying from low growing to tall woody-stemmed shrubs, and *Erica tetralix* (cross-leaved heath; Z3) is found on wet heaths in Britain. However all heaths and heathers will need the good drainage given by a raised bed in wet conditions.

Just mentionably, although these are not much cultivated, the North American *Lyonia lucida* (fetterbush; Z5), which grows to around 1.5 m (5 ft.), occurs along with *L. mariana* in swampy regions; the scandent, small shrubby Japanese *Phyllodoce aleutica* (Z2) grows in wet meadows; and *Pieris phillyreifolia* (Z7), a larger evergreen (to 1 m, 3.3 ft.), grows naturally with taxodiums.

Escallonia 'Iveyi'

ESCALLONIA

ESCALLONIACEAE

Escallonia occurs in South America, mainly in the Andes. All are evergreen and seemingly very tolerant of wet soils. I have grown a plant of *E.* 'Iveyi' for close to two decades against a wall in my Zone 8 garden on an extremely wet site, by springs; it makes a small tree (to about 3.5 m, 11.5 ft.), and in mid to late summer produces abundant racemes of white flowers that are seen in clear relief against its dark green leaves. The flowers are bisexual, with their floral parts mostly in fives.

With their tough leaves and robust growth, escallonias make good hedges, even regenerating young shoots from old cutback stems. Most grow 1–3 m (3.3–10 ft.). Their tubular flowers, in reds, pinks, and white, are attractive and freely produced but best appreciated at close hand. Some species are tender; *Escallonia tucumanensis* (Z9), from northwestern Argentina, with its masses of pendentracemed bright white flowers, remains one of my favourite plants, as does the rarely seen Kew-raised *E.* 'Caroline', the hardier hybrid from this plant. Most hybrids, in fact, are hardy to –10°C (14°F) or lower. Escallonias are generally easy-to-grow, tough plants. They can be propagated by semi-ripe or even hardwood cuttings.

EUCALYPTUS
GUM TREE
MYRTACEAE

With some 700 species *Eucalyptus* is an important genus of trees used for timber and essential oils, or grown for flower, with the bonus of nectar for honey production; many are grown just for the sheer beauty of their bark and foliage. The number cultivated in Zone 8 gardens has increased in recent years. All are quick growing, and the southeastern Australian *E. aggregata* (swamp peppermint) to 20 m (67 ft.), *E. ovata* (swamp gum) to 60 m (197 ft.), and its close relative *E. camphora* (mountain swamp gum) to 20 m (67 ft.) occur naturally on wet soil. These heights are for the plants in their natural habitats; in cultivation, they do not grow as tall.

The more commonly grown species, like *Eucalyptus perriniana* (spinning gum; to 9 m, 30 ft.) and also the very hardy *E. gunnii* (to 30 m, 100 ft.), a Tasmanian endemic, both occur on wet soils; however, when grown on cold wet soil, low temperature seems limiting for some of the hardier species, and they can die if the soil is fully saturated over winter. For warmer Mediterranean zone gardens, two Western Australian eucalypts, *E. occidentalis* (to 21 m, 70 ft.) and *E. spathulata* (to 9 m, 30 ft.) grow on naturally wet soils. For propagation, see Myrtaceae.

EUONYMUS
SPINDLE TREE
CELASTRACEAE

Although they are not tolerant of waterlogging, euonymus can grow happily on heavy soils, and are tolerant of dry soils (including the range from light chalk to acid sand). I have seen what I took to be *Euonymus hamiltonianus* in full fruit, on a very wet western Chinese mountainside, and, on the edge of Tibet, the rare *E. porphyreus* growing as a small riverside tree. And though it occurs in seasonally dry habitats, *E. velutinus* will grow on wet but well-drained soils. Those mentioned are hardy, but some tender species are in cultivation.

The wing-stemmed, bushy *Euonymus alatus* (Z4), from China and Japan, is one of the most spectacular for autumn colour, but the European spindle cultivar *E. europaeus* 'Red Cascade' (Z4), with its abundant fruit and good autumn colour, is now more popularly grown. The range available is considerable. Most, such as North American native *E. atropurpureus* (burning bush; Z4), are shrubby or small trees; some, like *E. fortunei* (Z5), are trailing or scrambling. The Japanese *E. japonicus* (Z7) is evergreen, and its many forms make desirable urban plants.

Euonymus flowers are small, white to green coloured, and have free petals alternating with stamens. Their fruit splits when ripe, opening its four or five lobes to reveal seeds, which are fully or partly covered by a brightly coloured, mostly red aril.

Seeds are sown when ripe, and stratified or otherwise kept cool and moist, but germination can be erratic. Softwood cuttings may be used for evergreen euonymus; for the deciduous species, semi-ripe cuttings set under mist is the preferred method. *Euonymus porphyreus* has proved very difficult to root from cuttings, but it and *E. velutinus* sucker, and *E. fortunei* will layer naturally.

FAGUS

BEECH

FAGACEAE

All beautiful in leaf, particularly in spring and autumn, beeches form a small genus of deciduous trees from the northern hemisphere that are often associated with warm light soils, both acid and alkaline, though they can also grow well on heavy soils. They do however require good drainage because, like the related *Castanea*, they are susceptible to, among several other diseases, ink disease fungi (*Phytophthora cinnamomi*, *P. cambivora*). Beeches can reach 40 m (131 ft.), though in eastern North America, as on Long Island, *Fagus sylvatica* (European beech; Z5) grows particularly vigorously. They make excellent hedging plants, with one annual cut sufficing, but their great attraction as a hedge is in holding their golden brown leaves over winter.

Beech mast needs stratification for six to eight weeks at 4°C (39°F), and seed containers must be protected against rodents. The many forms, from cut-leaf to golden and copper, may be increased by grafting.

Euonymus europaeus 'Red Cascade'

Fraxinus sieboldiana

FRAXINUS

ASH

OLEACEAE

Ashes vary in their ability to withstand wet soil. The lovely *Fraxinus ornus* (manna ash; Z6) from southern Europe and southeastern Asia is not exactly happy and grows more slowly on a cold wet soil, but it is one of the few plants I have seen recover from a distressed and flaccid condition after a period of saturation on a heavy soil. Another medium-sized flowering ash from central China, *F. mariesii* (now included with the Korean and Japanese *F. sieboldiana*; Z6) is as good as or better than *F. ornus* in flower, and though it tolerates heavy soil, I give it a slightly raised bed, for in nature, notwithstanding its occurrence in wet regions, such plants as I have seen have been growing on sheer-sided (well-drained) valley edges. My own plant, as with many of the ashes in cultivation, is grafted onto the stock of the more wet-soil-tolerant *F. excelsior* (common ash; Z4), which can grow 37 m (121 ft.) and seems tolerant of both damp and base-rich soils and, with abundant moisture, can grow quickly. This is cheering for wet gardens since its selection 'Jaspidea' is a favourite for its golden summer foliage, which contrasts against the somewhat uniform high summer green of other trees, and also for its lovely gold fall colour. Among the American ashes, *F. caroliniana* (Z6) occurs in wet depressions, and *F. pennsylvanica* (Z3) and *F. nigra* (Z7) may be found in woods by streamsides.

With their wind-spiralling seeds, the polygamous common ash trees can create weeding problems from abundantly produced seedlings, though, and in this respect more fortunately for gardens, some species of ash have separate male and female trees. Where only a single plant of such species is grown, seeding stops; this dioeciousness also limits the propagation of rare species in cultivation, and cultivars, to grafting. *Fraxinus excelsior* is the most frequently used rootstock, but judging from the many examples of swollen unions seen on specimen trees, this stock has a degree of incompatibility with other ashes.

GAULTHERIA

ERICACEAE

Some of the hardy shrubby gaultherias occur on wet soils—for example, the procumbent *Gaultheria hispidula* (Z6) from Japan and northern North America, and *G. procumbens* (Z4) in eastern North America—but they need good drainage in cultivation. Perhaps, because

TREES, SHRUBS, AND CLIMBERS

G. shallon (to 1 m, 3.3 ft.; Z5) from western North America has been so widely used for game cover, gardeners are less conscious of their value as tough, glossy-foliaged evergreens with attractive lily-of-the-valley flowers. For propagation, see Ericaceae.

GLEDITSIA

HONEY LOCUST
LEGUMINOSAE

The hardy central and eastern North American *Gleditsia triacanthos* (honey locust; Z4/5), of which several forms are grown in gardens because of their ability to cope with industrial climates, occurs naturally on rich soils and by rivers. It grows to 21–25 m (70–82 ft.) and it, and some other gleditsias, have noticeably large spines on their trunks. A related species, *G. aquatica* (water locust; Z6), has a more southerly range in the central and southeastern United States; this is a smaller tree (15–18 m, 50–59 ft.) with a one- to two-seeded pod, and it tends to be an even smaller, multi-stemmed tree in Britain. The several Asian species, and the Iranian and Transcaucasian *G. caspica* (Z6), can grow on heavy soils, and while all make attractive specimens, often with fine yellow autumn colour, their short racemes of small flowers are not showy. For propagation, see Leguminosae.

GORDONIA

THEACEAE

Gordonias grow much more vigorously than the related camellias, or at least that is my experience of this lovely genus of small trees. Of the seventy or so species, the two best known in cultivation are the Asiatic (China, Taiwan, and Vietnam) *Gordonia axillaris* and *G. lasianthus* (loblolly bay; Z8/9) from the southeastern United States. This latter species occurs naturally on wetland, and its bark has been used for tanning. Both have camellia-like white flowers and dark evergreen leaves, but *G. lasianthus* can be difficult to grow. Although rated hardy, gordonias are a little too tender for Britain other than for the mildest locations. For propagation, see *Camellia*.

GYMNOCLADUS

LEGUMINOSAE

Gymnocladus occur in eastern North America and eastern Asia, where they can be found growing on rich soils and along streams. *Gymnocladus dioica* (Kentucky coffeetree; Z4) is noted for having

Halesia monticola

wood that is resistant to decay. In the central and eastern United States it forms a broad tree 18–20 m (59–67 ft.) in height and is also tolerant of pollution; in Britain it makes a small, slow-growing tree that comes late into leaf but has lovely yellow fall colour. The Chinese *G. chinensis* (Z9) is similar but scarcely hardy. Both require well-drained sites. For propagation, see Leguminosae.

HALESIA
SNOWDROP TREE
STYRACACEAE

The flowers of the deciduous halesias are always a delight in spring as they come quickly into flower after bud break, and the species from the southeastern United States are widely cultivated. *Halesia carolina* and *H. diptera* (both Z5/6) tend to be shrubby, with the former having four-winged and the latter (as its epithet suggests) two-winged fruits; *H. diptera* var. *magniflora* is a larger-flowered form. Both their pendent flowers, which are mostly white, and fruits are produced abundantly. *Halesia monticola* (mountain snowdrop tree; Z5) can in time make a medium-sized tree; its white flowers are about 3 cm (1.2 in.) in diameter, and there is a rose-coloured form.

Both *Halesia carolina* and *H. diptera* occur naturally on stream-banks, and though able to grow on dry soils, droughts are limiting to their success. They thrive in moist open woodland. For propagation, see *Styrax*.

HAMAMELIS
WITCH HAZEL
HAMAMELIDACEAE

In their natural habitat, the deciduous, shrubby witch hazels grow along the edge of woodland and by streams, both in eastern North America (across to the Ozarks) and in China and Japan. They are all fairly hardy, with some flowering in autumn and others in early spring, before the leaves emerge. Flowering lasts for about one month, and the tolerance of these narrow-petalled flowers to frost is surprising. This, with their beauty and scent, makes them popular garden plants. They tend to flower more freely when growing on an open site but will do well in light woodland. The most popular garden hybrids, forms of *Hamamelis* ×*intermedia* (Z5), are crosses between the Chinese *H. mollis* (Z6) and Japanese *H. japonica* (Z5), and their bright flowering, of mostly yellows through to orange, brings great cheer in late winter. They respond reasonably to light pruning, as some like *H. japonica* 'Arborea' can make small trees, but all grow relatively slowly.

Selected garden forms are usually propagated by grafting (late winter side-grafts or summer budding) onto seedling stocks of the autumn-flowering American *Hamamelis virginiana* (Z4). Thus, one is actually judging the wet tolerance of this species rather than the hybrids or East Asian species grafted onto it; however, such grafted plants mostly grow well on wet soils. Layering is possible, as are semi-ripe cuttings given the use of mist-propagation and auxins. Seed raising for species is not easy as, even with natural winter stratification in a cold frame, the seed may take two years to germinate. Two months postharvest warm storage followed by three months chilling can help overcome germination blocks.

RELATED GENERA

Disanthus cercidifolius, from southeast China and Japan, may shrivel on summer dry sand soils, but equally grow poorly in dense unthinned moist woodland. However given a moist, sheltered, but open glade in woodland it can prosper in Zone 8, producing its narrow-petalled flowers in early autumn before its cercis-shaped leaves turn brilliant red. A hamamelis-sized shrub, it requires the same cultivation points.

There are many other fine garden plants in Hamamelidaceae, most thriving in cool, moist temperate woodland. *Corylopsis, Distylium, Parrotia,* and *Sycopsis* are also tolerant of drier soils; *Fortunearia, Fothergilla, Parrotiopsis,* and *Sinowilsonia* prefer moist woodland.

HEIMIA

LYTHRACEAE

Members of this small genus are not often grown, but *Heimia myrtifolia* from Brazil and Uruguay is available (along with *H. salicifolia*, which is sometimes considered a geographic variant of *H. myrtifolia*). The four-angled stems of heimias become woody at the base, making them reasonably self-supporting as garden plants. They are very tolerant of cultivation.

Heimia salicifolia (Z8/9) occurs naturally by streamsides or in grassy areas in Texas and Central and South America; in Mexico a hallucinogenic beverage is made from its leaves. It has yellow flowers and, as its epithet indicates, willow-like leaves on shoots that can grow 1–2 m (3.3–6.6 ft.). It needs a warm site to avoid its stems being cut back in winter, though it will regenerate new shoots from

TOP *Hamamelis ×intermedia* 'Pallida'
ABOVE *Disanthus cercidifolius*

its perennial rootstock. Heimias are easy to grow and raise in spring from seed sown at 15°C (59°F), or they can be propagated from basal cuttings in spring.

RELATED GENERA

The loosestrife family has several other bog or aquatic members. Ammannias are small submerged aquatics with a cosmopolitan distribution; some cupheas occur in wet soils; and the mauve-red-flowered *Decodon verticillatus* (swamp loosestrife) from eastern North America occurs in swamps and shallow water. *Lythrum virgatum* (Z4) from eastern Europe and Asia, including China, is similar to the pernicious weed *L. salicaria* but of a more slender appearance; several cultivars are available. Its flowers are particularly attractive to butterflies.

HIBISCUS

MALVACEAE

Only a few of the many hibiscus can grow well on wet soil. In the southeastern United States, several species are plants of marshy ground (the range of one, *Hibiscus moscheutos*, swamp rose mallow, also extends to the north); their large blossoms—15 cm (6 in.) in diameter—have inspired plant breeders to produce cultivars with even larger (20–25 cm, 8–10 in.) flowers of white, pink, or red, such as the deep red 'Southern Belle' and 'Lord Baltimore'. Depending on the parentage, these grow 1–2 m (3.3–6.6 ft.) in summer from a woody base. Though rated as hardy to Zone 5, they need summer warmth and are not best suited to temperate climates; limited to –5°C (23°F), they are sometimes grown as summer annuals. The yellow-flowered *H. diversifolius* (swamp hibiscus) from eastern Australia (New South Wales and Queensland) is of similar stature and requires similar conditions.

Generally these are quick-growing, short-lived plants that flower and grow well in full sun. The species can be seed raised without difficulty, and most will root easily from basal cuttings.

HYDRANGEA

HYDRANGEACEAE

Hydrangeas need no introduction as fine shrubs for damp soils, but unfortunately many will collapse if grown on saturated soils in summer. Their often-spectacular flower heads have outer sterile flowers with enlarged sepals, and many of the hortensia hybrids (Z6) have

TREES, SHRUBS, AND CLIMBERS

flower heads entirely composed of these ornamental sterile flowers. The approximately 100 species have a wide natural range, occurring in North and South America and from the Himalayas to Japan; still, not every site is suited to their taste, and, with several, hardiness is a factor. On a moist or damp soil, hydrangeas can be set in full sun, where they will flower magnificently, but they can also grow well on a dry soil, given shade—though too much shade on wet soil also seems deleterious. Usefully the popular Japanese *Hydrangea anomala* subsp. *petiolaris* (climbing hydrangea; Z4/5) will grow on a shaded side of a house in heavy wet soil, its aerial roots ensuring it clings tightly to walls. Though on a wet soil it can easily cover a wall 6–7 m (20–23 ft.) high, it normally needs only a light annual trim after each flowering to keep it in bounds. However in ideal conditions *H. anomala*, which also occurs in China, can reach 12–24 m (40–80 ft.).

Hydrangea aspera

The many forms of *Hydrangea macrophylla* (Z6) from China and *H. paniculata* (Z3) from Japan also prosper on heavy soils; but, when in doubt, planting on a slightly raised soil bed will ensure a good growth. This is good advice for *H. quercifolia* (oak-leaved hydrangea; Z5) from the southeastern United States, which in nature experiences a good deal of summer warmth; this species occurs naturally on moist woody slopes and also by streamsides. Another North American species, *H. arborescens* (Z3), thrives when set in open woodland, or on the shady, north side of an east-west wall, which is warmed by the sun on its south face (but not against a high wall, for it needs good light to produce an abundance of its massive white flower heads). *Hydrangea arborescens* and *H. paniculata* and its cultivars seem the most durable and successful in open wet woodland. Young shoots on all four of these species can be damaged by late frosts.

Some of the many forms of *Hydrangea aspera* (Z7) that range from the Himalayas to China and Taiwan are slightly more tender; certainly, in summer, the forested Asian mountain valleys where this species originates can be subtropically hot and humid. Some are very vulnerable to late spring frosts in their early years but grow away well, up to 4–5 m (13–16 ft.), once established and woody. To flower well, they do need moist but well-drained conditions in summer. Because of the tender nature of many hydrangeas, any pruning of their pithy young or exfoliating old wood is best left to spring.

Seeds are small and, when available, usually produce good results; however, the seedlings are also small and relatively slow growing, needing perhaps only 7.5 cm (3 in.) wide pots for their first season.

Hypericum maculatum
subsp. *obtusiusculum*

Most can be propagated from cuttings, using a rooting auxin, and taken as semi-ripe summer cuttings, but earlier softwood and later season hardwood may be tried. The climbers may be propagated from internodal cuttings or even layering if required. Note: the roots of all seedlings in this family are vulnerable to the larvae of mushroom flies.

HYPERICUM

ST. JOHN'S WORT
GUTTIFERAE

More than a quarter of the approximately 400 species of the genus *Hypericum* are cultivated, and all the species mentioned here are hardy. They have a cosmopolitan distribution but are mostly northern temperate shrubs or herbs, with simple, usually opposite leaves that are dotted with pellucid glands. Some are evergreen, but most of those cultivated are deciduous. The many stamened flowers are bisexual, invariably yellow, and the small seed is formed in either a dry capsule or a fleshy berry.

Several North American and European hypericums occur naturally in swamps or other wet situations. *Hypericum buckleyi* from eastern North America is tolerant of wet soil. Both the herbaceous *H. tetrapterum* (Z5) and *H. elodes* (marsh St. John's wort; Z8) are available in nurseries. The ubiquitous shrubby tutsan of gardens, *H. androsaemum* (Z6), occurs naturally in wet woods from western Europe to western Asia including North Africa, and has arrived spontaneously in all my own gardens, wet or dry. Its fleshy red berries, which ripen to a deep black, are attractive to birds, and the seed is spread by their agency. It grows 60–80 cm (24–31 in.), happy among shrubs or in the base of hedges, and is tolerant of very wet soil.

The smaller (30–50 cm, 12–20 in.), more sun-loving, herbaceous *Hypericum maculatum* (imperforate St John's wort; Z6), native in Britain, occurs naturally in my wet garden, in its subspecies *obtusiusculum*, which I quite enjoy, but I accept it is a plant for the enthusiast. Some of the larger shrubby Asian species prosper on wet soil—for example, *H. kouytchense* (Z6) from western China, which in addition to its large golden flowers forms attractive red-tinged seed capsules. All are fairly carefree in cultivation, transplant easily, and tolerate both summer and winter clipping if growing too large for their site. Many of the Asian species will grow to 1.5 m (5 ft.) or more on warm moist soil.

Seedlings can regenerate excessively around parent plants on wet

TREES, SHRUBS, AND CLIMBERS

soil. Seed exhibits good percentage viability; small samples are usually sown in pots placed in a cool frame. Seedlings transplant readily. Those that form a woody, suckering base (*Hypericum maculatum*, for example) can be divided. Semi-ripe summer cuttings present some difficulty unless good propagation facilities are available.

ILEX
HOLLY
AQUIFOLIACEAE

The genus *Ilex*, with over 400 evergreen and deciduous species of trees and shrubs, is surprisingly cosmopolitan. The leaves of some hollies, such as the tender *I. vomitoria* (yaupon) from the southeastern United States and *I. paraguariensis* (mate), contain caffeine and have been used to make teas.

Hollies have smooth barks, and their leaves are simple, with either entire toothed or spiny margins. Their small, usually white flowers are unisexual, and the plants are dioecious, though some bisexual forms occur. The fruit, the familiar holly berry, botanically a drupe, varies a little in size with different species, and the colour range extends from red to yellow and white, as well as blue and black. To achieve good fruiting with dioecious plants, both male and female trees are required, and for some American hollies, pollinating males are required that match the female's season of flower.

Ilex aquifolium (Z6)—native in Britain, invasive in the Pacific Northwest—can grow to 25 m (82 ft.); within its range, from Europe to North Africa and western Asia, it may be found on a variety of soils, from hot and dry to heavy, cold, and wet, and it copes well with sun or shade, though its limits are shown by its failure in the cold winters of the northeastern United States. The North American possumhaw, *I. decidua* (3–9 m, 10–30 ft.; Z5/6), occurs naturally on moist soils and along streamsides, though it too copes well with dry soil. Hollies are often seen as understorey forest plants, as with, for example, the slow-growing often shrubby *I. pernyi* (Z5) in western China and *I. fragilis* (Z7) in Nepal. The latter is deciduous and has established as a small plant in Ray Wood, a north-facing oak wood in North Yorkshire (Z8). I find that *I. verticillata* (winterberry; Z3), a tall shrub from eastern North America, grows well on heavy wet soils in cultivation; in nature, it grows in wet soils with alder. In the southeastern United States *I. cassine*, *I. coriacea*, and *I. myrtifolia*, which are evergreen shrubs to small trees, are all recommended for wet sites. All are Zone 7/8, as is the bushy *I. amelanchier*, which has bright red berries and grows on moist soil. Generally the American species are said to grow better on neutral to acid soils.

Hollies are very accommodating plants, and a great many hybrids and selected forms are in cultivation. The evergreens may be used to give shelter in woodlands, and they make fine formal hedges, needing only one cut (in high summer) each year. One slight hazard, though: the dry leaves that accumulate beneath *Ilex aquifolium* are very flammable, and a carelessly discarded match or cigarette during a dry period in summer can cause the whole tree to flare up like a Roman candle. Also, the larvae of the holly blue butterfly like to pupate among these fallen leaves.

Given good root balls, hollies can be transplanted successfully, even as largish stock. Very young seedlings are, however, vulnerable to being eaten by rodents, particularly voles, and larger plants can suffer severe damage through winter bark stripping by muntjac deer. Seed collected in late autumn will, after vernalisation, germinate more readily in spring if first given a short warm period of post-harvest ripening. Delayed dormancy in hollies can last from one to three years or more. Selected cultivars and male and female forms are increased by grafting, or semi- ripe cuttings taken in late summer and set under mist propagation.

ILLICIUM

ANISE TREE
ILLICIACEAE

An interesting genus of evergreen shrubs to small trees, with leaves and bark that are strongly and pleasantly aromatic. Their leaves are simple, mostly linear-ovate, and their many tepalled, generally scented flowers are freely produced. Fruits are woody, and star-like—hence, star-anise, *Illicium verum* (Z8), from southeastern Asia—and have a single seed in each segment. They occur in eastern and southeastern Asia and the southeastern United States, extending to Mexico and the West Indies. All seem reasonably tolerant of wet soil; the hardy Asian species are found naturally by streamsides in mixed mesophytic forest at around 2000 m (6562 ft.), and the North American species can occur on the edge of swamps.

Once established they become fine, easy-care garden plants and grow steadily to form bushes 2 m (6.6 ft.) high or more. Four species tolerant to at least −5°C (23°F) are commonly cultivated: the two Asian representatives are *Illicium henryi* (Z8) which occurs in both the upper and lower Yangtze regions, and has dark rose-coloured flowers, and *I. anisatum* (Z7) from China, Taiwan, and Japan, which has pale yellow flowers. From the southeastern United States are *I. parviflorum* (Z6/7), with green-yellow flowers, and the more widely grown *I. floridanum* (Z6), with maroon-purple (or, in one form, white) flowers. All require a moist sheltered site, with good drainage, and they generally require an acid organic soil. Seed is not often available, and when it is, it is short-lived, needing sowing on receipt. Semi-ripe cuttings may be taken in summer, but good propagation facilities are required for their successful rooting. Where no facilities exist, layering is an alternative.

ITEA

SWEETSPIRE

ESCALLONIACEAE

For wet soil use, the deciduous *Itea virginica* (Virginia sweetspire; Z5) is a prime candidate, ranging widely in eastern North America in wooded swamps. Though not often seen in temperate gardens, it has several cultivars and can make a fine free-flowering shrub (1.5– 3 m, 5–10 ft.). The racemes are 10–20 cm (4–8 in.) in length, more drooping than pendent, with flowers creamy white and scented. It shows good autumn colour. The evergreen *I. ilicifolia* (3–5 m, 10–16 ft.; Z8) from central China grew well at Kew for many years positioned, as it was, against the north wall of a conservatory; this sheltered, moister, aspect, with warmer winter soil, suited it well, and it annually produced a mass of its catkin-like racemes, 30 cm (1 ft.) long, with small greenish white flowers. Most iteas in cultivation, including *I. japonica* (Z8) and *I. yunnanensis* (Z8/9), need similar moist but well-drained conditions and light shelter, as given by open woodland. Raise from fresh seed or propagate under mist or in a bottom-heated frame, from soft (green) wood cuttings early in summer or semi-ripe later in summer.

KALMIA

LAUREL

ERICACEAE

Generally these evergreen shrubs need moist woodland, but the eastern North American *Kalmia polifolia* (bog-laurel; Z2), as its common name suggests, is bog-dwelling, and in cultivation this translates to constantly moist, well-aerated, organic litter, slightly raised above the saturated soil. It is a small-growing, small-leaved plant, to 30– 70 cm (12–28 in.), but very attractive, with clusters of purple-pink

Itea virginica at the New York Botanical Garden

flowers that are smaller but otherwise like the other North American kalmias with their shallow-cupped flowers and stamens held in little pouches. For propagation, see Ericaceae.

LAURACEAE
LAUREL FAMILY

This large family of tropical and subtropical trees and shrubs includes many economically important plants, such as avocado and bay. Leaves are leathery; the smallish flowers are often in panicles (or cymes or umbels) and may be bisexual or unisexual. Most have strongly aromatic leaves and also aromatic bark, as in cinnamon and sassafras.

Asian members of this family are frequent understorey components of broadleaf forest and as such are adapted to a moist environment. In cultivation most require good drainage, but several are very tolerant of wet soils. *Laurus nobilis* (sweet bay; Z8), for example, seems able to cope with both wet and dry soils. These true laurels will mostly form long-lived, slow-growing, trouble-free specimens, generally requiring neutral to acid soils.

By contrast, the eastern North American *Lindera benzoin* (spicebush; 1.5–4.5 m, 5–15 ft.; Z5) favours limestone. This species occurs in moist woodland, often by streams, and is grown for its clear yellow autumn leaves and red fruit. Though not so hardy, several other linderas are cultivated, including the large-leaved dioecious *L. megaphylla* from southern China and Taiwan and *L. umbellata* from China and Japan (both Z8). All are useful for moist woodland gardens. Though very rare and not usually seen in cultivation, *L. melissifolia* (southern spicebush) occurs naturally on wet soil in the southeastern United States; similarly and from the same region is the endangered shrubby *Litsea aestivalis* (pondspice).

The Asian litseas and neolitseas are rarely cultivated, as most require warm temperate conditions, but the tender subtropical *Persea* (avocado pear) has some members that can grow in the mildest (Z9) parts of Britain. *Persea borbonia* (red bay) from the southeastern United States can be a shrub or small tree (2–6 m, 6.6–20 ft.), and grows well on moist soils. In nature it may be found in swamps. *Persea ichangensis* comes from the other side of the world—a Wilson introduction (1901) occurring in central and southwestern China. It has proved itself hardy in Zone 8 on a moist but well-drained site, growing slowly to become a small (6–8 m, 20–26 ft.) evergreen tree.

The bay-like *Umbellularia californica* (headache tree, Californian laurel; Z7) from California and Oregon grows along watercourses and, like *Laurus nobilis*, can grow on both marginally wet and dry soils.

Seeds of Lauraceae are not long-lived: sow when fresh, at 16°C (61°F) for temperate species. Seed of hardy linderas can be set in a cold frame to overwinter; deciduous linderas can be propagated from early summer greenwood cuttings, and the evergreens by later season semi-ripe cuttings. The large seeds of *Persea americana* (avocado) are often germinated by home gardeners on a windowsill and, given a cover of leaf litter, will even germinate on a compost heap out-of-doors. Given bottom heat, bays and some other evergreens can be rooted from hardwood cuttings.

LEDUM

LABRADOR-TEA
ERICACEAE

The aromatically foliaged ledums often grow naturally in sphagnum bogs, *Ledum palustre* (syn. *L. groenlandicum*) across northern North America and northern Europe and Asia, and *L. glandulosum* in northwestern North America. They are hardy to Zone 6 and grow 1–2 m (3.3–6.6 ft.), though some dwarfed forms have been selected for gardens, and as with all these bog-dwelling ericoids, they need specialist care in cultivation. If set in a conventional woodland garden, they are easily overgrown by more vigorous plants; they need a light but moist situation, and the care given to such plants as when grown in acid organic beds in a rock garden or other alpine collection. For propagation, see Ericaceae.

LEGUMINOSAE

PEA FAMILY, BEAN FAMILY

Also known as Fabaceae. Plants in this very large (600 genera) family of trees, shrubs, and herbs usually have compound leaves, though sometimes, as with many acacias, the pinnate leaves are seen only on seedlings. Flowers are bisexual (sometimes monosexual). In subfamily Papilionoideae (*Galega*, *Trifolium*) they are mostly pea-like. In subfamily Mimosoideae (*Acacia*, *Neptunia*), they are wattle- or mimosa-like, with prominent stamens. In subfamily Caesalpinioideae (*Gleditsia*, *Gymnocladus*), flowers are simpler but often very beautiful. All genera produce a legume, a peapod-like fruit. The family is widespread and includes many important crop plants (peas, beans) and several timber trees.

Generally members of this family require free-draining soil where they can take full advantage of the nitrogen-fixing bacteria in their root nodules. A few occur on wet soils, but a number of the several genera considered in this directory come from warmer climates, and since cold wet is more damaging than warm wet, a moist, but reasonably well-drained soil is advised.

The hard-coated seeds of many legumes are long-lived and need scarification, by chipping or hot water soaking, to soften the seed coat and allow germination. Most legumes are difficult to propagate from cuttings, and grafting is used to propagate selected forms of trees. Some acacias can be rooted from semi-ripe cuttings taken in summer, cladastris can be propagated from root cuttings, and *Amorpha fruticosa* produces suckers. *Galega* and other herbs can be divided, with care.

LEPTOSPERMUM

TEA-TREE
MYRTACEAE

The Tasmanian and other southeastern Australian leptospermums appear hardier than those from New Zealand, which are mostly Zone 9, and some of these shrubs and small trees can cope well with heavy soil. Many attractive cultivars have been selected in New Zealand, and though they flower well in southern Britain, they lack the heavy weight of blossoms produced in San Francisco and other even warmer regions. In southeastern Australia both *Leptospermum juniperinum* and *L. lanigerum* (the latter can survive most mild winters) occur naturally on swampy soil, and several others too, such as *L. sericeum* from Tasmania, grow by streams and in damp places. Even the familiar *L. scoparium*, which can survive in sheltered sites, grows naturally in various habitats including riverbanks. Leptospermums are, however, susceptible to having their stems bent over by snow load. For propagation, see Myrtaceae.

LEUCOTHOE

ERICACEAE

The more robust leucothoes are popular garden plants, and they generally grow well on moist soils, often growing naturally in woodland by streams. The evergreen *Leucothoe fontanesiana* (dog hobble; Z5) forms dense arching clumps, 1–1.5 m (3.3–5 ft.) in height, and grows in slightly wet woods. For wetter soil, there is the deciduous but attractively flowered *L. racemosa* (swamp leucothoe; Z5–9) and

L. davisiae (Z9). All three come from North America, the first two from the southeast, the latter from California and Oregon. For propagation, see Ericaceae.

LEYCESTERIA

HIMALAYAN HONEYSUCKLE
CAPRIFOLIACEAE

The shrubby, Himalayan *Leycesteria formosa* grows vigorously on heavy soil, to 2 m (6.6 ft.) or more, and is especially attractive in late season when hung with panicles of claret-coloured bracts and reddish purple berries. It is tolerant of a range of soils and conditions but needs particular care in transplanting, as does the more frost tender, yellow-flowered *L. crocothyrsos* from Assam. Though hardy to −15°C (5°F), the tips of the hollow cane-like stems of *L. formosa* are very susceptible to winter frost damage. Since each stem may live for a few years only, one option is to stool back the plants in late winter. Seed is spread by birds and germinates on any bare wet soil. Alternatively, propagate by summer semi-ripe heeled cuttings.

LIQUIDAMBAR

SWEET GUM
HAMAMELIDACEAE

Liquidambar is sometimes included in Altingiaceae. Its common and Latin names refer to the fragrant resin its bark exudes (which has a medicinal use), but the trees are best known for the lovely autumn colours of their palmate leaves. Fall colour varies greatly from season to season and site to site, thus it is best to purchase a selected clone to ensure good autumn colour. Some seedlings of a northern provenance, which produced attractive fiery reds when raised in a Wealden nursery, changed to a medley of yellows, oranges, and reds when planted in Thames-side Surrey. Flowers are monoecious, but not very noticeable.

Of the liquidambars, the North American *Liquidambar styraciflua* (Z5), which ranges into Mexico and Central America, seems very tolerant of wet soils. This species can grow to 37 m (120 ft.) in North America but achieves little more than half this height here, where it is slow growing. Smaller-leaved and slower still in cultivation, becoming only a small tree, *L. orientalis* (Z8) is from southwestern Anatolia and Rhodes; usefully, though, this species occurs in river deltas that can be subject to seasonal floods. The southern Chinese and Taiwanese *L. formosana* (Z9) is a stately, sometimes massive, tree

TOP *Leycesteria formosa*
ABOVE *Liquidambar styraciflua*

of lower forests, but it struggles with the cold. The western Chinese forms, *L. formosana* Monticola Group (Z6), are more tolerant of cold. Also from China, the similarly hardy *L. acalycina* is sometimes seen in collections, and in its natural habitat it too can be subject to seasonal flooding.

Sow seed when fresh, and keep cool over winter, or stratify at 5°C (41°F) for nine to twelve weeks first. With good skills, it is possible to root semi-ripe cuttings in summer, but more often clones are bud- or side-grafted onto seedling stocks. Liquidambars are slow to recover from transplanting even when young.

LONICERA

HONEYSUCKLE
CAPRIFOLIACEAE

I have long been intrigued by the diversity of *Lonicera* (albeit most of the 180 some species and many hybrids have paired flowers and opposite leaves). While many honeysuckles can cope with seasonally dry conditions, many also cope with moist conditions. The small shrubby *L. nitida* (Z7), often used as a hedging plant, grows by rivers in western China; it is one of the few evergreens that tolerates occasional inundation. Most shrubby honeysuckles reach 2–3 m (6.6–10 ft.) in gardens.

The climbing Japanese honeysuckle *Lonicera japonica* (5 m, 16 ft.; Z4) has a greater eastern Asian range than its name suggests and seems very tolerant of wet soil. It is so vigorous that it is considered a weed in many parts of the world. Where freezing winter weather does not occur, it remains evergreen and ever growing, though it can be damaged by frost. The common European and west Asian *L. periclymenum* (woodbine; 4 m, 13 ft.; Z4) also grows vigorously on a heavy soil and can flag lamentably if the soil dries in summer. Some are noted for the scent as well as the beauty of their flowers, while many, such as the shrubby *L. xylosteum* (Z4), berry well.

Species may be propagated by seed, but most honeysuckles, including the hybrids and garden forms, come from summer stem cuttings. Climbers may root along stems where they lie on the soil.

MAGNOLIA

MAGNOLIACEAE

Magnolias are well known for their beautiful solitary bisexual flowers, some of which are highly scented. There are both evergreen and deciduous species, many suited to small gardens but others reaching 30 m (100 ft.). Over time I have become increasingly confident about the ability of magnolias to withstand wet soil, and notably, in nature, the eastern North American *Magnolia virginiana* (Z5) grows on wet soils. On my own cold wet soil, I find the Japanese *M. kobus* (Z5, but flowers may be frost damaged), *M. obovata* (Z6), and *M. stellata* (Z4) also grow and flower well. So do the Chinese Oyamas, *M. sieboldii* subsp. *sinensis* and *M. wilsonii* (both Z6); the Chinese Yulans *M. dawsoniana*, *M. sargentiana* (both Z7), and *M. sprengeri* (Z5); the very hardy (Z4) North American *M. acuminata* and *M. tripetala*; and, of course, hybrids from all these species.

Magnolia sprengeri is difficult to establish. Because it starts its new growth early in the season, it can be caught by late frosts, and to add to the woes of this species when young, seedlings are very susceptible to damage by herbicides, and also from slugs, which devour their leaves. Two-year-old plants can establish well but—particularly with *M. sprengeri* seedlings—I have, more than once, had to dig them up, repot, and return them to a cold greenhouse for recovery from a cold spring.

The related *Magnolia dawsoniana* grows at around 2000 m (6562 ft.) in wet forest in western Sichuan; and not far away in this land of panda and snow leopard, the lovely pendent-flowered *M. wilsonii* occurs at the same altitude. Interestingly this latter and the closely related *M. sieboldii* subsp. *sinensis*, which also occurs in this region, are much more tolerant of my garden conditions than most seed-raised Korean forms of *M. sieboldii*, which usually persist for just a few years before dying (although they will also do this on a dry soil). Sadly, much as I like this Oyama group of magnolias, none are happy on a very wet soil: they can yellow and die in wet summers, despite the fact that in nature they may be found by streams.

Growing magnolias in containers for two or three years, and overwintering them in a cold greenhouse, so that they form a woody stem before planting, has long been practised with *Magnolia macrophylla* (Z5), for example. Tennessee marks the northern end of the natural range of this species, but with a good stem it can survive further north. For those magnolias that come from warm regions, and occur in moist forested and sheltered valleys, which are almost subtropical in summer, hardiness is a general concern. Severe cold will cause loss of spring blossom or, worse, bark split and death.

TOP *Magnolia sieboldii*
CENTER *Magnolia* 'Roamer', an *M. sprengeri* hybrid seedling
ABOVE *Magnolia tripetala*

Planting and transplanting magnolias is often left until late winter or very early spring, when their fleshy roots are active and recovery hopefully swift. With young plants, I delay planting until all danger of frost has passed. On a wet site, a slightly raised bed is used for planting, and it is important to maintain a good ring of clear ground around the plant, because young magnolias cannot compete well with vigorous grass. Beware of using herbicides if the weather is warm and dry, since young magnolias are particularly sensitive. It is better to tolerate a few weeds rather than lose a plant. Magnolias form dense mats of surface roots, and weeds are thus better controlled by the use of mulches. Happily, early-flowering bulbs grow well under mulched deciduous magnolias; chionodoxas, for example, can flourish.

Curiously, the large trees of the Yulan group of magnolias are among the most wind tolerant of trees. In contrast, branches can be torn out of some forms of *Magnolia kobus* by high winds, but the wounds will heal. As a student I was taught that magnolias should not be pruned because they did not readily wound heal. While there is truth in this, and magnolias do not need pruning *per se*, some grow so vigorously that they soon exceed their allotted space, making pruning essential. Careful pruning, cutting away young in preference to older wood, does not seem to cause problems, and I have frequently pruned magnolias during the last thirty years. In China *M. officinalis* is regularly cut back to harvest its bark for medicinal purposes. As mature plants they can also recover well from frost-damaged shoot tips, regenerating from dormant lateral buds.

Magnolia carpels are arranged spirally on a central extended floral axis and split when ripe to release large (pea-sized) seeds that have a pink, orange, or red fleshy coating. These brightly coloured seeds hang from the carpels on short, thin threads, or funicles. Many are self-fertile and can set viable seed in cultivation. Some forms of *Magnolia grandiflora* (Z7) are grown for the beauty of their seed cones, and *M. kobus*, *M. obovata*, *M. sieboldii* subsp. *sinensis*, *M. sprengeri*, *M. tripetala*, and *M. wilsonii* set seed freely in gardens. Hybrids vary in this respect. Some, like those of *M. sprengeri*, set seed freely; others (*M. ×soulangeana* 'Lennei', for example) rarely do. Where species are grown in isolation their seedlings come fairly true, but in mixed collections the Yulans, for example, readily cross-pollinate, and in practise there are few barriers to crossing in magnolias. Magnolia seed should be sown when ripe (early to late autumn) using an organic compost that is kept moist and cool in a cold frame over winter. Germination occurs in late spring as the days warm. Initially the seedlings tend to produce a long, little-branched primary root and are best potted individually as soon as they can be handled. They can grow quickly, so need potting-on once or twice in their first season.

Several are propagated by means of summer softwood cuttings, but this is a skilled task requiring good propagation facilities, careful selection of material, and the use of wounding and rooting hormones. In private gardens, layering (that is, where branches are low to the ground) can produce the odd replacement plant, and in the past, layer beds were commonly used. Many selected cultivars are propagated by grafting onto seedling stocks of sometimes but not necessarily related species, using both chip-budding, and side-veneer grafting techniques. Grafted plants tend not to have the vigour of seedlings but will come into flower at an earlier age.

RELATED GENERA

The popular but tender (Z9) genera *Manglietia* and *Michelia* are increasingly grown in Zone 8; these too cope well with moist soils and require similar conditions, generally, to *Magnolia*.

MAHONIA

BERBERIDACEAE

Mahonia is taxonomically very close to *Berberis* (there is even a recorded hybrid between the two genera). Mahonias are all evergreen shrubs to small trees and valued garden plants. As with berberis, their familiarity often means their beauty is overlooked, particularly if the plants are set in dark shady corners; I'm thinking especially of *Mahonia aquifolium* (Oregon grape) or *M. japonica* from eastern Asia (both Z5/6). Grown as large specimens in a moist mild temperate climate, plants like the more tender broad pinnate-leaved *M. siamensis* or the longer-leaved *M. lomariifolia* (4–10 m, 13–33 ft.; Z8/9) from southwest China and Myanmar are very beautiful in flower. They are also welcome in the short days of late winter, their long racemes of yellow blossom contrasting vividly with the dark green of their leaves.

In cold temperate gardens the many hybrids from *Mahonia japonica* and *M. lomariifolia*, known as *M.* ×*media*, are very hardy (–15°C, 5°F, and lower), though they do not flower so well in heavily shaded woodland, preferring a more open situation. Woodland does however give some shelter to the more tender species such as *M. russellii* from Mexico, which can survive outdoors in Zone 8 given a close tree canopy.

While some species, such as the southern Californian *Mahonia nevinii*, prefer well-drained soils, most Asian species may be found in mountainous regions, usually at low altitudes, on the edge of moist forests or in scrub. In cultivation this seems to translate to a tolerance of conditions from dry sand to moist woodland and heavier soils.

Propagate from seed (as for berberis) or leaf bud cuttings of the large Asian members in late winter using a propagation unit. Some sucker; others form a stool that produces roots on basal stems. Cultivars must be vegetatively propagated.

MALUS

FLOWERING CRABAPPLE
ROSACEAE

Many hardy deciduous apples tolerate wet soil; if too wet and with impeded drainage, however, they are susceptible to root decay. Cultivated apples are mostly propagated by grafting, so, to some extent, tolerance of wet soils depends on the vigour of the rootstock. On a heavy wet soil, dwarfing rootstocks give poor anchorage, while the more vigorous rootstocks do not always produce as large a tree as might be expected. The major problem for many apples on wet sites is, however, their susceptibility to diseases such as scab, which disfigures fruit, and canker, which can kill branches or even the main stems of trees.

Disease aside, flowering apples are easy to grow and useful in gardens because they are mostly only small to medium-sized trees. They tolerate pruning, have good wound healing, and flower abundantly, producing either usefully edible or often ornamental fruit. They do however require an open unshaded site to flower well. *Malus baccata* is widespread in Asia, and in the arboretum at Castle Howard (Z8), a large group of the Korean form of this species, var. *mandshurica* (Z2), is set among pines; when in flower, the massed umbels of their startling white blossoms contrast strongly with the sombre green of the pines. The fruits of this latter species are small, dark, and pea-sized; those of *M. toringo* (Z5) from Japan are also small, though some forms can be red or bright yellow, and quite a feature until taken by birds. The Chinese *M. prattii* (Z7) may have dullish brown or rich pear-coloured fruits, and there are many brightly fruited species and cultivars. Many wild apples grow naturally on heavy soils. The western North American *M. fusca* occurs in moist woods, sometimes near water.

Species may be seed raised; clones are increased by budding or side-veneer grafting.

MYRICA
BOG-MYRTLE
MYRICACEAE

Though not commonly encountered, several shrubby myricas are cultivated for their sweetly scented leaves and small clustered fruits, which often hold on the bush over winter. Myricas occur in both wet acid bogs and dry habitats, and the distribution of the genus is almost cosmopolitan. *Myrica gale* (sweet gale; Z1) is a small deciduous shrub, up to 1.5 m (5 ft.), with an extensive range in the northern hemisphere, occurring in acid bogs from North America to western Europe and northeastern Asia. With its golden brown catkins (whether male or female), it is a welcome addition to the bog garden.

Three other larger-growing myricas from North America (sometimes included in the genus *Morella*) seem to be able to tolerate both moist and dry soils. The evergreen *Myrica californica* (California wax myrtle; Z8), which ranges from Vancouver Island to southern California, can reach 4–6 m (13–20 ft.) in favourable conditions but is often smaller (to 2 m, 6.6 ft.), and can be cut back by hard frost. The two other species come from the eastern side of North America. The evergreen *M. cerifera* (wax myrtle; to 3 m, 10 ft.; Z7) has an extensive range, often on sandy soil, and is noted for the wax granules that form on the plant. Similarly, the very hardy (Z3) deciduous *M. pensylvanica* (bayberry; to 2 m, 6.6 ft.) produces a wax that gives its fruit a grey-white surface. All require good drainage in cultivation.

Plants may be dioecious or monoecious. The unisexual flowers form in short catkins; they lack petals and sepals and are wind-pollinated. The fruit is a small drupe, often wax-coated. Fresh seed can be sown in containers and held in a cold frame. Softwood cuttings are difficult to strike without a good propagation unit, but myricas can be layered and sometimes sucker.

MYRTACEAE
MYRTLE FAMILY

This large, widespread, and diverse family of mainly tropical and subtropical trees and shrubs has concentrations of species in tropical America and Australia. Most possess aromatic oils and have evergreen, often opposite, leaves. Flowers are bisexual, and the numerous stamens noticeably extend beyond the petals on many.

While several genera of Myrtaceae occur naturally on wet soils, soil temperature is an interrelated and complicating factor. In a warm temperate garden (winter minimum −5°C, 23°F), many will form superb flowering trees and shrubs. However and unexpectedly, some of the shrubby callistemons and leptospermums can thrive on cold wet soils, and several can be grown in milder (Z9) maritime regions. The range of available plants has greatly increased; nevertheless, on wet soil, the use of raised planting sites is advised.

Southern South America provides many interesting evergreen myrtles for gardens. Sadly though, they are tender, prospering only in milder (Z9) gardens, and even then sometimes needing the shelter of a wall.

Amomyrtus luma from Chile and southwestern Argentina is sometimes cultivated and can be found naturally on somewhat wet soils, where it tends to produce aerial roots. In the southern evergreen forests of Chile it can become a tall tree, to 20 m (67 ft.), with a stem diameter of 50 cm (20 in.). More common in cultivation and from the same region is *Luma apiculata*, which has lovely cinnamon- and cream-coloured bark, making it a feature in warm temperate gardens; it occurs in evergreen forests, where it forms a 15–20 m (50–67 ft.) tree, and needs a moist, not saturated soil. *Luma chequen* (again, from the same region) sneeds similar conditions, and, though lacking the cinnamon bark, it is hardier. Both lumas will probably achieve only half the stated heights in temperate gardens. *Myrceugenia exsucca*, another southern South American tree, occurs on soils subject to seasonal flooding, and grows to 13 m (43 ft.), but it is tender and rarely cultivated. The shrubby, slightly hardier (to −10°C, 14°F) Chilean guava (*Ugni molinae*) is more often grown, but it needs a moist rather than a saturated soil.

Other genera offer species adapted to wet soils that are suitable for warm temperate gardens. From Australia there are *Baeckea* (similar to *Leptospermum*) and *Melaleuca* (similar to *Callistemon*), of which *M. gibbosa* and most of those occurring in Tasmania grow on wet soil. Some melaleucas inhabit coastal swamps. In New Zealand, *Syzygium maire* (tawake), a tree to 15 m (50 ft.), grows in swamp forest.

Many are self-fertile, setting viable seed in cultivation that can, as with *Luma apiculata*, regenerate freely on moist soil. The fleshy seeds are best sown fresh and kept moist at a temperature related to their origin. Seed from dry capsules, such as eucalyptus and callistemon, will store a little longer, but it is best sown as fresh seed in spring. Seedlings should be potted on at an early stage and root damage avoided. Eucalyptus seedlings can be grown on quickly (they make long roots) and planted in their final sites in their first year to increase anchorage. To root semi-ripe cuttings, a good propagation unit is required along with the use of rooting hormones. Some are very difficult to root; others, like callistemon, are relatively easy.

NOTHOFAGUS

SOUTHERN BEECH
FAGACEAE

The Chilean species of this southern hemisphere genus of moist forest trees are on the edge of hardiness; the evergreen *Nothofagus dombeyi*, however, does grow well in Zone 8. The species from Tasmania and New Zealand are best in milder regions (Z9), though New Zealand's mountain beech, *N. solanderi* var. *cliffortioides*, has grown for more than twenty years in Ray Wood in Yorkshire (Z8), albeit as a slight, sparsely foliaged tree to 6–7 m (20–25 ft.).

All need acid soil and can grow on fairly moist, heavy soils, in which some are susceptible to loss through root-invading fungi. At Castle Howard (Z8) this has happened with the deciduous Chilean *Nothofagus antarctica* and *N. pumilio*, which in a more favourable climate grow to 17 m (56 ft.) and 40 m (131 ft.), respectively. However, these deciduous species have good autumn colour, and their flowering in early season on bare branches is attractive as their massed male flowers exsert strongly coloured (yellow to red as they age) stamens. Nothofagus are monoecious and normally raised from fresh seed.

NYSSA

TUPELO
CORNACEAE

Grown for their spectacular fall colour, nyssas grow very slowly in their early years. They appear to grow faster when planted out, as opposed to being kept in pots, and do not respond well to transplanting. The largest *Nyssa sylvatica* (Z4) I have seen was massive and growing in a deep, wet hollow in the eastern United States. In the wild the Chinese *N. sinensis* (Z8) grows in the same wet forest as davidia. These two species are the most usually cultivated, but others, including the eastern North American *N. aquatica* (water or swamp tupelo), are worth growing if seed can be obtained. Tree height for nyssas varies with available moisture, to 15 m (50 ft.) on a dry soil to 30 m (100 ft.) or more on a wet soil. Seed should be sown

TOP *Nothofagus antarctica* flowering in spring
ABOVE *Nyssa sylvatica* in autumn

fresh in autumn and kept cool and moist over winter. Propagation from semi-ripe cuttings is possible.

OLEARIA

DAISY BUSH

COMPOSITAE

Olearia glandulosa from southeastern Australia and Tasmania and *O. virgata* from New Zealand occur on boggy ground; and both *O. furfuracea* and *O. rani* (also from New Zealand) occur by streams. Certainly they respond favorably to a well-drained moist soil in cultivation. They are relatively easy-to-grow shrubs, to 2–3 m (6.6–10 ft.), and flower well in full sun. Only *O. virgata* is hardy in Zone 8; the other three evergreens are slightly tender (Z9). Olearias root readily from soft or semi-ripe stem cuttings.

OSTRYA

HOP HORNBEAM

CORYLACEAE

There are some ten species of *Ostrya* in the northern hemisphere, all of which are medium-sized (to 25 m, 82 ft.) trees; their growth on wet soils is slow but matches *Carpinus* in this as well as in autumn colour and hardness of wood. As its common and Latin names suggest, *O. carpinifolia* (Z6), from southern Europe and Asia Minor, is hornbeam-like, similarly monoecious, and the seeds are carried at the base of swollen bracts, which look hop-like. The eastern North American *O. virginiana* (ironwood) is hardy to Zone 4. Fresh seed is the preferred method for propagation, but seed may also be stratified. Ostryas may also be grafted onto carpinus.

OXYDENDRUM

SORREL TREE, SOURWOOD

ERICACEAE

The lovely *Oxydendrum arboreum* (Z5) produces great racemes of pieris-like flowers and can grow to 25 m (82 ft.), but perhaps only half of that height in Britain, where it is slow growing. Though found in the eastern and southeastern United States on both wet and dry acidic soils, it is enigmatic in cultivation. Good drainage seems to be important for its survival, yet it can be killed by dry shade. Its time of splendour comes each autumn, when trees have a rich red gown of leaves. My memories are of an aged, but now lost, specimen tree at Kew, and also of an autumn day on a southern Appalachian mountainside, where the burning hues of a host of sourwoods were intensified by the accompanying fire-glow reds of *Acer rubrum*. It flowers well too, so while not a plant for wet soil as such, it is worth making an effort to grow it by looking for, or forming, a slightly raised site. Can be raised from seed or semi-ripe stem cuttings in summer.

OZOTHAMNUS

COMPOSITAE

Helichrysum once had some shrubby members, but these have long been separated into *Ozothamnus*. I had always treated the Tasmanian members of this genus, some of which grow to 1.5–3 m (5–10 ft.), with some care in cultivation, because they are slightly tender, and prefer moist but well-drained situations. However, when given a plant of *O.* 'Sussex Silver' I was delighted to find it very tolerant of warm, wet soil, in Zone 8, and I then noted with pleasure that *O. rosmarinifolius* (which is also in southeastern Australia, and a plant I had long grown on dry soil, where it is hardy to –10°C, 14°F) grows naturally on wet peaty heaths. Propagate from seed or summer stem cuttings.

PALMAE

PALM FAMILY

Palms form a large and very recognisable family of mostly tropical and subtropical woody evergreens with some 2700 species in 200 genera. A few are sufficiently cold tolerant to be enjoyed in temperate gardens, and a number can grow in wet soil and bogs. Economically, for a range of products, from the oil palm (*Elaeis guineensis*) to coconut (*Cocos nucifera*), they are very important.

Most are easy to grow in a garden or container but cannot easily be transferred between these options for, as young plants, palms "assess" their available soil resource and then "set" their stem diameter. Thus, if a palm has been in a container for many years and started to form a stem, when planted out, its stem diameter will increase, reflecting better conditions, but this subsequent heavier growth will be formed on the original narrower and thus weaker basal part of the stem. Similarly transplanting leaves a band of stem restriction as a permanent record of the palm's changed circumstances.

Palms are predominantly seed raised; their seeds are large, oily, and short-lived. For germination, seeds are kept constantly moist and at a temperature related to their natural environment. Their embryos develop slowly and germination can take months. The

Trachycarpus fortunei at Trebah in Cornwall

seedlings need careful handling since they are connected, for some while, to the rich seed endosperm by a hypocotyl stalk. A few, such as the date palm (*Phoenix dactylifera*), can be increased from sucker shoots.

Many palms from dry areas (*Phoenix* and *Washingtonia*, for example) will grow where their roots are either in streams or can reach underground water. Some of the many genera for moister soils follow.

Livistona. Large coryphoid palms, mostly from Asia. *Livistona australis* grows by rivers and in boggy areas in eastern Australia, and the widely grown *L. chinensis* also grows best with a moist soil. Z10.

Mauritia. Large tropical South American lepidocaryoid palms for wet soils. I recall seeing *M. flexuosa* in wet gullies in the Amazon region and wading through a razor grass swamp in Trinidad to collect some of this mauritia's golfball-sized seeds. Z11/12.

Phoenix. The pinnate-leaved dwarf date palm *P. roebelenii* (1–4 m, 3.3–13 ft.) from northeastern India and Myanmar grows along rivers; *P. paludosa* from India, Malaya, and Thailand grows in even boggier situations. Z10.

Ravenea. Tropical arecoid palms from Madagascar and the Comoro Islands including *R. rivularis* (25 m, 85 ft.), which grows by riversides, as does *R. musicalis* whose seed can initially germinate in water. Z11/12.

Rhopalostylis. With just three species, these large monoecious pinnate-leaved palms from New Zealand and Norfolk Island grow naturally in moist stream valleys. They survive outdoors on the Scilly Isles (off Cornwall). Z10.

For warmer climes, three further arecoid palms cope well with wet soil: the small (9 m, 30 ft.) *Chrysalidocarpus lutescens* from Madagascar; *Pinanga densiflora* from Sumatra and Indo-Malesia (most tropical Asian pinangas grow naturally by rivers and may occasionally be inundated); and *Ptychosperma macarthurii* from Australia and New Guinea.

As a footnote for lovers of palms, the hardy, slow-growing but eventually tall (20 m, 67 ft.) *Trachycarpus fortunei* (hemp palm; Z8) is tolerant of fairly wet soil if given good drainage.

PARTHENOCISSUS
VIRGINIA CREEPER
VITACEAE

Though not a plant of wet soils *per se*, I have been surprised by the tolerance of *Parthenocissus quinquefolia* to heavy wet soils, and the other parthenocissuses can also grow well on moist soils. They can be vigorous climbers, to 10–20 m (33–67 ft.), and are particularly self-clinging because the tips of their tendrils have adhesive disks. These woody vines are grown primarily for their fine autumn foliage, since their flowers and fruits are small and not usually very conspicuous.

The Chinese *Parthenocissus henryana* (Z7) has attractive three- to five-digitate leaves, with silvered markings following its main veins, in addition to a good autumn colour. This species can, however, be tender when young. Usefully, the much hardier *P. quinquefolia* (Virginia creeper; Z3) from eastern North America will grow happily on the shaded side of a house. In nature it can reach the top of deciduous hardwood trees and can soon reach 10 m (33 ft.) on buildings but will need an annual pruning thereafter. *Parthenocissus tricuspidata* (Z4), the understandably but confusingly (because it is a temperate Asian plant) named Boston ivy, has variable ovate or trifoliate leaves when young, settling into its familiar three-lobed leaves as it matures. It is the most self-clinging of these vines, particularly on walls, as in comparison others usually trail down loose shoots, and, because it is the best for autumn colour, a number of cultivars have been selected.

Seeds, if available, require cleaning and stratifying. The rooting ability of species varies; some are difficult, but many parthenocissuses can be propagated from summer leaf bud cuttings, aided by the use of a rooting hormone and bottom heat. Layering offers a simple means of propagation.

Photinia villosa in flower

PHOTINIA

ROSACEAE

A northern hemisphere genus of small trees and shrubs that has come to prominence with the recent popularity of such plants as *Photinia ×fraseri* 'Red Robin' (Z8), a hybrid between *P. glabra* (Z8) from China and Japan and *P. serratifolia* (Z6) from China and Taiwan, with its young evergreen leaves flushing bright bronze-red. Many other species also occur in eastern Asia, particularly China.

The shrubby (to 3 m, 10 ft.) and deciduous *Photinia davidiana* (Z8), which was for a long time in the genus *Stranvaesia*, is familiar in gardens for its scarlet autumn fruits. Less often seen is *P. villosa* (Z4) from China, Japan, and Korea; I have been quite taken with this plant, since all forms are good, specifically the Korean, which makes a pleasing large arching shrub (3–4 m, 10–13 ft.) that flowers well in summer and has showy fruit and yellow leaves in autumn. It seems very content on a heavy wet soil, given reasonable drainage, though it can cope in the short term with a saturated soil. Most cultivated photinias can grow on heavy soils, and the evergreen photinias can provide useful screens. The deciduous species can be increased from seed; if good propagation facilities are available, the clones and evergreens can be rooted from stem cuttings.

PHYLLOSTACHYS

GRAMINEAE

A popular genus of bamboos, coming mostly from China, but extending into India and Myanmar. Several of its sixty-odd species, including a number of impressively large plants, are cultivated, particularly in warm temperate climates, where they attain their greatest heights. However, even in southern Britain (Z8), *Phyllostachys viridiglaucescens* from eastern China can grow to 7 m (23 ft.). All seem tolerant of heavy wet soils. Many forms of the popular Chinese *P. nigra* (black bamboo) are available, and though in warm conditions the species itself can grow 6–10 m (20–33 ft.), with freely spreading rhizomes, in cooler climates it keeps to reasonably tight clumps of half this height. Both species are rated Zone 7.

PLEIOBLASTUS

GRAMINEAE

Bamboos of the genus *Pleioblastus* respond variably on wet sites. The striped-leaf *P. viridistriatus*, which reaches 0.9–1.5 m (3–5 ft.) in Zone 8, still keeps tight clumps (30–45 cm, 12–18 in. in diameter) after thirty years but doesn't look happy. The slowly spreading *P. linearis*, also from Japan, grows well in Zone 8 with dense linear leaves, 15–20 cm (6–8 in.) long, on culms to 3 m (10 ft.).

POPULUS

POPLAR
SALICACEAE

Much as I like poplars, I should hesitate to plant them in a garden for the dangers they often present, unless they can be set a good distance from any buildings. Their roots will get into drains, and they can also cause foundation subsidence, by drying out wet soil. Also they grow so quickly that a tree surgeon will be needed in relatively few years if the tree is badly sited. Forked main branches can also split out in wind. Worse in some ways, the lovely balsam poplar and many others are susceptible to canker, particularly in wet gardens.

However, if there is room for the mainly European (extending to North Africa) and west Asian *Populus alba* (to 30 m, 100 ft.; Z3), the silver sheen of its leaves can be enjoyed all summer, as can the shimmering long-petioled leaves of the much smaller-growing but suckering European aspen, *P. tremula* (Z2), which also occurs in Siberia and North Africa, or the similar North American *P. tremuloides* (Z1). Where size is a concern, *P. alba* 'Richardii', which has small golden leaves, is weaker growing and a very accommodating as well as delightful garden plant. Again ultimately a large tree, *P. nigra* 'Lombardy Gold' (Z3), introduced in 1974 by John Whitehead, has a feature use in gardens; the golden Lombardy poplar is slower growing than the Lombardy poplar.

The winter buds of poplars are distinct. The large sticky buds of *Populus balsamifera* (balsam poplar; Z2) produce the strong smell of balsam as they open. Poplars have a mainly northern temperate distribution, and most are very hardy. They are also dioecious and wind-pollinated; their seeds have cotton-like appendages. In North America *P. deltoides* (Z2) and others are known as cottonwoods: their heavy production of seed can cover the ground beneath and around the trees with white "cotton." Seed is short-lived, but I have seen fresh seeds of poplars germinate well on moist lint held in a glass-lidded Petri dish. Most poplar clones can also be rooted from hardwood cuttings, often produced from stool beds, and aspens will sucker. Not all poplars are easily propagated. Some are grafted onto seedling stocks; Wilson, the introducer of one such, the large-leaved *P. lasiocarpa* (Z5), reported it growing from stakes of its wood used for fencing in central China!

PRUNUS

CHERRIES AND OTHER STONEFRUIT
ROSACEAE

Apricots (*Prunus armeniaca*, *P. mume*), peaches (*P. persica*), cherries (*P. avium*), and plums (*P. domestica*) are not the happiest of plants on wet soils but can survive given raised planting sites. The 400 or so *Prunus* species are mostly small to medium-sized trees, and they are widely distributed in the world's northern temperate zones, extending down into more tropical areas on mountains. A great many are cultivated as ornamentals for their abundant flowering; *P. serrula* (Z5) and others are grown especially for their polished barks; others are commercially grown for their fleshy fruits or indeed nuts, as the seeds of *P. dulcis* (almond; Z7) are commonly known. Also in

Prunus spinosa in flower

this genus are some very familiar garden evergreens: *P. laurocerasus* (cherry laurel; Z6) with its many selected cultivars, and *P. lusitanica* (Portuguese laurel; Z7).

A few grow reasonably well on heavy wet soils, given some drainage. *Prunus spinosa* (blackthorn; Z4), best known as a spiny suckering hedge plant, is somewhat tolerant of heavy wet soils, and it has a wide natural range in Eurasia and North Africa. Some of the native wild plums of North America, such as *P. americana* (Z3), grow by the sides of streams and in the latter case, around the edge of swamps; and the sometimes scrubby *P. virginiana* (chokecherry; Z2) can also be found on moist soils.

Cultivating flowering cherries is now a problem because of the prevalence of blossom wilt (*Monilinia laxa*), which causes serious damage: infections result in a progressive shoot dieback that all but kills the trees. Where this disease is not a problem, some forms of the Japanese *Prunus jamasakura* (hill cherry; Z5) will grow on wet soil, as will the lovely pink-flowered and sumptuous, early autumn–foliaged, *P. sargentii* (Z4), notwithstanding their preference for good drainage. The further problem for these and for *P. padus* (bird cherry; Z3) and its other long-racemed relatives is that they can grow

TREES, SHRUBS, AND CLIMBERS

too quickly on a wet soil and are always thus vulnerable to attack by root-decaying fungi.

The beautiful hybrid Japanese flowering cherries simply do not flourish on wet soils. This state of affairs (which they have in common with sweet cherries) may partially relate to their rootstock, but oddly *Prunus avium* (Z3) itself, selections of which are used for cherry rootstocks, can grow well on heavy soils. Most species can be raised from seed (including stratification) without too much difficulty, though seedlings of otherwise hardy continental species can succumb to late frosts here in Britain. Some are bud grafted, as are the cultivars. If good propagation facilities are to hand, stem cuttings, both softwood and semi-ripe, can be used for some cherries.

PTEROCARYA

WING NUT
JUGLANDACEAE

The winged seed chains of the monoecious pterocaryas are ornamental. These large trees are also deciduous and often have rich yellow autumn colour. I recall once seeing a dense stand of *Pterocarya fraxinifolia* (Z7) filling a deep alluvial streambed in the mountains of northern Iran; this species also occurs in the Caucasus.

Pterocarya ×*rehderiana* (Z6), a hybrid between *P. fraxinifolia* and the Chinese *P. stenoptera* (Z7), grows extremely vigorously given warmth and moisture. Even in the cold conditions of North Yorkshire, it has become a robust, if suckering, waterside tree to 20 m (66 ft.) in forty years. In cultivation, *P. fraxinifolia* and *P.* ×*rehderiana* are sometimes confused, as they are similar, but both are well adapted to wet sites.

Sow fresh seed *in situ* in autumn or hold it in cold storage over winter for spring sowing. Rooted suckers can be removed in winter; and layering is sometimes used.

PYRACANTHA

FIRETHORN
ROSACEAE

With just half a dozen species of *Pyracantha* ranging from southeastern Europe to Asia, particularly the Himalayas and China, I had no great expectation of their tolerance of wet soil. Only because I had some spare seedlings of the western Chinese *P. rogersiana* (Z8), which can be found on well-drained limestone hills, in areas of high

A hedge of *Pyracantha rogersiana*, growing on a saturated site in the author's garden

rainfall, did I attempt to plant it as a mixed hedge (with willow) on a very wet site. To my surprise, two decades later, the willows have progressively died from lethal fungal infections, but the pyracanthas have proved unstoppable. The only problem is that when it is warm, on a wet site, they grow almost too well, needing cutting two or three times a year. This species is a useful dense evergreen with some spiny shoots and produces an abundance of small orange berries. The yellow and paler forms are slightly weaker growing. More vigorous free-berrying yellows are Pyracantha 'Renault d'Or' and P. 'Soleil d'Or'.

While pyracanthas do have thorns, they are not hooked and not sufficiently abundant to be a concern except when pruning. Their evergreen leaves have toothed margins and hold well over winter, but as with hollies, dead leaves constantly collect as litter below the plants. Individually, pyracanthas can grow to 5 m (16 ft.) or so and respond well to a warm sunny position on moist soil. They can be trained against walls and pruned, like espaliered apples. Sunlight is important for berry production; they flower and fruit much less well in shade.

Easily raised from seed, and often self-sows in temperate climes. Both mid-season and also later season semi-ripe stem cuttings will root under mist.

PYRUS

PEAR
ROSACEAE

Most of the approximately twenty-five species of wild pear are, like cultivated pears, deciduous, smallish to medium-sized trees, some with spines, and nearly all flower heavily in spring. If the wild species grown in gardens have been seed raised, they are more able to grow on heavy soils than pear clones grafted onto dwarfing quince rootstocks, since this latter does not prosper on wet soils. Such grafted plants have a tendency to blow over, often lying at forty-five degrees like cordons. Unfortunately pears also tend to suffer more with diseases, such as scab (*Venturia pyrina*), on wet sites, and though hardy, they really need warmth in summer to ripen wood and fruit. Fruiting pears are thus often trained against sunny walls.

The wild pears are handsome trees, 9–18 m (30–59 ft.), and a delight when wreathed in snow-white blossoms and seen against a pale blue spring sky. Some like the Korean *Pyrus fauriei* (Z5) and the northeastern Asian *P. ussuriensis* (Z3) can have fiery autumn foliage. The silver-leaved *P. salicifolia* 'Pendula' has become a bit of a designer cliché in formal gardens; I greatly prefer its hybrid, *P.* ×*canescens* (Z6), a cross between *P. salicifolia* (Z4) from southeastern Europe and western Asia and the southern European *P. nivalis* (snow pear; Z6). Similarly the upright 'Chanticleer', a selection of the Chinese and Korean *P. calleryana* (Z5), has been overused at times. Of the Chinese pears, I quite enjoy *P. pyrifolia* (sand pear; Z5), a Wilson introduction.

The two wild pears in Britain both form small hard fruits. Native to southern Europe, *Pyrus cordata* (Plymouth pear; Z8) exists in only a few sites in southern Devon and western Cornwall and has been subject to a conservation recovery programme, though its native status has been questioned. The other, *P. pyraster* (Z6), is an introduced plant with scattered populations elsewhere in central and southwestern Europe and western Asia; it is closely related to the culinary forms of *P. communis* (Z4), which is presumed to be an ancient hybrid.

As with other genera in this family, using raised planting sites helps with drainage, and most pears seem very hardy. Certainly, as on heavy soil in the arboretum at Castle Howard (Z8), the *Pyrus* collection has become a very attractive feature. Pears are normally propagated by grafting onto seedling rootstocks of *P. communis*. Their seed needs stratification.

Pyrus pyrifolia

QUERCUS

OAK

FAGACEAE

Oaks are the most widespread genus in their family, some 600 species occurring over much of the northern hemisphere and extending to southeastern Asia and central and South America. With such a diversity of oaks it is tempting to grow a wide range—given that one has a large enough garden! Two species native to Britain, *Quercus robur* (Z3) and *Q. petraea* (Z4), are able to grow on wet soil, even where there are springs beneath. The greatest diversity of oaks occurs in North America and Mexico; some of these are adapted to hot dry soils, while others occur naturally on wet soils. In biological matters I am always cautious about generalisations, but for the most part, other than the native British oaks, and some hybrids, all grow much more slowly on a cold wet soil. They should for preference be planted on raised mounds.

A magnificent *Quercus castaneifolia* (chestnut-leaved oak; Z6) grows at Kew on a site that has moist silt below from what was, in the eighteenth century, an ornamental lake formed from a backwater of the River Thames. With good drainage at the surface and moisture below, this tree is as large as any of its kind that I have observed in its Iranian homeland in the Alborz Mountains (and its range extends to the Caucasus).

Hardiness is a consideration for many oaks, and one that is difficult to evaluate. For example, the semi-evergreen *Quercus canariensis* from North Africa and Iberia and some Mexican oaks have proved very hardy, while others, such as some North American oaks, succumb to a cold British winter. The problem seems to relate to the lack of summer warmth here compared to continental summers, and also to the problem of the early-season growth of continental species being caught by late frosts that are much more damaging once sap has risen. Seasonality is also a factor; for example, the Japanese form (previously *Q. myrsinifolia*, but now combined) of the slower-growing, temperate Asian evergreen *Q. glauca* (Z7/8) makes new growth late in summer and autumn.

For warmer summers, the following American oaks are worth considering on wet soils: *Quercus bicolor* (swamp white oak; Z3), *Q. laurifolia* (laurel oak; Z7), particularly its diamond-leaved form, and *Q. michauxii* (swamp chestnut oak; Z6). In moist soils, *Q. imbricaria* (shingle oak; Z4), *Q. macrocarpa* (burr oak; Z2), *Q. nigra* (water oak; Z6), *Q. palustris* (pin oak; Z4), and *Q. shumardii* (Z5) grow well; and in nature the drought-tolerant *Q. nuttallii* (Z5) copes with occasional inundation.

Oaks are monoecious and mainly wind-pollinated, with male flowers in catkins and females solitary or in much shorter catkins. Leaves are stalked, alternately arranged and simple with varied leaf margins. The variation in acorns and their cupules can be a helpful guide to identification, but for propagation, the acorns of oaks are not long-lived and present storage difficulties. Many will start to germinate soon after collection—if kept warm and moist, often while still in their collecting bags. Cool, moist storage is needed until sowing in autumn or spring, but watch for damaged seed. With its large food store the seed is attractive to boring insects and consequent infection. Dropping the seed into water can quickly separate out nonviable seed, which floats. Another concern relates to hybridity: wind-pollinated oaks are promiscuous, so seed from cultivated plants and sometimes seed from wild plants can produce hybrid progeny. Sown seed will need protection over winter against rodents. Early spring grafting is the main means of propagating desirable forms.

While as seedlings oaks can be moved around in nursery beds, and transplant tolerably well when larger, there is every advantage in planting them when young so as to help develop good anchorage roots. For this reason oak seedlings, for example, were often grown on in deep pots, or "long toms"; nowadays root trainers are favoured. Tender species are best grown in containers for at least two to three years while the stem thickens and becomes more frost resistant. Planting depth is critical, for if set too deep, they will languish and fail to grow away. Oaks are currently threatened by sudden oak death, a disease caused by the pathogen *Phytophthora ramorum*.

RHAMNUS
BUCKTHORN

RHAMNACEAE

Through much of my working life I passed daily by a collection of *Rhamnus*, and I must admit they are not the most inspiring of garden shrubs and small trees, though their autumn colouring can be attractive. Buckthorns are obligingly tolerant of a wide range of soils and are now frequently planted for their wildlife value. Many birds eat their autumn fruits; the larvae of the brimstone butterfly (*Gonepteryx rhamni*) feed on both *R. cathartica* and *R. frangula*; and the caterpillar of the green hairstreak butterfly (*Callophrys rubi*) feeds on their flowers. Leaves are simple. There are both deciduous and evergreen species, and though cosmopolitan in distribution, they are found mainly in northern temperate regions. Many are hardy.

Frangula is now usually included within *Rhamnus*, being earlier distinguished in part by its bisexual flowers and lack of spines. *Rhamnus sensu stricto* tends to have unisexual flowers, with some plants carrying both male and female flowers while others are dioecious. The flowers are small, often greenish yellow, but the abundant fruits (drupes) will ripen through red to a rich black in some species. Others can be deep blue.

The European, Near East, and North African *Rhamnus frangula* (syn. *Frangula alnus*; Z2) forms a distinctive small tree, to 5 m (16 ft.), with fresh green leaves that turn yellow in autumn; it grows on damp peaty soils. As shrubs or small trees, *R. imeretina* (Z6) from the western Caucasus, *R. caroliniana* (Z5) and *R. purshiana* (Z7) from North America, and *R. cathartica* from Europe, northwest Africa, and Asia can all be found on damp soils. *Rhamnus frangula* makes

Rhododendron calophytum

reasonable extension growth each year, but many other species are slow growing. Extracts from *R. purshiana* ("cascara sagrada") and *R. frangula* have been used medicinally as very powerful laxatives.

Seed is frequently used to raise new plants, but it needs to be vernalised before sowing. Seed will germinate naturally in gardens, having been carried by birds. Semi-ripe stem cuttings are not easy to root and need specialist propagation facilities.

RHODODENDRON

ERICACEAE

In nature, rhododendrons are often seen on low islets formed among bands of rivulets flowing down mountainsides. One of the finest displays of hardy deciduous azaleas local to me has been created on an acid bog with raised beds. These are made from excavated peaty soil and are edged by shallow drainage channels that were formed by the excavation. This gives the plants constantly moist but not saturated soil. Several of the lovely native North American azaleas that can grow 1–4 m (3.3–13 ft.) in height occur naturally in moist soils. These include *Rhododendron canescens* (Z7), which also has fine autumn foliage; *R. vaseyi* (Z4), which grows in mountain bogs; and *R. viscosum* (Z3), the sweetly scented swamp azalea, from wet woodland bog areas.

Rhododendrons will fail on any soil if planted too deep. On a wet soil they should be very shallow planted or, better, set on low mounds with the base of their root balls close to the surrounding soil surface. These raised mounds or beds are then mulched both to suppress weeds and keep the raised soil moist. Rhododendrons respond to drought by rolling their leaf margins downward, and their leaves, particularly the undersides, are noted for their waxy blooms, hairs, or scales. I never cease to be amazed, for example, at the beautiful western Chinese (Z6) *Rhododendron calophytum*'s ability to withstand drought, its drooping and tightly curled leaves fully recovering after rain.

Given moist woodland, particularly one that only receives light frosts, large-leaved giants—like *Rhododendron sinogrande* (Z8) from western China and northern Myanmar, with its 80–100 cm (31–40 in.) leaves and large trusses of white flowers—can be enjoyed. The Asian giants of subsections *Grandia* and *Falconera* tend to occur at lower latitudes and altitudes, and in early season their flowers can be easily lost to frost. In contrast the small-leaved higher alpine species, such as *R. impeditum* (Z4) also from western China, and others in subsection *Lapponica*, need a more open situation in cultivation and are more frost tolerant. Generally, in drier regions, given moist soil, plants from subsections *Cinnabarina*, *Pontica*, and *Fortunea* are most likely to succeed, as are the old hardy and loderi hybrids.

In North America, the moist mild parts of the Pacific Coast offer greater opportunities for these plants than colder regions on the Atlantic side. Above all else, though, a neutral to acid soil is critical. For propagation, see Ericaceae.

RIBES

CURRANT
GROSSULARIACEAE

About half of the 150 species of *Ribes* are cultivated, including such popular soft fruits as black currants (*R. nigrum*), red currants (*R. rubrum*), and gooseberries (*R. uva-crispa*), whose ancestral species are of European and Asian origin. All ribes are small to medium-sized, mostly deciduous shrubs occurring in temperate regions of the northern hemisphere but extending down to the Andes. They are shallow-rooted, and many are at home in wet woods. *Ribes lacustre* (Z4) is the swamp currant of the northern United States.

Though several species are available, few are seen in gardens other than the widely grown *Ribes sanguineum* (Z6), introduced to Britain from western North America by Archibald Menzies in 1790. Its various cultivars make a bold statement if planted in a large group, and, though a gardening cliché, a group of a deep red form like *R. sanguineum* 'Pulborough Scarlet' can be spectacular.

Ribes can also grow strongly on wet soils; red currants for example have no difficulty in reaching a height of 2 m (6.6 ft.). The majority of ribes, including those mentioned, are reasonably hardy and also tolerant of pruning, and most are worth a trial. One of my favourites, though less of a natural wet soil plant, is *Ribes odoratum* (buffalo currant) from North America, which has smallish greeny yellow but deliciously scented flowers. It reaches 1–2 m (3.3–6.6 ft.) and is hardy to Zone 4; some selections are even hardier, but its use is restricted in some U.S. states because of its susceptibility to pine blister rust.

Flowers are usually bisexual, though some, such as the Chinese *Ribes laurifolium* (Z9), have unisexual flowers. The fruit is a berry, often juicy, with many seeds. These seeds are well adapted to distri-

bution by birds; seedlings arise freely on wet soils, frequently among other plants. Hardwood cuttings are popularly used to propagate soft fruit, but, for many, summer softwood cuttings set in a closed frame, or under mist, is a better option. Plants will also layer naturally where low branches touch the ground; and *R. odoratum* suckers.

ROSA
ROSE
ROSACEAE

Roses have to be the most popular of all small flowering shrubs and climbers in temperate gardens worldwide. Their beauty of flower, rich scent, and long flowering season (of modern hybrids) enhance their appeal such that they are produced annually by the millions.

For those on wet soil there is thus likely to be the hope that some may flourish in such conditions. Many are able to grow well on heavy soils; but if too wet, growth is then excessive in summer and wind rock is a likely outcome. This again relates to the rootstocks used in budding and grafting and is much less of a problem with plants that are grown on their own roots. Hardiness is not really a concern in southern Britain but is very limiting in northern continental Europe and North America, where stems are killed back by winter cold, and so earth is mounded over the base of the plants for protection.

With the warmth of a sunny wall, growth can be prodigious on a moist soil, and I delight in the mass of apricot-coloured, heavily scented, nodding blossoms of *Rosa* 'Climbing Lady Hillingdon', which I grow under such conditions. The genus *Rosa* is northern temperate and includes about 150 species and countless cultivars. A few of the species grow naturally on wet soils; for example, the pink-flowered *R. palustris* (to 2.5 m, 8.2 ft.; Z4) from eastern North America can grow in swamps, and *R. setigera* (prairie rose; 2–5 m, 6.6–16 ft.; Z4) can be found on moist ground. This latter species also has the advantage of a slightly later flowering season and good autumn foliage.

For the most part, wild roses can often be found scrambling through scrubby or hedgerow trees and shrubs, thus securing slightly drier conditions; however, wild species, such as *Rosa rubiginosa* (eglantine; Z4) and *R. arvensis* (field rose; Z6), flower and fruit abundantly on my wet soil. Similarly, given drainage, Chinese shrub roses such as *R. moyesii* (2 m, 6.6 ft.; Z5), *R. roxburghii*, and *R. sericea* (3 m, 10 ft.), which extends to the Himalayas, and hybrid cultivars of *R.* ×*odorata* (1.2 m, 4 ft.; Z7/8) all grow reasonably well on wet soil but can die if drainage is lost and the soil remains saturated. However they all seem to grow better than *R. glauca* (Z2) from central Europe, which needs good drainage and can only just survive on really wet soil.

Some of the older shrub roses such as *Rosa* 'Maiden's Blush' (2 m, 6.6 ft.; Z5) or *R.* 'William Lobb' (1.5 m, 5 ft.; Z6) are not concerned by wet soil and grow vigorously; but the forms of *R. gallica* suffer very badly from fungal infections if on a wet soil. Again, just raising the planting bed can help. For example, on a very wet spring-fed site, I made a small pile of gravel into which I planted the sweetly scented, pink-flowered *R.* 'Marchesa Boccella' (on its own roots); it has subsequently grown to 3 m (10 ft.) and flowered heavily for many years.

With more modern roses, results can vary. I have found the delightful Austin roses go the way of the gallicas, and the normally dependable *Rosa* 'Korbin' suffers heavily with leaf diseases. Even *R.* 'Frühlingsmorgen', *R.* 'Frühlingsgold', and other vigorous shrub roses, which may grow well for a few years, eventually succumb to stem decay on wet soils. On warm sites, however, to make up for other disappointments, the Japanese *R. rugosa* (1.5 m, 5 ft.; Z2) forms generally grow well.

Thus, a mixed story for roses on wet soil. Vigorous plants—the climbing *Rosa filipes* 'Kiftsgate' (Z5), the double white *R. banksiae* var. *banksiae* 'Alba Plena' (Z7), the large (2 m, 6.6 ft.) shrubby *R. roxburghii* (Z5)—do not turn a hair, while many others can be short-lived. And it is their susceptibility to diseases on wet soils as much as any other factor that limits the use of roses. Another aspect with climbers is that when trained against a house, those exposed to the warmth of sun on moist soil grow excessively, and the consequence is a frequent need to prune. Pruning tall climbing roses, more than almost any other plant save brambles, needs the use of protective clothing, particularly gloves and some form of safety glasses to protect eyes from thorns.

For propagation, *Rosa glauca*, *R. rubiginosa*, and some others can be seed raised (seeds should be stratified). *Rosa* 'Maiden's Blush' and *R. roxburghii* sucker freely. A great many roses (*R.* ×*odorata* cultivars, for instance) can be easily rooted from stem cuttings in summer. I get better success with a range of roses using late summer rather than hardwood winter cuttings, though most commercially produced plants are grafted by budding onto selected rootstocks.

Rubus 'Benenden'

ROSTRINUCULA

LABIATAE

Rostrinucula is a genus of two shrubby species, both endemic to China. Jim Russell, Hans Fliegner, and I collected the lovely *R. dependens* (Z9) at 1000 m, 3300 ft., on Fanjing Shan in Guizhou, western China, where it grows in wet forest along rivers, its flowering branches overhanging the water. Its silver-felted leaves and pendent, terminal, purple-tipped flower spikes make it an attractive plant for the mild garden; in warm temperate conditions, it can become a buddleja-sized shrub.

RUBUS

BERRY FRUIT
ROSACEAE

This large genus of shrubs and scramblers, many with thorns or bristles, is familiar from the common presence of garden raspberries and hedgerow blackberries. A surprising number of species grow well on wet soil, most needing good light and growing weaker in shade. In nature many can be found on the edge of wet woods and some on wet soil; examples include the eastern North American *Rubus hispidus* (swamp dewberry; Z3) and the western North American *R. spectabilis* (salmonberry; Z5). The circumboreal low-growing edible *R. chamaemorus* (cloudberry; Z2) grows on hummocks in peat bogs. *Rubus* has an extensive, almost cosmopolitan range; many species occur in northern temperate zones, and though those mentioned here are hardy, there are also tender evergreen species.

The familiar northern temperate red raspberry, *Rubus idaeus*, has biennial cane-like stems to around 1.5 m (5 ft.), is shallow-rooted, and copes well with wet soils if given reasonable drainage, as does the blackberry, *R. fruticosus*; and both raspberry and blackberry seed germinates freely on wet soil. Left to itself, *R. phoenicolasius* (wineberry; Z5) from northern China, Japan, and Korea, which has attractive soft red bristly tipped hairs and large clustered panicles of sweet orange raspberry-like fruits, indicated to me its preference for drier sites by progressively migrating up a bank—that is, producing suckers on its drier upper rather than lower wetter side. However the advantage of a moist soil can be seen in the tall (2 m, 6.6 ft.) and beautiful arched flowering canes of the Collingwood Ingram hybrid (1950), *R.* 'Benenden' (Z5) a cross between two western North American species.

The western Chinese white-stemmed bramble *Rubus thibetanus*

(Z6) and the similar *R. cockburnianus* (Z5) from China, as well as the white-flowered *R. biflorus* (Z7), from the Himalayas to southwestern China, have strong, but very thorny, arching canes, growing 2–4.5 m (6.6–15 ft.) on rich moist soils. Where the tips of these long canes can bend over to touch moist ground, they will root and produce plantlets. Not the nicest of plants to prune, but because the canes last only two seasons and lose their white bloom in their second season, it is necessary to enter the clump at least once a year in winter to cut out the old and dead stems.

Those that spread freely, whether by seed, suckers, or stolons, can become weedy. The evergreens are increased by semi-ripe stem cuttings set in a warm propagation unit. Cuttings from cane types can be difficult to root.

SALIX

WILLOW

SALICACEAE

The some 300 species of *Salix* occur in many parts of the temperate world but mainly in the northern hemisphere, and most are very hardy. Their wood is light; willow has long been used to make cricket bats. While most are easy to grow and can quickly give substance to a new garden, willows can often become too large. *Salix alba* (Z2) from Europe to North Africa and central Asia, for example, can reach 30 m (100 ft.). My favourite, *S. acutifolia* 'Pendulifolia' (pendulous Siberian violet willow; Z5) from Russia to eastern Asia, reaches 6–9 m (20–30 ft.); it has graceful growth and is not as susceptible to stem decay or leaf diseases. Trunks and branches tend to be slender and, under winter hoar frost or snow, its cascade of delicate branches sparkles white in low-angle sun. Catkins come early, like pearls strung on slender branchlets. Summer passes quietly, other than for wasps attracted by exudates, but beauty returns with the gold of its autumn leaves.

Willows are dioecious, with the different-looking male and female catkins on separate plants, and they are mostly insect-pollinated. Since they are easily propagated by cuttings, most cultivated selections are either predominantly male or female. There are lots of good catkin willows. *Salix gracilistyla* (Z5) from temperate northeastern Asia is perhaps one of the most endearing, with consistently abundant catkins and silvery foliage; little more than a shrub to 2 m (6.6 ft.), it is nevertheless too vigorous and spreading for a small garden. 'Melanostachys', its black-catkined form, also has a following.

TOP *Salix gracilistyla* 'Melanostachys'
ABOVE *Salix gracilistyla*

Salix magnifica in seed

The male clone of *S. kinuyanagi* (Korean osier; Z6) which is cultivated in Japan also has good catkins and a striking white underside on its leaves. When given a light open position on wet soil, it can hold a lovely silver sheen to its foliage over summer, but this effect is reduced where it is shaded by other trees. For strongly silver foliage, *S. exigua* (coyote willow; Z5) from western North America is perhaps the most attractive, although it is comparatively less root secure and more susceptible to disease on wet soil in Zone 8. The form cultivated in Britain has a delicate appearance and, growing upright to 4–5 m (13–16 ft.) with small narrow leaves, could be more widely used in gardens. Among small trees, *S. hookeriana* also has reasonably silvered leaves.

By water the pendulous willows arrest the eye of photographer and artist alike. *Salix* ×*sepulcralis* var. *chrysocoma* (Z6), which grows to 20 m (67 ft.) or more, needs a very large garden, though sadly it is often planted, and then butchered, in smaller gardens. The contorted *S.* 'Erythroflexuosa' (Z7) is better suited, growing to 5 m (16 ft.), but it produces an irritating amount of epicormic growth, which has to be pruned off to achieve the willow pattern form. Less contorted, and of similar size, *S. alba* 'Snake' offers a non-epicormic substitute, but both are sadly susceptible to the loss of leaves and shoots in summer from anthracnose. However this disease can just about be lived with and has the "benefit" of restricting overall growth.

Salix magnifica (Z7), from western China, makes a 3–4 m (10–13 ft.) clump and was thought to be a magnolia when first seen by E. H. Wilson. This is not surprising as its purplish-hued young leaves and buds are similar to those of a magnolia. Its foliage is the most appealing feature of this large shrubby willow, though its long flower spikes, produced on young leafy shoots, are attractive. It is the female form that is generally available, and its catkins go on to form fluffy cottonwool seedpods. This plant also shows that not all willows can survive very wet conditions, as it can die if saturated in summer.

Though many are able to regenerate if cut back (as in coppiced osier stools or pollarded willows), once willows are cut their soft wood is susceptible to decay, and they can quickly become dangerous trees. Thus pollarding or coppicing has to be continued once embarked upon. Also, many willows cannot be coppiced and die if cut hard back. The many beautifully winter-barked willows, particularly *Salix alba* var. *vitellina* 'Britzensis' and other forms of *S. alba*, are intentionally treated as osiers, cut back each spring to achieve a mass of brightly coloured young stems in winter.

One might expect more disease resistance from willows, since they are adapted to wet soils, but they are very vulnerable to many fungi, particularly silver leaf (*Chondrostereum purpureum*). Nor are willows the most stable of trees, and on wet ground they will blow over, but they have good regenerative powers, and will produce roots and upright stems from branches that touch the ground, often then forming a dense tangle of growth. Seed is short-lived and needs a constantly wet surface for germination, which makes the European to northeastern Asian *Salix caprea* (goat willow; Z4) a weed in many wet gardens. Most willows can be rooted from hardwood cuttings (25 cm, 10 in., or so); some can be rooted from large branches. Cuttings can be prepared in autumn, but I prefer to take them in early spring just before bud break and set them in pots in a cold frame. This avoids the winter loss of the easier rooting, pencil-sized cuttings; such careful timing is particularly needed for *S. magnifica*. *Salix exigua* produces suckers.

SAMBUCUS
ELDER
CAPRIFOLIACEAE

There are several species of elders in the northern hemisphere, and some in the southern. *Sambucus nigra* (common elder; Z5), a small deciduous tree to 10 m (33 ft.) from Europe to North Africa and southwestern Asia, has given rise to dissected, golden, variegated, and purple-leaved garden forms. It is such an obliging plant, tolerating the full range from very dry to wet soils; with good foliage and handsome white, dinnerplate-sized flower corymbs in early summer, and later hung heavy with fruit, it has much to offer. The purple fruits of *S. nigra* make a heady wine of the same colour, the flowers a refreshing cordial, and even the pith from young stems can seemingly be boiled and eaten (I have enjoyed the wine and cordial but not tried the pith). The leaves, bark, and green fruits, however, are mildly toxic, as are the berries and roots of *S. ebulus* (dwarf elder; to 2 m, 6.6 ft.; Z3), from Europe to Asia Minor and Iran.

The smaller-growing red-berried European and western Asian elder *Sambucus racemosa* (Z5) is also represented in gardens by many interesting cultivars, but neither this species nor *S. nigra* are long-lived plants and seem shorter-lived and more susceptible to fungal attack of their main stems when growing on wet soils. The latter particularly is, however, useful as a quick-growing filler or screen and has a value for wildlife. The frequently stoloniferous and very

Sasa veitchii, new green growth and previous summer's brown-edged leaves

hardy *S. nigra* subsp. *canadensis* (Z3) from eastern North America again has many cultivars, some with different fruit colour, and notably grows naturally by springs in wet woods. Some of the more herbaceous elders from the Himalayan and Sino-Himalayan region, though spectacular in fruit, which can be very brilliant red, are difficult to manage in gardens as they spread by underground stems. The woody elders too can be weedy: their seed is distributed by birds and will germinate freely in any small patch of bare soil. Species may be seed raised; cultivars are propagated by softwood or heeled hardwood cuttings.

SARCOCOCCA

BUXACEAE

Sarcococcas are useful and undemanding evergreen understorey plants. They grow 1–1.5 m (3.3–5 ft.) on cane-like branching stems and can sit all year unobtrusively among other shrubs, providing a valued dark foil for small flowering herbs. They will tuck in anywhere, even under alders or evergreen oaks, and they grow happily on a permanently moist soil. Some, but not all, will reward a less competitive but still sheltered situation by filling the air in late winter with sweet scent from small white dioecious flowers. The sixteen or more *Sarcococca* species occur in the Himalayas from Afghanistan east and across into eastern China. Some are tender, but both *S. confusa* and *S. ruscifolia* are reliably hardy (Z7/8). The even hardier *S. hookeriana* var. *digyna* (Z6) will sucker to some extent, but generally propagation is by division of those with clumps, or by stem cuttings.

SASA, SASAELLA

GRAMINEAE

Some of the smaller species of these broadleaved, thin-stemmed hardy bamboos are useful as dense ground cover plants; the Japanese *Sasa veitchii* (to 100 cm, 40 in.; Z8) is one example. But in a good moist soil, they can become excessively invasive. This is equally true for the related but narrower-leaved *Sasaella ramosa* (Z6), also from Japan, which has stems to about 60 cm (2 ft.). The long thin rhizomes of both genera are incredibly tough and difficult to remove; they are, however, indisputably tolerant of a wide range of soils, including heavy wet. For propagation, see bamboo.

SCHEFFLERA

ARALIACEAE

A large genus of evergreen shrubs or small trees that grow well in moist woodland, where they gain from the frost protection afforded by the canopy. Most are tender, but a few verge on hardiness. One such is *Schefflera bodinieri*, from western China to Vietnam; I recall collecting cuttings from this species on Fanjing Shan in Guizhou, where it grew on a riverbank in moist forest at low altitude (500 m, 1600 ft.), and surprisingly it has survived the last sixteen years in Ray Wood in North Yorkshire (Z8), where it has grown to about 2 m (6.6 ft.). *Schefflera digitata* (Z10) grows by riversides in New Zealand, to 8 m (26 ft.). For propagation, see Araliaceae.

SORBARIA

ROSACEAE

These vigorous, deciduous, pinnate-leaved shrubs form a small genus of about ten species; those in cultivation are mostly of Asian origin. They tolerate both dry sands and wet soils, but since some sucker and seed freely, they can become weedy in gardens; three species are now naturalised in Britain.

Noticing sorbaria used as a hedge in a mountain village in western China, I thought to use *Sorbaria sorbifolia* (1.5–2 m, 5–6.6 ft.; Z2), from northern Asia to Japan, similarly and find it works effectively, tough enough to grow even under limes (though it is then slightly reduced in size). Given a light moist site, growth and flowering for all the sorbarias, with their large terminal inflorescences of many small creamy-white flowers, can be impressive. Their cane-like, but woody, stems are a little more perennial than many rubus, but they are not very long-lived. The temperate Asian *S. kirilowii* (Z7) is taller than *S. sorbifolia*, reaching 2–3 m (6.6–10 ft.) with proportionately larger white panicles.

Many years ago, I tended a bed of these hardy shrubs in a formal part of a garden, pruning them hard each winter, back to about two-thirds of their height, so as to reduce summer height and increase flowering shoots. The bed was top dressed annually with organic waste and was also densely underplanted with crocus. Both the sorbarias and the crocus grew and flowered prolifically.

My only concern with sorbarias is their persistent spread, so I cannot recommend them, other than for areas where this is a requirement rather than a nuisance. But they can grow well on very wet soil. Increase by seed, suckers, or, if needed, from semi-ripe cuttings.

TOP *Sorbus caloneura*
CENTER *Sorbus vilmorinii*,
early-season fruit colour
ABOVE *Sorbus khumbuensis*,
faded fruit colour

SORBUS

ROWAN, WHITEBEAM
ROSACEAE

For gardens this is an important northern hemisphere genus of small deciduous trees: they are easy to establish, fairly quick growing, and attractive throughout the year—particularly so in fruit in late summer, and later in autumn garb. The clustering fruits (actually small pomes) vary greatly in colour, particularly among the rowans, and include shades of white, yellow, orange, pink, red, and crimson. Many are apomicts giving rise to uniform seedlings, though interestingly intergeneric hybrids have occurred with *Amelanchier*, *Aronia*, and *Pyrus*. Birds keenly seek their fruits; the fruit of *Sorbus torminalis* (service tree) was once used to make checkers, a type of beer.

Plant size varies. Some, such as the Himalayan *Sorbus microphylla* (Z5), are little more than alpine shrubs, whereas *S. torminalis* from Europe, Asia Minor and North Africa and *S. domestica* from southern Europe and southwestern Asia (both Z6) are trees to 20 m (67 ft.). Under favourable conditions, even *S. aucuparia* (mountain ash or rowan; Z2) and the large, silver-reverse-leaved Himalayan whitebeams such as *S. cuspidata* (Z7) can become substantial trees. For the home garden, smaller plants such as *S. cashmiriana* (pearl-white fruits), *S. scalaris* (carmine-red), or *S. khumbuensis* or *S. vilmorinii* (ruby-red fading to pink) are all Zone 5, and ideal garden trees.

The growth of young plants can be so rapid that, if wished, seedlings can be planted out just a year after germination. The pinnate-leaved rowan group (section *Aucuparia*) start more quickly than the more simple-leaved whitebeams (section *Aria*), but the latter catch up, some fruiting when just a few years old, and both types then seem to slow, particularly on heavy wet soils. They are susceptible to fungal root decay on wet soil, though they can equally succumb on acid sand. Many are associated with limestone, where growth rates are slower. Sorbuses grow well in light woodland but open sunny sites allow more flowering and fruiting. There is great diversity within this genus, with its many apomicts and microspecies from restricted habitats; it is hard to generalise, but overall I find the whitebeams and micromeles (section *Micromeles*) are the most tolerant groups for wet soils.

Having collected both *Sorbus keissleri* and *S. caloneura* (both in section *Micromeles*, and both Z6) more than twenty years ago in Guizhou, western China, I have been interested to watch their progress.

TREES, SHRUBS, AND CLIMBERS

The former makes a more upright tree, while the latter is spreading; both are very tolerant of heavy wet soil. *Sorbus keissleri* was expected to be hardy, but *S. caloneura* generally grows at lower altitudes (1000 m, 3300 ft.), where summers can be very warm, and it shows the tropical habit of producing red-coloured spring foliage. The intensity of this colour varies from seedling to seedling, from an orangey brown to a darker red, but in mild winters it can be produced as early as late December or January on some plants, more usually March. However, in no case have I seen these precocious young leaves damaged by frost. While the fruit of *S. keissleri* is apple-green with a slight red flush, *S. caloneura* has more noticeable pear-coloured pomes with lighter lenticels.

Sorbus seeds germinate fairly freely, some seedlings arising straightaway if sown when ripe in early autumn, but most need vernalising: keep them cool and moist over winter, for spring germination. Some however, particularly if dry stored, may take two years to germinate. Selected forms are budded or grafted.

SPIRAEA

SPIREA

ROSACEAE

As many as sixty species of this large genus of hardy, mainly deciduous shrubs are cultivated. Leaves are often small and simple, and though the individual flowers are also small (and can be bisexual or unisexual), they are abundantly produced: *Spiraea prunifolia* (1–2 m, 3.3–6.6 ft.; Z4) from eastern Asia is a snowy mass of flowers in spring. This adaptable species (it has naturalised in the United States) needs good drainage and is better on dry soils.

Spireas are distributed throughout the world's northern temperate regions. Some occur naturally in moist woodland. Three such—the western North American *Spiraea douglasii* (Z5) from bogs and damp meadows; the closely related eastern North American and northern and central European *S. tomentosa* (Z3), with dense panicles of white or pinkish purple flowers; and *S. alba* (2 m, 6.6 ft.; Z5) from eastern North America—have naturalised in Britain. The often-seen arching eastern Asian *S. thunbergii*, however, will decay and die if grown on waterlogged soil.

Can be seed raised, and some sucker, but generally increased from stem cuttings.

STEWARTIA

THEACEAE

Stewartias deserve to be more widely grown. Most are attractively barked deciduous trees, producing white flowers in mid summer and the bonus of autumn colour. Occurring naturally in moist temperate forests, they tolerate a range of soils and moisture levels, though if grown on dry light soils they will flag in summer and under more extreme conditions can shed buds and flowers. They may also drop flowers in moister conditions but usually a succession of buds open. Moist woodland suits them well. They are not quick growing, eventually forming large shrubs or small trees.

Happily most are hardy and all are garden-worthy. With its brownish purple to cinnamon peeling bark, the Chinese *Stewartia sinensis* (Z6) has long been one of my favourites; in natural forest conditions, however, its striking bark, covered with mosses, lichens, and algae, may go unnoticed. The flowers of this and other East Asian species—*S. pseudocamellia* (Z5), *S. monadelpha* (Z5), *S. serrata* (Z7)—are all white. The smaller-growing *S. malacodendron* (Z7) from the southeastern United States has the most striking flowers; they are large (6–8.5 cm, 2.5–3.3 in.) with a central boss of purple filaments and bluish anthers. Another attractively flowered smaller American species, *S. ovata* (mountain camellia; Z5), can be found naturally by streams in woods and on floodplains. Stewartia flowers tend to open facing down or outward and are best viewed at close hand; they are less noticeable from a distance.

Seed requires three months' postharvest ripening followed by three months of cool, moist conditions for spring germination. With good propagation facilities, softwood or semi-ripe cuttings can be used.

STYRAX

STORAX
STYRACACEAE

The range of the approximately 120 species of *Styrax* includes North America, Asia, and Europe. With their small stature and free-flowering habit (even when young), they make ideal garden trees for neutral to acid soils yet are rarely seen outside plant enthusiasts' gardens. True, their white flowers must be viewed from below, as they hang down under obscuring leaves, and cold resistance in some is less than stellar, but otherwise they are trouble-free plants.

Both the large-leaved *Styrax obassia* from Japan, which has good autumn colour, and the free-flowering Chinese, Japanese, and Korean *S. japonicus* and its several cultivars are hardy to Zone 5. They grow readily on a heavy wet soil, up to 10 m (33 ft.), but all are susceptible to late spring frosts when young. The shrubby American snowbell tree, *S. americanus* (Z5), can be found growing naturally in swampy ground, with taxodiums and nyssas; however, it is difficult to grow and slightly tender here, just about surviving in Ray Wood (Z8). *Styrax officinalis* (Z9/10), which occurs in southeastern Europe, Asia Minor, and California, may survive in mild gardens; it grows to 7 m (23 ft.).

RELATED GENERA

Pterostyrax species from eastern Asia are grown for their fragrant pendent panicles of flowers; the two most commonly seen, *P. corymbosa* and *P. hispida* (both Z7) from China and Japan have an even greater requirement for moisture than halesias. Of the less frequently seen small genera, the slightly tender (Z8/9) *Rehderodendron* from Indo-China and China, and hardier (Z6–8) *Sinojackia* from China, with just two species, grow well in moist, temperate gardens. These too are all small trees.

Most are propagated by seed, sown when fresh, with temperatures following the natural warm temperate pattern: a post-ripening autumn period (three months or more) followed by a cool (just above freezing) winter period (two to three months of cold stratification) for spring germination. Unfortunately, some of the seed will not be viable, but the occasional seedling will germinate. Young plants are frost tender and will need protection. Given good propagating facilities, semi-ripe summer cuttings can be rooted.

SYMPHORICARPOS

SNOWBERRY
CAPRIFOLIACEAE

Grown for its attractive berries (drupes), which hold well over winter, this small genus of deciduous shrubs occurs both in the New World and China. *Symphoricarpos albus* (common snowberry; Z3) comes from dry to moist open forests; its var. *laevigatus* from western North America is the form most frequently encountered in gardens (and also naturalised in Britain). It grows to 1.5 m (5 ft.) or more and tolerates both dry shade and much moister soils. Seeing the pretty

TOP *Styrax japonicus*
ABOVE *Symphoricarpos orbiculatus*, a plant raised from seed collected in the southern Appalachians

S. orbiculatus (coralberry; Z2) in the Smoky Mountains of Tennessee and North Carolina, I was inspired to try growing it on my wet soil; however, I found that seedlings vary considerably, some fruiting better than others, and they need good summer warmth to fruit well. As an object lesson, I grew a small row of these plants (all of one good fruiting clone) on a sloping, very wet site with a spring at its lower point. For a few years, the plants at the wetter end were only half the size (60 cm, 2 ft.) of those at the drier end, but after about eight years they caught up. All species sucker, giving the option of removing rooted shoots; plants can also be raised from cuttings or seed.

TILIA
LIME
TILIACEAE

Though in nature many grow along streams, lime trees (also known as lindens or basswood) are adaptable, tolerating both dry and wet soils. Related to jute (*Corchorus*), limes too form bast fibres beneath their outer bark which in the past have been used to produce coarse ropes. Their deciduous leaves are simple, palmate-veined, and mostly broadly ovate to cordate.

Because many of the forty-five or so species that occur in the northern temperate zone look similar and hybridise freely, there is a tendency to think they will all grow as well as the native British limes, *Tilia cordata* (small-leaved lime; 38 m, 125 ft.) and *T. platyphyllos* (large-leaved lime; 34 m, 112 ft.), and their naturally occurring hybrid, *T. ×europaea* (46 m, 151 ft.), all hardy to Zone 3. But there is much variation; for example, in northern Britain, some North American and Asian limes struggle to grow well; some grow very slowly; others fail to establish. Such trees need a warmer continental climate, though a good range can be grown in southern Britain.

Where space allows, limes are popular additions to large gardens and parkland. At one time, they were popularly coppiced, and on a heavy soil, over a couple of decades, limes can regrow multiple stems to a height of 10 m (33 ft.) or more with basal diameters of 25–30 cm (10–12 in.). Limes are often used to form avenues, which can last for two or three centuries if the trees are well maintained. *Tilia ×europaea* in particular is widely planted in civic areas; it is especially tolerant of very wet soils, but if permanently waterlogged, its roots and butt are vulnerable to decay fungi. Careless tree surgery (for avenue trees are often crudely pollarded) can quickly lead to decay, with pathogens entering through torn or badly positioned cuts; any consequent regrowth of heavy branches is then attached to a decaying base and becomes a potential danger. Once a tree has been pollarded, it is necessary to revisit and prune it back at least once every ten years to prevent heavy branches forming. Because of their flexible stems and ability to regenerate new shoots, limes are often pleached and trained in various ways as features in formal gardens.

Limes form extensive surface root systems that dry out the surrounding soil in summer. On a dry soil, it is difficult to grow much beneath them, but on moist soil more is possible, particularly spring flowers and bulbs. *Tilia* ×*europaea* attracts large summer infestations of aphids that drift honeydew down upon every surface in the immediate vicinity—often within minutes, on a sunny day. Black moulds soon develop on this sugary film. Also this lime produces an abundance of suckers on its main stem—particularly at its base, a feature it shares with its parent *T. platyphyllos* that suckers to a lesser extent.

On a warm sunny day when limes are in flower the attraction of their scented flowers to bees is such that an audible hum surrounds each tree. The lovely weeping silver lime *Tilia* 'Petiolaris' (Z5) with its silver reverse leaves makes a magnificent specimen, but its flowers can narcotise bees, many of which can consequently be found as "fallen dead" beneath these trees.

Lime flowers form on a slender stalk that is fused on its lower half to a linear bracteole. The upper half of the bracteole is set at an angle to the flower's stalk but dries and falls with the ripe seed to act as a wing, spinning the seed slightly away from the parent plant. These small, woody, pea-sized seeds are much sought-after by wood mice and other rodents. If stratified or sown fresh, and kept cool and moist over winter, most limes will regenerate well from seed but can take two seasons. As an indicator of their requirements, while natural regeneration on dry soils is scarce, *Tilia platyphyllos*, for example, germinates readily on moist to wet soils particularly in gravel. Clones are grafted. Layering has sometimes been used, as have rooted suckers, extensively, but trees raised from suckers will also sucker.

ULMUS

ELM

ULMACEAE

Many elms form large vigorous trees, though there are smaller-growing species and cultivars. The ease with which a few of the approximately forty-five species, distributed throughout Eurasia and North America, produce suckers allowed their extensive propagation from the seventeenth century, and pastoralists once used elms as winter fodder for livestock as well as for timber. Thus many elms and their hybrid clones became familiar as hedgerow trees, particularly on the heavy clay lands of the Midlands and southern England.

But I sadly miss these evocative, dome-headed trees, two to three centuries old, that populated the fields and gardens of my earlier years. Elms in Europe and North America have suffered badly from Dutch elm disease (*Ophiostoma ulmi*), which is spread by elm bark beetles (*Scolytus*). A more lethal strain of the disease was introduced to Britain from the 1960s and still holds sway, with 20 million or more trees killed. At one time, I was involved in setting up a rescue programme that propagated all the more important forms of these trees in England, ahead of the advancing disease, which has similarly damaged *Ulmus americana* (American elm; Z2) in the United States. In British tree collections, precious few elms have survived, other than the notably smooth-barked, stately, western Himalayan *U. villosa* (Z5).

That said, where disease is not an issue several elms can be grown in wet gardens, since a good few are trees of bottomlands. The wych (= supple) elm, *Ulmus glabra* (Z5), with a range extending from northern and central Europe to western Asia and native in Britain, formed large (37 m, 120 ft.) wide-spreading trees, but it has a smaller-growing pendulous form to 12 m (40 ft.), *U. glabra* 'Camperdownii', with large leaves, which survived in several gardens. The recommended "resistant" species are the smaller-leaved *U. parvifolia* (Chinese elm; Z5), an attractive medium-sized tree from China, Korea, and Japan, and the smaller and less arboriculturally desirable *U. pumila* (Siberian elm; Z4), whose forms (both shrubby and medium-sized trees) range beyond Siberia into northern China, Mongolia, Korea, and Turkistan. The most popularly promoted resistant clone is *U.* 'Sapporo Autumn Gold', raised in the United States from seed received from Japan of *U. pumila* crossed with *U. japonica* (Z5). This latter species occurs in Japan and more widely in northeastern Asia.

Elms have alternate leaves with distinct asymmetric bases and mostly small clusters of mainly bisexual flowers that appear before the leaves. In *Ulmus procera* (English elm), for example, bright red anthers on the exserted stamens make the flowers attractively colourful. A few, such as *U. parvifolia*, are autumn flowering.

The wood of elms has a distinctive smell. Its strong interlocking grain ensures it does not split readily, and it can be easily worked—characters that gave it many uses. Most curiously, perhaps, it was used underground to form water conduits (before metal, and now plastic pipes, were used); and seemingly, in such use and conditions, it could last for more than two centuries—whereas, when used as fenceposts, it rots relatively quickly. Similarly, mature elm trees are very susceptible to trunk decay following careless branch pruning.

The fruit, a nutlet, is winged (a samara). With species, seed should be sown when ripe. A few seedlings may germinate soon after sowing; ungerminated seeds should be kept cool over winter, or more practically stratified in a moist medium for nine to thirteen weeks at 5°C (41°F) before sowing for germination in spring. Semi-ripe stem cuttings can be rooted in summer, though (as for most woody cuttings) they will be more likely to root if taken from young plants. Grafting is also used (that is, budding in summer or side-grafting in winter), and the now-lost hedgerow elms were propagated from suckers.

RELATED GENERA

Most of the approximately seventy species of *Celtis* (hackberry) occur on dry and well-drained soils, but others, such as the medium-sized North American *C. laevigata* (Z5) and *C. occidentalis* (Z2/3), can grow on wet alluvial soils. *Planera aquatica* (water elm; Z6) from the southeastern United States forms a smallish tree 10–13.5 m (33–45 ft.) with an attractive flaking bark; it occurs in wet soils but, though easy to grow, is rare in cultivation.

VACCINIUM

BILBERRY

ERICACEAE

Vacciniums are neat, small to tall bushes that have a mainly northern temperate distribution and are often cultivated for their fruits. *Vaccinium macrocarpon* (cranberry) can be found in sphagnum bogs in eastern North America; *V. corymbosum* (highbush blueberry), of which there are many cultivars, grows from 2–3 m (6.6–10 ft.), often in upland bogs in the same region. The small *V. oxycoccus* has a circumboreal distribution. All three are evergreen and rated Zone 2.

VIBURNUM

CAPRIFOLIACEAE

This large genus of 150 or more species from the temperate and subtropical regions of Asia, Europe, North Africa, and North America provides a great range of good garden shrubs. Most popular are

Viburnum ×burkwoodii

the deciduous, winter-flowering viburnums, such as *Viburnum farreri* (to 1.5 m, 5 ft., in gardens) from northern China and the larger *V. ×bodnantense* (both Z5 or lower). The more heavily scented early-spring-flowering *V. ×burkwoodii* (to 2 m, 6.6 ft.; Z4) is often planted, because on a still sunlit day its heady perfume can fill a small garden. They grow well in an open situation on a fertile soil but tolerate woodland on a dry sandy soil, while also coping with heavy wetter soils. In Spain the evergreen, winter-flowering *V. tinus* (Z7) from southern Europe and North Africa grows beneath stone pines—it is a plant that can take abuse. *Viburnum lantanoides* (syn. *V. alnifolium*; hobblebush; Z3) from eastern North America, *V. furcatum* (Z5) from Japan, Korea, and Taiwan, and *V. nervosum* (Z6) from western China are large-growing (3–4 m, 10–13 ft.) viburnums that thrive in damp woodland and look attractive in flower, and their large leaves turn a fine butter-yellow in autumn.

In the southeastern United States, *Viburnum nudum* (smooth witherod; Z5) is sometimes promisingly called the swamp-haw; 'Winterthur' and 'Pink Beauty' are among its improved selections. But most viburnums can be more surely accommodated in a wet garden by raising their planting bed above the general soil level. The native British guelder-rose, *V. opulus* (4 m, 13 ft.; Z3), in its range through Europe and into North Africa and northern and western Asia, seems equally at home on hot dry soils as wet bog. Having grown it in both conditions, I'd say it grows more slowly in saturated soil, a characteristic widely shared in Caprifoliaceae. Notable for its bright, translucent berries, it is self-fertile; many other fine fruiting viburnums, however, such as the Chinese *V. betulifolium* (3 m, 10 ft.; Z5), can be self-incompatible, and thus fail to berry if a single clone is grown.

Viburnums tolerate what little pruning is required. Those mentioned are generally very hardy, though there are tender species; for example, *Viburnum bitchiuense* (Z6) from southern Japan and Korea and the much larger (to 6 m, 20 ft.) evergreen *V. cinnamomifolium* from western China are not hardy with me. For propagation, *V. farreri* has a tendency to form thickets from which plants can be separated, and while viburnums may be seed raised, most in cultivation, including the hybrids, are increased by deciduous softwood, evergreen semi-ripe, or hardwood stem cuttings in a propagation unit.

TREES, SHRUBS, AND CLIMBERS

VITIS

GRAPEVINE

VITACEAE

Bearing in mind the dry Mediterranean conditions under which *Vitis vinifera* is usually cultivated, it is fortunate for wet gardens that a number of grapes grow naturally on wet soils. Most of the more than sixty species occur in temperate Asia and North America, though they extend into the Near East and down to South America. Some are grown for their fruit, others for their foliage and autumn colour, and usefully several hardy North American grapevines can be found on wet soil, including *V. palmata* (red grape; Z5), which occurs in taxodium swamps. Others that grow on alluvial soils and in wet woods include the vigorous muscadine, *V. rotundifolia* (to 30 m, 100 ft.; Z5) and *V. riparia* (Z2), which, as its name suggests, occurs along the banks of watercourses. The related *V. vulpina* (frost grape; Z5) can grow to 20 m (67 ft.) on trees.

Vigour varies, but most respond well to pruning, which is a task for late summer or winter, as wounds will weep if cut in early season when the sap is rising. Leaves are alternate, and tendrils form opposite to leaves. The panicles of small, unisexual or bisexual flowers give rise to fleshy grapes (technically berries). Many grapes can be propagated from "eye" cuttings, formed from a short piece of stem with but a single bud; grafting onto disease-resistant rootstocks is necessary for many grapevines. The ornamental species can also be layered or rooted from hardwood cuttings using a propagator with soil warming. Seed requires stratification.

Xanthorhiza simplicissima

XANTHORHIZA

YELLOWROOT

RANUNCULACEAE

Though not often seen in gardens, the slow-growing, deciduous *Xanthorhiza simplicissima* (Z3) grows naturally in damp soils in the southeastern United States, and seems equally at home in Westonbirt Arboretum's heavy soil, where this shrubby plant makes an interesting feature. It forms thick stems, to 1 m (3.3 ft.), with large overwintering terminal buds, reminiscent of a tree peony, and in spring has panicles of small spidery purple flowers and good autumn foliage colour. Normally seed raised, this species is easy to grow, transplanting readily when young, and will produce suckering shoots.

Yucca recurvifolia

YUCCA

AGAVACEAE

The combination of their symmetry, uniformly thick stems, and long leaves allows yuccas to be used like statues in gardens; they make good feature or focal points, and associate well with buildings, though beware of the spiny leaf tips on some. My plants (two forms of *Yucca recurvifolia*) are growing in heavy wet clay on the north side of my house, and I have been surprised by their tolerance of this situation, though they grow more slowly, and flower later in the year, than they would on warmer soil. A raised bed might be considered where there is doubt! Yuccas have a succulent appearance, and though most can withstand dry conditions, several also tolerate heavy and constantly moist soils; for example, the low-growing *Y. flaccida* (Z4), from the Appalachians, grows naturally in cold damp conditions.

There are monocarpic yuccas, but these grow on drier soils, so seed raising for wet soils will be limited to new introductions. *Yucca recurvifolia* (to 2.5 m, 8 ft.; Z8), from the southeastern United States, and others produce offsets. These can be carefully removed, trimmed (reducing their leaves in number and size, to reduce water loss), and inserted into a narrow container of light soil. They are slow to root. Suckering forms can be propagated from root cuttings.

ZENOBIA

ERICACEAE

The lovely glaucous-leaved, anise-scented, white-flowered shrubby *Zenobia pulverulenta* (Z5) can grow to 2 m (6.6 ft.) but is very tolerant of pruning. Native in the southeastern United States, where it occurs in bogs and damp areas, it nevertheless requires good drainage in gardens; and though it is evergreen in warmer climates, it becomes deciduous in cold weather, with good autumn colour. This species has happy Kew associations for me: not only was it my early introduction to the wide range of Ericaceae that could grow well there in the more consistently moist climate of the mid-twentieth century, but Zenobia, so named, one of the last carthorses at Kew, was still in harness when I came to work there. For propagation, see Ericaceae.

CHAPTER 6
Herbaceous plants and bulbs

ACHILLEA

SNEEZEWORT

COMPOSITAE

Most achilleas are plants of the temperate northern hemisphere. *Achillea ptarmica* (Z8) ranges over Europe and western Asia and occurs naturally on heavy wet soil in the arboretum at Castle Howard in Yorkshire. One of its several selections, 'The Pearl', a double sneezewort, seems relatively oblivious to both dry sand and wet bog and is fully hardy to Zone 5. Growing 60–80 cm (24–31 in.), it produces a mass of small pearl-like flowers in high summer that stand out against its dark green foliage.

The newer *Achillea millefolium* hybrids do not seem to persist on wet soil, but *A. filipendulina* 'Cloth of Gold' (to 90 cm, 36 in.; Z3) with its large heads of flowers, seems durable. The white-flowered *A. grandifolia* from the Balkans and Turkey is somewhere between 'Cloth of Gold' and the millefolium hybrids in durability. Hybrids between *A. filipendulina* and *A. ptarmica* also occur (the yellow *A.* 'Schwellenburg' is one). All mentioned here are deciduous, hardy perennials and propagated by division.

ACONITUM

MONKSHOOD

RANUNCULACEAE

Many hardy perennial monkshoods grow on moist soils. In particular, the tallish (1–2 m, 3.3–6.6 ft.) Wilson Group of *Aconitum carmichaelii* cope as well with wet soil in cultivation as do their progenitors in rain-sodden western Chinese foothills. Similarly I have noted *A. hemsleyanum* climbing 3–5 m (10–16 ft.) in extremely wet forest in western China.

Aconitum lycoctonum (wolf's-bane), which has a wide Eurasian

Achillea ptarmica The Pearl Group

171

Acorus gramineus 'Ogon'

range, occurs naturally by streams and in woods; its subsp. *vulparia* is naturalised in Britain and occupies similar moist habitats. Many wolf's-banes are yellow-flowered, but there are purple, lilac, and cream forms.

Though noted for its toxins (which seem to do little to limit the feeding of vine weevil larvae!), this genus offers a good range of species and cultivars, and it is worth a gardener's time and effort to try to grow them on wet soil. Propagation is mainly by division; do wear gloves whenever handling these plants.

ACORUS

SWEET-FLAG

ACORACEAE

Two of the three species in this small genus of hardy rhizomatous herbs are widely cultivated. Their flowers are densely packed on a short spadix (5–10 cm, 2–4 in.) that grows at an angle to the stem, but it lacks the spathe seen on most aroids. *Acorus calamus* (Z3) is of uncertain origin in southeastern Asia but had been introduced to Europe from western Asia by the sixteenth century; this plant, now naturalised both here and in eastern North America, is a triploid. Its scented, iris-like leaves, which were strewn on floors, grow 50–125 × 2.5 cm (20–50 × 1 in.) long and wide, and are deciduous. The fertile diploid form occurs in North America and Siberia.

The more diminutive *Acorus gramineus* (Z5) from China and Japan and its many cultivars are more frequent in gardens. With their neat, fan-like, linear leaf arrays on thin rhizomes, the variegated forms make handsome features. Leaves are evergreen and up to 40 × 1 cm (16 × 0.4 in.), persisting over winter. They are subject to damage by severe cold.

Sweet-flags grow naturally around the edges of ponds and watercourses. Both *Acorus calamus* and *A. gramineus* can grow in shallow water (to 10 cm, 4 in.), but they will also grow on damp soil. The rhizomes and leaves have a strong tangerine and vanilla smell when crushed, and extracts from the rhizome of *A. calamus* have been used in medicine, perfumery, and flavourings.

Propagate by division as growth commences in spring; if set in moist soil, divisions will be well established by autumn. The fruit is a fleshy berry. Seed, if available, can be sown in a cold frame. Triploids are mostly sterile.

HERBACEOUS PLANTS AND BULBS

ALCHEMILLA

LADY'S MANTLE

ROSACEAE

Surprisingly perhaps, *Alchemilla* is a genus of some 300 species, mostly small herbaceous perennials, with a very wide distribution in Eurasia, the Andes, and the higher elevations of Africa. Most ubiquitous of the two dozen or so that are cultivated is the large-clumped (60 × 30 cm, 24 × 12 in.) *A. mollis* (Z4) from Asia Minor, grown for its thin-stemmed, massed sprays of lime-green flowers which, though lacking petals, are particularly attractive. So are its tough, glaucous-green leaves, from which water can run, as with the sacred lotus, in droplets like mercury. Alchemillas self-sow freely on wet soils, particularly if these are thinly overlain with gravel; flowering stems are therefore best clipped off after flowering, before plants become weedy.

Alchemilla mollis is deciduous, but plants form a tough and extensive, if shallow-rooted, rootstock, making them useful as ground cover around the base of birdbaths or plinths, or under roses and other shrubs. Its dense growth effectively suppresses weeds, but it does not compete well with coarse grass on wet soils unless planted as a good-sized clump, and it will die out if heavily shaded by trees. Otherwise, it is a durable and dependable plant for wet soils. Can be raised by seed or division.

Allium schoenoprasum

ALLIUM

ONION

ALLIACEAE

The 700 or so species of *Allium* occur around the world's northern temperate zone, with many using their bulbous resting phase to survive in seasonally arid or cold regions. But alliums are environmentally flexible—the attractive *A. cristophii* (Z9) has an altitude range of 900–2250 m (3000–7400 ft.) in the mountains of northern Iran—and though many will die out, several can cope with wet soil. Garden vegetables like garlic (*A. sativum*) and leeks (*A. porrum*) are all very tolerant of winter-wet soils; the wild progenitor of chives (*A. schoenoprasum*) grows in damp, grassy meadows in high northern latitudes; and *A. ursinum* (bear garlic; Z5) naturally inhabits both wet and dry woods and hedgerows.

A slightly raised bed, over moist subsoil, with full sun exposure suits many flowering alliums, such as the popular, but expensive,

Allium 'Globemaster', and is particularly successful for plants like *A. karataviense* (Z8) from central Asia. Several will shed viable seed in quantity, and this often germinates close to the parent plants. Such successful regeneration can make alliums weedy; some caution is needed when naturalising, for example, *A. ursinum* in grass. Many species have escaped from cultivation; moist Cornish hedgerows are decked each spring with the white bells of *A. triquetrum* (three-cornered leek; Z8), originally from the western Mediterranean.

Seed raising is straightforward. Seed germinates freely when fresh, and seedlings can be pricked out and grown on without difficulty. Some alliums produce bulbils (often in quantity) on their flowering shoots; others are comparatively slow to increase from their subterranean bulbs.

ALTHAEA, SIDALCEA

MARSH MALLOW
MALVACEAE

Althaea officinalis (Z3) occurs in coastal salt marshes in Europe and southern England and is naturalised in the eastern United States, where it also grows in marshy ground. This perennial is better known for the mucilage found in its roots, which has many medicinal uses. The straight species, with stems to 1.5 m (5 ft.) and lilac-pink flowers, is not frequently seen in gardens; more often encountered is its selection, the shorter 'Romney Marsh', whose white flowers have a pink centre. *Sidalcea oregana* (Oregon checker mallow) is sometimes grown in gardens; it occurs in wet meadows in western North American, as does *S. malviflora* subsp. *virgata* (rose checker mallow, marsh hollyhock). Both are Zone 5.

Mallows tend to be short-lived perennials with a woody rootstock, and their branchlets are often very thin and fibrous, and susceptible to dieback in winter. Raise from seed or basal cuttings.

ANEMONE

RANUNCULACEAE

The many species of *Anemone* vary in their requirements, but several will grow on moist soils. Certainly the visual effect of drifts of the clear blue southern European *A. apennina* (Z6) growing to 20 cm (8 in.) high in moist woodland is a particular pleasure. The tough thin rhizomes of *A. nemorosa* (wood anemone; Z5), which is native to Britain, are very competitive, spreading and flowering freely in

174

Anemone nemorosa establishing a claim to wet grassland

coarse grassland on wet soil; the pale lavender-blue 'Robinsoniana', one of its loveliest forms, withstands even the occasional inundation, though it does not grow well under such conditions. Also, it builds up its clumps more slowly than *A. nemorosa* and holds its leaves nearly through the summer. I find *A. nemorosa* 'Robinsoniana' divides best when in very early growth, as it takes a year or two to reestablish from dormant rhizomes, as does the more delicate yellow European *A. ranunculoides* (Z4). The taller, and equally hardy American *A. virginiana* (thimbleweed) has dull, greenish white flowers and can withstand flooding (but dies back in a wet summer despite good drainage!); *A. canadensis* (Z3) also copes with wet soils. So too does *A. rivularis* (Z7) from northern India and southwestern China; this more garden-worthy species grows to 60–90 cm (24–36 in.), with a fine display of clear white flowers and darker violet reverse and anthers.

The vigorous autumn-flowering anemone hybrids (60–90 cm, 24–36 in.; Z6), mostly derived from the western Chinese *Anemone hupehensis* and *A. vitifolia*, (which ranges across the Himalayas from Afghanistan to western China) tolerate a wet, but not saturated, soil. In China's Guizhou Province, both pink and white forms grow in damp hillside meadows; further north, in Sichuan, growing on wet mountainsides at 2743 m (9000 ft.), is a form whose dark, smaller outer tepals form an almost chocolate-brown cross on the reverse of the blossom. Anemones can be seed raised, but most are increased by division.

ANEMOPSIS
SAURURACEAE

Anemopsis californica, as its name suggests, is native to western North America, where its range extends from California south to Mexico. It grows freely in wet soil or shallow water, tolerating alkaline conditions. It is not fully hardy, dying out over winter on a wet soil, but is sold in garden centres as a bog plant. Thus the rhizomes would need to be below water to survive even a mild (−5°C, 23°F) winter. It produces a rosette of leaves to about 20 cm (8 in.), and small bisexual flowers form on a dense spike with a whorl of petal-like bracts below. As with strawberries, stout surface runners produce a plantlet at each node; a single runner may produce three or more transplantable plantlets in one growing season.

ANGELICA
UMBELLIFERAE

Most of the approximately fifty species of *Angelica* occur in northern temperate regions by streams or in damp meadows and woodlands. Though large-leaved (30–90 cm, 12–36 in.), these herbs are happily in proportion and make a strong visual statement when in flower. Most are hardy biennials, but even many of the longer-lived plants are monocarpic. They thus need to be seed raised, but the seed is short-lived.

Angelica sylvestris has a Eurasian range; it can grow 50–200 cm (20–80 in.), with its flower spike forming many umbels 15 cm (6 in.) across. Its flowers are mostly white or pinkish; 'Purpurea' is an attractive dark wine-red selection, and, when well grown, the form 'Vicar's Mead' can be a truly spectacular plant. Several other species are grown. One of the more popular is *A. gigas* from China, Korea, and Japan, which has dark red-purple flowers and stems. The impressive *A. archangelica* (Z4) from northern and eastern Europe and beyond has many medicinal and culinary uses, and its stems can be candied. It has greenish yellow flowers held in 25 cm (10 in.) umbels on 2 m (6.6 ft.) stems.

Several other genera in Umbelliferae grow well (some too well!) in wet soils. *Aegopodium podagraria* (ground elder) is a gardener's nightmare weed (see "Pernicious Weeds" in chapter 3). Be that as it may, *A. podagraria* 'Variegatum' (Z6) is often sold and grown as a variegated ground cover; it is an adaptable plant, growing on light dry soils under trees but also tolerant of wet soils.

Apium graveolens (wild celery; Z8/9) accepts wet soils. The pink-and-white-splashed leaves of *Oenanthe javanica* 'Flamingo' (Z9) have made it a popular if slightly tender plant. Likewise popular is the anise-scented and ferny-leaved *Myrrhis odorata* (sweet cicely; Z5); this European perennial herb seeds freely and lives happily in damp but light parts of the garden. *Sium latifolium* (greater water parsnip; Z8), also from Europe but including Britain, a bog plant to 1.2 m (4 ft.), is sometimes grown.

Seed raising for annuals and biennials is straightforward where plants do not self-sow. *Oenanthe javanica* 'Flamingo' and clumped perennials can be divided.

ANTHRISCUS

CHERVIL
UMBELLIFERAE

Anthriscus cerefolium, the chervil of France, is the most likely species from this small Eurasian genus to be encountered in formal cultivation, but *A. sylvestris* (cow parsley; Z7) makes a fine, naturally regenerating addition to the wilder parts of the garden. Its dissected young green leaves appear early in the year, with snowdrops, and any not welcome can be easily be spotted and immediately weeded out. The plants are mostly biennial to short-lived hardy herbaceous perennials, forming a much-forked, tuberous, parsnip-coloured root system. Flowering stems also arise early, to flower in late spring, at a height of about 90 cm (3 ft.). Their branching umbels spread their flowers to join with the flowers of neighbouring stems: the wayside appearance of these white-flowering drifts seals spring's arrival. There are several selections, including the dark-foliaged 'Ravenswing', and darker-leaved forms sometimes arise in the natural population.

Anthriscus sylvestris can be suppressive of other herbaceous plants, and seeds so freely that it is best cut down after flowering. Plants will grow on moist soils, light or heavy, and tolerate partial shade, but are at their best on sunny sites, close to trees or hedges, on moist soils.

AQUILEGIA
COLUMBINE
RANUNCULACEAE

Aquilegias can make a good attempt at growing on moist soils, particularly those that have the genes of the violet-blue European columbine, *Aquilegia vulgaris* (Z4), which grows to 60 cm (2 ft.) or more on moist peaty soils. Seedlings are short-lived, forming a small rosette of leaves in their first season to flower the following summer, mostly dying back after seeding.

ARISAEMA
COBRA LILY
ARACEAE

Sometimes snake-like, and generally of curious appearance, the inflorescences of arisaemas have contributed to their increasing popularity in gardens. They are plants of moist forest, or occasionally more open hillsides, where they grow among trees and scrub. In China, and elsewhere, their tubers are extensively collected from the wild for their medicinal value, but they are also eaten. I have in the past partaken of them in China as a diced vegetable in soups. They respond well to cultivation, given deep compost on a soil that stays constantly moist under light shade, and their summer growth dies right back in autumn, the plants perennating over winter as tubers. Though many are northern temperate, their range extends down to Mexico and tropical Asia, and thus hardiness is a consideration, with some species being tender. Conservation is now a concern for the rare species, threatened by overcollecting and habitat loss, and plants of unknown source should not be purchased.

For wet gardens, the eastern North American *Arisaema triphyllum* (jack-in-the-pulpit) and its several distinct varieties are deserving of wider notice. Also from even wetter woods in North America is *A. dracontium*, distinguished by its leaves having five to fifteen leaflets. Both are hardy to Zone 4. I admit however to a preference for the Asian species: the cobra-like east Himalayan *A. griffithii* (Z8) with its strongly ribbed, large-hooded, brown-purple 10–25 cm (4–10 in.) spathe and long trailing spadix; or the crisp black-lined, white-throated *A. sikokianum* (Z5) from China and Japan, which I first saw in its variety *serratum* in Guizhou, western China. Unfortunately this last and several others can have their perennating organ damaged by heavy frost.

The flesh should be cleaned from seed before sowing. If growing well, plants will produce offsets.

ARISARUM
ARACEAE

Arisarum is a small genus of aroid-like perennial herbs from the Mediterranean region. The woodlander *Arisarum proboscideum* (mouse plant; Z7), with its long mouse-tailed inflorescence, occurs naturally in Italy and Spain and will grow on moist soils. It is sensible to keep this small plant in a raised bed near one's residence so that it can be both seen and cared for, particularly since its leaves, 10–20 cm (4–8 in.) in length, die off from late summer. Its spreading rhizomes allow easy increase by division.

ARTEMISIA
WORMWOOD
COMPOSITAE

The aromatic artemisias include many silver-foliaged plants for dry soils, but the mauve-purple-leaved *Artemisia lactiflora* Guizhou Group is very tolerant of wet soils, flagging in summer if the soil dries. Jim Russell, Hans Fliegner, and I collected seed of this white-flowered herbaceous perennial in 1985 on Fanjing Shan in Guizhou Province, western China, where it grew on the edge of wet forest at 2000 m (6562 ft.). Its deciduous stems grow to about 1 m (3.3 ft.). Seedlings vary slightly, but I have grown plants of another seedling from this taxon ever since on my wet soil. It is hardy in Zone 8 and will probably take lower temperatures.

ARUM
ARACEAE

A genus of tuberous perennials that occurs in Europe, the Mediterranean, and across to the Himalayas, often in seasonally dry conditions. *Arum maculatum* (cuckoopint; Z6) is native from Europe to the Caucasus; in earlier times its small tubers were widely used to obtain laundry starch, and it was said to crack the skin of those who employed it thus. It lives and self-sows happily on heavy soil, and though its flowers and leaves have a quiet attraction, it is not often cultivated, apart from in native plant gardens. Its bright red seeds are clubbed, like a drumstick on a short stalk, and are just as attractive as the more popular *A. italicum* (Z6), though both need sun to

TOP *Artemisia lactiflora* Guizhou Group
ABOVE *Arum maculatum*

fruit well. This latter species has many cultivars, one of which, the marble-leaved *A. italicum* 'Marmoratum', makes a useful ground cover as its new foliage emerges in midwinter; it dies off in late summer, but this is a small price to pay for the pleasure it gives earlier in the season. The cormous tubers of both species produce offsets; *A. maculatum* is increased from seed.

ASARUM, SARUMA
WILD GINGER
ARISTOLOCHIACEAE

Asarums are low-growing rhizomatous herbs from northern temperate regions, with shiny, dark green, often ornately marked leaves, some evergreen, some deciduous, and selected forms are prized as pot plants in Japan. Their dull flowers are often rendered inconspicuous by their shades of green and brown, but plants can make a low (15 cm, 6 in.) and beautifully dense ground cover under shrubs. Asarums occur naturally in moist shaded forests and tolerate heavy wet soils but, having seen them firsthand in wet forest in western China, I am surprised by their tolerance of dry conditions. They are obliging plants to grow, needing little attention, and slowly expanding the size of their clumps over years. Their roots have antibiotic properties and were used in North America as a ginger substitute. In Europe, the evergreen *Asarum europaeum* (asarabacca; Z4) was used medicinally. The small herbaceous yellow-flowered *Saruma henryi* (Z8), which occurs from northwest to southwest China, may also be tried in moist woodland.

Both genera can be increased by seed, when available, but asarums are usually propagated in early spring, by division of their rootstock.

ASCLEPIAS
MILKWEED
ASCLEPIADACEAE

The distinctive flowers of *Asclepias*, carried in umbels, are adapted to insect pollination, producing much nectar and having their pollen in pollinia. The plants are also characterised by having milky latex and seedpods that split to reveal silky plumed seeds. Many asclepias are suited to dry soils; however, several North American perennial asclepias provide candidates for wet soils: *A. purpurascens* (purple milkweed) from the eastern United States; the closely related *A. speciosa*, with its calotropis-like leaves, from moist grassland in the prairies;

A. lanceolata (red milkweed), which ranges from Nebraska to the swamps and wet pine savannas of Louisiana; and the widely distributed rose-flowered *A. incarnata* (swamp milkweed), to 1.5 m (5 ft.), also from the eastern United States. This latter has a white-flowered form (*A. incarnata* 'Alba'); both it and the type do well in gardens where they are given reasonable drainage. These and *A. speciosa* are hardy to Zone 3; the others cope with at least Zone 5.

Though on the tall side, more than 1 m (3.3 ft.) in height, these asclepias are useful for wet meadows or pond borders, requiring full sun and constant moisture when in growth. With their deep root system, transplanting is difficult but can be achieved with careful lifting. Asclepias are usually seed raised but can be propagated from early-season basal stem cuttings.

ASTELIA

ASTELIACEAE

Generally the southern hemisphere astelias grow naturally in damp places on peaty soils. Some are epiphytes, and some of the Australian species are high mountain plants, but it is the slightly more tender (Z8/9) New Zealand species, such as *Astelia chathamica* and *A. grandis*, that appear most frequently in temperate gardens. These rhizomatous herbs form large clumps with attractive long keeled leaves that often have a very silver appearance—for example, in the cultivated forms of *A. chathamica*, which, as its epithet suggests, comes from the Chatham Islands. In mild, moist conditions the leaves of this species can reach 2 m (6.6 ft.), though 60 cm (2 ft.) is not unusual in less favoured gardens. Its flowers are greenish; its 1 cm (0.4 in.) berries are orange. Astelias may be raised by seed or division.

ASTER

COMPOSITAE

Around the world in temperate regions are a number of perennial asters that grow in wet habitats (such as the lilac-flowered *Aster puniceus* from the southeastern United States), and these may be worth seeking out by the enthusiastic wet-soil gardener. In more familiar territory, the northeastern North American Michaelmas daisy, *A. novi-belgii*, and its hybrid relatives seem very tolerant of wet soils and are hardy to Zone 4 or lower. I selected out a small, light blue-flowered seedling many years ago for its resistance to mildew (since surpassed in this character by numerous cultivars); it grows successfully on a very wet soil, but I have to remember to remove its flower

stems before seed is set and distributed, otherwise a myriad seedlings arise. The delicate but floriferous *A. ericoides* cultivars and the strong-stemmed (to 80 cm, 31 in.) *A. trinervius* (Z7), very like a Michaelmas daisy, from temperate Asia, also grow well on wet soil.

ASTILBE

SAXIFRAGACEAE

Astilbe is a small genus of a dozen or so clump-forming species and a great many hybrids. Most species in cultivation come from northeastern Asia; others occur in the Himalayas and North America. Generally they grow well on moist soils, but I have to admit that some cultivars, such as *A*. 'Bronce Elegans', a small-growing simplicifolia hybrid (to 25 cm, 10 in.), do not grow that well on a boggy soil, though summer temperatures may be a factor, as with warmth they grow better on a wet soil. Many hybrids are popular for their small but vibrantly coloured flowers, densely packed on branched inflorescences. These range through red to pink and white and are often a striking feature of summer flower shows. There are also many coppery-red foliage forms.

Though some are very hardy, to Zone 4, in bog beds late spring frosts can be very damaging to young shoots and flowers. My experience of them in the wild is limited to *Astilbe grandis* (Z6) in western China and *A. thunbergii* (Z7) in Japan, in which countries both grow on wet mountainsides. I find that these two grow equally well on wet soil, with flower panicles on both to about 75 cm (30 in.). Flower colour is very variable in seedlings from *A. grandis*.

Flowers are mainly bisexual, but can be unisexual, and leaves are either of three leaflets or more pinnate. Astilbes are mostly increased by division, but the small seeds of species usually germinate readily.

ASTILBOIDES

SAXIFRAGACEAE

Astilboides tabularis (syn. *Rodgersia tabularis*; Z6) is a rhizomatous perennial that requires moist but not waterlogged soils. Like rodgersias, it is not easily established in gardens, though it grows naturally by lakes and streams in northeastern China and North Korea. Flowers are small (8 mm, 0.3 in.), creamy-white and borne on spike-like cymes (to 1.5 m, 5 ft.), and the large lobed leaves grow to around 90 cm (36 in.). It comes into growth slightly later than rodgersias and like them can be increased by division.

BIDENS

This cosmopolitan genus offers a number of moisture-loving species, some of which have become popular in cultivation. Most have yellow-rayed flowers, but some, particularly the annuals, are very weedy. The low-spreading tender *Bidens aurea* occurs in the southern United States to Central America, where it grows in marshy areas; and *B. ferulifolia*, with a similar range, is used in summer bedding, particularly for hanging baskets. Both are hardy in Zone 9. The much hardier *B. cernua* (nodding bur-marigold) is a widespread wild plant in the northern hemisphere; the North American name for this species, nodding beggartick, is more usefully descriptive: it is a reference to the fruit, an achene with a pappus of three or four branched bristles, which cling tightly to clothing or fur, causing irritation. *Bidens cernua* var. *radiata* occurs in my Zone 8 corner of Britain, on the muddy fringes of ponds and rivers. Plants can be propagated from seed; perennials can be propagated from stem cuttings or divided.

BORAGINACEAE

BORAGE FAMILY

Popular in gardens, these are mostly deciduous perennial herbs (with some annuals, and a few small shrubs and trees) with a widespread distribution, mainly in the northern temperate zone. Several of the 150 genera in this large family—*Myosotis, Pentaglottis, Pulmonaria, Symphytum, Trachystemon*, and to some extent *Brunnera, Cerinthe, Echium, Mertensia*, and *Omphalodes*—tolerate wet soil. Many of these will also grow on drier soils. The stems and leaves of the herbaceous borages are often covered with bristly hairs, and their five-lobed flowers are bisexual. They have small fruits, formed either as nutlets with one to four seeds or as a drupe.

Seed is small and hard, and may need scarifying, but where fresh seed of a borage is available, it is readily germinated using conventional sowing practises. Some annuals, such as cerinthes, will self-sow, thus reducing their raising requirements to either the occasional thinning or transplanting to preferred sites. Cut flowering stems of *Myosotis scorpioides* will quickly produce roots in a vase of water; division or offsets can be used to increase most others mentioned. On cold wet sites this is best undertaken in early spring, when warm days are still to come. This allows good establishment, but division can be undertaken at other times, particularly if the ground is moist.

BRUNNERA
BORAGINACEAE

The forget-me-not-blue-flowered *Brunnera macrophylla* (Z6 or lower) from the Caucasus and Turkey is an accommodating garden plant that needs little attention, dividing easily and flowering freely, as do its several notable variegated cultivars, which are sometimes used for spring bedding. As a border plant, however, it can leave a summer gap, particularly as its leaves flag and shrivel when the soil becomes dry. Flower stems are about 45 cm (18 in.) high.

CALAMAGROSTIS
SMALL-REED
GRAMINEAE

Small-reeds occur in northern temperate regions, many in wet habitats, and some are cultivated, particularly the Eurasian *Calamagrostis epigejos* (wood small-reed; Z7), which occurs in damp woods and fens and grows to about 1.8 m (6 ft.). Several cultivars of the hybrid *C.* ×*acutiflora* (*C. arundinacea* × *C. epigejos*) are grown in gardens, but they can spread and should thus be carefully sited. Increase by division.

CALTHA
MARSH MARIGOLD
RANUNCULACEAE

The herbaceous perennial *Caltha palustris* (kingcup; Z3) is of almost circumboreal distribution—northern Europe, Russia, and North America—and is much at home in very wet soils, growing to 45–60 cm (18–24 in.) or more. Though widespread and familiar, when its clear golden blossoms open in spring they still bring cheer to the poorest spirit, lighting up boggy areas. Since my childhood years, when I first saw it growing in an old countryman neighbour's garden (it was his pride and joy, set in a redundant kitchen sink that was filled with water and framed by a leafy arbour), I have always had it in my own garden. It is a variable plant, and several polyploid forms occur naturally, some quite large. Garden selections include the double 'Flore Pleno' and var. *alba*, a white form prone to mildew. Kingcup has a stocky rhizome but can be divided readily and grown at the pool edge, in very wet soil, or in a moist border.

Some other species are grown: the narrower petalled *Caltha poly-petala* (Z4); the silvery white-flowered *C. leptosepala* (Z3) from western North America (coastal ranges and Rockies), which is roughly the size of a small *C. palustris*; and the white-sepalled *C. natans* (Z2) from North America and Siberia, which is an aquatic. All calthas require similar (wet) conditions, and most are increased by division.

CAMASSIA

CAMAS
HYACINTHACEAE

Camassias are great plants for a wet garden, blooming regularly and memorably each May, their electric-coloured flowers borne on spikes to 30–90 cm (12–36 in.). Those in cultivation come from western North America, where the indigenous people (whose words *quamash* and *camas* mean "sweet") at one time ate the bulbs of *Camassia quamash* (small camas; Z5), having steamed them for twenty-four hours to release their sugars. They often flower well if grown in a warm moist bed in full sun. The pale steel-blue-flowered *C. cusickii* (Z5) from northeastern Oregon can be naturalised in grass but does not flower if shaded by trees. It is probably members of *C. leichtlinii* subsp. *suksdorfii* Caerulea Group (Z3) that are best suited to naturalising in grass; there are other cultivated forms of *C. leichtlinii* (large camas), a species distinguished by its sepals, which twist to cover and protect the fruit capsule. Fresh seed germinates with normal care, but the resultant seedlings are very slow growing, and best left undisturbed for their first year. Full development to flowering size can take several years, thus daughter bulbs are the preferred means of increase. Camassias, if growing well, can increase from one to forty bulbs in a decade.

CANNA

INDIAN SHOT
CANNACEAE

Canna has about fifty-five species, all from the New World, and many grow naturally in wet places. Given a frost-free environment, some like *C. glauca* can be grown in shallow water; *C. flaccida* (golden canna) grows in marshes and swamps in southwestern United States; and the widely cultivated *C. indica* is now naturalised in some marshy areas of the United States as well as in the Old World. All are perennial rhizomatous herbs, producing leafy shoots 0.5–3 m (20 in.–10 ft.)

TOP *Camassia cusickii*
ABOVE *Camassia leichtlinii*
Caerulea Group

in height, with terminal inflorescences. Their broad leaves have a sheathing base, and flowers are mostly large and brightly coloured. Some of the apparent petals are staminodes.

Breeders have seized upon these vibrant flowers and easily cultivated plants, producing cultivars that offer an array of flower and leaf colours and size. These may be seen at their summer best at Longwood Gardens in Pennsylvania, at which famous gardens in the 1970s Robert J. Armstrong bred a vast number of new cannas, including a range of "water cannas" with *Canna glauca* as a parent that can grow in 30 cm (1 ft.) of water.

Cannas are popular bedding plants: from spring establishment in pots in a cool greenhouse, they are planted out in early summer. The problem with this had been that cannas, usually just coming to their peak of flowering in late summer, were then cleared to make way for winter bedding; climate change, however, has increased their popularity. Where freezing winter temperatures apply, they are better grown in containers for summer use out of doors, or added to a mixed border where they can stay, like dahlias, until the first leaf-curling frosts demand their removal. Usually the plants are then cut back and the rhizomes overwintered in a frost-free place.

In a frost-free environment, cannas can be kept growing and flowering over a long period; in subtropical gardens, lifting and dividing every six months will keep them in active growth and flower. The more delicate stemmed growth of *Canna indica* (1–2 m, 2.3–6.6 ft.), from tropical and subtropical regions of Central and South America (including the West Indies), makes it a graceful poolside plant.

Division of dormant rootstock is the normal means of propagation for all species and cultivars. The hard seed, formed in a three-valved capsule, may need chipping or soaking in water for a day before sowing at minimum temperatures of 15°C (59°F).

CARDAMINE

BITTERCRESS
CRUCIFERAE

Several herbaceous cardamines are plants of wet meadows and open woods, and the genus is familiar to many through the charming lilac-pink flowers of *Cardamine pratensis* (cuckooflower; Z4), which has a wide northern temperate distribution. Aside from the alpine species, cardamines seem very tolerant of wet soil, and, though some are weeds, several are sought-after garden plants.

The low perennial trifoliate-leaf mats of *Cardamine trifolia* (Z7) from central and southern Europe are often seen in rock gardens, and they look well as an early-season ground cover under bulbs. The short (15–30 cm, 6–12 in.) racemes of small white flowers contrast well against the leaves, which emerge light green and darken as the season progresses. It is an "obedient" plant for the garden, staying where it is put for years, whereas *C. pratensis* rarely forms a large clump and tends to "move around," with new plants arising randomly though usually not far from the original. The several cultivars include doubles with a limited colour range; my favourite is *C. pratensis* 'Flore Pleno', a pale lilac seventeenth-century selection, with flower stems to about 30 cm (1 ft.).

Bittercresses with fleshy underground rhizomes (sometimes placed in the genus *Dentaria*) also tolerate wet soil. One, *Cardamine enneaphylla* (Z7) from mountains in central and southern Europe and northwest Balkans, has yellowish white pendent flowers in 20–40 cm (8–16 in.) panicles; another from central and western Europe, *C. pentaphylla* (Z6), offers white or lilac flowers on 30–50 cm (12–20 in.) stems.

Flowers are usually bisexual, and the fruit is a dehiscent capsule, but the ability this gives for ejecting seed has also contributed to the success of many cardamines as persistent weeds. Seed, when fresh, germinates readily. Both *Cardamine pratensis* and *C. trifolia* are easily propagated from leaf cuttings. Division of those with either dense or extended rhizomatous clumps is best undertaken in spring just as growth commences. Where suitable material is in short supply, several can be propagated from basal stem cuttings.

CARDIOCRINUM

LILIACEAE

The Himalayan *Cardiocrinum giganteum* (Z8) grows all the larger with sufficient shelter, a rich compost, top dressing, and, when in growth, a good water supply. In the past—perhaps because their flowering spikes can reach 4 m (13 ft.)—these giant lilies were seen only in large gardens, but they are becoming more widely grown. The western Chinese form, *C. giganteum* var. *yunnanense*, contributes to this by having smaller 1–2 m (3.3–6.6 ft.) flowering stems; as a further advantage, its stems are often a dark blackish purple, with the sweetly scented flowers also carrying this colour, only more chocolate, on their inner tepals. This Chinese variety usually occurs at lower altitudes, 2438–2743 m (8000–9000 ft.); I have seen it growing on Fanjing Shan in Guizhou, in seemingly constant rain and

TOP *Cardamine pratensis* 'Flore Pleno'
ABOVE *Cardiocrinum giganteum* var. *yunnanense*

mist. In western Sichuan on the Hengduan range, it occurs in forest clearings on the eastern, wetter side of these impressive mountains, and I was amused once to see a plant growing epiphytically, on the large mossy trunk of a fallen tree, a metre or so above the ground. Eastern Chinese and Japanese forms of *C. cathayanum* and *C. cordatum* are also now becoming available. All are well worth the effort of a raised bed.

Monocarpic (that is, the bulb flowers just once), these lilies can fail to produce daughter bulbs after flowering and die out as a consequence. Also, the bulbs are susceptible to damage from cold wet conditions in winter because the bulbs grow naturally with their noses at, or just above, soil level. The large cordate, mostly basal leaves of cardiocrinums can be, particularly on young plants, an attractive dark red in spring, becoming greener as the season progresses. It takes time to build up a flowering-sized bulb from seed—three or four years for the smaller plants, and up to seven years for the very tall forms.

Seeds are light and papery and produced in quantity, and the old flower spikes are very durable, their cylindrical, trilocular capsules splitting with a fringe of "teeth" that make them desirable for use in dried flower arrangements. It is usual to vernalise seed over winter in a refrigerator for spring sowing, but the best germination I had was from seed collected and sown in early summer (May); most of the papery seed disperses by autumn but a few seeds remain in the old capsules over winter, and this naturally vernalised seed germinated freely.

CAREX

SEDGE
CYPERACEAE

With their grass-like form, sedges are increasingly popular, but only a small proportion of the great many species are cultivated. They are easy to grow and increase, and though winter cold can be a problem for some of the warm temperate species, this is nevertheless a very useful genus for wet temperate gardens, providing both fine foliage and flowering specimens for group plantings with all-year-round appeal. Most are perennial herbs having a clumped or creeping rootstock, with stems or culms triangular in cross section; the linear leaves are sometimes reduced to sheaths. Flowers are not very conspicuous (though the full inflorescence can be attractive with its spikes of florets) and are wind-pollinated.

The large (to 1.5 m, 5 ft.) and impressive *Carex pendula* (Z5), native to Britain, has a range extending through Europe to west Asia and North Africa. Its tall inflorescences bend gracefully as the catkin-like flower spikes expand, and it often arrives of its own accord in gardens. As its range suggests, this species can also tolerate hot dry conditions, but these restrict its size to almost half of that achieved in wet soil. It is reasonably long-lived for a carex, lasting several years, and conveniently, I find, produces the occasional seedling replacement.

Another common native British sedge, *Carex riparia* (greater pond-sedge; Z6 or lower) can be an invasive weed of shallow waterways, but its attractive variegated ('Variegata') cultivar is less competitive and can be used as a ground cover in very wet soils, where it quickly forms dense but running clumps. The young inflorescence glumes form attractive blackish brown "paintbrushes" contrasting well with its variegated foliage (60 cm, 2 ft., or more), which is made lighter by some shoots having fully white leaves. *Carex riparia* has a wide range through Europe to the Caucasus, North Africa, and west Asia. Nearly as widespread, *C. elata* (tufted-sedge; Z7 or lower) produced a fine golden-leaved form, *C. elata* 'Aurea' (earlier known as 'Bowles' Golden', after E. A. Bowles, the gardener and author who found it in the Norfolk Broads).

Carex riparia 'Variegata'

Several species from New Zealand are now cultivated in the northern hemisphere. *Carex buchananii* (Z7), with its dark coppery brown curled-tipped foliage, is popular. The inflorescences of this are more upright than those of the similar but more arching-leaved *C. comans* (to 60 cm, 2 ft.; Z8), which are lax and hidden by the dense foliage. Both species frequently produce naturally regenerating seedlings on bare wet soil. The foliage of *C. comans* varies from green to dark red and dark bronze, and the leaf colour of seedlings also varies a little but is broadly true to their parent. The light green and white *C. comans* 'Frosted Curls' with its squat swirls of leaves, 30 × 60 cm (1 × 2 ft.) high and wide, comes uniformly true from seed; this plant is completely at home in wet soil and ideal for forming attractive groups. *Carex comans* can be caught by frost (−8°C, 18°F, or lower) and killed, so all forms are best regarded as short-lived—perhaps two to three years, before being replaced. Otherwise *C. c.* 'Frosted Curls' looks well year-round, as does the hardier Japanese *C. morrowii* 'Variegata', which has a neat and tidy habit, if small (20 × 40 cm, 8 × 16 in.). Even smaller (6 in., 15 cm), the evergreen, variegated *C. conica* 'Snowline' is popular in gardens.

Many regenerate readily from seed, the cool temperate species needing vernalisation over winter before spring sowing. The warmer temperate species are best sown under glass, though as indicated, they can germinate out-of-doors in temperate regions. Division is used for most. Spring is the best time, because divisions can then recover and grow away in summer. For hardy species, division can be undertaken *in situ* in the garden using a sharp spade or knife.

RELATED GENERA

Of the tender Australian native Cyperaceae, *Isolepis nodosa*, a tufted rush that occurs throughout the southern hemisphere; *Gahnia melanocarpa* (saw-edge) from eastern Australia; and *Lepidosperma gladiatum* (sword rush) from temperate Australia all grow to about 1 m (3.3 ft.) and are among several suited for wet garden use (Wrigley and Fagg 2003).

CENTAUREA
KNAPWEED
COMPOSITAE

Most members of this herbaceous genus are adapted to dry soil, but the European perennial *Centaurea nigra* (black or common knapweed; Z5) tolerates both wet and dry soils. It grows to 60–80 cm (24–31 in.) or more and, since it is well able to survive in very wet grassland, makes a superb addition to the wild garden or meadow, where its thistle-like mauve flowers are a great attraction to insects. It regenerates even in very boggy soil, is simple to maintain, can be divided in the dormant season with a spade, and can also be mown over in winter—using a high cut to trim off the old flowering stems but to leave the basal clump of leaves. The blue, summer-flowering *C. montana* (Z3) from the mountains of western Europe and northwest Balkans also seems reasonably tolerant of heavy and wet soils, and has several cultivars.

CERINTHE
BORAGINACEAE

A pleasant surprise on my wet soil has been the regular regeneration of the Mediterranean *Cerinthe major* (honeywort). In summer its very glaucous-leaved selection 'Kiwi Blue' grows vigorously on damp soil, especially where surfaced with gravel, forming a much-branched, bushy plant, 60 cm (2 ft.) or more tall. Sometimes grown as an annual, it can also behave as a biennial, with its self-sown late summer and autumn seedlings overwintering on wet soil. Some plants will survive the occasional frost (−8°C, 18°F), though stem damage can result.

CHAEROPHYLLUM
CHERVIL
UMBELLIFERAE

These attractively flowered hardy biennial or perennial herbs from northern temperate regions are reasonably tolerant of moist soils. Their dissected leaves are fern-like and their umbels of flowers may be a light lilac-mauve or white. *Chaerophyllum hirsutum* 'Roseum' (Z5) will grow on wet soil, even tolerating winter wet; the parent species comes from central and southern Europe and across to southwestern Russia and the Caucasus. The effect of wet soil is that this perennial then spreads more slowly, flowers on shorter stems, perhaps to 30 cm (1 ft.) rather than 60 cm (2 ft.), and is shorter-lived. Thus a moister soil, or a slightly raised bed on wet soil, is needed to give it permanence. Propagate by seed or division, with care, as recovery can be difficult.

CHELIDONIUM
PAPAVERACEAE

Chelidoniums are not everyone's favourite plants, especially on a dry soil, where they can be a bit weedy. The widespread *Chelidonium majus* (greater celandine; Z6), which occurs from Europe through to western Asia, has several cultivated forms, such as one with double flowers and another with more dissected foliage. They are persistent hardy perennials, growing to 60–90 cm (2–3 ft.), and their young foliage is very attractive. If established under trees on wet soil, they are less weedily aggressive and sometimes welcome in gardens. When damaged they exude a deep yellow-orange sap that contains toxic alkaloids whose powers were earlier recognised in folklore for killing warts. Once established, chelidoniums should regenerate naturally from seed, particularly if on moist gravel.

CHELONE
TURTLEHEAD
SCROPHULARIACEAE

As is often the case, the establishment of plants on a cold wet soil can be a lengthy process, and the lovely eastern North American chelones, which grow by streamsides and in wet woods, are a case in point.

TOP *Cerinthe major* 'Kiwi Blue'
ABOVE *Chaerophyllum hirsutum* 'Roseum'

Chionochloa rubra

I grew *Chelone obliqua* (Z6), the most popular of the four species, in a winter wet bed, but it took two years to produce its first flowering stem and eight years to form a decent-sized flowering clump (stems to 75 cm, 30 in.), though perversely it flags to the point of shrivelling in a drought. Some of the other species have an even lower hardiness rating.

It can be raised from seed or summer cuttings but is usually increased by division. Slow to establish in cool climates; in such areas, it is best to establish divisions in a cool greenhouse.

CHIONOCHLOA

SNOW GRASS, TUSSOCK GRASS
GRAMINEAE

The evergreen New Zealand tussock grasses form beautiful arching clumps, and the hardy *Chionochloa rubra* grows even in woodland. On my wet soil, I give it a slightly raised bed, which also shows off its dense fountain (to 1 m, 3.3 ft., high and wide) of long thin leaves, which are of a greenish brown hue. It flowers freely, the lax culms curving within the lie of the leaves, and seedlings regenerate naturally from single specimens. *Chionochloa flavescens*, which can grow slightly larger, is also suited to damp sites. Raise from seed.

CHRYSOSPLENIUM

GOLDEN SAXIFRAGE
SAXIFRAGACEAE

Chrysospleniums have a range that covers Europe (including two species in Britain), Asia, North Africa, North America, and temperate South America. Most, but not all, occur in moist places, such as riverbanks, bogs, and woodland. They are low-growing herbaceous plants spreading by horizontal stems or rhizomes. Their flowers are borne on flat cymes, and some are of a striking lime-yellow supported by similarly coloured leafy bracts. These are plants for the specialist. Several very hardy species have been grown, but the colourful *Chrysosplenium davidianum* (Z7) from western China is now freely available. In nature it grows on the wetter eastern side of high mountains, forming large flowering mats in light woodland glades with rhododendrons and *Salix magnifica* at around 3000 m (10,000 ft.). Can be increased from seed but usually by division in spring.

HERBACEOUS PLANTS AND BULBS

COLCHICUM

AUTUMN CROCUS

COLCHICACEAE

My first impression of colchicums in cultivation was of plants well adapted to seasonally dry conditions; this was confirmed by seeing my first wild colchicum growing on dry scree in Crete amid spiny verbascum cushions. But the European native *Colchicum autumnale* (Z5) occurs in damp meadows, and when I later saw *C. speciosum* (Z6) likewise situated by springs and streams in the Alborz Mountains of northern Iran, above 2250 m (7400 ft.), I felt more confident about trying some of these bulbs in moist sites.

Colchicum is a large genus of some sixty-five species of perennial herbs that have corms covered by tunics and lanceolate leaves formed into a sheath. In autumn, and sometimes spring, the crocus-like flowers arise separately from the leaves. They are usually held within a pointed sheath, from which they emerge sequentially. Among other characters, they are distinguished from crocuses by their possession of six stamens. Their distribution extends from Europe, through the Mediterranean, to central and western Asia, through northern India, western Pakistan, and western China.

Colchicum autumnale 'Nancy Lindsay'

The National Collection of colchicums grows close to my home in Norfolk, but it is on a light free-drained soil with a Mediterranean type of climate (moderated by the proximity of the sea), and the plants grow superbly. As anticipated however, *Colchicum speciosum* is happy on my heavy wet soil. Sun seems important, too, since *C. tenorei* for example doesn't compete too well with other herbs in a border. Also, on heavy soil, the grass growth is generally too competitive. While some species fail, as I write this, *C. autumnale* 'Nancy Lindsay' is thrusting up its late summer flowers, reminding me that it is worth the effort of trying. For the more difficult species, a bed under high-pruned trees, which will dry more in summer and also let in more light, might extend the range on a wet soil.

Gardeners with small or well-controlled gardens often resent the space taken by the foliage of these bulbs, which can stand from winter to mid-summer. However if grown in a border, behind say hellebores, then the summer-dying foliage is scarcely noticed, and the ginger-like pseudostems of leaves formed by the larger-growing species are not unattractive.

Seeds are sown when ripe (mid-summer). The corms usually produce extra daughter corms each year, some increasing by two to three new corms over two seasons. Generally corms are large, surprisingly so when compared to a crocus.

COLOCASIA

COCOYAM

ARACEAE

This small genus of herbaceous perennials comes from tropical Asia. The tropical East Asian *Colocasia esculenta* is cultivated as a crop around the world in rich, moist but well-drained soils for its edible upright cormous rootstock, which needs peeling and cooking to reduce its toxic contents. With its long-stalked leaves, this cocoyam (or taro) is similar in appearance and size (to 1.8 m, 6 ft.) to some alocasias and tolerates boggy conditions, even shallow water for limited periods. Many forms have been selected for differing "tuber" qualities; and 'Fontanesii', with purple leaf stalks and veins, and several other dark-foliage forms are now much used for summer bedding. Tubers can overwinter in mild areas (Z9/10) but are best lifted and stored frost-free. They are normally increased by the removal of offsets.

COMPOSITAE

DAISY FAMILY

Also known as Asteraceae. This is among the largest plant families, with almost every new taxonomic survey increasing the number of recognised genera and species. One of the most recent indicates over 1500 genera and 22,000 species—I take these figures on trust! Biologically it is certainly a very successful family, with daisies, in all their many forms, occupying a wide range of habitats and having a truly cosmopolitan distribution.

The herbaceous form predominates, though there are a few trees and shrubby members. As learned in school botany, daisies are compound flowers. The flower head or capitulum has many small flowers crowded onto its disk-like head. These flowers (sometimes called florets) have two forms: the ray flowers, usually the outer, have an extended ligule, while the inner disk flowers have a tubular form. The capitulum may have both ray and disk flowers or just one or the other, and though most composites have bisexual flowers, some are dioecious, with separate male and female plants. Most usually, the disk flowers are bisexual, and the ray flowers are bisexual, female, or sterile (neuter).

This family provides many valued plants for wet gardens, particularly temperate: they offer masses of late summer colour when in flower, most are easy to grow, and composites are adaptable, with a good many able to grow in both wet and dry soils. Treating them as subjects for bedding can usefully extend the range of composites suited to temperate wet gardens—that is, use tender annuals (sunflowers, tagetes) or tender perennials (chrysanthemums, dahlias) for summer display, since such plants cope well with warm moist soils in summer; then remove them to store (as seed, rootstock, or tuber), thus avoiding winter's deleterious cold wet conditions. The biggest problem is their freely produced seed, which is mainly windborne. Remove flowering stems before seed is distributed, or be prepared to weed away many seedlings.

Of other genera not mentioned elsewhere, *Cicerbita* (blue sowthistle; Z3–6), from the mountains of Europe, Asia, and North Africa, is a genus of herbs, often erect, with a milky sap, which grow in damp places. Species of *Doronicum* (leopard's-bane) from southeastern and western Europe into southwestern Asia are relatively unobtrusive and often overlooked until they flower in early summer, when their clear yellow daisies on 45 cm (18 in.) stems catch the eye. They tolerate moist shade but do not survive long on very wet soil. Such as I have tried from *Microseris*, which genus has some wet-soil-tolerant herbs with large leaves and hawkweed-like flowers, have died over winter. *Bellis perennis* (lawn daisy; Z4) can grow on wet soils, though it is a more noticeable weed of dry soils, where the grass is less competitive; it is native to Europe and western Asia, and the many large-flowered bedding hybrids derived from this daisy are also tolerant of heavy soils. *Sinacalia tangutica* (Chinese ragwort; Z5) is more invasively successful at growing in damp shady places and is naturalised in parts of Britain.

Several other genera of composites grow naturally in moist soils and may be candidates for the wet garden, but since I have not grown them in wet soil, I simply mention them here for reference: the herbaceous arnicas from western North America and *Boltonia* from northeastern Asia and North America. Experience suggests that no matter how likely a candidate from wet habitats might be, whether or not it will persist over years on wet garden soil can only be tested by trial and error.

The ability of many composites to set viable seed by self-pollination, if their preferred cross-pollination fails, ensures that seed may be set from only a single plant. This undoubtedly contributes to their success in gardens, and often, it seems, to their tendency to naturalise. Most hardy genera will self-sow in temperate gardens; for the more tender species, and particularly the woody members, a cold frame may be used. Division is the preferred means of increasing most herbaceous composites. Basal herbaceous cuttings are sometimes used, and softwood cuttings provide a simple means of increasing the woody composites.

CONVALLARIA, MAIANTHEMUM
CONVALLARIACEAE

The familiar convallaria is a perennial herb with simple, usually unbranched stems and small bell-like flowers; its fruit is a berry. In temperate gardens, both 'Fortin's Giant', a vigorous selection of *Convallaria majalis* (lily-of-the-valley), and the similar *Maianthemum bifolium* (false lily-of-the-valley) can spread their rhizomes aggressively in a leafy soil, and thus be used to good effect as ground cover in a moist woodland garden. Both genera have a delicate scent; the former is stronger, but the latter, in compensation, has more noticeable small white-stamened flowers and sculpturally veined leaves. Both are also widely distributed in northern temperate regions to Zone 4. *Smilacina* is now included with *Maianthemum*, and these are all fine plants for moist woodland, with the North American *M. racemosum* (Z4) perhaps the most popular; it grows to 90 cm (36 in.) and has striking, creamy flower heads.

All are normally increased by division, though they are slow to reestablish. With maianthemum, for example, it is easier to grow small divisions in pots in a cold frame, planting out later in the season, when they should be growing strongly. By comparison, divisions made *in situ* will probably sulk for a year or so. For seed propagation, see *Disporum*.

CORTADERIA
PAMPAS GRASS
GRAMINEAE

Pampas grasses are very tolerant of wet soil. I have grown, for example, the dwarf Argentinean *Cortaderia selloana* 'Pumila' (to 2 m, 6.6 ft.; Z5) on both very dry and very wet soils, for many years, with equal success. These large tufted perennials can produce female plants, though some are bisexual. In cultivation it is often the female forms that are selected because their inflorescences are broader and last longer. Several cultivars of *C. selloana* (to 3 m, 10 ft.) are available, but I favour the more graceful beauty of the New Zealand cortaderias, such as *C. richardii* (Z8), which grows to about 2.4 m (8 ft.). The form of the latter in cultivation is bisexual and sets viable seed. Propagate by division, but wear gloves to protect hands from the sharp-edged leaves.

CRINUM

AMARYLLIDACEAE

Though many species are plants of seasonally dry conditions, bog and aquatic crinums occur in both the Old and New Worlds; in the southeastern United States *Crinum americanum* is known as the swamp lily, and similarly in Central America, crinums may be found in low marshy areas. Many of the large showy-flowered crinums grow well on wet soils, given warmth. In Zone 8 Britain this means planting against the south-facing exterior wall of a heated building. The South African *Crinum moorei* and *C. bulbispermum* (Orange River lily) grow well in such conditions (the latter grows naturally in swampy ground and along riverbeds); happily, they have passed their tolerance of wet soil onto their hybrid, *C. ×powellii* (to 90 cm, 3 ft.), with its pink and, slightly superior, white forms.

Like most amaryllids, crinums reestablish slowly after transplanting or repotting, and they like each other's company, flowering better when in tightly packed clumps. Their large bulbs, with tightly wrapped leaf bases, which extend the neck of the bulbs above the ground, can grow deep so that, with their densely matted root systems, dividing and transplanting can involve quite an excavation—though such depth protects the growing point of the bulbs from frost.

Seed is the size of a large pea, with a corky waterproof coat. Germination begins with the production of a hypocotyl shoot (in the case of *Crinum bulbispermum*, while the seed is still on the plant), which then forms a protobulb at its tip, from which roots and leaves develop.

CROCOSMIA

MONTBRETIA

IRIDACEAE

Crocosmias are of African origin, mostly from South Africa, and all are very tolerant of wet soils. Because of their long-established popularity in gardens, a great many hybrids that are hardy to Zone 5 have been developed, as exampled by Alan Bloom's fiery, more recent

TOP *Cortaderia selloana* 'Pumila'
ABOVE *Crinum ×powellii* 'Album', benefiting from the warmth and shelter of a south-facing wall

Crocosmia 'Lucifer' to the golden-orange, century-old *C. ×crocosmiiflora* 'George Davison', named after the head gardener of Westwick Hall, Norwich, who raised this plant. Some, such as the slightly tender *C. ×crocosmiiflora* 'Solfatare', flower well in warm sunny conditions. I have mostly failed with the brilliant orangey-red *C. masoniorum* (Z6) on my wet soil but recall seeing it succeed in a well-drained soil bed warmed by being against a greenhouse wall; I say "mostly," because after dying out in one spot and sulking for years in another, this latter has flowered after a warm July, so temperature is a factor. Curiously, one of its supposed progeny, the lovely yellow *C.* Jenny Bloom (= 'Blacro') (Alan Bloom 1980) flowers well in a very damp north-facing (Z8) border. Most crocosmias grow naturally in grassland, and several, including *C. pottsii* (Z6), have naturalised in parts of Britain. The latter can be found, among other places, by rivers and lakes. They come freely from seed and produce tight horizontal chains of corms.

CYPERUS

UMBRELLA SEDGE
CYPERACEAE

This large genus of perennial herbs has many temperate species, particularly in North America. Almost all umbrella sedges, or galingales, can be found in wet soil, and many are emergent aquatics. Most have a clumped or creeping rootstock, and triangular stems in cross section; their small bisexual flowers are usually carried in branched terminal umbels, as in the beautiful mop-headed *Cyperus papyrus* (Egyptian paper reed). This tall-stemmed cyperus has a considerable range from Israel (Galilee) in the north to southern Africa; its tropical forms reach 3–4 m (10 ft.–13 ft.), taller than the northern forms. In cultivation it is slow growing, needing at least Zone 10 warmth, and its rootstock extends very gradually from year to year. It can be divided, but care is needed to successfully reestablish offsets. It is sometimes grown in shallow water in large waterproof pots but grows better if a peat bed can be formed for it at water level in a pool. It grows best if water temperature is held around 24°C (75°F).

Cyperus involucratus (umbrella plant) is a popular and easily grown pot plant that tolerates cooler conditions: it can survive out of doors in summer and overwinters in very mild (Z9) regions. Others cultivated include *C. eragrostis* (pale galingale; Z8) from southern Mexico and southern North America, which has grass-like leaves (to 60 cm, 24 in.) and brown globose flower spikes. The galingale itself, *C. lon-*

gus (Z8 or higher) from southern Britain and more widely in northern temperate regions, has stems to 1 m (3.3 ft.) and grassy foliage with brownish branching flower heads. Like *C. eragrostis* it is reasonably frost hardy and useful for stabilising banks.

Propagation is mostly by division as seeds are rarely available. The tops of the flowering stems of *Cyperus involucratus* and others can be taken as cuttings.

CYPRIPEDIUM
SLIPPER ORCHID
ORCHIDACEAE

Slipper orchids occur in the northern hemisphere, extending their range down to Mexico in the Americas and to Southeast Asia. Most grow well in moist woodland, often on hillsides among shrubs, but happily for wet gardens the very showy *Cypripedium reginae* (Z4), with its rich pink pouch and white petals, grows in wet soils—as I found on my first sight of this plant in the wild, which was in the northeastern United States: I should have been warned by the presence of sarracenia but, keen to photograph the plant, I soon found my legs sinking into a peaty bog. This species forms slender, perennial rhizomes, and in spring its pleated leaves emerge in tight rolls; its flower racemes can grow up to 75 cm (30 in.).

Joining *Cypripedium reginae* in a requirement for moist soil are *C. acaule* and *C. guttatum* (Z4/5), though for the latter this can also be wet calcareous meadows. For conservation and propagation, see Orchidaceae.

CYRTANTHUS
AMARYLLIDACEAE

Cyrtanthus elatus (syn. *Vallota purpurea*; Scarborough lily) occurs naturally at high altitudes in the western Cape Region of South Africa, often by forest streams. In cultivation it is very tolerant of moist soil, and flowers abundantly if containerised. I have grown it in a pot with minimal attention for fifty years; it has never failed to flower in late summer and can withstand a few degrees of frost if sheltered over winter (it does lose its evergreen leaves if the frost is harder). A pair of spathes enclose and shield the flower buds, and its bright orange-red flowers are borne on 45 cm (18 in.) stems. The smaller though equally tender, scented and white-flowered *C. mackenii* also occurs in damp habitats in South Africa. Both can be increased by daughter bulbs, though the initial stock of species might be seed raised.

Cyrtanthus elatus

Darmera peltata in late summer

CYRTOSPERMA
SWAMP TARO
ARACEAE

Cyrtosperma merkusii (Z10) from the South Pacific and beyond is a large (4 m, 13 ft.) alocasia-like aroid (but with prickly petioles) cultivated for its large tuberous rhizomes, which are made edible by cooking. It can grow in very wet ground. For the tropical garden, the smaller *C. johnstonii* (Z10) from the Solomon Islands is sometimes cultivated for its attractive red-veined leaves, even though its petioles are slightly spiny. Increase from offsets.

DACTYLORHIZA
MARSH ORCHID
ORCHIDACEAE

Thirty or more species of *Dactylorhiza* are distributed in Eurasia, North Africa, and Alaska; several are in cultivation, most of them relatively easy to grow. They are terrestrial perennials, dying down after seeding to overwinter as digitate tubers, and when dormant they can be transplanted, establishing best if taken with soil rather than bare root. The blotched leaves are spirally arranged, and flower spikes are densely packed with attractively marked, mostly pink and white, small flowers. Spikes vary in height (roughly 15–60 cm, 6–24 in.), depending on the species and habitat, though some, such as the Mediterranean *D. elata* (Z7/8), are taller. Most grow in very moist, sometimes calcareous soils. For conservation and propagation, see Orchidaceae.

DARMERA
SAXIFRAGACEAE

The herbaceous perennial *Darmera peltata* (Z6) is a wetland plant from western North America, where it grows naturally by streamsides and in bogs. Given a light moist position in gardens, it soon forms a dense mat of rhizomes from which, in early season, its pink clustered flowers arise on sturdy, 30–60 cm (12–24 in.) leafless stems; these early-produced flowers can be damaged by late frosts. The large deciduous parasol leaves follow on long 60–90 cm (24–36 in.) stalks but can grow to twice that height if conditions are favourable. Easily increased by division of its thick rhizomes.

HERBACEOUS PLANTS AND BULBS

DESCHAMPSIA

HAIR-GRASS

GRAMINEAE

Deschampsia cespitosa (tufted hair-grass; Z5) is widespread in northern temperate regions and high montane Asia and Africa, forming tussocks 20 cm to 2 m (8 in. to 6.6 ft.) in height, with delicate golden flowering culms on wet moorland and meadows. I had a lovely clump of *D. cespitosa* 'Bronzeschleier' that grew well until inundated by a summer flood of short duration; it languished thereafter—a pity, because there are many other tempting cultivars of this species. Also (and without the justification of inundation) *D. flexuosa* 'Tatra Gold' seemed less than happy on wet soil, though this wavy hair-grass occurs in the "drier parts of bogs." Increase both by division.

DICENTRA

BLEEDING HEART

PAPAVERACEAE

Certainly the Asian *Dicentra spectabilis* (Z8) needs good drainage, and the late frosts that occur in wet hollows can be damaging to this species; however, in moist and sheltered conditions, the many garden forms of *D. formosa* (Z5), which comes from moist forests and streambanks in Washington, Oregon, and California, will spread under trees in leaf litter to form a fine ground cover, particularly on acid soil. Their flowers (stems to 30–45 cm, 12–18 in.) are the main attraction, but their delicately divided leaves also have a special charm. Over the years I have increased the number I cultivate by always providing these hardy woodlanders with a slightly raised bed. They are easily increased by division in early spring.

DISPORUM

CONVALLARIACEAE

Disporum has a wide northern temperate distribution, and several choice species are relatively easily grown in sheltered, moist and shaded gardens down to Zone 8, as shown by a vigorous twenty-year-old clump of *Disporum hookeri* var. *oreganum* (syn. *Prosartes hookeri* var. *oregana*) with stems to about 60 cm (2 ft.), in Ray Wood. These herbaceous perennials can persist without attention for many years, but a well-prepared site with regular weeding and division of clumps best provides for disporums.

Seed, when available, should be cleaned before sowing in pans using light organic compost and then held in a cold frame for germination. Green seed can oblige with spring germination; otherwise, from an autumn sowing, seedlings may take up to eighteen months to emerge (that is, after two winters). Seedlings can be difficult to grow.

RELATED GENERA

Though they boast some very hardy species, drainage is a factor for all these genera. I have collected *Polygonatum orientale* in wet soil in north-facing woodland in the mountains of northern Iran and witnessed the very rare *P. pendulum* growing as an epiphyte, trailing its sickle-like leaves and small white flowers from high up on the branches of a large tree in western Sichuan, albeit in a constantly moist forest. This general requirement for moist well-drained conditions also applies to *Tricyrtis* and *Uvularia*. The fleshy roots of uvularias are susceptible to rot if purchased when dormant, and their rhizomes will need careful reestablishment in pots for a year or two before planting. Once set out, the wiry-stemmed *U. perfoliata* (Z4) from the eastern United States spreads freely in a leaf mould rich soil in partial shade. A sawfly specific to Solomon's seal (*Polygonatum*) can quickly skeletonise foliage; look out for its caterpillars in summer.

DODECATHEON

SHOOTING STARS
PRIMULACEAE

Almost all the fourteen or so species of this herbaceous genus are cultivated, along with a number of cultivars, and this is not surprising, for the flowers of shooting stars, with their reflexed, cyclamen-like petals, are very attractive. These are borne on stout stems either singly or in terminal racemes. Plants form a basal rosette of leaves on a perennial rootstock, and some produce bulbils. Also, like many primulas, some die back to a dormant resting phase after flowering and seeding. Most occur in North America, mainly on the Pacific side, also extending into northeast Asia.

Candidly, dodecatheons will not persist in temperate gardens unless given good care, a moist organic soil, and regular repropagation. Some species occur in wet meadows, but others require drier situations. The two most often seen are *Dodecatheon meadia* (25–60 cm, 10–24 in.) from the mid and eastern United States, where it grows on woodland banks and in prairies; this species is for well-drained sites. More germane, *D. jeffreyi* (Sierra shooting star) can be found as large clumps in wet meadows and on streambanks in the mountains of western North America. Both are hardy to Zone 7 or lower. Increase by seed or division.

ECHIUM
BUGLOSS
BORAGINACEAE

The tall, blue-flowered *Echium pininana* comes from the Canary Islands, where it occurs in moist laurel forest at 600 m (2000 ft.) on Las Palmas. It has grown for me on a heavy soil, regenerating seedlings that, despite the wet, can overwinter if temperatures stay above –5°C (23°F). It is a seed-raised biennial, producing its large, terminal, witch's-hat-like inflorescence on the overwintered stem.

EOMECON
SNOW POPPY
PAPAVERACEAE

If its site suits the eastern Chinese *Eomecon chionantha*, this lovely, deciduous perennial takes off, its long underground rhizomes spreading quickly, producing a succession of single long-stalked glaucous leaves, to 15 cm (6 in.). Its white flowers come less freely in a shaded spot, but it tolerates somewhat moist soils and is hardy to at least –10°C (14°F). Raised from seed or increase by division.

EPIPACTIS
HELLEBORINE
ORCHIDACEAE

A group of terrestrial perennial orchids that are mainly northern temperate but extend to warmer regions in the Old and New Worlds, helleborines are more variable in their requirement for moist soil, many needing good drainage. *Epipactis palustris* (marsh helleborine; Z6) is often found on wet calcareous fens and marshes; it has a wide range over Eurasia and North Africa and is beautiful, flowering on 30–90 cm (12–36 in.) stems. It is easy to grow on a wet soil, forming an easily divided spreading rhizome, and produces its new season's shoots late, in early summer; stems die down after seeding. It is a parent to the very striking hybrid *E*. 'Sabine'. I must again emphasise that vulnerable wetland plants such as this orchid should only be obtained for gardens from cultivated stock.

Epipactis palustris

ERANTHIS

WINTER ACONITE
RANUNCULACEAE

The low-growing perennial *Eranthis hyemalis* (Z5) and its groups, with their familiar snowdrop-time, yellow-sepalled flowers, seem able to tolerate both hot and dry and damp and cold soils. Among shrubs or under trees, their brittle rhizome spreads slowly, forming large clumps. However they do not seem to be able to cope with the competition of other plants in more open situations. Winter aconites are widely naturalised but range naturally in southern Europe and temperate Asia. Divide after flowering in early spring. Can self-sow on limestone soils.

ERIOPHORUM

COTTON-GRASS
CYPERACEAE

Eriophorums grow mainly in the colder regions of the northern hemisphere; common species such as *Eriophorum angustifolium* (Z4) and *E. latifolium* (Z8) are widely distributed through Europe, to Siberia and North America. They are plants of acid bogs, spreading extensively from a creeping rootstock to form large colonies that can arrest the eye with masses of their white cottonwool-like seedheads. In cultivation this effect is diminished, perhaps by their reduced planting scale, though their narrow dark green leaves, which grow to 60 cm (2 ft.) or so, make a useful ground cover on boggy soil. Tolerant of neutral conditions, long-lived, and easily divided.

ERYNGIUM

ERYNGO
UMBELLIFERAE

Starting with the thought of the waxy-leaved, deep-rooted *Eryngium maritimum* (sea holly) growing happily on seaside shingle banks does not lead to any expectation of wet soil tolerance in the genus. But there are some 230 eryngiums with an extensive distribution in Eurasia and North America, with many in Central and South America.

A colleague, who was not keen to grow it because of its prickly-edged leaves, gave me a plant of the large *Eryngium pandanifolium* (Z8). Its evergreen leaves can each grow 1–2 m (3.3–6.6 ft.) in length and though they appear very tough are easily torn at their base. Interestingly, this plant has been cultivated in South America for its fibres, known as *caraguata*. It has a large, black kniphofia-like rhizome, from which offsets arise to form an ever-extending clump of tightly packed rosettes, perhaps becoming 2–3 m (6.6–10 ft.) wide in a decade, and its equally tall flower spikes develop in late summer. Thimble-like flower cones form on a candelabra rather than an umbel. This species is slightly tender, but this is only a concern when young, newly taken divisions are exposed to winter frost. The previous season's leaves are hardy to at least –10°C (14°F), and the rosette is protected by a mass of leaves that persist, in a papery form, long after they have died. It seems very tolerant of wet soils and can best be divided in early spring.

Seedlings transplant readily, and division of the clump-formers is usually successful.

EUPATORIUM
THOROUGHWORT
COMPOSITAE

These herbs, and there are some shrubby eupatoriums which can reach 3 m (10 ft.) or more, have a range extending both to Asia and South America, but wet soil tolerance varies. I recall a natural stand of the European *Eupatorium cannabinum* (hemp agrimony; Z5) flowering profusely on tall (0.75–1.5 m (2.5–5 ft.) stems, on an inundated site in Cornwall; more memorable, though, was the fluttering sea of butterflies visiting these flowers. Similarly the eastern North American *E. purpureum* (Joe Pye weed; to 2.1 m, 7 ft.; Z4) grows naturally on moist ground and swampy meadows. However, whereas *E. cannabinum* seedlings arise naturally in my garden, the white form ('Alba') of *E. purpureum* is seriously set back by winter cold and wet—it is probably yet another composite that needs warmth with its moisture, and it now grows happily with me on a better-drained, sheltered site. Sadly too I find the dark-leaved *Ageratina altissima* 'Chocolate' (previously *E. rugosum* 'Chocolate') seems even more vulnerable to winter cold and wet. For propagation, see Compositae.

EUPHORBIA
SPURGE
EUPHORBIACEAE

Their flowers most distinguish euphorbias: what superficially appears to be a single flower is actually a cyathium, a compact inflorescence with separate male flowers, each reduced to a single stamen,

Eryngium pandanifolium

around a reduced female flower with a single ovary and three carpels. The nectaries sometimes develop petal-like extensions, making a cyathium look even more like a single flower.

Among the hardy herbaceous spurges I grew *Euphorbia schillingii*, from Nepal, cautiously at first on my Zone 8 wet soil, since it was a plant given to me by its collector, Tony Schilling. I was then surprised by how well it took to a north-facing border on all-year-round wet clay, so much so that seed germinated freely nearby. These seedlings quickly form deep roots and a perennial, fleshy rootstock; they should thus be transplanted when very young. In high summer the mature plants form yellow cyathia that are enhanced by lime-yellow upper leaves, giving a fine display that lasts for several weeks.

Subsequently I have found that the eastern Himalayan *Euphorbia sikkimensis* (Z6) grows equally well on wet soil, as does the vigorous *E. palustris* (marsh spurge; Z5) from northern and southern continental Europe across to west Asia. This latter and *E. schillingii* have flowering stems to 60–90 cm (24–36 in.) with me, but *E. sikkimensis* is taller, and in warmer conditions all can reach 90–120 cm (3–4 ft.). The large, central Asian *E. soongarica* (Z7) and European *E. villosa* (Z5) also favour wet soil, and the scarce *Euphorbia hyberna* (Irish spurge; Z9) occurs naturally on streambanks.

I suspect that even a few of the euphorbias adapted to dry conditions will tolerate wet soils. I have grown the biennial *E. lathyris* (caper spurge; Z6) from southern and eastern Europe and northwest Africa, with some success on a pretty moist soil, though it is floppier (that is, less root-secure) when in moist shade. More pleasingly the shrubby (to 1.5 m, 5 ft.) *E. mellifera* (Madeira honey spurge), which also occurs in laurel forest in the Canary Islands, where it reaches up to 15 m (50 ft.), has prospered for many years on my very wet heavy clay, and seedlings regenerate naturally. The limit to euphorbia possibilities on wet soil is soon reached, however, with *E. characias*, which slowly fades away.

The milky latex of these plants is generally toxic and a skin irritant, so take care when handling them. Semi-ripe summer cuttings are used to propagate many; among the deciduous herbaceous some, such as *Euphorbia sikkimensis*, spread by rhizomes, and the clump-formers can sometimes be carefully divided—though not all can be so easily increased. Seed may be forcibly dispersed, causing seedlings to arise variously, and seed usually germinates readily if fresh.

FARFUGIUM

COMPOSITAE

In damp woodland the herbaceous *Farfugium japonicum* produces its bright yellow (4–6 cm, 1.6–2.4 in.) flowers on 60–75 cm (24–30 in.) stalks and has colt's-foot-like leaves. It comes from Korea and Japan, where a number of spotted and variegated leaf forms, such as 'Aureo-maculatum', have been selected; they survive to about –5°C (23°F) or slightly lower. For propagation, see Compositae.

FILIPENDULA

ROSACEAE

All the hardy herbaceous perennials in this small genus occur naturally in northern temperate regions, and happily, such as I have grown survive and even prosper on the wettest of sites. Filipendulas are rhizomatous or tuberous, forming tight clumps that keep out other plants, and are thus useful for naturalising. They are also deciduous; but while the foliage of North American *Filipendula rubra* (queen of the prairie) and European *F. vulgaris* will disappear over winter, the Eurasian *F. ulmaria* usually retains some overwintering leaves. New leaves and flowering stems arise in spring, and, though their individual flowers are small, a great many are held on each panicle.

Filipendula rubra 'Venusta'

Filipendula ulmaria (meadowsweet; Z2) is a common wayside plant on wet soils, with flower stems to 90 cm (2 ft.). Its foliage and that of other species release a heady antiseptic smell when cut or crushed, and its flowers were the original source for salicylic acid, which substance is also found in—and takes its name from—willows. The name of the drug in which it is used, aspirin, derives from *Spiraea*, the earlier generic name for the filipendulas.

Filipendula vulgaris (dropwort; Z3), of which there are several cultivars, grows naturally on drier soils but copes with wet and is particularly useful as a pondside plant in a sunny position. Its milfoil-like foliage and white-flowered (45 cm, 18 in.) racemes have a delicacy which can be overshadowed by the more spectacular, large blowsy pink panicles of *F. rubra* 'Venusta' (Z3) which, given a warm sunny site on a moist soil, can grow to about 1.8 m (6 ft.) in temperate gardens, and up to 2.5 m (8.2 ft.) in warmer climates. The species itself can occur in swampy calcareous meadows and, though now more widespread, occurs naturally in some parts of the central and eastern United States.

Of other Zone 3 plants, the white-flowered Asian *Filipendula palmata* (to 1.2 m, 4 ft.) has several cultivars, and *F. camtschatica* (giant meadowsweet) from eastern Asia can look luxuriantly impressive, reaching 3 m (10 ft.) in good conditions. All divide readily, and some will regenerate naturally, if sporadically, from seed in gardens. Some forms of *F. ulmaria* are vulnerable to mildew that deforms the flower raceme; this is not easily controlled, and since there are resistant forms, mildewed plants are best removed and burnt. Increase is mostly by division, but some will self-sow.

FRAGARIA

STRAWBERRY

ROSACEAE

The familiar cultivated strawberry, so associated with sun and summer, is surprisingly tolerant of wet soil, albeit at the price of increased fruit rot. The widespread wild *Fragaria vesca* (Z5) of northern temperate zones is most often seen on hedgerow banks or in light woodland, but its selection 'Semperflorens', with small, very tasty and long season "alpine strawberries," grows happily on slightly wet soils. I find it is very persistent; a clump can last many years, and seed germinates frequently. For good fruiting, it needs a warm sunny spot. Similarly, cultivars of the runner-producing, cultivated hybrid strawberry *F.* ×*ananassa* will spread very freely on moderately wet soil.

Fragaria Pink Panda (= 'Frel'), grown for its flowers, is recorded as being raised by crossing a strawberry with the pinkish-flowered, avens-like *Potentilla palustris*, and then back crossing. It should thus be even more tolerant of wet soils, though I have not tried to grow it, because I do not find it appealing. I *have* grown the diminutive yellow-flowered, east Asian *Duchesnea indica* (Z8), which was at one time included in *Fragaria*; with its tiny, but tasteless, bright strawberry fruits, it makes a useful ground cover, as it spreads readily by runners.

Most strawberries will increase prolifically from runners on a wet soil, and *Fragaria vesca* 'Semperflorens', though lacking runners, seeds around.

FRITILLARIA

FRITILLARY

LILIACEAE

Though the arrestingly large (to 60 cm, 24 in.) flower stems of the western Asian *Fritillaria imperialis* are cultivated successfully on moist fenland soils, I find it persists on my heavy wet soil only if given a raised bed. Fortunately though, the European *F. meleagris* (snake's head fritillary; Z4) is a plant of wet meadows. I have some that are set in a permanently wet site, where they grow well, but there seems to be some clonal variation: within a batch of bulbs, some will fail while others prosper. Happily the successful forms, even if reduced to a few, eventually increase by daughter bulbs, and seedlings too should regenerate naturally. Fritillary bulbs, particularly *F. imperialis*, have a foxy smell that is obviously a deterrent of sorts to some but not all of its potential pests.

Fritillaries occur across Eurasia and western North America, and more than 80 of these species, and many cultivars, are available in cultivation. Very few are really suited to wet gardens, most requiring a summer "bake"; however, *Fritillaria camschatcensis* (Z4) occupies moist habitats like *F. meleagris*, and *F. uva-vulpis* (Z7) grows in moist soils in Turkey, northern Iraq, and western Iran.

GALANTHUS
SNOWDROP
AMARYLLIDACEAE

Snowdrops, which occur naturally from eastern Europe through Turkey and east to northwestern Iran, can grow well on damp heavy soils, though botrytis and other fungal diseases are sometimes a worry and in areas subject to winter flooding they may die back. On a light sandy soil, bulbs persist better if given a light dressing of clay—the ancient practise of marling. On wet soils, they respond well to life under limes or hazels (whose tree roots dry out the soil in summer), and the cover given by woody plants also suppresses otherwise competitive weeds; such shelter allows bulbs to flower earlier than they would if planted in grass. On wet soils, grass is really too competitive for snowdrops—though they survive. Richard Nutt, an acknowledged authority on *Galanthus*, told me that it is often the case that a garden favours either singles or doubles but rarely both. Mine favours doubles, *G. nivalis* f. *pleniflorus*, which have probably been here since the eighteenth century. The doubles are a bit looked down on in some circles, but I enjoy them.

Galanthus nivalis is hardy to Zone 4, and most other species (including *G. ikariae*, a Great Plant Pick in the Pacific Northwest) are hardy to at least Zone 8. Snowdrops seem to be sufficiently toxic to deter consumption by rodents. Given a surface of leaf mould with no competitive weeds, they will regenerate naturally, but where partic-

TOP *Fritillaria meleagris* (dark chequer form)
ABOVE *Fritillaria meleagris* (white form)

ular plants are required, seed can be taken when ripe and sown and grown on initially in a cold frame. To extend a planting, bulb clumps can be divided regularly after flowering.

GALEGA

GOAT'S RUE

LEGUMINOSAE

The deciduous perennial *Galega officinalis* (Z4) seems very able to tolerate wet soils: here, it has naturalised and can be found growing by riverbanks. It is not a long-lived plant in such conditions in temperate gardens, however, and needs regular propagation. In moist soils, its stems can reach 1.5 m (5 ft.), but when heavy with flower, the otherwise stiff stems are very vulnerable to collapse in wind. The range of *G. officinalis* in central and southern Europe extends to western Asia. A number of garden forms are grown, as is the similar *G. orientalis*. Both can be raised from seed or divided.

RELATED GENERA

Some of the North American baptisias, in the same subfamily (Papilionoideae), are cultivated. *Baptisia alba* var. *macrophylla* (white

HERBACEOUS PLANTS AND BULBS

wild indigo; Z6) can grow to 1.2–2 m (4–6.6 ft.) on wet soils in meadows and along streamsides.

GERANIUM
CRANESBILL
GERANIACEAE

Observing a stand of pale blue-flowered *Geranium pratense* (meadow cranesbill; Z5) growing with a foaming mass of meadowsweet (*Filipendula ulmaria*) on a very wet streamside alluvial soil in Yorkshire gave confidence. Meadow cranesbill, which can grow to 60 cm (2 ft.) or more, and has a wide range in Eurasia, also has many forms, including the old double pictured, all of which provide a dependable display of flowers each year for a garden on heavy soil. However one soon finds the limits of wet tolerance in these herbaceous, mostly perennial, favourites. *Geranium phaeum* (dusky cranesbill; Z5) from the mountains of central and southern and western Europe, for example, grows reasonably well on wet soil but soon diminishes if growing on fully saturated soil over winter. A raised bed can overcome this problem and also allows the cultivation of its many garden forms, such as the blotched-leaf *G. phaeum* var. *phaeum* 'Samobor' and descriptively named 'Blue Shadow' and 'Rose Madder', though these are weaker growing; *G. phaeum* 'Album' seems particularly poor on a wet soil.

Geranium macrorrhizum (Z4) from southern Europe grows well as a ground cover in wet woodland, and it is reasonably tolerant of wet soil. Its many cultivated varieties—the intense magenta-flowered 'Czakor', the lighter magenta-pink 'Bevan's Variety', or (my favourite) the rose-pink 'Ingwersen's Variety', originally collected in Montenegro—all have this species' aromatic swollen rhizomatous stems and mounds of soft green foliage, and all grow well in both sun and partial shade on wet soil. And, using a slightly raised bed, the list extends with *G. clarkei* 'Kashmir White', *G. endressii* from the western Pyrenees, and *G. himalayense* 'Gravetye' (all Z4), which are long-lived on wet, but not saturated soils, as are *G. gracile* (Z7), *G. nodosum* (Z6), and *G. sylvaticum* (Z7). More surprisingly, one of the giant herb-roberts, a hybrid of the short-lived *G. maderense* and *G. palmatum*, both from Madeira, overwinters and flowers on permanently moist soil in Zone 8 and, though it dies after flowering, its seedlings will regenerate freely on wet gravel.

The familiar weedy northern temperate herb-robert itself, *Gera-*

TOP *Geranium phaeum*
ABOVE *Geranium pratense* 'Plenum Violaceum', a double form

A nursery selection of
Geum ×*intermedium*

nium robertianum (Z6), can withstand both moist shade and sunny dry soils, as can many of its compatriots. A word of warning, however: some hybrid geraniums, such as *G.* ×*oxonianum* (*G. endressii* × *G. versicolor*), can, on a moist soil, grow so excessively that they swamp all around, as can the Himalayan *G. procurrens*. This latter is a parent of *G.* 'Ann Folkard', which seems very slow to establish on my wet soil, and its leaves are chlorotic early in the season, suggesting it would prefer more warmth than received in Zone 8. More difficult, though, is the task of finding companion plants that can harmonise with its strong magenta-coloured flowers.

Seed is small and often explosively ejected from the seedpod, while the pod itself is characteristic (and gives cranesbills their common and generic names). With the hardy perennial and biennial species, seed can be sown when fresh or held over winter in cold storage for spring sowing, though some such as *Geranium sylvaticum* are very variable from seed. *In situ* division of the clump-forming perennials can be undertaken at most times—if it is cool and moist. The divisions will collapse if it is too hot and dry. Spring is the best time for regeneration when many plants are required and the divisions can be reduced to single shoots. If a cold frame is available, numbers can be quickly bulked up.

GEUM
AVENS
ROSACEAE

Many of these useful and hardy, clump-forming herbaceous perennials are grown in gardens for their long season of flower, and some can hold their leaves over winter. They are widespread, occurring in the temperate zones of both hemispheres. Geums tolerate drier soils but are not then so long-lived; some of the montane species need good drainage.

Geum urbanum (wood avens) can become very weedy in gardens. It has small yellow flowers on stems to around 70 cm (28 in.) and forms a globose seedhead of hooked achenes, which catch on fur or clothing and thus can spread widely. I let this native European (also in western Asia and North Africa) grow where it pleases in the wilder parts of the garden, but it establishes best under trees where soil is moist and competition from other plants is limited. The smaller *G. rivale* (water avens; 20–40 cm, 8–16 in.; Z3), which occurs widely in Europe, Asia Minor, and North America, has larger attractively nodding flowers, and the several cultivated forms show a range of colours from dusky pink or purple-red to yellow and apricot, with its sepals adding a contrasting colour, often purplish. It is much more a plant of wet soils but not often seen in gardens. The hybrid *G. ×intermedium* occurs naturally where these two species meet, and selected forms for gardens combine the most attractive characters of both parents' flowers, having large yellow petals with brownish purple sepals. Happily, it also grows well on wet soils, keeping winter leaves.

Most garden hybrids, including those from the southern European *Geum coccineum* (Z5), are happy on wet soils and are easily propagated by division in spring. Those that include the parentage of *G. chiloense* (Z7/8), from Chile and Peru, form more open attractive flowers and also keep their leaves in winter. *Geum* 'Dolly North' has deep orange flowers, and the semi-double; *G.* 'Mrs. J. Bradshaw' has scarlet flowers. Geums can be seed raised, and some cultivars come true, but many are increased by division.

GLADIOLUS

IRIDACEAE

While the sumptuous, large-flowered, hybrid gladioli find a place in temperate gardens worldwide, their half-hardy nature means that they are frequently treated like expendable summer bedding, and few gardeners attempt to grow the many charming species. Fortunately several species tolerate wet soils. I have been amazed by the performance of *Gladiolus papilio* (Z8) from Natal, which has grown vigorously for me over the last ten years in a stodgily winter-wet but sunny bed, flowering abundantly in late summer. The flower spikes grow to 1 m (3.3 ft.) or more, and the flowers are a subtle fusion of purple and green. Producing new bulbs on underground runners, it soon spreads to form a large clump.

In central Europe *Gladiolus palustris* (swamp gladiolus) and *G. imbricatus* (both Z6) inhabit damp to boggy upland meadows. Some South African gladioli are also tolerant of wet soils; these include *G. cardinalis* (crimson waterfall gladiolus), *G. angustus* (which grows by streams and marshes), and the sweetly scented *G. tristis* var. *concolor*, a small but reliably hardy clump of which grew at Kew among the roots of *Magnolia virginiana* in the 1950s.

Gladiolus tristis, known in the Cape as the marsh Afrikaner, occurs in marshy ground in winter rainfall areas, at altitudes up to 1800 m (5906 ft.). Imagine, then, my joy in finding that it has not only survived for some years on my wet soil but flourished, producing

Gladiolus tristis var. *concolor*

masses of creamy blossomed spikes in early summer and regenerating small bulblets all around. I planted it outside, close to the outer wall of an unheated greenhouse, thinking it would thus get some extra reflected light and shelter, particularly since it keeps its foliage in winter. Such are my life's pleasures. Increase from daughter bulbs.

GRAMINEAE

GRASS FAMILY

Also known as Poaceae. The grasses form a very large family of cosmopolitan distribution, and one that has great economic value, as crop plants (cereals, sugar cane), forage grasses, construction materials (bamboos, thatching stems), and amenity for sports turf and lawns. A number of other grass-like plants, sometimes grouped in cultivation with grasses, belong to the families Cyperaceae, Juncaceae, and Typhaceae.

Grasses may be annual or perennial, tufted or rhizomatous herbs, or perennials with woody culms (flowering stems) and rootstocks. Most, but not all, have stems with solid nodes and hollow internodes, and, as is seen in many monocots, each node possesses a bud or growing point. Leaves are linear, lance-shaped, and mostly alternate and two-ranked. The distinctiveness of grasses is seen particularly in their leaves, which consist of three parts, the sheath, ligule, and blade. Flowers are mainly bisexual, though some are dioecious, and an upper and lower bract (glume) encloses each grass flower. The inflorescence is invariably terminal and formed as a spike or spikelets. Pollen is wind-borne and often a trigger for hay fever.

Grasses are adapted to many habitats and, happily for wet gardens, those that grow well on wet soil are mostly large and impressive perennials. These large grasses tend to be long-lived, requiring little attention other than division when they become too large for their allotted sites. Generally grasses are undemanding garden plants, and a gardener's main concern must relate to their potential invasiveness. The annuals, for example, seed freely, and weeding out grasses from other plants—or worse, among other grasses, which means spotting and identifying them as seedlings—can be a demanding task. Grasses with running rhizomes are very invasive, so those used in flowerbeds should be of the tufted or short rhizome types. Where unwanted seeding, or pests and diseases, are a problem, then the plants may be clipped over in autumn. However, most gardeners like to leave the culms over winter for their frost-tinged

beauty (and the birds), clipping off dead growth in late winter or early spring.

Seed should be sown when fresh, unless it is kept in a cold store under controlled conditions, since viability falls quickly after one season. Cuttings may be used for some tropicals. Division, using a sharp knife or spade (depending upon the size of the clump), is the most popular means of propagating hardy grasses; with cold wet soil, this is often better left until spring, when plants can subsequently recover and grow away.

Less familiar grasses for wet situations come from several genera. Starting with hardy genera, *Beckmannia syzigachne* (American slough-grass; Z5) is a wide-ranging annual or short-lived perennial, growing 50–100 cm (20–40 in.); it occurs as a casual introduction in Britain.

Bromus ramosus (wood brome; Z5) from Eurasia has 1.2–2 m (4–6.6 ft.) culms and grows in damp woodland.

Hierochloe odorata (vanilla grass; Z5), which occurs by riverbanks in Ireland and Scotland, Eurasia, and North America, forms compact 20–50 cm (8–20 in.) tufts of notably fragrant leaves (when cut) and golden brown spikes.

The perennial *Holcus mollis* (creeping soft-grass; Z5) is seen by gardeners as a weed of lawns and borders. Its tough, string-like rhi-

A wet summer meadow with *Holcus mollis* and docks, in flower

zomes can be a concern, but it grows well on heavy soil (20–100 cm, 8–40 in.), and its pink and white flowering culms can give a lovely effect in a meadow. Also, it usefully binds the surface of wet soils and is often an early coloniser of open soils (it is later shaded out by trees). Its less vigorous variegated form 'Albovariegatus' is often grown in gardens, as is 'White Fog'. Similarly attractive in flower is *H. lanatus* (Yorkshire-fog).

Three large American grasses for wet sites are *Spartina pectinata* (prairie cord-grass; Z5), which can grow to 1.8 m (6 ft.) in warmer conditions (thus the weaker variegated 'Aureomarginata' is preferred for gardens); *Tripsacum dactyloides* (eastern gamma grass; Z6), which grows by streamsides and can reach 3 m (10 ft.) in summer warm climates; and *Zizania aquatica* (1–2 m, 3.3–6.6 ft.; Z6), the annual wild rice. All have a shorter (by about one-third) stature when grown in cooler temperate regions. Seed of wild rice is much sought by wild fowl; it germinates in damp soil, and seedlings grow on in shallow (5 cm, 2 in.) water.

Among tropical grasses, two that tolerate wet soils and are seen as good pot plant subjects in temperate regions are *Oplismenus hirtellus* 'Variegatus' and *Stenotaphrum secundatum* 'Variegatum'. The oplismenus is a small, thin-stemmed trailing grass with attractive green and white striped leaves, useful in hanging baskets or to trail over and hide the sides of large plant tubs; it can easily trail 60–80 cm (24–31 in.) in one season. If kept too dry it tends to take on a reddish purple hue. Under glass, it is readily propagated early in the year from simple herbaceous stem cuttings. The stoloniferous stenotaphrum (St. Augustine or buffalo grass) can be used as an ornamental lawn grass in the tropics (minimum 5°C, 41°F). Coincidentally, the growth of many temperate lawn grasses slows to a standstill below this temperature.

GUNNERA

GUNNERACEAE

Gunnera manicata, from Colombia and southern Brazil, was uncommon in private gardens before the fashion for strong or architectural plant form increased its popularity. It is usually set by a pond but tolerates drier soil if given shade. In a warm boggy site, the leaves can grow to 2 m (6.6 ft.) or more, and its large, narrow-conical flower spikes can reach 1.5 m (5 ft.). The leaves are susceptible to, and blackened by, the first heavy frost of autumn, but its large, horizontally growing rhizome-like stem is fairly hardy. Though formerly

Gunnera manicata

it was usual to protect the overwintering stems from severe cold by thatching the plant with straw or other herbaceous material, this species is now grown in Zone 8 without winter protection. On a wet soil, it spreads quickly to form a 4–5 m (13–16 ft.) wide clump. With such large spiny leaves, plants should be sited well back from paths, as well as away from any smaller plants that will be suppressed by the early season's leaves slowly lowering to the ground as the summer progresses. Growing this gunnera under the shade of trees can reduce its size by about one-third, which makes it more manageable—if less spectacular. *Gunnera tinctoria* (Z7) from Argentina and Chile is very similar but forms a smaller clump (1–2 m, 3.3–6.6 ft.).

There are about forty-five species of *Gunnera* in the southern temperate regions. All are rhizomatous perennial herbs, some clump-forming, some trailing, and their leaves are stalked and have stipules. Of the smaller species, the mat-forming *G. magellanica* (Z7) from southern South America, with leaves to 9 cm (3.5 in.), is more frequently cultivated than *G. prorepens* (Z8) from New Zealand, which needs winter protection.

The polygamous inflorescence of *Gunnera manicata* is formed as a very large densely branched spike or panicle of many small flowers; these are zoned, with the upper flowers being male, and the lower

TOP *Hakonechloa macra* 'Aureola'
ABOVE *Hedychium densiflorum*

female, with sometimes bisexual flowers between these two zones. Some are dioecious. Seed, if available, is sown in a cold frame and kept moist, but division is the usual method of increase. With *G. manicata* the thick branching stem often forms tennisball-sized buds at its base and these quickly produce root initials. These buds can be cut off and grown on. It is also possible to transplant large clumps successfully using a large tractor's hydraulic bucket! As another approach to *in situ* propagation, the growing end of the main stem can be easily cut off with a saw when dormant and used as a giant cutting; though slow to recover (and the terminal bud may die), lateral buds will then emerge and grow away after about a year.

HAKONECHLOA

GRAMINEAE

The image of a variegated hakonechloa arching its thin stems of narrow, forward-facing leaves over mossy rocks in a Japanese garden epitomises this lovely plant. In this genus, there is but a single, rhizomatous, small-growing (30 cm, 12 in.), deciduous-stemmed perennial species from Japan, where it occurs in wet mountain forests on Honshu. *Hakonechloa macra* (Z5/6) merits the effort of finding it a moist but reasonably drained site in any garden. Several different, and very attractive, variegated leaf forms are available in cultivation. Increase by division.

HEDYCHIUM

GINGER LILY
ZINGIBERACEAE

Increasingly popular of late, these erect-stemmed, rhizomatous herbs form their attractive inflorescences at the end of a long leafy shoot. Leaves are usually two-ranked, and the fruit is a capsule. The subtropical and heavily perfumed *Hedychium coronarium* (Z9/10) will grow happily in boggy conditions in a subtropical garden. Though originally ranging from India to Indonesia, it has since naturalised in Central America and other damp places worldwide. Interestingly, this species has hybridised with others including the very weedy but beautiful *H. gardnerianum* (Z9/10).

Most other hedychiums grow well on very moist soils. In a frost-free environment, the stunning Himalayan (Bhutan, Sikkim, Assam) *Hedychium greenii*, with its bright red blossoms and maroon reverse to its leaves, grows to about 2 m (6.6 ft.) tall, whereas if planted against the outside wall of a heated building in Zone 8, it only just survives

HERBACEOUS PLANTS AND BULBS

with its summer shoots reaching about 60–90 cm (2–3 ft.). Several Himalayan hedychiums are now grown in warm sheltered temperate gardens, tolerating a few degrees of frost. The pseudostems of *H. densiflorum* (Z8/9) and other hardier species are deciduous, which for colder gardens makes it easier to lift and store the rhizomes over winter.

Most are propagated by division of the rhizome. Where the pseudostems die back fully in winter, this becomes a simple operation, if dealt with when repotting into fresh soil ahead of the new growing season. *Hedychium greenii* produces small aerial plantlets (bulbils) around its inflorescences, which can be detached and grown on. Seed, when available, is best cleaned of its outer coat and sown early in the year at 18°C (64°F) minimum or warmer.

Helenium 'Rubinzwerg'

RELATED GENERA

More and more moist-soil genera (*Roscoea, Zingiber*) from the ginger family may be tried, and not just in subtropical climates. For example, *Cautleya spicata* 'Robusta', with rich maroon-bracted heads and orange-yellow flowers held on 60 cm (2 ft.) stems of dark green leaves, is now seen even in Zone 8 gardens.

HELENIUM

COMPOSITAE

A splendid and long-lasting summer display from *Helenium* 'Rubinzwerg', a hardy perennial helenium on a wet but not saturated soil, came as a pleasing surprise, though the yellow-flowered American parent of this and most hybrids, *H. autumnale* (45–120 cm, 18–48 in.; Z3), occurs in moist open places, including wet ditches and streambanks. Increase *H. autumnale* hybrids by division. Happily, my skin is not in any way allergic to these plants, though some people are affected.

HELIANTHUS

SUNFLOWER
COMPOSITAE

The New World sunflowers offer several wet-soil-tolerant, hardy perennials as well as some that are slightly tender. The familiar *Helianthus ×multiflorus* (*H. annuus × H. decapetalus*; Z5) and *H. ×laetiflorus* (*H. pauciflorus × H. tuberosus*; Z4) are both able to live in very moist soil. *Helianthus angustifolius* (Z6) is the swamp sunflower, *H. decapetalus* (Z5) occurs in wet pine savannas, and *H. heterophyllus*

Helleborus ×*hybridus* flowering in snow

(Z8/9) is the bog sunflower from Louisiana. The only concern I have noted with these plants on wet soil is the occasional loss of stems to fungal infection. Given a warm sunny site, they can grow from 90 cm (36 in.) up to 2 m (6.6 ft.), giving great value to the summer garden, flowering profusely as they do over a long period. Increase mainly by division.

HELLEBORUS

HELLEBORE
RANUNCULACEAE

Hellebores are justly popular herbaceous perennials, offering a huge array of cultivars. The short-stemmed *Helleborus foetidus* can make a large impressive woodland ground cover and will seed around. This is fortunate, because on damper soils, it is susceptible to disease and is anyway short-lived; it is happier on light soils over chalk and limestone. Similarly, though they are tolerant of wet soil, neither the larger-stemmed *H. argutifolius* (Corsican hellebore) and its hybrid progeny nor *H. niger* (Christmas rose) grow well in heavy wet conditions. Fortunately *H. orientalis* (Lenten rose), from northern Greece, northern Turkey, and the Caucasus, has crossed with other species to produce a complex group of hybrids and segregates in cultivation that cope well with a damp soil. These *H.* ×*hybridus* forms respond well to fertilisers by producing a strong flowering display and are hardy to Zone 6, with clumps surviving for many years.

Seedlings of *Helleborus* ×*hybridus* germinate in abundance around the parent plants. They will also usefully grow in borders on the north and east face of building walls. Seedlings take two to three years to reach flowering size, thereafter increasing in size and the number of flowers they produce each year. Little troubles them but, since most very young seedlings are likely to be eaten by molluscs, any required are best lifted and pricked out into pots. Unless seedlings are particularly required (and they do come fairly true to their parent), it is best to clip off the seedpods before they ripen. Ants distribute the seed of some hellebores. Clonal forms are increased by division of the rhizomatous rootstock after flowering.

HELONIAS

MELANTHIACEAE

Helonias bullata (swamp pink; Z6) from the eastern United States (New York State and at higher elevations from Pennsylvania south to east Virginia) is a clump-forming, rhizomatous perennial herb.

Its small bright pink flowers with blue anthers are formed as a tight head on small stems (35–45 cm, 14–18 in.) that hold them well above its ground-hugging foliage. At home in bogs and swamps, when in flower it can form an unusual waterside planting, and it has overwintered with me for several years on a cold, wet soil. Clumps increase slowly, but division is possible, and best in spring, as the new leaves emerge.

HEMEROCALLIS

DAYLILY
HEMEROCALLIDACEAE

A genus of more than twenty species of herbaceous perennials mainly from the temperate Far East. Their lax linear leaves may persist over winter in some species and hybrids, while others die down completely, and these deciduous daylilies tend to be hardier. Species mentioned here are hardy to Zone 4, and some hybrids are rated Zone 2. Daylilies have short rhizomes, often with some swollen or fleshy roots. Their colourful flowers are short-lived, "one-day opening," either nocturnally (evening and night) or diurnally. A number (the fragrant *Hemerocallis citrina*, some hybrids) have a flower-opening period that extends from late afternoon to noon the following day. The tepals are united at their bases, and the flowers are held on a raceme or panicle.

Hemerocallis can be found growing naturally in wet meadows along river valleys and on mountainsides, or as part of the ground flora in mixed forests. In northern China, *Hemerocallis minor* (grass-leaved daylily), which has a range beyond China's boundaries, is an important plant of wet meadows, while the tall *H. lilioasphode-lus* (syn. *H. flava*; lemon daylily) occurs in larch (*Larix gmelinii* var. *olgensis*) swamp forest in northeastern China. Some species, such as the small (30 cm, 12 in.) grass-like *H. forrestii* from Yunnan, tolerate slightly dry periods. All the specialist books play safe by recommending a free-drained soil for daylilies. While this is wise advice in the pursuit of optimum growth and flowering, I find, as a group, hemerocallis are extremely tolerant of wet soils in cultivation.

There are literally tens of thousands of cultivars now registered, and these represent a wide range of forms in terms of size, flower type, and colour. The Royal Horticultural Society gives Awards of Garden Merit (AGMs) to the best cultivars, but I do not find all modern cultivars grow as well on my wet soil as do the species and older hybrids, which are very tough plants, surviving even in neglected

TOP *Helonias bullata*
CENTER *Hemerocallis* 'Hyperion'
ABOVE *Hemerocallis* 'Chicago Picotee Lace'

gardens where borders have returned to weeds and grass. Some of the more vigorous are thus thought of as weedy, but many diminutive cultivars have been produced for small gardens. Though tolerant of shade, they all flower better with sun and moisture, and a neutral to slightly acid soil is preferred. The early spring emergent shoots on some may be chlorotic until the days warm, when they turn green, and a sustained temperature above 16°C (60°F) will initiate flowering.

My first "encounter" with hemerocallis in eastern China was a salad that included their fresh, pea-flavoured flower buds; later in Sichuan, I enjoyed the young buds stir-fried in a wok with garlic in oil. Nowadays, I can only just bear to lose my own flowers by such disbudding—not for eating, but to remove the hemerocallis gall midge (*Contarinia quinquenotata*), which has recently appeared on one of my plants and lays eggs in the young flower buds, preventing their further development. If this does not prove effective, treat the ground around the plant with a persistent but safe insecticide; alternatively, choose later-flowering cultivars.

Division is the usual means of increase. This simple operation is best carried out in early spring, when new growth starts, though full flowering recovery may take two growing seasons. To keep the clump flowering, divide plants every three years, digging manure or compost into the soil before replanting. Scarce cultivated forms are often micropropagated.

Fresh seed may be sown in autumn and held in a cold frame over winter for germination in spring, or the seed can be refrigerated over winter for spring sowing. Seeds will germinate as the temperature rises. Seedlings may be grown on in pots or a nursery soil bed, and they transplant readily. First flowering may take three to four years. However, seedlings from hybrids will vary in flower from their parent.

HEUCHERA
CORAL-BELLS
SAXIFRAGACEAE

Few of the approximately fifty-five species of *Heuchera* are seen in gardens; it is the many cultivars of these small herbaceous perennials that are popularly grown, chiefly for their attractive, often-marbled foliage, which is more or less evergreen in sheltered situations. Plants form compact clumps, and flowers are held on thin stems, 10–40 cm (4–16 in.) tall. Breeding has intensified both flower and foliage colours. Though ranging widely in North America, most species come from the western mountains and the Appalachians, where they generally grow in woodland, some along streambanks, others in drier situations. They grow well on my wet soil in summer, but winter wet in cold conditions can cause problems, and this tends to make them short-lived. On cold wet soils, therefore, it is essential to site them on a raised bed and divide them regularly, though most are hardy to Zone 6 or lower; they seem otherwise very amenable to cultivation. They do need reasonable light levels to flower well and can die back where there is too much competition from large trees. Regular division keeps all heucheras growing and flowering well. Given good recovery conditions, offsets can be removed throughout the growing season, and summer cuttings can also be taken. Seeds and seedlings are small and slow growing and will take a year to form a plant large enough to plant out.

Several good intergeneric hybrids with *Tiarella* have been raised, and these (×*Heucherella*) too grow well on moist soils.

Hordeum jubatum

HORDEUM

BARLEY
GRAMINEAE

I must confess it was with some trepidation that I planted *Hordeum jubatum* (foxtail barley; Z5) on wet soil. Not suitable for barleys, was my thought. But this grass has given me great pleasure every year since, behaving as an overwintering biennial. Its beautifully curving long-awned heads (12.5 cm, 5 in.) shatter early, and the seed germinates, even in the wettest spots, to provide overwintering seedlings that flower the following summer. Growing to 30–45 cm (12–18 in.), it occurs naturally in North America down to Mexico and across in northeastern Asia; I was pleased to note, however (in confirmation of its behaviour with me), that in Alaska it occurs on riverbanks. Seedlings have lightly glaucous, upright leaves, which helps differentiate them from weed grasses.

HOSTA

PLANTAIN-LILY
HOSTACEAE

The familiar hostas are clump-forming, rhizomatous herbs from China, Japan, and Korea. Most are grown for their attractively pat-

Hosta 'Halcyon'

terned long-stalked basal leaves, though some have been selected for their bell- or trumpet-shaped flowers, in shades of blue or white, which form a loose head on an erect, usually unbranched stem.

Hostas are really tough and obliging plants in cultivation, able to grow in many situations while, each year, the size of the clump increases. They are generally unperturbed by heavy soils and seem to thrive in moist, shaded sites, though some exposure to sun is needed for good flowering and strong leaf colour. In this last character particularly, the gardener is spoilt for choice: the range of foliage colours is extraordinary. Two hostas that have been with me all my gardening life, on both dry and wet soils, are the spring gold of *Hosta fortunei* var. *albopicta* f. *aurea* and the vigorous (25–38 cm, 10–15 in.) glaucous-leaved *H. sieboldiana* var. *elegans*, with lavender flowers on 60 cm (2 ft.) stems. For fragrant flowers, the pale-green-leaved *H. plantaginea* from southern China has white flowers on stems 60 cm (2 ft.) or taller; one of its hybrids, *H.* 'Honeybells' has robust racemes up to 100 cm (40 in.) that carry a light fragrance from its pale white, lilac-lined flowers. All are hardy to Zone 4.

Most who grow hostas are all too aware of the many garden molluscs that can reduce their attractive leaves to netted skeletons, and though the leaves will come again next spring, the shredded remains are unsightly. Controlling slugs and snails is, however, a worry: poisonous baits have an effect on other wildlife. One option, where large numbers of slugs exist (as often happens on wet sites) is to grow the plants in large containers, which reduces attacks and makes control easier. As the use of garden chemicals is ever more restricted by legislation, it is at least encouraging to know that molluscs are severely deterred by garlic oil! Ferric phosphate formulations, too, are safer and can be effective. Biological control in the form of nematodes is also now available but not always effective. For my own garden, I encourage mollusc-eating song thrushes, hedgehogs, and amphibians, and tend to plant thicker-leaved, "mollusc resistant" hostas.

Because most seedlings will not carry their parent's particular leaf variegation or colours, division is the normal practise. For hostas, this is a simple process, and clumps can readily be divided from autumn on, whenever the ground is workable. The clumps are tightly bound and may need to be cut; a large clump can provide a dozen or more separate pieces for immediate replanting, but it is worth remembering that hostas are slow to recover. Larger pieces will give quicker recovery and effect.

HOUTTUYNIA

SAURURACEAE

Houttuynia cordata (Z5) ranges from the Himalayas to far-eastern Asia; its many selected forms include the widely grown 'Chameleon', with its red, cream, and green variegated leaves, and one that is double-bracted. The species grows to 50–60 cm (20–24 in.) on thin stems, and its white-bracted terminal inflorescences are attractive. It occurs naturally as a perennial ground cover herb in both broadleaf and evergreen rainforest in China. Useful on wet soil, and at the water's edge, it can also tolerate drier parts of the garden. It needs summer warmth to grow well, and its new shoots can be caught by frost.

Its underground runners are strongly aromatic and spread freely. They have been served to me several times as a cooked dish in remote parts of Guizhou, western China—at least I was told it was this plant, though its cooked runners are not readily identified other than by their strong taste! An acquired taste, seemingly. The aromatic leaves are also eaten. Because of houttuynia's ready production of runners, it is normally propagated by this means.

HYACINTHACEAE

HYACINTH FAMILY

To my surprise I have found that most hyacinths tolerate a heavy wet soil with part shade; the dark blue cultivars of *Hyacinthus orientalis* (which species occurs naturally from Turkey to Iran) have flowered well for me in such a position for more than twenty years. Over this time, as is usual, the flower spikes have become more open, but they are still attractive and sweetly scented.

Given a warm climate, some southern African bulbs from this family can also grow on somewhat moist soil—*Galtonia* and *Eucomis* (pineapple lily), for example. If topped with gravel, or set in slightly raised beds, other genera—*Chionodoxa, Muscari, Ornithogalum, Puschkinia, Scilla*—can all be grown on an otherwise wet site. *Eucomis comosa* includes marshes within its range of natural habitats; and against the rules, self-sown *E. zambesiaca* seed not only germinated in my garden on open ground, but the bulbs grew to flowering over three to five years, unprotected on a cold wet, but not waterlogged, soil.

TOP *Houttuynia cordata* 'Chameleon'
ABOVE *Ornithogalum umbellatum* (star-of-Bethlehem), from Europe and the eastern Mediterranean, naturalises well in part shade but needs sun to open its flowers.

HYACINTHOIDES

BLUEBELL
HYACINTHACEAE

The bulbs of the western European bluebell, *Hyacinthoides non-scripta* (Z5) grow well in light woodland, on both dry sandy and heavy wet soils. So too does the more robust *H. hispanica*, from southwestern Europe and North Africa. Flower spikes (to 50 cm, 20 in.) of *H. non-scripta* are one-sided with curving tips, contrasting with *H. hispanica*'s larger broader flowers on an upright spike, but these two hybridise.

Increase is by division and can conveniently be undertaken as the young shoots emerge from the bulbs in winter. Natural spread by seedlings depends upon the presence of suitable mycorrhizal fungi. In woodland, *Hyacinthoides non-scripta* requires only moderate shade (as under oaks); plants will gradually die out under very competitive shade.

HYMENOCALLIS

SPIDER-LILY
AMARYLLIDACEAE

The lovely, usually deliciously scented and white-flowered *Hymenocallis* species from the New World can grace tropical and subtropical gardens with moist soils, forming clumps 60 cm to 1 m (2–3.3 ft.) in height. As with most amaryllids, their flowers are formed in umbels; less commonly, a corona, formed like a small cap, joins the bases of the stamens.

In the southern United States, *Hymenocallis caroliniana* (Z9) occurs naturally in wet places; further north, while a few of the deciduous species can grow in warm and sheltered sites (even in Britain), their late-season flowers can be caught by frost. Thus, species such as the small *H. harrisiana* (Z10) from Mexico are best grown in containers and held dry in a cold frame over winter, though they still need some warmth to get them started in summer. All the many evergreen species from the West Indies and South America are worth cultivating in warm regions. They increase naturally from daughter bulbs.

IMPATIENS

BALSAM
BALSAMINACEAE

Brightly coloured *Impatiens* hybrids now make their appearance in temperate countries as popular plants for summer bedding and hanging baskets. Many species are denizens of wet forest margins and riversides. Most occur in Asia, from the Himalayas to India, China, and Japan, and southeast to New Guinea and the Solomon Islands. They also occur in tropical and subtropical Africa; one reaches into Europe, and half a dozen occur in North America down to Mexico. Although none are frost hardy, the Indian *I. flaccida*, the East African *I. walleriana*, and the New Guinea hybrids derived from *I. schlechteri* are all widely cultivated for their long season of flower. Hardier species survive winter cold as seed or tubers; the annual species, with their efficient seed dispersal, can become weedy. Such is the case with the lovely tall (1–2 m, 3.3–6.6 ft.) pink-flowered *I. glandulifera* (Himalayan balsam; Z7), which has established along riversides here, and with the North American *I. capensis* (orange balsam; Z2), a plant of damp shady places in its natural habitat. Some of the Indian species, such as *I. campanulata* (Z10), form tuberous roots, as does the African *I. tinctoria* (Z9), which is cultivated in warm spots in temperate gardens, with its rootstock lifted and stored frost-free over winter.

Impatiens are mostly annual or perennial herbs, though some are almost shrubby, with a single or simply branched stem that is thickened and often watery-translucent. Their stalked leaves have a simple blade and may be alternate or whorled, and their leaf stalks often have noticeable glands. The resupinate flowers are readily recognisable as balsams because of the long or short spurs formed from their lower sepal. Of their five petals, the laterals may be fused into two pairs with the fifth free petal often forming a hood. Their fruit is mostly a fleshy capsule that explodes at the touch when ripe, flinging out its seeds with force.

Balsams grow well with good light, warmth, and moisture. Cold weather and wind depress growth, and their soft stems and foliage make them susceptible to attack by aphids and red spider (the latter particularly if plants are grown dry). The firmer-stemmed perennial species will rot if kept too wet in low temperatures; those with soft succulent stems collapse when desiccated. Almost all the perennials root readily from soft stem cuttings, even if just set in a jar of water. Seed is used to raise annuals and many of the bedding plants—but first you have to catch it! With a bag to hand, almost-ripe capsules can be very carefully picked and put into the bag to explode later, or the ripe capsule can be covered by a small bag before touching or detaching the pod.

INULA

YELLOWHEAD
COMPOSITAE

Inula helenium (elecampane) has long been cultivated for its medicinal properties (it is used to treat respiratory diseases), but the inulas are also spectacular summer-flowering herbs, some with flowering spikes towering 1.8 m (6 ft.) or more, bearing thin-liguled yellow daisy flowers. These compound flowers are large, 12.5–15 cm (5–6 in.) in diameter. Most inulas prefer moist soils, but some, like *I. magnifica* (2 m, 6.6 ft.) from the Caucasus, tolerate very wet soil and compete successfully when naturalised among coarse grasses. *Inula orientalis* (60–90 cm, 24–36 in.) is often seen in gardens, but it is not as tolerant of cold wet soil as *I. magnifica*; and certainly smaller-growing species like the Himalayan *I. hookeri* (60 cm, 24 in.), which prefer damp soil, seem to need reasonable drainage, fading away over winter in very wet soils. Where bare soils or gravel occurs, seedlings will regenerate naturally, or use division. All are hardy to Zone 6.

IRIS

IRIDACEAE

Irises are essential to wet gardens but, beyond avoiding the popular bearded irises, I do not see the need to restrict one's choice to water irises. The most unexpected iris success for me has been with the bulbous Dutch irises that are often seen as florist's flowers. They are hybrids of *Iris xiphium* (Spanish iris), from southwest Europe, and the related North African *I. tingitana*. The sky-blue Dutch iris 'Ideal' never fails in my wet soil beds, flowering and increasing over decades. Each year it renews its shining green, U-channelled leaves (to 70 cm, 28 in.) in October, and these hold crisply over winter, not fading until well after late spring flowering. With the protection of a house wall, Dutch irises can flower two to three weeks earlier than plants grown out in an exposed open bed. *Iris latifolia*, the parent of the now little grown but related English iris cultivars, occurs in wet meadows in the Pyrenees and Cantabria.

Winter-flowering *Iris unguicularis* (Z7/8) and its forms and relatives, from North Africa and around to Syria and Turkey, expect warm dry conditions, such as against the wall of a heated house, if they are to flower well. I have one clone that thrives in such a spot on my wet soil, but when grown in moister conditions it tends to produce more leaf. This iris has short rhizomes and tufts of lax leaves to about 60 cm (2 ft.). The smaller-flowered *I. lazica* from northern

TOP *Inula magnifica*
ABOVE *Iris confusa* from Niba Shan, western Sichuan

Turkey and the southwestern Caucasus is also slightly more tolerant of wet soils.

For a boggy soil, the range of suitable hardy rhizomatous iris is considerable. The blue *Iris spuria* (30–90 cm, 12–36 in.; Z5), which is naturalised locally in fens and distributed from southern Europe and Algeria across to the west Himalayas, produces especially interesting forms in Turkey and Iran, where it grows in saline meadows as well as by riversides. There are several bog irises in North America. The violet-blue-flowered *I. versicolor* (Z3) comes from eastern North America; its selection 'Kermesiana' has purple-red flowers. *Iris versicolor* is sometimes called the northern blue flag to distinguish it from *I. virginica* (southern blue flag), which is considered to be of borderline hardiness though its range extends to the Great Lakes region. *Iris versicolor* is naturalised in parts of Britain, as is *I. ×robusta*, the hybrid between it and southern blue flag; *I. ×robusta* 'Gerald Darby' (Z4) has a dark purple colouring on the lower part of its leaves, and flowering stems to about 60 cm (2 ft.) with me.

The beautiful red iris from Louisiana, *Iris fulva* (copper iris; to 90 cm, 36 in.; Z7), is worth trying as it extends the iris season by flowering perhaps a month after mid-summer; also known as the bronze iris, it grows around marshes in Missouri. Even more tender and smaller is the zigzag-stemmed *I. brevicaulis* from southern Louisiana, another denizen of pond or swamp margins. A great many fine cultivar Louisiana iris hybrids have been raised, and these ensure that irises can be grown in the wettest of warm temperate gardens.

Continuing around the northern temperate zone, in which the world's 250 species of *Iris* occur, I find the delicate pale blue flowers of the East Asian paddy-field iris *I. laevigata* (Z4) entrancing, especially in its form 'Variegata', where the striped foliage provides a harmonising foil for the flowers on 45 cm (18 in.) stems. In Zone 8 it dies right back in winter and grows well in boot-suckingly wet soil. In Japan the many cultivars of *I. ensata* are very popular. These bold flowers demand attention and are held high on stems up to 1 m (3.3 ft.). They too will grow in permanently wet soil, and they set abundant viable seed from which seedlings can be raised to flower in two years. I grow some shocking purple seedlings raised from wild plants growing in Hokkaido.

TOP *Iris ×robusta* 'Gerald Darby'
ABOVE *Iris sibirica*

Similarly happy on boggy soil is the yellow-flowered *Iris forrestii* (Z6) from eastern Tibet, southwest Sichuan, and northern Yunnan. For wet soil, as opposed to submerged or standing water, these and the delicate Siberian irises are another delight. There are dozens of fine cultivars of *I. sibirica* (Z4), but the blue-flowered species itself remains my favourite plant; it grows naturally in wet meadows and wood marsh in Europe and Siberia, but it is becoming less abundant. As with most Iridaceae, Siberian irises need full sun to flower well and will lapse to lax leaves and no flowers if overshaded by a tree.

In a consistently moist (but not sodden) and preferably warm soil, the crested fan irises, such as *Iris wattii* (1.2 m, 4 ft.; Z8/9), can give pleasure. Their foliage, which can often be browned at its tips by winter cold, is better given a warm summer. The fan-like growth of *I. japonica* (Z7/8) benefits from the shelter of, say, a shrub rose; and though its rhizomes are very persistent, its spreading habit is manageable and not too competitive. Of similar hardiness is the richer blue *I. confusa* from western Sichuan in China, which grows on very wet hillsides; its cane-like stems reach 60–70 cm (24–28 in.) or more, but it can double its height in warm temperate conditions. The light blue-flowered form I grow was raised as seed I collected from Niba Shan, where it grows at 2000 m (6562 ft.) with *Magnolia wilsonii*, but in seasonally vague climates, it too needs a little shelter to do well.

Species can be readily raised from seed, and the stemmed and rhizome sorts by division or, more usually, single stem or rhizome cuttings with a trimmed-back fan of leaves.

JUNCUS

RUSH

JUNCACEAE

Rushes—mostly tufted perennial herbs, cosmopolitan in distribution—are good indicators of wet soil and impeded drainage, and several interesting cultivars of various species are now cultivated. *Juncus effusus* (soft-rush; Z4), native to most areas of Britain and a widespread temperate species, is known in gardens for its several forms, such as *J. effusus* f. *spiralis* (corkscrew rush). The type has smooth erect stems that are glossy when young; it can reach 1–2 m (3.3–6.6 ft.) in good conditions but will seed around. Increase forms by division.

KNIPHOFIA

RED-HOT POKERS

ASPHODELACEAE

Kniphofias are herbaceous perennials from central and southern Africa and Madagascar, where they are often found along the banks of streams and rivers, or in damp uplands. Their flower scapes are simple, erect (50–200 cm, 20–80 in.), with a cluster of tubular flowers formed at the tip. *Kniphofia rooperi* (120 cm, 48 in.) may be found in marshy places, and *K. laxiflora* (75 cm, 30 in.) occurs naturally on heavy clay soils. Many, including *K. triangularis* (60 cm, 24 in.; Z4), grow and flower well on moist soils in cultivation. Kniphofias have thick rhizomes (rarely stems) and form dense clumps of long, linear tapering leaves.

They are easy to grow plants, and most of those cultivated are happy in a wide range of garden soils. All flower better given an open sunny position, but they do not demand frequent division to continue being floriferous, since, as the clumps enlarge, so the number of flowering spikes increases. At least this has held true for my twenty-year-old clump of *Kniphofia uvaria* 'Nobilis' (Z6). Thus division is undertaken when it is either desired to increase the number of plants grown or the plant has grown too large for its site. The more deciduous, often smaller species can be readily grown to flower in pots or other containers. Between the species and the now many hybrids, a lovely range of flower colours is available—red, orange, yellow, cream, and green. The lower flowers on the scape open first, their colour fading as they age, so giving a two-colour effect. Flowering period varies, and both species and cultivars can be chosen for summer or even autumn flowering.

For the large-growing evergreen kniphofias, division can be a major operation, even though their roots lift reasonably easily. On cold wet soil, they can take two or three years to recover, and hardiness is also a factor. In temperate countries, early spring is probably the best time to undertake division. Kniphofias hybridise readily, and much of the seed offered for sale comes from hybrid swarms. With so many lovely cultivars available, it is worth purchasing named clones.

Kniphofia triangularis

LABIATAE

MINT FAMILY

Also known as Lamiaceae. Members of this large and widespread family of perennial and annual herbs, with some shrubs, have simple, frequently aromatic leaves and mostly four-angled stems. The two-lipped flowers are usually bisexual, and the fruit is a four-seeded nutlet or more rarely a drupe. Most are well adapted to dry soils, but a few grow well in wet soil.

The lovely little *Ajuga reptans* (bugle; Z8) and its many cultivars tolerate a moist soil but need good drainage (sadly, they die out with

TOP *Prunella vulgaris*
ABOVE *Salvia uliginosa*

me). In contrast the dull gypsy-worts, such as *Lycopus americanus* and *L. virginicus* from North America and the European *L. europaeus* (all Z5), grow happily on wet soil, spreading weedily. The North American physostegias are also plants of wet soil; the popular *Physostegia virginiana* (obedient plant; 60–90 cm, 2–3 ft.) is a delightful upright perennial with several good cultivars, particularly the variegated form. True, they have consistently failed in my wet soil, but I plan to try again, this time with a raised bed. The self-heals are a little more persistent; several selections of *Prunella grandiflora* (Z5) from Europe, with its attractive upright flower spikes (15–30 cm, 6–12 in.), are available. The smaller-flowered *P. vulgaris* (Z3), native throughout Britain and widespread in Europe to the Himalayas, establishes freely on mown wet lawns, forming a tight mat of small leaves; some of its cultivars are also grown in gardens. When not mown, its flower spikes grow to 50 cm (20 in.).

Other wet-soil-tolerant labiates include the bright blue-flowered *Salvia uliginosa* (Z7), from Argentina, Uruguay, and Brazil, which, with its tall (1–2 m, 3.3–6.6 ft.) but lax flowering spikes, is a very attractive plant. Among the skullcaps the North American, European, and Siberian *Scutellaria galericulata* (30–60 cm, 12–24 in.; Z5) can grow on wet ground.

Propagation is straightforward, either from seed, herbaceous cuttings, or semi-ripe cuttings of the shrubs, or division of the herbaceous perennials.

LAMIUM

DEAD-NETTLE
LABIATAE

The several hardy perennial dead-nettles can be usefully grown as low herbaceous ground cover among shrubs, particularly *Lamium album* (white dead-nettle; 60 cm, 24 in.; Z4), native to temperate Europe and west Asia, which is a good source of nectar for bumblebees. Both the equally hardy *L. purpureum* (red dead-nettle) from northern Europe and *L. galeobdolon* (syn. *Lamiastrum galeobdolon*; yellow archangel; 50 cm, 20 in.) can cope with wet soil, and both are also native in Britain. The former is an endearing, small, spreading herb, readily weeded out when not wanted, with attractive reddish purple flowers produced over a long season and from early in the year; still, with its free-seeding and spreading habit, it is best confined to the wilder parts of the garden.

Lamium galeobdolon subsp. *galeobdolon* is now a rare native plant

HERBACEOUS PLANTS AND BULBS

in Britain; subsp. *montanum* is much more common. The species is widespread in Europe and into western Asia; cultivated forms, like the silver-flecked-leafed 'Hermann's Pride', have seemingly been selected from eastern European forms and are vigorous, needing clipping when used as a ground cover on wet soil. Of the many cultivars of the southern European and North African to west Asian *L. maculatum* (Z3), I find the silver-foliaged 'Beacon Silver' a well-behaved ground cover among peonies and, usefully, bulbs can be planted beneath its dense, spreading, low-growing mat of stems. It grows well on wet soils but is susceptible at times to mildew, though it holds its leaves all year round. Seedlings can arise freely on gravel; these vary a little—some with white flowers, others purple—while the foliage on some reverts to type. For propagation, see Labiatae.

LATHRAEA

TOOTHWORT
SCROPHULARIACEAE

Lathraea clandestina (Z6) from western and southwestern Europe is interesting, occurring on heavy soils as a root parasite on willow, poplar, and alder, most commonly. From a distance, its purplish clustered flowers, emerging leafless in spring, look like small crocuses. The less ornamental European *L. squamaria* (Z6) is found growing on elm and hazel roots, and also on alder and beech on moist soils; its creamy flowers are tinged pink or purple. Toothworts lack chlorophyll and form an underground rhizome-like structure. They do not seem to be very species-specific, as a partial ring of *L. clandestina* used to emerge each spring among the roots of an aged black walnut (*Juglans nigra*) at Kew, and at Wakehurst it can be seen on maples and rhododendrons. Introduction is usually from seed sown in the root zone of a potential host tree.

LEUCANTHEMUM

OXEYE DAISY
COMPOSITAE

Leucanthemums vary in their tolerance of wet soils, for whereas the lovely British native *Leucanthemum vulgare*, which ranges through Europe and temperate Asia, is very short-lived on wet soil, the much larger *L.* ×*superbum* (Shasta daisy; to 90 cm, 36 in.; Z5) will grow and persist on wet soil, regenerating seedlings all around (though seedlings from the double forms usually revert to singles). The original Shasta daisies were raised by Luther Burbank as selections of

Lathraea clandestina

L. *lacustre* from Portugal, possibly also crossed with *L. maximum* from the Pyrenees, and he named them after Mt. Shasta in northern California. Many of these and later cultivars are grown, but they are so vigorous on moist warm soil that they spread and crowd out more delicate neighbouring plants. Careful placement is needed to ensure their spread can be readily controlled. Increase by division.

LEUCOJUM

SNOWFLAKE
AMARYLLIDACEAE

Leucojum aestivum (summer snowflake; Z4), which occurs from western Europe to Iran, will even grow submerged in water; and, as its natural habitats include flooded meadows and riverine forest, its seeds are adapted to water dispersal. In wet soil, bulbs steadily increase from year to year, coming into growth (60–80 cm, 24–31 in.) very early in spring, though not flowering till late spring. They can be readily divided when not in full leaf. The much smaller European *L. vernum* (spring snowflake), which flowers earlier, at snowdrop time, also tolerates wet soil and the occasional inundation. Despite their possession of toxic alkaloids, my plants of the Hungarian *L. vernum* var. *vagneri* (Z5), with their twin-flowered scapes, are very susceptible to slug damage.

LIBERTIA

IRIDACEAE

Interesting, rhizomatous perennials, libertias have many devotees. All occur naturally by watersides or in damp meadows (the small *Libertia pulchella* from southeast Australia, for example, is found on mountains, often by streams); thus they require moist soils. They are accommodating, easy-to-grow plants with attractive foliage set off by crisp clusters or panicles of small white or blue flowers. *Libertia formosa* from Chile, where it grows by lakes and coasts, is on the borderline of hardiness, whereas the smaller Chilean *L. elegans* is actually naturalised in parts of cool, moist Scotland. Species from New Zealand—the evergreen *L. grandiflora*, *L. ixioides*, and the orangey brown (to bronze, in some cultivars) *L. peregrinans* (45 cm, 18 in.)—are also on the borderline of hardiness, though now, because of climate change, they grow well on my wet soil, with *L. peregrinans* spreading considerably, albeit with sparser growth. *Libertia pulchella* is a Zone 9 plant, the others are Zone 8; but they all make attractive ground fillers. Propagate by seed or division.

TOP *Leucojum aestivum* 'Gravetye Giant'
ABOVE *Libertia grandiflora*

LIGULARIA

LEOPARD PLANTS

COMPOSITAE

Ligularias are large and impressive perennials mostly from wet woodland and streamside habitats in Europe and central and eastern Asia, but this does not translate directly to gardens (I have consistently failed on wet soil with the tall thin-spiked *Ligularia* 'The Rocket', and I note it flourishing on thinner soil over limestone). Happily *L. dentata* (Z4), from China and Japan, with its 1–1.2 m (3.3–4 ft.) stems of bright and garish orange daisies, grows well in wet soil, as do its several selections, some of which have a deep purple colour on both leaf surfaces and stems. It also produces masses of seedlings. Others such as *L. hodgsonii*, *L. japonica* (especially in its selected form, 'Rising Sun'), *L. veitchiana*, and *L. wilsoniana* (all Z5) are best in moist soil. Increase mainly by division.

LILIUM

LILY

LILIACEAE

When thinking of plants from this family for my own wet garden, lilies did not instantly come to mind, but the success of the leopard lily, *Lilium pardalinum* (Z5), from Oregon and California encouraged me. Its scaly rhizome-like bulb increases prolifically on even very wet soils, and its orange recurved flowers form in summer on 1–1.5 m (3.3–5 ft.) stems. In warmer conditions than my garden offers, they can grow taller; and there is a variety, *L. pardalinum* var. *giganteum*, that has 3 m (10 ft.) flowering stems. This species is a parent of the Bellingham and other hybrids, but the hybrids are not quite so tolerant of wet soils.

Other lilies that grow naturally in moist soils but seem to need good drainage include the western North American lily *Lilium occidentale*, and from eastern North America *L. canadense* and *L. grayi*. For areas with little winter frost, there is the curiously beautiful *L. catesbaei*, which inhabits wet pine savannas from Virginia to Louisiana. It is rare and something of a challenge to grow, its flowering stems reach about 60 cm (2 ft.), and its flower has long, lax, tapered yellow to orange tepals. All are Zone 5.

Using the extra shelter and soil dryness given by trees, I have extended my range to include *Lilium martagon* (Z4), which, to my surprise, has withstood a summer flood; but, as might be expected, *L. candidum* (Madonna lily) dies out if too wet. *Lilium sargentiae* (Z6),

TOP *Ligularia japonica* 'Rising Sun'
ABOVE *Lilium sargentiae* collected from Erlang Shan, western Sichuan, pot-grown with *Dahlia* 'Bishop of Llandaff'

a sweetly scented trumpet lily, grows well to about 1.5 m (5 ft.) or more, and though not of wet soils, it does occur on the slopes of the wetter eastern side of Chinese mountains. I collected several forms in Guizhou and Sichuan which vary in outer tepal colour from green to dark crimson. Its main problem in temperate regions is the susceptibility of its emerging new season's growth to damage by late frosts, but usefully, *L. sargentiae* is readily propagated from its freely produced bulbils. Across China, trumpet lilies are plants of lower altitude, where summers are almost subtropical but winters are bitter, while the hardier Turk's-cap species, such as *L. taliense*, occur at much higher altitudes.

Some lily species germinate like onions (epigeal germination), while others are hypogeal (that is, the cotyledons remain below ground). Where bulbils are produced, they can be taken from the plants in late summer, by which time they have often already formed a primary root; and if pricked out, as for seedlings into trays, they will make several leaves and roots by autumn. Trumpet lilies, given frost-free conditions, will often continue to grow over winter; with frost, they will die down until spring. With regular potting-on in the growing season, such plants can achieve a flowering-sized bulb in two to three years. My early training has conditioned me to pricking out three seedlings or bulbils to a pot 7.5 cm (3 in.) in diameter for their first move, but they probably grow better potted singly. They can then be combined later if a large flowering container of bulbs is required. Commercially lilies are mass-produced from bulb scales. Some are stoloniferous; many slowly increase from the production of daughter bulbs.

LOBELIA
CAMPANULACEAE

Lobelia is often separated into its own family, Lobeliaceae. Of the wet-soil-loving lobelias, I started with the striking (or vulgar, depending on one's taste) violet-purple-flowered *L. ×speciosa* 'Vedrariensis', which comes true from seed and has 80–100 cm (31–40 in.) flowering stalks. From its sometimes seemingly dead bases of last year's stalks, fresh shoots arise in spring; however, to keep a good flowering group, regular attention must be given, particularly early in the year, when the clumps can be moved around, dividing and gapping-up as required.

Other bog lobelias include one of the latter's parents, the striking but short-lived *Lobelia cardinalis* (Z3) from North America. This species occurs naturally by the borders of streams and in wet places (it even tolerates total submersion); and there are several forms, including plants with white, red, rose, or vermilion flowers. The blue-flowered *L. siphilitica* (1 m, 3.3 ft.; Z4), another North American native, seems better suited to temperate gardens. Its natural distribution includes wet soils in pasture and woods, and its flower colours range from blue to purple and white. Lobelia flowers are bisexual and resupinate.

There are now a great many hybrid cultivars of these lobelias available as named clones, and also some good seed strains. The dark red-leaved *Lobelia cardinalis* 'Queen Victoria' (Z7) has long been popular in cultivation, as is the more recent *L. ×speciosa* 'Tania'. Hardiness of the cultivars varies; Zone 7 is the lower limit for some. As an insurance, it is sensible to keep either the odd clump or young plants in a cold frame over winter.

The flowering stems of lobelias such as *Lobelia ×speciosa* 'Vedrariensis' can be cut into sections (leaf-bud cuttings) after flowering, but with varying degrees of success. Those with overwintering rosettes can be divided. Care is needed when handling some lobelias as many possess milky latex, and the sap can be a painful, long-lasting irritant if it contacts an eye.

LUZULA
WOOD-RUSH
JUNCACEAE

Several luzulas are well suited to wet gardens, and though cosmopolitan, most of these herbaceous perennials are native to northern temperate regions. The frost hardy *Luzula nivea* (snow-white wood-rush; Z5/6) from Europe has attractive pubescent, dark green foliage and from a small division can grow slowly over two or three years to form a good-sized tufted clump, 50 cm (20 in.) in diameter, not much more than 20 cm (8 in.) high. Its delicate white inflorescences, to about 50 cm (20 in.), are a summer attraction, but it can be short-lived on wet soil and needs regular repropagation.

Larger growing, with broader lighter green leaves, the European *Luzula sylvatica* (great wood-rush; Z4), a plant of woods and moorland, makes a fine ground cover for a woodland garden. Given a sunny site on moist soil, it flowers well with 80 cm (31 in.) spikes of brownish flowers; and its lighter flowered selection 'Taggart's Cream' forms many young bleached leaves in spring. The cosmopolitan *L. campestris* (field wood-rush; Z6) is common throughout temperate

Europe and Asia; it has small (15–25 cm, 6–10 in.) erect flowering stems, and its silky-haired leaves show up within the mown grass of wet lawns.

Most luzulas can be propagated by division. On wet soil *Luzula sylvatica* seeds prolifically, and in beds, seedlings abound. It is thus better confined to a ground cover role.

LYCHNIS
CATCHFLY
CARYOPHYLLACEAE

Lychnis flos-cuculi (ragged robin), from bogs and wet meadows from Europe to Siberia, is an often-recommended catchfly for wet soils. Growing to about 60 cm (2 ft.), it can be an attractive meadow or streamside flower, and several cultivars have been selected for gardens. It is fussy about site, however, growing best on a moist, fen soil; it will not grow on all wet soils. Despite its silvery-felted leaves, which suggest dry soil and sun, *L. coronaria* from southeast Europe is shallow-rooted and operates well as a biennial in open sites on wet soil. And while some will be lost over winter, an annual seed sowing in summer can refurnish stock, the cerise, white, and pinkish forms all coming true from seed. Other lychnises, like *L. chalcedonica*, are also valued but tend to be short-term additions to a wet garden. All are Zone 4. Propagate by seed, basal stem cuttings for *L. chalcedonica*, or division for perennials.

LYSICHITON
SKUNK CABBAGE
ARACEAE

Lysichitons are fashionable stream and lakeside plants for many temperate gardens, popular for their large (30–35 cm, 12–14 in.) golden or white-spathed inflorescences. What limits them in small gardens is not their flowers but their large (1.5 × 0.5 m, 5 ft. × 20 in.) leaves, which are formed as a basal rosette; however, the white-spathed *Lysichiton camtschatcensis* has more modest (60–100 cm, 24–40 in.) leaves. These waxy leaves are attractive but surprisingly soft, and thus liable to be eaten when young by waterfowl. The plants need constant moisture and are very deep rooted—hence, not easily transplanted. They are therefore most often seed raised and then planted into their permanent sites, but offsets can be taken for propagation.

TOP *Lychnis flos-cuculi*
ABOVE *Lysichiton americanus*

HERBACEOUS PLANTS AND BULBS

The golden-flowered *Lysichiton americanus* comes from coastal western North America (Alaska to northern California) and also inland, whereas *L. camtschatcensis* is from the other side of the Pacific, from northeastern Siberia and Kamchatka to central Honshu in Japan. In gardens, where both are grown, vigorous hybrids can arise, but these cream-coloured forms are, to me, less satisfactory than either parent. All are Zone 5.

LYSIMACHIA
LOOSESTRIFE
PRIMULACEAE

This genus of about 180 species is widely distributed in the northern hemisphere, extending to South Africa; though relatively few are cultivated, most that are grown are herbaceous and tolerant of wet soil. The hardy *Lysimachia nummularia* (creeping Jenny), a plant of my childhood garden on wet clay, came accidentally to my current garden, in among the roots of some other plant, but it quickly established itself in the wettest of beds, forming dense mats of its trailing stems and overpowering other perennials. The golden yellow flowers are attractive, but only when seen close, and for greater effect the golden-leaved 'Aurea' is often grown.

The yellow-flowered *Lysimachia ciliata* (fringed loosestrife) from North America grows naturally at the edge of ponds and in other wet places, but with me, it grows more weakly than, say, *L. punctata*. Its red-leaved selection, *L. ciliata* 'Firecracker', is so vigorous and spreads so aggressively that it is best naturalised in a more remote part of the garden; in a flowerbed, it will suppress more delicate plants. It is hardy and can easily hold its own in a wet meadow (as can *L. punctata*) and can be mown down with the long grass in late autumn.

Lysimachia clethroides (gooseneck loosestrife) seems able to grow on both wet and dry and acid and alkaline soils. When in flower, it is a pleasing plant, especially those forms where the sturdy inflorescence spike forms an almost right-angled curve with its flowers opening sequentially. The individual white flowers are small but densely packed on the terminal part of the inflorescence. Several eastern Asian forms are cultivated. The newly emergent shoots of those from Guizhou, western China, can sometimes be caught by a late frost, and the plant can die back if too wet in winter; however, this form was found growing as a forest edge plant at about 1000 m

TOP *Lysichiton camtschatcensis*
ABOVE *Lysimachia clethroides*
Guizhou form

Lysimachia punctata

(3300 ft.), which is really warm temperate. It forms a creeping stem-like rootstock that reddens when exposed to light, and the leaves similarly may take on this colour in autumn.

Lysimachia punctata, which occurs in southeast and central Europe through to Turkey, is a very tough, hardy, and familiar garden plant. Because little else can grow among its dense mat of stems and roots, it is best naturalised in meadow or bog, where it will give a bold display when densely clothed with its yellow flowers. The variegated *L. punctata* 'Alexander' is a more popular choice. Established clumps will spread but not as fast as *L. ciliata* 'Firecracker'.

Lysimachias divide readily and will often self-sow on wet sites. All mentioned are Zone 4 (but note my comments on *Lysimachia clethroides*).

MENTHA

MINT

LABIATAE

Mints occur naturally around northern temperate regions and extend to South Africa and Australia. Obviously most are grown as perennial culinary herbs, but they are not unattractive in flower; and since so many are not only hardy but very tolerant of wet soils, they can be useful additions to the wet garden. Growth tends to be upright (60–80 cm, 24–31 in.), becoming twiggy at the base later in the season, and flowers form in terminal spikes or sometimes in a more whorled arrangement. The soft variegated foliage of *Mentha suaveolens* 'Variegata' (Z6) has an appeal with its floppier stems, which associate well with the more poker-straight stems of 'Goldsturm' coneflower (both persist in an extremely wet flowerbed here). It rewards further when its stems fall onto the grass, giving off a delicate lemony-pineapple scent when the mower trims them back.

Like many in this family, as well as subterranean rhizomes, mints can produce horizontally growing stems, on the surface, which can root and shoot from every node. Thus on a wet soil they need to be confined; largish pots or containers, sunken or stood on a paved area, work well. Mints can persist for many years in a large pot if given a little fertiliser each year, and they even tolerate indifferent watering. In small beds set in paved areas they are easily managed, but where there are looser surfaces, mint seedlings will arise.

The Eurasian *Mentha aquatica* (watermint; Z6) can stabilise waterside banks, and in bog gardens it is possible to grow blocks of mint with lysimachias and fleabane. In my own garden, mints are kept in place by a water-filled channel on one side and mown grass on the other. They are easily increased from rhizomes or seed.

MERTENSIA

BLUEBELLS
BORAGINACEAE

Mertensias inhabit northern temperate regions, particularly in North America. Many, especially the montane species, need good drainage, but most tolerate moist soils. The delicate *Mertensia ciliata* (to 30 cm, 12 in.; Z4) from the Rocky Mountains has grown happily with me on wet soil for fifteen years but needs some care, as it does not compete too well with more vigorous wetlanders. *Mertensia paniculata* (20–150 cm, 8–48 in.; Z4) grows naturally in wet meadows and along streambanks in northwestern North America. *Mertensia virginica* (Virginia bluebells; Z3) does not seem to grow quite as robustly in Britain as in its native home, where it can deck the woodland floor as does *Hyacinthoides non-scripta* here. For propagation, see Boraginaceae.

MILIUM

MILLETGRASS
GRAMINEAE

Since the perennial *Milium effusum* (wood millet; Z5) occurs naturally in my garden along a shady hedgerow, I thought I should try its selected form 'Aureum' (Bowles' golden grass). I find its leaves are best in spring, as their colour fades later in the year. The species itself has attractive leaves, lax and flat, in small clumps 60 cm (2 ft.) high and wide, with longer (to 80 cm, 31 in.) slender culms. It is a pleasing plant, increasing slowly by seeding around among bluebells and primroses. Bowles' golden grass (30–60 cm, 12–24 in.) is less vigorous but happy on a wet soil; I grow it on the north side of my house, where it has the benefit of extra shade. There is also a variegated form. The species has an extensive range in North America, Europe, and temperate Asia. 'Aureum' comes true from seed (but rarely produces seedlings naturally) and can be divided.

MIMULUS

MONKEY FLOWER
SCROPHULARIACEAE

Many monkey flowers revel in wet surroundings. *Mimulus guttatus* is an attractive yellow-flowered, soft-stemmed herb, and it and

TOP *Mertensia virginica* in a Delaware garden
ABOVE *Milium effusum* 'Aureum' in summer

the glandular-pubescent-leaved *M. moschatus* (musk flower), both from North America, are now happily naturalised in many parts of Britain. The latter species was a David Douglas introduction, from around 1828, and prized for its musk scent, since lost by its progeny in cultivation (though native populations are not always musk-scented). The many species in this genus occur in both the Old and New Worlds; some are annuals, but most are short-lived perennials, and only a few are cultivated.

More popular are the bedding (smaller matted) forms derived from crossing North American with Chilean species, such as *Mimulus cupreus* (Z9) and *M. luteus* (Z8). Though these hybrids seed around, and flower heavily as short-lived perennials in gravel paths, they do not persist if transferred to a bog bed. In contrast *M. guttatus* (Z8) itself is very durable, its lower stems spreading freely on wet soil and rooting from the nodes; seedlings also arise in any damp spot. The wet-soil-loving *M. cardinalis* (Z6), which occurs in southwestern North America, is nevertheless susceptible to frost (at least its southern Californian provenance is), and in areas with cold winters it is best overwintered under glass as freshly rooted young plants. In a good summer, a single such overwintered plant can form a clump 1 m (3.3 ft.) in diameter within a few months. Seedlings will arise naturally, but they do not grow much until the days warm sufficiently and are often better started by growing on initially in pots in a cold frame.

MISCANTHUS

GRAMINEAE

As the years pass I have become more attached to miscanthus, mainly because their tall (1.5–2 m, 5–6.6 ft.) graceful flowering stems hold so well over winter; in December and January, they still glow silver when the long-haired spikelets are backlit by low-angled sun. The only downside is in late January and February, when they start shedding their long leaves, which catch the wind and blow around the garden. Their thin reed-like stems form tight clumps, and it takes three years or so for the newly planted arrivals to grow to their full height. In nature, as in western China, they grow on open, damp mountainsides at low levels, but they can also cope with drier soils. The most popular species, with over seventy available cultivars, is *Miscanthus sinensis* (Z4); all seem content on wet soils. The genus itself is distributed through central, eastern, and southeastern Asia

HERBACEOUS PLANTS AND BULBS

and Polynesia. Division of their densely matted clumps requires the use of a very sharp spade.

MYOSOTIS

FORGET-ME-NOT
BORAGINACEAE

The easiest to grow genus for moist soils must be *Myosotis*. The seedpods of garden forget-me-nots cling so readily to clothing and animal fur that their arrival in a moist garden is just a matter of time, and once established, plants proceed to colonise any area of bare earth. They make excellent fillers, and so it is worth introducing a good flowering cultivar of *M. sylvatica* (woodland forget-me-not; Z5). For the enthusiast there is a wide range of species, from temperate Eurasia, African mountains, the Americas, and Australasia, and these occur in both dry and wet habitats, some as marginals in water. 'Mermaid' and the brilliantly variegated Maytime (= 'Blaqua') are selections of the perennial *M. scorpioides* (water forget-me-not; Z5); this species, native in much of temperate Eurasia and North Africa, is a plant for wet situations, occurring in both alkaline and slightly acid water.

Like *Myosotis sylvatica*, the many bedding cultivars seem to be short-lived biennials, seed-raised one year to flower the next. The only disadvantage of these short-lived forget-me-nots is that they become tatty after flowering: they are susceptible to mildews (both downy and powdery) and die off after forming seed. If grown in more formal areas, the dead plants will need clearing from June, and so their best use is as temporary fillers and ground cover in newly planted herbaceous beds. In more mature plantings, other plants soon mask their waning growth. Forget-me-nots can also be established as a seasonal ground cover in light woodland.

NARCISSUS

DAFFODIL
AMARYLLIDACEAE

Narcissus pseudonarcissus (Z4), native in its various guises to Britain and western Europe, is often to be found in river valleys, mostly among trees, or along woodland edges. It appears tolerant of a range of soil types but not too wet (I find it less than happy on my wet soil). Many of its cultivars grow well on a wet soil, as do others, particularly those possessing the genes of *N. triandrus* (Z4) or the diminu-

TOP *Miscanthus sinensis* 'Silberfeder'
ABOVE *Miscanthus sinensis* 'Variegatus'

tive *N. cyclamineus* (Z6) from wet meadows in northwestern Spain and Portugal, which is one of the earliest to flower, on scapes to 20 cm (8 in.). Even the sweetly scented Mediterranean to Iranian *N. tazetta* (Z8) persists in wet soil given a warm site.

Naturalising hardy daffodil species can be achieved by broadcasting fresh seed onto turf, though the resultant seedlings may take seven years to flower. Separation of bubs, when dormant, is the main means of increasing stock.

NERINE

AMARYLLIDACEAE

Most species of *Nerine* and many of the hybrids are tender. Unexpectedly I find the late-summer-flowering Barbara Cartland–pink *N. bowdenii* (Z9) from South Africa has grown unperturbed in my wet beds for nearly twenty years. It is relatively hardy to –15°C (5°F), though the bulbs do not increase or flower as freely, with scapes to 45 cm (18 in.), as when baked by summer sun and given better drainage. Increase from daughter bulbs.

TOP This natural population of *Narcissus pseudonarcissus* has to cope with changing river levels.
ABOVE *Narcissus cyclamineus*

HERBACEOUS PLANTS AND BULBS

OENOTHERA

EVENING PRIMROSE

ONAGRACEAE

Because oenotheras, which originate in the New World, are generally well adapted to dry soils, I was surprised to find that the widely naturalised, large-flowered evening primrose, *Oenothera glazioviana* (Z3), a vigorous biennial (to 1.8 m, 6 ft.), was very able to sit out a British winter as vigorous seedlings on a wet soil, flowering and seeding prolifically the following summer. This species can, however, become weedy. *Oenothera* 'Apricot Delight' (Z5) is a more manageable biennial (to about 60 cm, 2 ft.) and can also tolerate wet soil, though perhaps less happily, and it also seems to seed less freely. Their small seeds germinate readily *in situ*, but for the deep-rooted oenotheras, it is easier to raise young plants in pots ready for setting out into their flowering sites.

OMPHALODES

NAVELWORT

BORAGINACEAE

Of the several species of navelwort, the hardy *Omphalodes cappadocica* (Z6) from the Caucasus and Turkey is a challenge worth taking on moist soils: I shall long remember a vivid blue drift of omphalodes adorning a garden border at Heslington near York. Both it and its several good cultivars do not thrive if the soil is too wet and boggy in winter; however, without competition from surrounding plants they can have a long and useful flowering season on moist soil. Flower stems rise to about 25 cm (10 in.) from mostly basal leaf clusters. Increase by division.

ORCHIDACEAE

ORCHID FAMILY

This is among the plant kingdom's largest families, with 835 genera and somewhere in excess of 20,000 species, all perennial herbs with a cosmopolitan distribution. The deciduous temperate and subtropical species form tubers or sturdy rhizomes, and the evergreens from tropical and subtropical regions may have swollen stems or rhizomes. The latter forms may also possess pseudobulbs—swollen stem organs. Leaves are mostly simple, and usually tough and thickened in the evergreens. Most epiphytes, and many scrambling types, have thickened aerial roots that can both adhere to bark and other surfaces and absorb moisture from the atmosphere.

TOP *Oenothera* 'Apricot Delight'
ABOVE *Omphalodes cappadocica*

Disa uniflora

The beautiful and diverse flowers of orchids are long lasting, though they fade quickly after pollination. Within the flower, the column (gynostemium) is formed from both male and female parts of the flower, and the pollen is combined into masses (pollinia). Some orchid flowers are resupinate, and the then lower petal may become a spur, pouch, or other specialised form, very different from the remaining, usually more simple petals and sepals. The very sophisticated form of orchid flowers relates to their highly evolved relationships with their insect pollinators.

Most cultivated orchids require well-drained, aerated soils, but several grow in bogs. Though plants may occur naturally on wet soil, this requirement does not always hold in cultivation. For example, the beautiful terrestrial disas from Africa and Madagascar include several bog and wet-soil species, but in cultivation they are given conventional free-draining orchid compost. The best display I have seen of *Disa uniflora* (red disa) from the southwest Cape was in Munich's botanic garden. Here the grower diligently attended to their watering, carefully filtering the water through peat and moss before use, and, during their growing season, the plants were kept moist but not saturated. Regular repotting is thought to reduce the chance of the compost becoming stagnant. But these enigmas are what drive people to grow these beautiful yet demanding plants.

Because of their beauty and often restricted range, habitat loss and overcollecting has brought—and is still bringing—many species to the verge of extinction. There are now severe conservation controls on the collecting and trade in rare plants. It is very important to be aware of what is now complex worldwide legislation and only to purchase or acquire plants from *bona fide* sources that observe CITES and other legislative requirements—there is much illegal trade.

Happily there are a great many orchid hybrids available in cultivation, and, for wet gardens in warm moist regions, there is the opportunity to grow many of the beautiful epiphytic forms. Those cultivated are mostly tough plants, and the epiphytic phalaenopsis (moth orchids) and terrestrial cymbidiums show this in their ready tolerance as houseplants in temperate climes.

Similarly, hardy terrestrial orchids cannot be taken from the wild, and only cultivated stock should be used for gardens. Purchase only known cultivars, particularly hybrids, for these are easier to grow, and such action helps protect wild plants. Sometimes such orchids can be present naturally in a wet garden; dactylorhizas (marsh orchids), for example, are still common in Britain, and managing the habitat for their benefit can be a rewarding challenge.

In nature, the dust-like orchid seed needs an endotrophic fungus to aid successful germination and growth; consequently, most orchid seedlings are raised *in vitro* (that is, in aseptic conditions on prepared media). This is not a difficult technique but one that now tends to be left to specialist growers.

For most gardeners, division when the plants are dormant represents the easiest means of increasing the hardy terrestrials; however, since such orchids resent being transplanted, it is best done when the plants are about to come into active spring growth. Divided plants should not be left to dry but replanted promptly. Division is also used for most other orchids; cymbidiums, for example, can be increased from single, green back bulbs.

PACHYPHRAGMA

CRUCIFERAE

The hardy *Pachyphragma macrophyllum* (syn. *Thlaspi biebersteinii*; Caucasian pennycress) from woodlands of the Caucasus and northeastern Turkey has much in common with cardamines. A semi-evergreen, rhizomatous perennial, in early spring it produces corymbs of scented white flowers on 20–40 cm (8–16 in.) stems. Very tolerant of wet ground, it has become naturalised in parts of Britain, and in gardens forms a useful ground cover among shrubs. Propagation is mostly by division, but it can also be raised from seed or stem cuttings in spring.

PAEONIA

PEONY
PAEONIACEAE

With their large, attractive flowers and ease of cultivation, peonies are accommodating garden plants, long-lived and flowering year after year with little attention. All will grow on acid sands or even chalky soils. Flowering early in summer, their foliage continues to hold until autumn, sometimes giving autumn tints, but it then turns black and hangs on the plants, requiring the tidy gardener to cut down the herbaceous peonies and to clip the leaves off tree peonies.

Wild peonies have a Eurasian range extending from Spain to Japan. In nature, many are associated with warm seasonally dry soils; but some of the northern Asian species and hybrids are more

Paeonia lactiflora seedling

tolerant of moist soils, and some can even withstand inundation. The western Chinese and east Tibetan *Paeonia veitchii* (Z6–8), for example, occurs in very moist mountain regions, usually under the shelter of woody shrubs (no surprise that it grows particularly well in cool, moist Scotland). As a matter of routine, however, I form a slightly raised bed for all peonies on wet soil.

Unfortunately peony blight (*Botrytis paeoniae*) is common, which is a problem since fungi generally are hard to control. It arrives like potato blight, without introduction, and spreads as quickly. Most of my seed-raised plants, despite a damp site, were free of fungal problems for a few years, but infections have subsequently become apparent, and I now space plants widely to reduce the likelihood of fungal cross infection. With an initial infection, the diseased parts can be cut off and burnt. With a more severe infection, as may happen in a wet summer, additionally spray routinely with a systemic fungicide.

Given a bed of their own, healthy peonies respond well, flourishing with just an annual organic mulch, particularly if it is well-rotted manure. And peonies associate happily with anemones, fritillaries, and other bulbs, bringing forward the flowering season of the bed. Tree peonies can start into growth when winter's snow has scarcely melted, and they then flower on the newly produced soft young shoots before the summer foliage has fully developed. This young growth can be caught by late heavy frosts; siting peonies on the shaded, north (in the northern hemisphere) side of the house or wall can help reduce such damage.

The thirty or so species in cultivation are, almost without exception, attractive plants, offering a range of flower forms and colours from white to yellow to peach and pink and many shades of red; some also have handsome foliage. The many *Paeonia lactiflora* hybrids (Z7), which tolerate wet soil given a slightly raised bed, can grow tall (80–100 cm, 31–40 in.), and since their stems can be flattened by wind, often just as they are coming into flower, it is best to stake them. Individual plants can be held with wire frames, pea sticks, or just three canes and some twine or wire to encircle the clump. Canes to about two-thirds the height of the flowering stems should be sufficient, and if set before summer growth progresses, these supports will soon be disguised by foliage.

The shrubby tree peonies (to 1.5 m, 5 ft.), once scarce in Western gardens, are now readily available. Most large tree peonies are hybrids: peonies have a long history of cultivation in China. What we have known as cultivars of *Paeonia suffruticosa* (Z7) are now considered to be the progeny of three or four distinct Chinese species. Of these, *P. rockii* (Z7), with its large single basally blotched flowers, was rare in gardens until recently. The single red-flowered *P. delavayi* (Z6) from Yunnan, the vigorous yellow-flowered *P. delavayi* var. *delavayi* f. *lutea* (formerly *P. lutea*), and *P. ludlowii* (Z6) from the Tsangpo Gorge (Tibet) are reasonably tolerant of moist to wet soils, as are many of the suffruticosa hybrids and *P. rockii*.

Transplanting three- or four-year-old tree peonies is a very satisfying task: so often on damp soils, the soil falls from a plant when lifted, but tree peonies form a dense mat of roots and soil and transplant without a check. The herbaceous forms have more extensive roots, can be difficult to dig out, and, if divided, may take up to two seasons to recover flowering. Remember, though: deep planting on a wet soil is the quickest way to kill a plant.

Seedpods persist over winter, forming in threes and fives, sometimes less, and standing upright on a disc at the top of the flowering stem. The hard-coated, Indian shot– to pea-sized seeds are mostly black when ripe. Flowers are bisexual, and the species produce plenty of viable seed, the hybrids less so, particularly in an Atlantic climate. Seedlings of *Paeonia delavayi* var. *delavayi* f. *lutea* often occur near the parent plant. Fresh seed should be sown in autumn, and the seed pots can then be held in a cold frame. Seed of peonies has what is known as epicotyl dormancy, that is, a seed will produce just a root in its first spring, but not usually until the second spring will its first shoot develop. At this latter stage, seedlings are easily handled, and I prefer to put them individually into small pots, once the first leaf has started to emerge. They are not too fussy as to compost—any standard compost suffices—but may take three to four years to flower.

Autumn division of the dormant rootstock is the most common method of propagation for herbaceous species, though a few, such as *Paeonia peregrina* (Z8), can regenerate from root cuttings. Tree peonies can be propagated from stem cuttings, but this is a difficult process, even with good facilities; grafting has been the alternative technique, using a scion from the tree peony grafted onto the root of an herbaceous peony, such as *P. lactiflora* or its hybrids.

PAPAVER
POPPY
PAPAVERACEAE

The often large, colourful, paper-thin petals of the poppies have long made them popular garden plants, but they are not the first thought

Papaver 'Beauty of Livermere'

when plants for wet gardens come to mind. The annual *Papaver somniferum* (opium poppy) is reasonably tolerant of damp soil (and seeds so freely that it is hard to remove once established), but it is among the perennial poppies that real wet tolerance exists. The great red blooms of *P.* 'Beauty of Livermere' (Oriental Poppy Group) can be almost dinnerplate-size on a warm moist soil, given shelter, and it persists better than the smaller *P. orientale* cultivars. Its floral stem bracts show its relationship to *P. bracteatum*, a plant I have seen growing naturally in moist mountain meadows at 2400 m (8000 ft.) in the Alborz Mountains, northern Iran. On my moist site this poppy, which also occurs in eastern Turkey and the Caucasus, grows best with a sheltering yew hedge on its west side. The much smaller, orange-flowered Moroccan *P. atlanticum* is very persistent on wet gravel in an open site. All are Zone 7.

Poppies resent being transplanted. The small seed may be sown thinly when ripe and can germinate naturally in late summer, autumn, or spring. Autumn seedlings should be pricked out and held cool and well ventilated over winter. The oriental types are more often raised by division, and also root from cuttings.

PELTANDRA

ARROW ARUM
ARACEAE

Peltandra is a small genus of bog plants from eastern North America, occurring down into the southeastern United States. They have long-petioled, arrow- or hastate-shaped leaves that arise from a sturdy rhizome, and while *P. virginica* can grow to 1 m (3.3 ft.) in warm conditions, it reaches perhaps little more than half that height in more northern temperate climes. The inflorescences are pale green, with yellow to white edges in *P. virginica* (Z5); the smaller *P. sagittifolia* (Z7) has white spathes and red berries. Increase by seed or division.

PENTAGLOTTIS

BORAGINACEAE

Since converting to gardening on wet soils, I have become attached to many borages for their excellent ground-covering characteristics; their growth is so dense and competitive that little else thrives among them. *Pentaglottis sempervirens* (green alkanet), a southwestern European now widely naturalised in Britain, can grow vigorously, with large basal leaves (38 cm, 15 in.) and flower stems rising to 70–100 cm (28–40 in.), on a variety of soils, from dust-dry to wet,

HERBACEOUS PLANTS AND BULBS

in sun or shade. It turns up unannounced in gardens and is hard to remove, but I allow it full head as a ground cover in one shaded site amid the dense white canes of a Himalayan bramble, wherein I do not often wish to venture. With its dense tufts of hirsute leaves and meagre though not unattractive spikes of anchusa-blue flowers, it has a value: it is a case of matching the plant to the needs of the site. Green alkanet seeds around freely and also produces many offsets.

PERSICARIA

KNOTWEED
POLYGONACEAE

Though persicarias (now including *Bistorta*) are members of the dock family, a good many species and cultivars are grown, the great majority of which grow well on wet soils and are controllable in gardens. The word "persistence" comes to mind, for they are very durable, mostly hardy herbaceous plants. I have grown some for twenty years or more, in the same site with minimal attention, and they still provide a good display of flowers each year. Cultivars of the popular trailing *Persicaria affinis* (Z3) are often seen in gardens. I use *P. affinis* 'Superba' in a partly shaded wet border, but it has been allowed to escape onto nearby wet gravel in full sun, where it flowers more freely. Other than the use, once a year, of shears or sometimes a spade to constrain its further spread, it rewards with an annual display of flowering and seeding lasting several months.

I first saw *Persicaria bistorta* (bistort) in the 1950s, growing wild in a Yorkshire meadow. Its cultivar 'Superba' has been with me too for many years, growing happily on both dry and boggy soils (my own plants are in a boggy site that gets regularly flooded), and I also find it naturalises well in heavy grass. The species itself ranges across Europe into Asia, and temperate Asia has provided several other good garden persicarias, such as the Himalayan *P. campanulata* (Z6), which carries its delicate tracery of pink flowers over a long season. *Persicaria virginiana* (Z3) from Eurasia and eastern North America provides a useful foliage plant in the unusually variegated 'Painter's Palette'. I have grown the Guizhou form of *P. virginiana* for twenty years; it has the attractive V-marked foliage of its kind but needs more warmth than my garden provides, as it frequently gets frosted at the end of the season just as its small flowers are developing. Its stems are deciduous and replaced each spring by new growth, for, like many in its family, it has a tough woody rootstock.

Knotweed flowers generally are small but noticeably attractive

TOP *Persicaria affinis* 'Superba'
ABOVE *Persicaria campanulata*

when produced in quantity on large inflorescences. As a group, knotweeds are distinguished by their membranous stem sheaths (ochrea), which are formed from stipules, and they have a winged appendage or appendages around their seeds. These appendages are often brightly coloured, giving the old flowering stem an extended season of beauty. Persicarias can be raised from seed but are mostly increased by division. *Persicaria affinis* roots along its prostrate stems, and thus branched pieces can be detached and grown on *in situ* or rooted in pots.

PHALARIS
CANARY-GRASS
GRAMINEAE

Phalaris arundinacea (reed canary-grass; Z4), native to Britain and widely distributed in the northern hemisphere, is found in wet areas by rivers, lakes, and marshes. An aggressive coloniser, it is better known for its variegated forms, popularly called gardener's garters. *Phalaris arundinacea* var. *picta* has long been in my own garden. It is unassuming, usefully filling spaces between shrubs all summer long with its variegated foil of leaves. Growing to 2 m (6.6 ft.), its wild parent is very vigorous, but the variegated forms are weaker. My plants (possibly the selection 'Feesey') grow to about 60 cm (2 ft.). Many garden writers warn about this variegated perennial's invasive rhizomes, especially on wet soils, but—and this may shock the reader—if my clumps start to spread where not required, they are restricted by carefully dripping a narrow band of glyphosate on young spring shoots along the desired boundary for the clump. Not a recommended practise, but one that works for me, as this grass is very easily killed. Increase by division.

PHORMIUM
NEW ZEALAND FLAX
PHORMIACEAE

There are two species of *Phormium* in New Zealand: the smaller *P. cookianum* (mountain flax; Z8), which has more flaccid arching leaves (to 1.5 m, 5 ft.), and the upright *P. tenax* (leaves to 3 m, 10 ft.; Z8), which is also distinguished by its large, keeled, erect seedpods. The flowers, which have protruding stamens, are formed on tall (1.5–4.5 m, 5–15 ft.) branched spikes. In recent years a great many coloured leaf forms have been selected or hybridised. Plants are valued for their toughness and toleration of both dry and very wet soils—even wet soils in colder climates. The linear, persistent leaves have strong fibres, and these are extracted to make a flax-like material. Sadly, and though introduced for this purpose, New Zealand flax became an invasive weed on the mountainsides of the remote South Atlantic island of St. Helena, which has a unique flora.

Forget to water a phormium in a container and it will usually "sit there," not flagging until remembered; yet planted in constantly soggy soil, it seems to grow equally happily, albeit becoming a much larger plant. They are fairly winter hardy in temperate climates, particularly in coastal regions, and can give good form to a bed or border in the dormant season. Phormiums are difficult to kill and may just get too large for a small garden. Division of their tough, large, rhizomatous clumps requires a sharp spade and a strong arm. It is easier to cut out small offsets, which will normally carry a young root or two.

PODOPHYLLUM

BERBERIDACEAE

Podophyllum is a small genus of hardy herbaceous perennials that have short (25–40 cm, 10–16 in.) stems carrying just one or two relatively large, usually deeply lobed leaves, which are attractively mauve-blotched when emerging in spring. The 5 cm (2 in.) flowers may be either solitary or clustered; and the yellow or red plum-like berry has seeds carried in a pulp. These are interesting, if curious, plants for cool, moist woodland gardens, such as can be found in the Pacific Northwest or Scotland. In nature, the Himalayan and western Chinese *P. hexandrum* (syn. *P. emodi*; Z6) may be found at high elevations (3000 m, 10,000 ft.) in subalpine scrub; its berry is bright red. The North American *P. peltatum* (May apple; Z4) has a wide latitudinal range from Quebec to Texas, growing in marshy woodland yet also tolerating drier conditions. Podophyllums may be readily raised from seed, which should be cleaned of its seed coat, and either sown fresh or stratified. The rhizome may also be divided.

POTENTILLA

CINQUEFOIL
ROSACEAE

Several members of this large northern hemisphere genus of herbaceous plants and small shrubs are cultivated, and a few of these occur on wet soils. The very popular shrubby *Potentilla fruticosa* has produced many variants over its wide range around the northern

Phormium 'Sundowner'

temperate zone, and a great many hybrids have been raised in cultivation. They regenerate best on moist soil over limestone and, being well adapted to cool, moist montane (Z3) conditions, they really need good drainage.

Several of the herbaceous potentillas—the circumboreal *Potentilla palustris* (marsh cinquefoil), for example—grow on moist soil, but they are scarcely garden worthy. Also, and despite having silver foliage, the common silverweed *P. anserina*, which also has a circumboreal distribution, sometimes occurs naturally on wettish soils. More suitable for gardens, the small, prostrate, but vigorously spreading *P. ×tonguei* (a hybrid between *P. anglica* and *P. nepalensis*) thrives on gravel laid over wet soil. Given a raised bed, many others can be grown, such as the bold yellow-flowered *P. megalantha*, a Japanese species with large strawberry-like leaves. All these are Zone 5. Increase herbaceous forms by division or from runners; *P. ×tonguei* roots along its trailing stems.

PRIMULA

PRIMROSE
PRIMULACEAE

Polyanthus and other primrose hybrids must be planted by the millions each year in temperate gardens, and the cheer they bring during the dark days of winter does lift the soul. The flowering of *Primula vulgaris* (primrose; Z6), which ranges through Europe to west Turkey and the Caucasus on moist woodland edges or along moist hedgerows, is also eagerly awaited as a harbinger of spring.

Primula offers gardeners a luxurious range of species and cultivars, a number of which grow well in bogs, though many others need good drainage, particularly high alpine species. Generally primulas prefer a moist soil, and most are easy to grow. In many the five petals of the flowers join to form a basal tube. They are insect-pollinated and are mostly heterostylous—that is, the flowers are of two types, pin-eyed and thrum-eyed, descriptions that relate to the relative length of style and stamens, a variation designed to ensure cross-pollination. They also frequently hybridise. The height of the flowering stem on many introduced primulas noticeably varies with the pattern of spring temperatures. I have read that ants distribute primrose seed (which has an insect-attracting elaiosome), and certainly hybrid seedlings can often appear randomly in many parts of a garden.

Primula vulgaris grows best on moist north-facing banks, while the European and northern Asian *P. veris* (cowslip; Z5) is more often found in wet meadows but also appears under shrubs. With *P. elatior* (oxlip; Z5), all three of these British native species and their various hybrids are very tolerant of wet soils. All are also yellow-flowered; but *P. vulgaris* subsp. *sibthorpii*, from northern Greece, the Caucasus, Balkans, and Turkey to Armenia, has very early (even late winter) lilac flowers, and has proved to be a very durable plant in cultivation.

I find the very commonly grown and vigorous *Primula denticulata* (drumstick primula; Z5), which occurs across the Himalayas from Afghanistan to western China and down to Myanmar, thrives in wet sticky soil. Others can be a challenge, such as *P. vialii* (Z7) from Sichuan and Yunnan, which has eye-catching flower spikes with a small spire of crimson flower buds that open to lilac-blue. Dying all too readily over winter, it seems to be short-lived and needs to be regularly re-raised from seed. Failure of primulas in gardens can have many causes. In nature the montane species will rest under a protecting layer of snow for much of the year, and though they have plenty of moisture in the growing season, they will rot if kept wet in winter. And for the large southeast Tibetan cowslip *P. florindae* (Z6), which is otherwise easy to grow, its susceptibility to vine weevil damage can prove terminal.

The group of Asian primulas popularly known as candelabras are valued bog garden plants and where successfully grown can form sheets of bright colour when in flower. Most are hardy to Zone 6 and have 60 cm (2 ft.) flower stems; like primroses, they hybridise readily and will seed around. Two of the more commonly grown are from China: *Primula beesiana*, with rose-carmine flowers that have a yellow eye (now considered a subspecies of *P. bulleyana*, which is mostly sold in its golden-orange-flowered form), and *P. pulverulenta*, an attractive mealy plant with crimson-purple flowers, though I prefer its paler pink Bartley Group. *Primula prolifera*, which is a good yellow, also comes from China, but it has a wider range, occurring in Assam, Burma, and Indonesia. I have often seen the small orange-red-flowered *P. cockburniana* (Z5) growing in very wet conditions on mountains in western and southwestern Sichuan, where it benefits from winter snow cover; it is short-lived in cultivation.

Primula japonica, another candelabra, arrived unaided in my garden in a wet bed under the shade of a large shrub, and the puzzle is how it got there, with no other primulas around. Some years there

OPPOSITE TOP *Primula denticulata*
OPPOSITE BOTTOM *Primula pulverulenta* Bartley Group
ABOVE *Primula vialii*

are several seedlings, and other years just one or two. There are some good selections of this species, such as the vibrantly coloured 'Miller's Crimson' and also 'Postford White'.

As a group, candelabras do not seem to stand strong competition. In nature they are usually found in wet situations among the light cover afforded by scrubby trees and shrubs, or in wet, usually grazed, grassland. Good displays require good gardening (that is, weed and pest control), re-raising, and regularly adding replacement seedlings, or dividing when necessary—along with the provision of a moist, rich soil. To some extent, it is a matter of luck as to whether or not any particular wet garden naturally provides ideal conditions, but if it does, candelabras will produce many seedlings each year.

Seed of hardy primulas should ideally be sown when ripe and given cool, moist conditions over winter to assist spring germination. The very small seedlings can be susceptible to damping-off diseases, so extra care is needed, but they transplant and divide readily. Division in spring is favoured; with *Primula vulgaris* and others, this may be undertaken either in late winter or after the plants have flowered. Basal cuttings or rooted offsets can also be used.

PULICARIA

FLEABANE

COMPOSITAE

The herbaceous pulicarias are well adapted to wet soil. *Pulicaria dysenterica* (common fleabane; Z7), native from Europe to North Africa in wet situations, consolidates boggy ground with its densely matted, spreading rootstock. It grows to about 60 cm (2 ft.), and its bright-yellow, mid to late summer flowers are a great attraction to butterflies, such as the small fritillaries and skippers. I still grow a good patch of it near a large pond, and the only maintenance it receives is a late winter mow-off of its old stems. It seeds freely, especially on wet sites. If seedlings occur in a bed with other plants, it is important to weed them out early before their runners spread beneath the soil to establish permanent residence, for they can intertwine and engulf whatever else is planted.

PULMONARIA

LUNGWORT

BORAGINACEAE

Pulmonarias are popular early-flowering plants; many have the bonus of attractively marked leaves, and they will persist on moist soils. They can be sited with deciduous shrubs and taller herbs, so that after the sheltered flowers are enjoyed, their foliage can die down in summer, unnoticed among other plants. My favourite player in this role is the azure-blue-flowered European *Pulmonaria angusti-folia* (Z3), which is good at skulking and keeping close to the ground among other herbage but, if given a sunny open site on moist soil, quickly transforms itself to a taller (to 25 cm, 10 in.), more normal-looking pulmonaria (the commonly cultivated clone to which I refer is apparently not a good match for the species). This deciduous species can cope with very winter wet soil, but others that have overwintering rosettes, such as *P. rubra* (Z3) and *P. saccharata* (Z5), require good drainage. Increase by division.

RANUNCULUS
BUTTERCUP
RANUNCULACEAE

This large genus is aptly named for wet soils (*rana* is Latin for "frog"), and within its 600 species there are many attractive hardy herbaceous garden flowers. However, it also provides some of the most tenacious weeds, especially once they get among perennials. I confess to giving space to the double form (var. *pleniflorus*) of one

Ranunculus ficaria under light oak cover

such, the widespread European *Ranunculus repens* (creeping butter-cup; Z3), which makes a good ground cover.

The low-growing *Ranunculus ficaria* (lesser celandine; Z5), which ranges from Europe to western Asia and North Africa, has many devotees, particularly for its cultivated forms, but it can be difficult to remove as a weed in borders, since most forms produce small tubers on their roots, all of which can regenerate. Where naturalised in damp grassland, under oak cover, it makes a welcome addition to the early spring garden—a golden carpet of blossom whenever the sun shines sufficiently to open its flowers. For such a weedy plant, it is choosy about the sites in which it will persist, though it can settle to a lightly shaded border or mown grass. Happy in winter damp, it dies down by mid-summer, but it does not seem to compete too well with vigorous grass or cope with full sun or deep shade under trees.

Ranunculus lingua (greater spearwort; 50–150 cm, 20–60 in.; Z4), native to Britain and ranging from central Europe to central and western Asia, and the smaller, also native, and equally wide-ranging *R. flammula* (Z5) are strong-growing bog plants that can spread very quickly in shallow water by means of their underground rhizomes. A single shoot of *R. lingua*, given warm, nutrient-rich water, can spread to cover 250 sq.m (269 sq.ft.) in just a few years, but it is fairly easy to control. There is also an octoploid, *R. lingua* 'Grandiflorus', whose larger flowers might be preferred. Both species tolerate slightly acid to slightly alkaline water.

Ranunculus aquatilis (white water-crowfoot) from Europe and *R. circinatus* also from Europe and northern Asia can be annuals or perennials (both are Z5). These are less frequently seen now than they were, but they are worth seeking out for the pleasures of their white flowers and delicate foliage. On water, their trailing stems can grow to a length of 2 m (6.6 ft.). Water-crowfoots can be propagated by means of cuttings or seed.

Any hesitation about growing buttercups is soon overcome by the double form of the Eurasian meadow buttercup *Ranunculus acris* 'Flore Pleno', for it is an easy-care plant that gives a long flowering display and doesn't produce seedlings. The only difficulty is in being able to spot other buttercups that may germinate among the clump. It is set back but not killed by inundations, and flowering stems are about 38 cm (15 in.). The smaller-growing *R. constantinopolitanus* 'Plenus', of which the species occurs from eastern Europe to northern Iran, can also tolerate a moist soil but is fussier over its situation, and seems to need a sunny bed. Another for damp soils is the attractive, tall (90 cm, 36 in.) white-flowered *R. aconitifolius* 'Flore Pleno' (Z5) from central Europe. North America also has its own native wet-soil buttercups, such as *R. hispidus* (northern swamp buttercup).

For most buttercups, division, or naturally produced runners are the most often used means of propagation. Seed can be sown as soon as ripe. Note that several are poisonous and can blister skin.

RESTIO

RESTIONACEAE

Mostly perennial herbs with rush-like growth, the many restios, which occur in South Africa, Madagascar, and Australia, have their leaves reduced to sheaths, and their green stems undertake photosynthesis. The decorative-looking *Restio tetraphyllus* (Z9) from eastern Australia and Tasmania is sometimes called the feather plant for its tussock (to 1 m, 3.3 ft.) of bright green stems with clusters of fine branchlets; *R. complanatus* is another but smaller (to 60 cm, 24 in.) Australian species. Both require damp soil. The endemic Tasmanian *R. oligocephalus* is common on damp heaths; it is a plant for damp rather than wet soil. Most are dioecious; seed may set when both male and female plants are grown, but division of the rhizomatous clumps is the usual method of increase.

RHEUM

RHUBARB
POLYGONACEAE

The hardy herbaceous rheums have both culinary and medicinal use, and generally respond well to moist soils. Some, as one sees in the mountains of Iran and Turkey, are adapted to withstand a dry summer by perennating; but others, such as *Rheum alexandrae* (Z5), from western China and Tibet, grow in constantly moist soil that is under snow from late autumn. This species, with its rosette of relatively small (20 cm, 8 in.) entire leaves, looks very little like the more familiar garden rhubarb; nor does the more photogenic, central to western Himalayan *R. nobile* (Z7), with its inflorescence column of startling, whitish cream overlapping bracts, which completely shield its flowers. Both are more difficult to grow than the vigorous red-leaved cultivars of *R. palmatum* (Z6), a species from northwestern China that grows particularly well on moist soil in full sun with flower spikes to 2 m (6.6 ft.) or more. Rheums can be raised from seed but, because they hybridise in cultivation, are mostly increased by division.

Rheum palmatum, a spring shoot

Rodgersia aesculifolia from Erlang Shan, western Sichuan

RODGERSIA

SAXIFRAGACEAE

Though only a small genus of bold-foliaged, eastern Asian, hardy herbaceous perennials, its members are well represented in gardens. Their long (60–90 cm, 2–3 ft.) stalked leaves are variously palmate or pinnate, and their tall inflorescences can be impressive. In this my thoughts return to a side valley of the lower Min River in Sichuan, where an area of damp grassy hillside is flecked white in May by cascades of the large flat-topped flowering cymes of rodgersias. Individually, flowers are small and, though they do not have petals, coloured sepals achieve their floral effect.

Normally found on wet forested mountainsides, rodgersias form a tightly packed clump of rhizomes. Their foliage dies down in autumn, and the Japanese and Korean *Rodgersia podophylla*, whose leaves take on attractive reddish brown tints when mature, can die down earlier, in late summer or early autumn. The popular *R. pinnata* from western China seems happy enough in a wet soil, but I am a little more cautious with *R. aesculifolia* from northern and western China and southeastern Tibet, which in my garden is given a raised bed. All three species are Zone 5. Seedlings are slow growing, but individual seedling vigour seems variable. I found *R. aesculifolia* took six years or more to form a mature flowering clump. Can be divided with care.

RORIPPA

YELLOWCRESS
CRUCIFERAE

For the fortunate with a clear water stream or spring, the growing of one's own watercress is possible. *Rorippa nasturtium-aquaticum* (syn. *Nasturtium officinale*; Z7) has a wide distribution in Eurasia and North Africa and is introduced in North and South America. It is reasonably hardy, dying back in winter, and grows readily to 60 cm (24 in.) in shallow water and on wet mud. Normally grown as a crop in spring-fed clear chalk streams with a water temperature of around 10°C (50°F), it can then grow through winter; it also tolerates more neutral water. In a wet garden, it can be grown as a salad green using a shallow moist trench for summer and pots stood in water in a cold frame over winter. Once established, it will seed around and spread (stems root readily at the nodes when in water), becoming a weed in flowerbeds.

RUDBECKIA

CONEFLOWER
COMPOSITAE

Many rudbeckias are at their best on wet soils, giving a dependable massed display of flowers later in summer. There are about 25 species in North America, where they occur as plants of meadows and streambanks, and most are worthy of a place in wet gardens. *Rudbeckia fulgida* var. *sullivantii* 'Goldsturm' (to 60–70 cm, 24–28 in.; Z4) will even tolerate the occasional inundation, while also able to grow on dry soils.

Rudbeckia laciniata 'Goldquelle' died out with me, but *R. l.* 'Herbstsonne' (Z3) has, over the years, become a firm favourite in my garden. I disregarded it when I grew it on a dry soil, but in a warm site, on a moist soil it grows luxuriantly to about 2 m (6.6 ft.) and, if space permits, then the outer stems can be allowed to fall (staking to about half the plant's height) to produce masses of its large, golden-rayed flowers from the ground up. Its dense advancing growth will suppress other plants around the clump, so I pair it with earlier season plants (Dutch irises, perennial poppies) that will be dying back as the rudbeckia swamps them. In a warm moist situation its golden cascades can hold for weeks, and many colourful Vanessa butterflies will be attracted to these flowers. Perennial coneflowers die back in winter to a resting rootstock; *R. laciniata* may die out on wet soils that are very cold (below –10°C, 14°F) in winter. Increase by seed or division. *Rudbeckia fulgida* var. *sullivantii* 'Goldsturm' seeds around.

RUMEX

DOCK
POLYGONACEAE

Docks and sorrels are little cultivated other than the broadleaved garden form of *Rumex acetosa* (common sorrel; Z3), which is grown as a vegetable. But even outside the vegetable garden, this species gives me great pleasure every year when the mass of its maroon flowering spikes mixes with flowering grasses to tinge my meadow. The Eurasian *R. sanguineus* var. *sanguineus* (red-veined dock; Z6) and the more vigorous *R. hydrolapathum* (great water dock; to 1 m, 3.3 ft.; Z5) are sometimes cultivated; however, most gardeners will be more familiar with the weedy docks (broadleaved dock, *R. obtusifolius*, for example), which are deep-rooted, free-seeding perennials on heavy and wet soils. As a child, like most other children of my day, I used

TOP *Rudbeckia fulgida* var. *sullivantii* 'Goldsturm'
ABOVE *Rudbeckia laciniata* 'Herbstsonne'

dock leaves to calm the skin irritation caused by stinging nettles (*Urtica*). Most come freely from seed.

RELATED GENERA

The northern temperate *Oxyria digyna* (mountain sorrel; Z2) can grow in moist, if well-drained, soil, and some forms can be very attractive in fruit.

SANGUINARIA

BLOODROOT
PAPAVERACEAE

Sanguinaria canadensis (Z4 or lower) occurs widely in eastern North America, and its white flowers can be seen along hedgerows in spring. The pretty many-petalled double, f. *multiplex*, the form most frequently encountered in cultivation, grows well on a wet soil if given a raised bed. It forms an attractive, low-growing (leaves to 30 cm, 12 in.) herbaceous perennial, slowly increasing the size of its clump each year. If damaged, the roots of sanguinaria exude a red sap that has a natural bactericide now used as a toothpaste additive to control plaque. Plants are most readily increased by *in situ* division in spring or late summer.

SANGUISORBA

BURNET
ROSACEAE

Several of these interesting, northern temperate perennial herbs are grown. Some occur on dry soils; others tolerate moist meadows. *Sanguisorba canadensis* (Z4) extends from east to west in northern North America; in the west it is separated as *S. stipulata*, with a range extending on into temperate Asia, and it is naturalised in Britain. It can be grown on somewhat wet soil, making a 25–100 cm (10–40 in.) tall plant with spikes of attractive green to yellowish white flowers, which, though petal-less, have pronounced stamens. The giant burnet, *S. officinalis* (to 1–2 m, 3.3–6.6 ft.; Z4) has a Eurasian and North American range; its maroon-sepalled flowers form in a shorter cluster. Happily, I find the bright pink-flowered *S. obtusa* (Z5) from Japan and Russia and *S. hakusanensis* (Z7), also from Japan and extending to Korea, grow well on my wet soil. The pink inflorescences of the latter species are lovely—dense, pendent, 10 cm (4 in.) in length, and heavily stamened. Increase by seed or division of rhizomatous rootstocks.

TOP *Sanguinaria canadensis*
f. *multiplex*
ABOVE *Sanguisorba hakusanensis*

HERBACEOUS PLANTS AND BULBS

SAURURUS

LIZARD'S TAIL

SAURURACEAE

Both species of *Saururus* are at home in swamps and wet-soil gardens. *Saururus cernus* (Z5) has a wide range in eastern North America; *S. chinensis* (Z6) is the eastern Asian species. Like the related houttuynias, they spread by runners, but their flower spikes (white in *S. cernus*, more cream in *S. chinensis*) are much longer. They also grow taller, *S. cernus* to 0.6–1.5 m (2–5 ft.). Flowers are small and bisexual. Propagation is by division in spring.

SAXIFRAGA

SAXIFRAGE

SAXIFRAGACEAE

Saxifraga is a large genus of some 440 species of annuals, biennials, and perennials, many of which, particularly the montane and woodland species, will grow well on wet soils. A large-flowered form of the well-named stoloniferous *S. stolonifera* (Z6) collected in eastern China has persisted on my wet soil for more than twenty years, having spent an earlier decade on a dry soil. Its natural montane habitat is very moist; there it survives long winter's snow and freezing mist, with rosettes sitting lightly on the soil surface. Others—*S. spathularis* (St. Patrick's cabbage; Z5) from Ireland, *S. umbrosa* (Pyrenean saxifrage; Z6), and their hybrid *S. ×urbium* (London pride; Z6)—are similarly surface-rooting and thrive in shady borders on wet soil (in confirmation, the latter has naturalised in woods by streams in Britain).

I particularly enjoy seeing the delicate white spring flowers of the European (extending to North Africa) *Saxifraga granulata* (meadow saxifrage, fair maids of France; Z5) growing in old meadows, churchyards, and ancient hedgerows. It is found mostly on soils that are reasonably drained, and in my own garden, where it is native, it grows well under trees. Flower stems rise 8–20 cm (3–8 in.), but leaves and flowers die down by mid to late summer. The dormant clumps enlarge each year, mostly by bulbils and, given mild weather in late autumn, they regrow small ground-hugging leaves, which persist over winter. At this stage in their growth, it is easy to increase the clumps by division.

Still, having lost saxifrages, I hesitate to recommend any for a wet site unless the plant can be well tended, regularly repropagated by division, stem cuttings, runners, or seed, and any competition from other plants controlled.

Saxifraga granulata

Several genera in this family are suited to moist soil. The most popular—*Astilbe*, *Astilboides*, *Chrysosplenium*, *Darmera*, *Heuchera*, *Rodgersia*, and *Tiarella*—have separate entries. Enthusiasts may want to try *Boykinia* (Z6–8) from eastern Asia and North America, the southwestern South American francoas (Z8/9), the western North American lithophragmas (Z8), the two Japanese peltoboykinias (Z6/7), and *Tellima grandiflora* (Z6), a clumping perennial from western North America with an 80 cm (31 in.) spike of green flowers. The hardy mitellas from North America and eastern Asia are low-growing (to 25 cm, 12 in.) spreading perennials, with small, attractive, greenish flowers on thin spikes; they too require a damp, cool, shady location.

SCHIZOSTYLIS

IRIDACEAE

Fully hardy and quite obliging for wet gardens, the lovely rich, satiny red-flowered *Schizostylis coccinea* (30–50 cm, 12–20 in.; Z6) from southern Africa grows well on my own wet soil, though I know from other gardens that it can be grown on a hot, dry soil. Several very good cultivars of this rhizomatous perennial have been selected, among them 'Red Dragon'; they flower in late summer and autumn, which makes them especially valued. 'Major', the larger form, holds its blossoms into early winter; these can withstand frosts of up to −5°C (23°F) without much damage, though snow, sleet, or hail will force a conclusion to flowering. The odd pink seedling will arise naturally if only a red form is grown. Of the various sites I have tried, schizostylis grows best where it has seeded itself in gravel over wet soil that catches full sun in summer but, though open, is shaded from the winter sun that can otherwise damage frozen growth. Can be seed raised, but clones are increased from offsets.

SCROPHULARIA

FIGWORT
SCROPHULARIACEAE

The native scrophularias of Eurasia and North America are mostly perennial herbs with a curious sort of beauty. Several occur naturally in wet places, along ditches and by open water; in these situations, their strong, upright, apple-green shoots catch the eye in late spring, but their tall (to 1 m, 3.3 ft.) flower spikes give rise to an expectation that is not quite fulfilled by their small brownish flowers. While not particularly a promoter of variegated plants, I recognise their value, especially for shady spots, and the hardy *Scrophularia auriculata* 'Variegata' (Z5) takes advantage of this west European and North African species' best characteristics. Scrophularias seed around, but not profusely with me, producing just the extra plant or two. Cutting off seedheads before plants distribute their seed is a very sensible practise on wet sites, with this and many other plants (for 'Variegata', such action has the advantage of stimulating foliage growth). Propagate 'Variegata' from early-season basal stem cuttings, or division.

RELATED GENERA

The woody New Zealand hebes (Z8) persist on very moist soil, and further genera in Scrophulariaceae, such as the herbaceous perennial temperate and subtropical gratiolas and New World micranthemums (Z9), are aquatic or will grow on very wet soils.

SENECIO
COMPOSITAE

Senecio is a large and variable genus; its species occupy many habitats, and several are xerophytic. Somewhat tolerant of wet soil and dependably hardy to −10°C (14°F) is *S. smithii* (Z7) from southern South America and the Falkland Islands; its broad spear-shaped leaves have a structural beauty, and their dark green contrasts well with the dense spikes of white daisy flowers. In sun, it grows to about 60 cm (2 ft.), making it a useful addition to the wet garden's range of herbaceous perennials. It is on my "quiet favourites" list. For propagation, see Compositae.

SILENE
CAMPION
CARYOPHYLLACEAE

I like having the widespread European *Silene dioica* (red campion; Z6) around. It "enjoys" my wet garden, where it is native, sowing itself into a range of sites and mostly behaving as a biennial. Among shrubs and along slightly shaded ditch edges, it makes large clumps, flowering from spring well into summer, with stems to 75 cm (30 in.) or more. It grows best with a western aspect (morning shade, afternoon sun). Logic said that its attractive compact selection 'Richmond' ought to grow similarly well, but it proved short-lived in a wet bed; and curiously neither the white campion, *S. latifolia* subsp. *alba*, or *S. ×hampeana*, the white campion's pink-flowered hybrid with

TOP *Senecio smithii*
ABOVE *Silene dioica*

S. dioica, will persist on my soil. The perennial *S. fimbriata* from the Caucasus, with its attractively inflated blossoms, is just about persisting on a wet but reasonably drained site, though it does not look permanent.

The fruit is a capsule with numerous, small hard seeds, and fresh seed usually germinates freely. Seedlings can be pricked out when small. For perennials, careful autumn or spring division of clumps usually succeeds.

SOLEIROLIA

MIND-YOUR-OWN-BUSINESS
URTICACEAE

A monotypic genus. Previously included in *Helxine*, *Soleirolia soleirolii* (Z9) is a low-growing, mat-forming, slender, creeping perennial with tiny round leaves and inconspicuous unisexual flowers. It comes from the western Mediterranean islands, notably Corsica and Sardinia, where it grows in damp shady places but also needs good drainage. It is just about hardy in temperate gardens, where its pale green mats make a useful but vigorous ground cover, with each trailing stem rooting from nodes. There are two popular cultivated selections, the golden-leaved 'Aurea' and the silver-variegated 'Variegata'. It is usually increased by division.

SOLIDAGO

GOLDENROD
COMPOSITAE

Solidagos, once so common in gardens, are now not often seen, perhaps because by self-seeding they can become very weedy. They are reasonably tolerant of wet soils, and for gardens there are many hybrids resulting, for example, from crosses of the Eurasian and North African *Solidago virgaurea* (Z5) with the North American *S. canadensis* (Z3). The thin stems of these herbaceous perennials grow up to 1 m (3.3 ft.). The sparsely flowered North American *S. patula* occurs naturally in swampy ground, and *S. riddellii* (syn. *Oligoneuron riddellii*; Z4) occurs in damp meadows. Increase by division.

SPATHIPHYLLUM

PEACE LILY
ARACEAE

The thirty-five or so species of *Spathiphyllum* range widely, but most occur in central and tropical South America. They are evergreen and can make largish handsome clumps, with the long-stalked leaves of some species reaching 1 m (3.3 ft.); the spathes, mostly white or green, are of similar or slightly greater height. Peace lilies grow well in warm moist conditions in a tropical border, and, having seen *S. cannifolium* growing naturally along the edge of rivers in Trinidad, I feel confident about their tolerance of wet soil. With their delicately scented, long-lasting white spathes, cultivars of the small, Central American *S. wallisii* are popular houseplants in temperate countries, but the species needs more light than provided by most building interiors to flower continuously. As with many aroids some people are allergic to the sap of spathiphyllums. All are Zone 10 and are easily increased by division.

SPIGELIA

PINKROOT
LOGANIACEAE

Most spigelias are native to the warm regions of the Americas and not often cultivated. The exception is *Spigelia marilandica* (woodland pinkroot; Z8), which herbaceous perennial grows naturally in damp rich soil and can be found in moist woods and along streambanks in the eastern and central United States. It forms a multi-stemmed clump (30–60 cm, 1–2 ft.) and has vivid red trumpet-shaped flowers that are yellow within. Increase by fresh seed, if available, or by division.

SPIRANTHES

LADY'S-TRESSES
ORCHIDACEAE

Lady's-tresses are small, mainly terrestrial orchids with an elongated, twisted inflorescence that carries many small white flowers. Several grow on damp ground, be it *Spiranthes aestivalis* (summer lady's-tresses) from Europe and North Africa (now extinct in Britain, alas), *S. sinensis* in India, China, Southeast Asia, and Australia, or *S. vernalis* from North and Central America. They appear to respond well to cultivation in pots or gardens, but gardeners should choose only cultivars, such as the vigorous and fragrant *S. cernua* var. *odorata* 'Chadds Ford' (Z5). For propagation, see Orchidaceae.

Spigelia marilandica

STACHYS

WOUNDWORT

LABIATAE

A large and widespread genus, with species of varying environmental need. Those that do tolerate wet soil are not, however, the most ornamental members of *Stachys* and are better suited to the wild garden. *Stachys palustris* (marsh woundwort; Z5), from Europe and North America, grows in swampy ground; it has attractive, pale blue flowers and is sometimes available from nurseries. Something more of an acquired taste, the weedier *S. sylvatica* (hedge woundwort; Z5), a British native with a Eurasian range, occurs naturally in my garden. This plant is extremely tolerant of wet soil, and I allow it to establish among bulbs under trees. Its small claret-coloured flowers form on 60–80 cm (24–31 in.) spikes, but its foliage is unpleasantly aromatic. If it gets into a formal area, it is hard to eradicate because of its long underground rhizomatous stems.

STOKESIA

STOKES' ASTER

COMPOSITAE

Stokesia laevis (Z6 with good drainage), a lovely perennial aster originating from pinewoods and savannah in the southeastern United States (North Carolina to Florida), grows well on wet ground, to 60 cm (24 in.). Besides the light and dark blue forms, white, yellow, and pink cultivars are now available; however, as with many moisture lovers from warmer latitudes, the cold wet of a less temperate, more northern winter can be fatal to its overwintering rosette of leaves, and in such places, a raised bed will be required. Both the species and the pale yellow-flowered *S. laevis* 'Mary Gregory' survive well in my garden on a slightly raised bed but may be counted on to flower more freely on a well-drained warm soil. Increase by division.

TOP *Stokesia laevis* 'Mary Gregory'
ABOVE *Strelitzia reginae* flowering on Christmas Day, RBG Kew

STRELITZIA

BIRD OF PARADISE

STRELITZIACEAE

The vivid orange and blue-tepalled *Strelitzia reginae*, from the East Cape region of South Africa, is grown worldwide in warm temperate gardens with a winter minimum of 10°C (50°F). The leaf blade of the closely related *S. juncea* is absent, giving its remaining long petiole a succulent appearance. Both can grow in either moist or dryish soil.

HERBACEOUS PLANTS AND BULBS

The taller (7–10 m, 23–33 ft.), more banana-like perennial *Strelitzia nicolai* (Z9/10) grows naturally along riverbanks in South Africa. In this species the upright tepals are white, and the sagittate "tongue" is blue. It is easily grown and has long been cultivated. Also with two-ranked, long-petioled, fan-like leaves, and large distinctive flowers in a large beak-like spathe is the closely related *Ravenala madagascariensis* (traveller's palm; to 16 m, 53 ft.) from Madagascar and the similar *Phenakospermum guianense* (to 10 m, 33 ft.) from tropical South American rainforest; both are Zone 10 and require warm temperate to tropical conditions. All three plants require moist but well-drained soils and shelter.

The arillate seed—bright blue in *Ravenala*, orange in *Phenakospermum*, red in *Strelitzia*—is best sown when ripe in a warm (21°C, 70°F) propagation frame. Most can be increased from young basal offshoots.

Stylophorum diphyllum

STYLOPHORUM
WOOD POPPY
PAPAVERACEAE

Stylophorums are perhaps the best woodland poppies for a cool, moist soil. The perennial, eastern North American *Stylophorum diphyllum* (Z6) tucks in under shrubs or trees, where its crisp, young oak-like leaves herald small golden poppy flowers to be followed by glistening, swollen, oval seedpods before it disappears for the winter. Seeds sown when ripe and kept cool usually germinate the following spring, as they do for the central and eastern Chinese species *S. lasiocarpum* (Z5). Also buttercup-yellow-flowered, this is a much larger plant (to 45 cm, 18 in.) but usually a shorter-lived though vigorous biennial. Its seedlings will germinate readily on a gravel drive, and they also transplant relatively easily when young, unlike some other poppies. Any root damage so caused, however, will become immediately obvious from the oozing orange-red sap that flows from any wound. Its happiness varies from site to site, and it is perhaps better to accede to its self-selected needs, allowing a large batch to regenerate naturally where it grows well. It has a long season of growth, but if it lives beyond two years, its leaves can become tatty. The western Chinese *S. sutchuenense* is similar but not often seen in cultivation. All are relatively easy to raise from seed, and transplant tolerably well.

Symphytum caucasicum

SYMPHYTUM
COMFREY
BORAGINACEAE

Probably subconsciously inspired by the drifts of *Symphytum* 'Hidcote Blue' (Z5) in the lovely gardens of that name, I use the herbaceous perennial symphytums similarly. I had been warned about the invasiveness of *S. caucasicum* (Z4), which, as its epithet suggests, comes from the Caucasus and Iran, where it grows in wet meadows, but thought first to increase stock of it by growing it on for just a year in my vegetable garden—a bad mistake. All its many thick roots possess innumerable tiny detachable scales, each of which is capable of regeneration: after removing every piece I could find, I had to continue to weed for two years to clear the remainder. Lesson learned! Among and under trees in grass, it makes a fine ground cover (to about 60 cm, 24 in.), producing masses of its startlingly blue flowers in early summer; it is easily kept in place by mowing (that is, cutting the grass up to the predetermined line chosen for the extent of its spread). I have also used the lower-growing *S. ibericum* (Z5) from the Caucasus and northeastern Turkey as ground cover in wooded areas; but again, because of their invasiveness on a moist soil, avoid putting them into formal flowerbeds! Increase by root cuttings or division.

SYMPLOCARPUS
SKUNK CABBAGE
ARACEAE

Symplocarpus foetidus (Z4), another perennial skunk cabbage of boggy gardens, well earns its epithet as the greenish to purple-brown flowers emerge in early spring and open to emit a foetid odour. Smell aside, the flowers have a beautiful form; they grow close to the ground with the spathe forming an enclosing snailshell-like globe around the spadix. The spadix can generate considerable warmth, which helps to transmit its fly-attracting "scent" and also protects the flower from frost. Needing similar conditions in cultivation to the lysichitons, its leaves are on a similar scale, if smaller, and more ovate, about 45 × 30 cm (18 × 12 in.). Its distribution ranges in northeastern North America from southern Canada and south through the United States at higher elevations; it also occurs in northeastern Asia. Seed, if available, is the preferred means of increase. Division is possible if carefully accomplished.

TANACETUM

TANSY
COMPOSITAE

Tanacetum parthenium (syn. *Chrysanthemum parthenium*; feverfew; Z6), now widely naturalised in northern temperate regions but originally from southeastern Europe and the Caucasus, grows well on wet soils. There are several good garden forms; I have almost an embarrassment of the double ('Plenum') on my wet soil. It flowers so abundantly and seeds just as freely, its seedlings then arising on any bare soil. Feverfew is shallow-rooted and grows quickly, as the new season warms, to produce its 40–60 cm (16–24 in.) or taller mid-summer flowering stems from its overwintering clump of leaves, but plants tend to be short-lived, almost biennial, becoming scruffy if they survive into their third year. The species itself is increasingly popular, perhaps because its foliage is considered to have migraine-relieving properties.

THALICTRUM

MEADOW-RUE
RANUNCULACEAE

Thalictrum flavum subsp. *glaucum*

Some thalictrums (there are about 330 species worldwide) grow well in wet soil. *Thalictrum flavum*, native to Britain and through Europe to North Africa, the Caucasus, and Siberia, may be found in fens, streamsides, and wet meadows, and in North America several species, such as *T. dasycarpum* (purple meadow-rue), occupy similar habitats. In temperate gardens it is often the Iberian (and northwest African) *T. flavum* subsp. *glaucum* that is cultivated. As in thalictrums generally, its coloured sepals fall as the flower opens, leaving a conspicuous display of stamens. On wet soil its flower spikes can reach 1.5 m (5 ft.), and it will regenerate naturally, though not profusely. In western China the lovely blue-flowered *T. delavayi* can reach nearly 2 m (6.6 ft.), but this is when drawn up among forest trees. It occurs naturally in damp woods where the soil is rich in humus, but in cultivation it can be tricky to overwinter in a cold wet soil. 'Hewitt's Double' is its more frequently grown selection.

Thalictrums are easy to raise from seed; indeed, I trim off old flowering heads of *Thalictrum flavum* to prevent its self-sowing. Those mentioned are hardy to Zone 5, but the choicer alpine species need a lot more care and control of competition from other plants. Some are dioecious; selected forms, including *T. delavayi* 'Hewitt's Double', can, with care, be divided.

TIARELLA

FOAMFLOWER

SAXIFRAGACEAE

Low-growing, clump-forming hardy perennials from eastern Asia and North America, tiarellas occur naturally in moist woodland and along streambanks and, like the related heucheras, they have attractive foliage and delicate flower stems to 30–80 cm (12–31 in.) or so. Growing over a range of latitudes and altitudes, they tolerate captivity but really need a raised bed in a wet garden, as they suffer in cold wet winters. Flowers are mostly small and white, sometimes pink or green. Several species are grown, among them *Tiarella trifoliata* (Z5) from western North America and *T. wherryi* (Z4) from the southeastern United States. Many cultivars have been selected, particularly from the eastern North American *T. cordifolia* (Z3) or produced by hybridisation with all three. Increase by seed or division, *T. cordifolia* from plantlets on its spreading runners.

TRACHYSTEMON

BORAGINACEAE

As a perennial ground cover, *Trachystemon orientalis* (Z5) from the Caucasus, Turkey, Greece, and eastern Bulgaria is well appreciated. It grows naturally in dampish woods (and has naturalised in southern Britain) but can be cultivated on both damp and dry soils. This species was first recommended to me by George Brown, who was keen to find ground cover plants that could grow under trees; in cultivation, it will establish even under limes. Once the ground has been cleared of perennial weeds, its dense summer foliage (to 60 cm, 2 ft.) keeps even nettles, hogweed, cow parsley, and docks at bay; and in early spring, before the separate leafy shoots expand, comes the bonus of its borage-like flowers, produced on shoots to 15 cm (6 in.) or more. Propagate by division.

TRIFOLIUM

CLOVER

LEGUMINOSAE

The Eurasian *Trifolium ochroleucon* (sulphur clover) can be found on wet soils, and the pleasingly attractive, taller (60 cm, 24 in.) *T. rubens* from central and eastern Europe, with its large, dark red terminal flower heads, grows well with me on wet soil in full sun. Clumps of this strong, deep-rooted perennial have persisted for nearly twenty years in a slightly raised bed. Self-sown seedlings establish readily in gravel over wet soil, but they have to be moved when young. Because it seeds freely, it is sensible to clip off flower heads before the seeds are distributed. Both are Zone 6.

TRILLIUM

TRILLIACEAE

Trilliums are mainly North American deciduous woodland perennials that occur on a variety of soils, and many of the thirty or so species are in cultivation. *Trillium cernuum* (nodding trillium) from eastern North America, which has pink, reddish brown, and occasionally white-flowered forms, grows naturally in moist, peaty soils by swamps. Several, such as *T. grandiflorum*, grow on calcareous soils; *T. undulatum* occurs on free-drained, acid soils. *Trillium ovatum* (western trillium) is a plant of wet woods and streambanks. The little three-leaved, small green-flowered *T. tschonoskii* occurs in the Himalayas, western China, and Japan, usually in moist woodland soil and sometimes by streamsides. Constant moisture and cool summer growing conditions are a common requirement, and in cultivation all must have good drainage. Those mentioned are hardy to Zone 5, except *T. cernuum*, which is Zone 6.

Flowers are terminal and usually have three green sepals and three coloured petals. Ants are attracted to the elaiosome, an oily appendage on the seeds; they carry the seed back to their nests, eating the appendage and discarding—and thus distributing—the seed. Seed requires vernalising, and some seed exhibits double dormancy. Seedlings grow slowly, taking from five to seven years to flower. To induce more offsets, growers sometimes ring the tuberous rhizome at the juncture of old and new growth and then replant. All divisions reestablish slowly.

TRITELEIA

ALLIACEAE

Two species of interest are from western North America. *Triteleia hyacinthina* grows naturally in wet meadows, and *T. laxa* and its selection 'Koningin Fabiola' are even tolerant of winter-wet soils, especially so where the small bulbs are exposed to a baking sun in summer. These thus flower better and persist for many years given a slightly raised bed, and can also be naturalised in grass. Both are frost hardy in Zone 8, and probably lower.

Triteleias have flowers in umbels, on 35–45 cm (14–18 in.) scapes for *Triteleia laxa*. Increase from daughter bulbs is slow, but they

TOP *Trifolium rubens*
ABOVE *Triteleia laxa* 'Koningin Fabiola'

regenerate readily from seed, with the seedlings growing on to flowering size in two or three years.

TRITONIA
IRIDACEAE

A cormous, perennial genus from tropical and southern Africa, which includes the pink-flowered *Tritonia disticha* subsp. *rubrolucens* (Z8) of the Drakensberg. This deciduous taxon grows to about 60 cm (2 ft.) and seems tolerant of wet soil, in which condition its corms increase quickly. It is intolerant of an alkaline soil over limestone, where its foliage becomes chlorotic and weak. Propagate from seed or division of corms. Regular division and replanting are needed to keep a group flowering.

TROLLIUS
GLOBEFLOWER
RANUNCULACEAE

These hardy herbaceous perennials are not grown as frequently as they deserve, particularly as all grow in wet soil and flower well in good light conditions. The many orange- to yellow-flowered hybrids from the Asiatic species, which grow to about 60 cm (2 ft.), are readily available, but the less common lemon-yellow *Trollius stenopetalus* from western China and northern Myanmar also makes a fine garden plant. Forms of the soft yellow circumboreal *T. europaeus*, native in northern Britain, may have slightly lank flower stems (to 90 cm, 36 in.) and have to fight harder for a place. *Trollius yunnanensis* and *T. pumilus* are more diminutive species from wet yak-grazed turf in western China, the latter extending to Tibet and the Himalayas. Globeflowers are hardy, mostly to Zone 5, though *T. stenopetalus* is regarded as Zone 6. They are usually increased by division, as seed may take two years to germinate, and seedlings are slow growing.

UNCINIA
HOOK SEDGE
CYPERACEAE

The perennial uncinias come mainly from the southern hemisphere, but with its lovely foliage, which can run from bright to deep red over the season, *Uncinia uncinata* is frequently grown on the edge of hardiness. It grows to about 30 cm (1 ft.) high, its long leaves arching to the ground. Its flowers are unisexual (both male and female form on a long spike, with males at the top), and the fruit is solitary and

TOP *Trollius europaeus*
ABOVE *Trollius stenopetalus*

HERBACEOUS PLANTS AND BULBS

triangular. But be careful of the ripe inflorescence: each seed awn is equipped with a pair of fine hooks that will catch on clothing or the fine hairs of skin. The running *U. rubra* and clumping *U. egmontiana* are similar; all three are from New Zealand, and all are Zone 8/9.

Uncinias make good container plants, and seedlings regenerate naturally in my garden. Still, seed is best sown at minimum temperatures of 16°C (61°F). Plants can be easily divided but need warmth, which means both recovering divisions and keeping fresh stock over winter in a cold frame. Old winter-damaged plants can become a dead mat in summer, with perhaps a few sparse new leaves.

VANCOUVERIA

INSIDEOUT FLOWER
BERBERIDACEAE

This genus of three, epimedium-like perennial herbs with long slender rhizomes occurs in the Pacific Northwest of North America. Though spurned by some gardeners, *Vancouveria hexandra* (Z5) is charming as a ground cover, its small white flower sprays held above deep green, three-pinnate leaflet leaves. Low-growing (15–40 cm, 6–16 in.), this is a fine plant for moist woodland use. Increase by division or fresh seed.

VERATRUM

FALSE HELLEBORE
MELANTHIACEAE

Veratrum is perhaps the most widely cultivated of the many little-known genera in Melanthiaceae. Often, those who grow these deciduous, mostly hardy perennials take as much (if not more) pleasure from their accordion-folded leaves as they do from their flowers. These many-veined leaves are distinctive and very attractive when young. Their star-shaped flowers have perianth segments of equal length, and the colour varies from white or green, to maroon and chocolate. They are mainly bisexual, though some cultivated veratrums are male. The flowers are gathered together in dense racemes or panicles atop a long stalk, and their numerous seeds are formed in capsules. These plants are toxic (their toxins irritate the skin of some people), but they are extensively used in folk medicine, particularly, for example, *V. viride* by the indigenous peoples of western North America.

Veratrum has a northern temperate distribution; several species grow naturally in wettish soils, but they are not exclusive to this

Veronica beccabunga

habitat and can be found in moist forest—for example, *V. album* (Z5) and *V. nigrum* (Z6) occur in the larch swamp forests of northeastern China, and both the North American *V. viride* (Z3) and *V. californicum* (Z7) grow naturally in wet thickets, meadows, bogs, and swamps. I recall *V. maackii* in Guizhou Province, growing on an open, south-facing but moist mountainside at just over 2000 m (6562 ft.), and I was delighted, some five years later, to see one of its progeny flowering at Kew with a spray of gorgeous chocolate-brown flowers on a 60 cm (2 ft.) stem.

Veratrum album is distributed from Europe to North Africa and northern Asia; *V. nigrum* occurs from southern Europe to Siberia and northeastern Asia. Both are impressive garden plants; the former has been cultivated in Britain from 1548, and the latter offers flowering spikes of from 60 cm (2 ft.) to 1.8 m (6 ft.) in good conditions. *Veratrum viride* (Indian poke) occurs in both eastern (from southern Canada to the Georgia uplands) and western North America (Washington to Mexico), producing tall (60–200 cm, 2–6.6 ft.) heavily laden flower spikes with thin drooping branches of musky-scented pale green flowers that have darker centres. While this is an impressive plant, the similarly sized *V. californicum*, which ranges up to Washington, is preferred for its larger whitish flowers, and its branchlets do not droop.

Most veratrums are hardy, though the flowering of some is erratic, even in nature. Where seed is available it is best sown in autumn and kept cool and moist over winter for spring germination. Seedlings do not grow rapidly, and as these plants only slowly increase the size of their rhizomatous clumps, material for propagation is often limited to root and bud cuttings. Spring division is the usual recommendation for the plant's quicker recovery, but, since many veratrums start growth early in the year, autumn division may be preferred. Some may produce bulbils on damaged flower spikes.

VERONICA
SPEEDWELL
SCROPHULARIACEAE

A few veronicas require wet conditions: *Veronica beccabunga* (brooklime; Z5) from temperate Eurasia and North Africa and also naturalised in North America; and *V. americana* (Z2), native to North America and northeastern Asia, for example. The pretty, pale blue-flowered *V. gentianoides* from the Crimea (Ukraine), Turkey, and the Caucasus tolerates a moist soil but dies out if it is too wet. *Veronica chamaedrys* (germander speedwell) often occurs in lawns, and *V. fili-formis* (threadstalk speedwell), originally from Turkey and the Caucasus, is a lawn weed *par excellence* in North America and the British Isles; since it rarely sets seed, its spread may be attributed to its ability to regenerate from mown pieces. It is a matter of taste, I suppose, but I have always enjoyed seeing the blue flowers of speedwells in informal lawns in spring, and I particularly admired such a blue sheen in the lawns of Munich's botanic garden. More usefully for the border, *V. longifolia* (Z4) from Eurasia is a good garden plant with many cultivars; it grows to around 90 cm (36 in.).

Once established *Veronica beccabunga* freely self-sows. Division increases most perennials. Stem cuttings can also be easily rooted.

VERONICASTRUM
CULVER'S ROOT
SCROPHULARIACEAE

The perennial *Veronicastrum virginicum* (1.2–2 m, 4–6.6 ft.; Z3) is well adapted to moist soils, as its habitat range in eastern North America includes wet meadows. Its leaves form attractive whorls on stiff stems. Hebe-like terminal inflorescences are produced in high summer; they can be long, with flowers ranging from white to pale pink, pale blue, lilac, and purple-rose. The genus also occurs in eastern Asia. Veronicastrums generally flag very quickly if the soil dries. Mainly propagated by division, though note: new shoots often arise late from the rootstock in spring.

VIOLA
VIOLET
VIOLACEAE

The approximately 500 species of *Viola* have a wide northern temperate distribution but also occur in the southern temperate regions of the world, in various habitats on a variety of soils. Several species occur naturally in wet habitats. One such, the perennial *V. palustris* (marsh violet; Z1), is widely distributed in northern Eurasia and North America; it has pale lilac flowers and is sometimes cultivated. Another example of moist soil tolerance is seen in the pretty western North American *V. glabella* (stream violet; Z5), whose range extends to Alaska and to northeast Asia. The perennial *V. riviniana* (dog violet; Z5), widespread in Europe extending to Russia and North Africa, also persists on wet soils, as do its cultivars.

Violas are readily recognised by their long-stalked, bisexual, five-

TOP *Veronicastrum virginicum*
'Lavendelturm'
ABOVE *Veronicastrum virginicum* 'Temptation'

petalled, spurred or pouched flowers; a few are scented. They can grow well on a wet soil, if it is raised to give drainage. For many years I had some charming bicolours that arose naturally from a cross between a cultivated pansy and the weedy and widespread annual field pansy, *Viola arvensis* (Z4/5), which regularly regenerated and flowered on my wet gravel drive.

Viola odorata (sweet violet; Z8) is native in Britain but is also wider ranging and frequently introduced. It grows well on wet soil in hedge bottoms or under trees, where it finds slightly drier conditions. Several colour forms occur naturally from a dark blue to white, and this perennial forms tough, low-growing (to 15 cm, 6 in.) spreading clumps. It also self-sows, making it well suited to the wilder parts of a garden. More usefully, the semi-evergreen, dark-purple-leaved form of dog violet, *V. riviniana* Purpurea Group, which was long known in gardens by the misapplied name of *V. labradorica*, takes to wet soils with relish, spreading vigorously and also regenerating by seed, especially on gravel over wet soil.

By the use of pots or containers, wet gardens need not be denied the many pleasure of violets, or the smiling faces of pansies derived from several *Viola* species, the *V.* ×*wittrockiana* hybrids. There is a host of free-flowering colour forms, with particular selections for winter or summer, such that pansies can be had in flower in most seasons. Also for gardens in areas with only light or no frost, the blue-and-white-flowered *V. hederacea* (ivy-leaf violet; Z9/10) is easy to grow. Preferring moist soil and shade, it soon spreads to form a large clump, and it has a long flowering season. It has an extensive range in nature from Tasmania to Queensland and also Malaysia.

Violets set seed freely. The small seeds form in sometimes explosive dry capsules; some have a small protruding oil body, which attracts ants that thus help with distribution. If high temperatures are avoided, seed should germinate readily. Modern pansy cultivars are treated as annuals or biennials. Perennial violas may be increased by division; herbaceous stem cuttings are used for those with trailing stems.

WAHLENBERGIA

ROCK BELLS
CAMPANULACEAE

The cultivated wahlenbergias are generally short-lived perennials, mostly from the southern hemisphere. The procumbent, western European *Wahlenbergia hederacea* can establish itself on wet acid lawns. Another, *W. gloriosa* (royal bluebell; Z9) from Victoria and New South Wales, spreads by underground stems to form a matted clump, with shoots rising only to about 10 cm (4 in.). The spreading perennial wahlenbergias respond well to regular division.

XANTHOSOMA

TANNIA

ARACEAE

Of the several tropical American species, *Xanthosoma violaceum* (blue tannia or taro; Z10), from southern North America through Central and South America, is widely cultivated in even temperate gardens in summer as a foliage plant as well as for its edible pinkish-fleshed rhizome. Easily grown and coping well with wet (though not saturated) conditions, it quickly produces its attractive alocasia-like, long-petioled leaves, which have a waxy bloom. With large leaves (70 cm, 28 in., or more) and stalks of 85 cm (34 in.) or longer, plants can reach 2.5 m (8 ft.). Increase from offsets.

Zantedeschia aethiopica

ZANTEDESCHIA

ARUM LILY

ARACEAE

Zantedeschia includes some eight species native to southern Africa. In my younger days I grew large pots of the South African *Z. aethiopica*, which proved good standby plants for the flowering conservatory. Out of doors, this species can survive in warm sunny sheltered spots in Zone 8, such as against a house wall, its aerial parts dying back from winter frost to recover in the warmth of late spring. In a bed in a warm temperate garden, the commonly cultivated form remains evergreen and, in wet conditions, grows luxuriantly to 1 m (3.3 ft.). It can be grown in shallow water. The golden yellow-spathed *Z. elliottiana* (Z9), which has white-flecked leaves, has likewise long been cultivated.

I also grew some of the tuberous South African species in pots in a cool greenhouse, including the now popular Swaziland arum, *Zantedeschia rehmannii* (Z9), paler and white forms of this purple-red-flowered species occur naturally. I have seen this species set in standing water when in growth (in its native habitat it grows in swamps), and it also grows well with partial shade. Generally, these tuberous species need a winter resting period in cultivation.

There has been much breeding and selection from several species, to the extent that gardeners now have a choice of fifty or more culti-

Zephyranthes candida

vars. Arum lilies can make attractive groups in gardens where there is little or no frost, and in harder climates their dormant tuberous rhizomes can be lifted and overwintered in frost-free conditions.

On occasion I have found *Zantedeschia aethiopica* seedlings on the moist soil of my garden, but separation of offsets is the usual means of increase.

ZEPHYRANTHES

ZEPHYR LILY
AMARYLLIDACEAE

A genus of small, attractively flowered bulbs from the warm regions of temperate North, Central, and South America, often cultivated in regions with little frost. In nature, they can be found along riversides and in areas subject to seasonal wetness. The white-flowered, crocus-sized *Zephyranthes candida* from Argentina and Uruguay is lately sold as a bog plant. Though tolerant of such conditions, as where it grows naturally by the Rio de la Plata, it needs either Zone 9 or a border by a heated building to overwinter. Like most zephyr lilies, it survives and flowers better if grown in a container and kept warmer and drier through winter. Propagate by division of daughter bulbs. Seed raising is fairly straightforward.

CHAPTER 7
Aquatic Plants

This brief directory of aquatic plants includes some ferns as well as several tropical species to give a flavour of the diverse range of plants available for water areas, from aquaria to lakes.

ALISMA
WATER-PLANTAIN
ALISMATACEAE

Bog and shallow-water herbaceous perennials, often with spear-shaped emergent leaves and tiered flower panicles (20–100 cm, 8–40 in.) in early summer. *Alisma plantago-aquatica* (Z5) is from northern temperate regions. Increase by seed or division.

ANUBIAS
ARACEAE

Tender, tropical African bog or shallow-water aroids with creeping rhizomes grown for their clusters of bright orange berries borne on short (15 cm, 6 in., or less) stalks. *Anubias afzelii* from central to tropical West Africa has long-stalked leaves, to 60 cm (2 ft.), and is grown in tropical pools. Increase by seed or division.

APONOGETON
WATER-HAWTHORN
APONOGETONACEAE

A genus of aquatic perennials, many of them tender, with submerged and floating leaves and delicate white flowers. The tuberous rhizomes of the southern African *Aponogeton distachyos* (Z8/9) are tolerably hardy; leaves are to 25 cm (10 in.). Usually increased by division.

Nymphaea 'Colossea', a 1901 Marliac hybrid, in the National Collection at Pocklington

BUTOMUS
FLOWERING RUSH
BUTOMACEAE

A shallow, emergent, rhizomatous perennial growing 0.6–1.5 m (2–5 ft.). *Butomus umbellatus* (Z8) forms attractive umbels of flowers. It has a wide distribution in Europe, central western Asia, and North Africa. Seedlings grow slowly, so increase is mostly by division.

CABOMBA
FANWORT
CABOMBACEAE

The New World cabombas have lacy, fan-shaped, submerged leaves on long (to 2 m, 6.6 ft.) stems often with tiny peltate floating leaves. Flowers (1–2 cm, 0.4–0.8 in.) open above water. Cabombas are useful oxygenators and give shelter to fish in aquaria and pools. *Cabomba caroliniana* needs warm (minimum 18°C, 64°F) water for growth but can overwinter in temperate regions. Increase by stem cuttings.

CALLA
WATER-ARUM
ARACEAE

The attractive white-spathed *Calla palustris* is a small (15–30 cm, 6–12 in.) temperate bog aroid with a creeping rhizome; it occurs around the northern temperate zone and is considered hardy but short-lived. Grow it in mesh containers set 7.5–22.5 cm (3–9 in.) below the water surface. Increase by seed or division.

CALLITRICHE
WATER-STARWORT
CALLITRICHACEAE

Widespread, mostly annual and perennial herbs with submerged leaves that are longer and thinner than emergent leaves (1–2 cm, 0.4–0.8 in.). Flowers are small, naked, and unisexual. *Callitriche hermaphroditica* (Z6–8) from northern temperate regions is used in aquaria but can dominate in ponds. Increase by stem cuttings.

CERATOPHYLLUM
HORNWORT
CERATOPHYLLACEAE

Widespread, almost rootless, long-stemmed (up to 1.8 m, 6 ft.) submerged aquatics. The older stem parts decay as new shoots grow, and the dichotomously divided leaves form in whorls. Plants are monoecious and flowers inconspicuous. *Ceratophyllum submersum* (Z8), native to Eurasia and North Africa, forms overwintering buds or turions. Increase from these or stem cuttings.

CERATOPTERIS
WATER-SPRITE
PARKERIACEAE

Tropical and subtropical floating ferns. Given a warm (20°C, 68°F) pool, *Ceratopteris thalictroides* from Southeast Asia can float on water, or grow on wet mud, producing fronds up to 1 m (3.3 ft.) in length, though it is usually smaller in cultivation (15–45 cm, 6–18 in.). Increase from plantlets on leaves.

CRYPTOCORYNE
WATER-TRUMPET
ARACEAE

Grown for their ovate to spear-shaped leaves, 5–20 cm (2–8 in.) in length, in colours ranging from brown and dark red to olive-green, these small perennials from tropical Asia are often grown as marginals in tropical pools (water minimum 18°C, 64°F) or heated aquaria. Leaves can be submerged or emergent, but their small-spathed inflorescences need to be above water for pollination. Division of their multi-stemmed rhizomatous clumps can easily increase species such as *Cryptocoryne beckettii*.

ECHINODORUS
ALISMATACEAE

Mostly emergent tender perennials (some with mainly submerged leaves), with conspicuous white flowers on tall scapes to 60 cm (2 ft.) and more, for warm-climate garden pools. Almost all the cultivated species come from the Americas. Mainly increased by division, occasionally seed. Z9.

EGERIA
ARGENTINEAN WATERWEED
HYDROCHARITACEAE

The attractive, densely foliaged stems of *Egeria densa* (Z9) from South America, up to 2 m (6.6 ft.) in length, have made it a popular aquatic for aquaria and ponds. It has naturalised around the world. Increase by stem cuttings.

EURYALE

NYMPHAEACEAE

Euryale ferox is the Southeast Asian counterpart of the South American giant waterlilies. Its leaves (0.6–1.5 m, 2–5 ft.) do not have an upturned rim but do have spines on their upper surface, and its flowers are violet. Grown as an annual in pools with a water temperature of 18–21°C (65–70°F). Seed raised, see *Victoria*.

HOTTONIA

WATER-VIOLET
PRIMULACEAE

Two species of perennial aquatics with attractive, mostly submerged, pinnatifid leaves. The Eurasian *Hottonia palustris* has lilac, primula-like flowers on aerial stems to 30 cm(12 in.); the eastern North American *H. inflata* is smaller, with greenish white flowers. Slightly tender, they can overwinter under water as turions. Increase by these, division, or seed. Z8/9.

HYDROCHARIS

FROGBIT
HYDROCHARITACEAE

A small floating perennial with suborbicular leaves (2 cm, 1 in., across) and attractive white, yellow-centred flowers, *Hydrocharis morsus-ranae* (Z7) is widespread though in decline in Europe, North Africa, and western Asia. It is dioecious and spreads mainly by stolons.

HYDROCLEYS

WATER-POPPY
LIMNOCHARITACEAE

A stoloniferous perennial with small (5 cm, 2 in., across) waterlily-like leaves and three-petalled, yellow flowers, *Hydrocleys nymphoides* from Central and tropical South America is often grown in heated (winter minimum 10°C, 50°F) pools. Increase from rhizome sections with leaves.

LIMNOBIUM

HYDROCHARITACEAE

The floating New World limnobiums are similar and related to *Hydrocharis* (frogbit) and also spread by runners. The tropical and subtropical *Limnobium spongia* (American spongeplant; Z10) is sometimes grown in aquaria and pools. Mostly increased from runners.

LIMNOCHARIS

LIMNOCHARITACEAE

Limnocharis flava from tropical South America has umbels of attractive yellow flowers and long-stalked (60 cm, 24 in.) leaves. It is a valued tender emergent perennial for warm (18°C, 64°F) pool margins. Mainly increased by division.

MARSILEA

WATER-CLOVER

MARSILEACEAE

These curious small amphibious ferns, with leaves superficially similar to four-leaved clovers, grow in shallow water. Most marsileas are tender (Z10), but the warm temperate Eurasian *Marsilea quadrifolia* (Z6) has naturalised in North America (and is potentially invasive in New England). The pH of both water and compost should be on the acid side of neutral. Increase from spores or division of the creeping rhizome.

MENYANTHES

BOG BEAN

MENYANTHACEAE

Menyanthes trifoliata (Z3) is a widespread, northern temperate, bog and shallow-water herbaceous perennial. It is an attractive plant for poolsides with its long-stalked, broadbean-like leaves and racemes of white-fringed flowers held on 50 cm (20 in.) stems. The thick rhizomatous stems often break off naturally and float away to reestablish elsewhere.

NELUMBO

SACRED LOTUS

NELUMBONACEAE

Wonderfully exotic, the pink-flowered sacred lotus *Nelumbo nucifera*, which is widely distributed in Asia down to Australia, has a yellow-flowered counterpart, *N. lutea* from eastern North America to Central America and northern South America. Though tender, their rhizomes can survive mild winters under water, buried in mud. In temperate regions, sacred lotuses are best grown in a soil bed in shallow

Menyanthes trifoliata, lining the edge of a lake at Castle Howard

water at 18°C (64°F) in summer and kept frost-free in damp mud in winter. Smaller cultivars such as *N.* 'Momo Botan' can be grown in half barrels kept in a warm sunny spot in summer and moved to over-winter in a frost-free environment. They resent root disturbance; for vegetative increase, the long rhizomes are grown over and then pegged to a prepared pan of compost and not separated until well-established roots form in the pan. Leaf stalks can reach 2 m (6.6 ft.), and water runs off the beautiful glaucous parasol leaves like mercury. The pea-sized and long-lived edible seeds form in an inverted-cone-shaped pod. Scarify the hard-coated seeds before sowing.

NEPTUNIA

LEGUMINOSAE

Tender, tropical bog and aquatic subshrubs for pools at or above 18°C (64°F). The Central American *Neptunia plena* forms long floating stems (to 1.5 m, 5 ft., or more) with sensitive mimosa-like and -sized leaflets and flowers. Floating stems with roots are used as cuttings.

NUPHAR

SPATTERDOCK
NYMPHAEACEAE

Also known as yellow waterlilies, from the colour of *Nuphar lutea*'s petaloid sepals, the vigorous, rhizomatous perennial nuphars come from the northern hemisphere. Their submerged leaves are flimsy, but their floating leaves are waterlily-like. Increase by division of their large rhizomes, which are 10 cm (4 in.) by 2 m (6.6 ft.) wide and long. Z4/5.

NYMPHAEA

WATERLILY
NYMPHAEACEAE

Tropical waterlilies hold their exotic blossoms on short stems above the water's surface; most temperate species hold their flowers closer to the surface. Hybrids of both groups are plentiful. High numbers of wildfowl can prevent the establishment of waterlilies, but once established, plants grow large. To keep a good floral display (as opposed to masses of leaves), grow plants in containers that can be removed when required from the water. Small formal pools with waterlilies are usually cleared in early winter, and waterlilies in containers may be divided and repotted at the same time; a loam

and sand mix is preferred to organic composts since the latter produce marsh gas when they decay. Also, keeping smaller individual clumps allows more flowering crowns in a given area. A single plant can soon overfill a 2 m (6.6 ft.) pool, but many smaller forms have been raised for home gardens. Increase by division of rhizome, or young shoots from the corm-like rhizome of tropicals, or seed. The tropicals are grown with a water temperature around 21°C (70°F), but can rest over winter in cooler water or be stored in damp sand in a warm greenhouse. Many of the colourful hardier hybrids need Zone 8 to grow well, but some northern species and their hybrids are hardy down to Zone 4.

NYMPHOIDES

FRINGED WATERLILY
MENYANTHACEAE

Nymphoides has a cosmopolitan distribution. Plants have small waterlily-like leaves and attractive yellow- or white-fringed flowers. Some are tropical, but there are hardier species—such as the Eurasian *N. peltata* (Z8), with leaves 5–10 cm (2–4 in.) in diameter—that can spread extensively in ponds. Increase by taking rosettes with rhizomes.

TOP *Nymphaea* 'James Brydon', raised in 1899 by Dreer's Nurseries, Riverton, New Jersey
ABOVE *Nymphaea* 'Moorei', raised in 1900 by Adelaide Botanic Garden

ORONTIUM
GOLDEN CLUB
ARACEAE

Orontium aquaticum (Z7) is a small deciduous bog or shallow-water perennial from eastern North America with soft, 15–45 cm (6–18 in.) leaves and an unusual inflorescence: the golden club, formed from a spathe-less, 7.5 cm (3 in.) spadix with golden flowers at its tip, contrasting with its clear white stalk. Difficult to transplant, it is often grown in baskets. Increase by division.

PONTEDERIA
PICKERELWEED
PONTEDERIACEAE

A small New World genus often grown in the tropics. *Pontederia cordata* (Z8) is a useful perennial for pool margins with its crisp lance-shaped leaves and spikes of azure flowers; it can just about survive mild winters if the rootstock is at least 10–12.5 cm (4–5 in.) below the water surface. Increase by division.

SAGITTARIA
ARROWHEAD
ALISMATACEAE

With their attractive white-flowered scapes and crisp, often arrow-shaped leaves, members of this easily grown small genus of temperate and tropical perennials find a place as shallow-water marginals, to 50–100 cm (20–40 in.), in many pools. Of the hardy species, three from North America have naturalised in Britain, and *Sagittaria sagittifolia* (Z7/8) from Eurasia is widely cultivated. All overwinter as tubers, which can be used to increase stock. Offsets can be taken in the growing season.

SALVINIA
SALVINIACEAE

Floating ferns from the tropics and subtropics with a thin stem and pairs of buoyant rounded leaves; a third submerged leaf with each pair is much divided and acts as the plant's roots. In *Salvinia auriculata* (Z10) from South America, each floating leaf is about 4 cm (1.6 in.). Salvinias are heterosporous and form sporocarps. Increase from pieces of stem with leaves.

TOP *Pontederia cordata*
ABOVE *Sagittaria sagittifolia*

UTRICULARIA
BLADDERWORT

LENTIBULARIACEAE

This genus of epiphytes and terrestrial species, as well as aquatics, occurs widely in tropical and temperate regions. The yellow-flowered *Utricularia gibba*, which has an extensive warm temperate and subtropical distribution, is often grown in aquaria (minimum water temperature 7°C, 45°F) for its dense but attractive foliage. It is protected in several U.S. states. It and all utricularias trap tiny creatures in their small hollow bladders.

Aquatic species need clear (preferably filtered) water to limit the buildup of algae on their fine foliage. They are sensitive to algaecides, so some growers add peat to the water (which acidifies the water and is suitable for some, but not all) to limit algal growth. Utricularias are rootless but sometimes form simple rhizoids; they can hold fast on stones, and others may run through the mud at the bottom of ponds. Many temperate aquatic utricularias are propagated from overwintering buds (turions) that drop to the bottom of the pool in autumn. Clumps can be divided.

VALLISNERIA

TAPE GRASS

HYDROCHARITACEAE

The long (to 2 m, 6.6 ft.) ribbon-like leaves of the tender *Vallisneria spiralis* will be well known to holders of aquaria and others who grow it in frost-free pools for its foliage. Its flowers are small and reduced, the male flowers breaking off and floating to the female flowers to effect pollination. This Old World species has a New World counterpart, *V. americana*. Increase by division.

VICTORIA

GIANT WATERLILY

NYMPHAEACEAE

Fun to grow if you have a large tropical or heated pool, giant waterlilies are gross feeders, and a full-sized plant needs a bed with up to three tons of loamy compost to see it through its growing season. The organic content of the compost should be limited because marsh gas from its decay is trapped under its leaves, causing necrosis.

The largest of the two species, *Victoria amazonica* from Brazil, has in nature from flat to slightly upturned leaf margins. *Victoria*

Victoria amazonica growing in a seasonally flooded meadow (*várzea*) along the Amazon above Manaus

cruziana from northern Argentina has smaller leaves with deeply upturned margins; it can be grown in slightly cooler water.

Seed of these short-lived perennials is stored in water at 16°C (60°F) and is sown in mid January at 29°C (85°F) for planting in its growing bed in May. Once plants are established, the water temperature may be lowered to 24°C (75°F); by late summer, a single seedling of the vigorous hybrid between the two species, *Victoria* 'Longwood Hybrid', is capable of covering a pool with leaves 2 m (6.6 ft.) in diameter.

BIBLIOGRAPHY

Bean, W. J. 1988. *Trees and Shrubs Hardy in the British Isles*, 8th ed., 4 vols. and suppl. John Murray, London.

Blackwell, L. R. 1999. *Wildflowers of the Sierra Nevada and the Central Valley*. Lone Pine Publishing, Auburn, Wash.

Brown, G. E. 2004. *The Pruning of Trees, Shrubs and Conifers*, 2d ed., revised and enlarged by T. Kirkham. Timber Press, Portland, Ore.

Brummitt, R. K. 1992. *Vascular Plant Families and Genera*. Royal Botanic Gardens, Kew.

Chadde, S. W. 2002. *A Great Lakes Wetland Flora*, 2d ed. PocketFlora Press, Laurium, Mich.

Cullen, J., ed. 2001. *Handbook of North European Garden Plants*. Cambridge University Press.

Farjon, A. 2001. *World Checklist and Bibliography of Conifers*, 2d ed. Royal Botanic Gardens, Kew.

Foote, L. E., and S. B. Jones, Jr. 1989. *Native Shrubs and Woody Vines of the Southeast*. Timber Press, Portland, Ore.

Hansen, R., and F. Stahl. 1993. *Perennials and Their Garden Habitats*. Cambridge University Press.

Huxley, A., ed. 1992. *The New RHS Dictionary of Gardening*, 4 vols. Macmillan, London.

Irish, M., and G. Irish. 2000. *Agaves, Yuccas, and Related Plants*. Timber Press, Portland, Ore.

Jones, D. L. 1987. *Encyclopaedia of Ferns*. Timber Press, Portland, Ore.

Kruckeberg, A. R. 1996. *Gardening with Native Plants of the Pacific Northwest*, 2d ed. University of Washington Press, Seattle.

Krüssmann, G. 1984–86. *Manual of Cultivated Broadleaved Trees and Shrubs*, 3 vols. Batsford, London; Timber Press, Portland, Ore.

Lord, A., ed. 2006–07, *RHS Plant Finder*. Dorling Kindersley, London.

Mühlberg, H. 1982. *The Complete Guide to Water Plants*. E. P. Publishing, New York and London.

Phillips, R., and M. Rix. 2002. *The Botanical Garden*, 2 vols. Macmillan, London.

Pojar, J., and A. MacKinnon. 1994. *Plants of Coastal British Columbia*. Lone Pine Publishing, Auburn, Wash.

Polunin, O., and A. Stainton. 1984. *Flowers of the Himalaya*. Oxford University Press.

Preston, C. D., and J. M. Croft. 1997. *Aquatic Plants in Britain and Ireland*. Harley Books, Colchester, U.K.

Rice, G., ed. 2006. *RHS Encyclopedia of Perennials*. Dorling Kindersley, London.

Rickard, M. 2000. *Garden Ferns*. David and Charles, Newton Abbot, U.K.

Salmon, J. T. 1996. *The Native Trees of New Zealand*, 2d ed. Reed Books, Auckland.

Stace, C. 1997. *New Flora of the British Isles*, 2d ed. Cambridge University Press.

Stewart, J. 1992. *Orchids at Kew*. Her Majesty's Stationery Office, London.

Stewart, L. 1994. *A Guide to Palms and Cycads of the World*. Cassell, London.

Trelawny, J. G. 2003. *Wild Flowers of the Yukon, Alaska, and Northwestern Canada*, 2d ed. Harbour Publishing, Madeira Park, B.C.

Willis, J. C. 1980. *A Dictionary of the Flowering Plants and Ferns*, 8th ed. Cambridge University Press.

Wrigley, J. W., and M. Fagg. 2003. *Australian Native Plants*, 5th ed. Reed Books, Australia.

USDA HARDINESS ZONE MAP

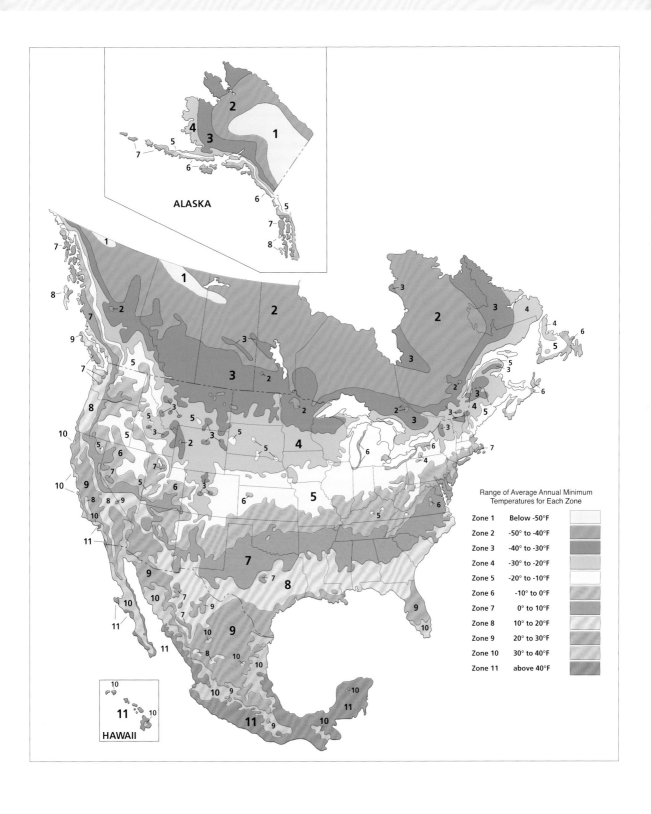

ALASKA

HAWAII

Range of Average Annual Minimum
Temperatures for Each Zone

Zone 1	Below -50°F
Zone 2	-50° to -40°F
Zone 3	-40° to -30°F
Zone 4	-30° to -20°F
Zone 5	-20° to -10°F
Zone 6	-10° to 0°F
Zone 7	0° to 10°F
Zone 8	10° to 20°F
Zone 9	20° to 30°F
Zone 10	30° to 40°F
Zone 11	above 40°F

PLANT INDEX

sylvestris 'Vicar's Mead', 176
Angiopteris evecta, 75
anise tree. See *Illicium*
Anthemis punctata subsp. *cupaniana*, 43, 60
Anthriscus cerefolium, 177
    sylvestris, 54, 61, 177
    sylvestris 'Ravenswing', 177
Anubias afzelii, 281
Apiaceae. See Umbelliferae
Apium graveolens, 177
Aponogeton distachyos, 281
Aponogetonaceae, 281
apple of Peru. See *Nicandra physalodes*
apricot. See *Prunus armeniaca*, *P. mume*
Aquifoliaceae, 123
Aquilegia vulgaris, 178
Araceae, 178, 179, 194, 200, 238, 250, 266, 270, 279, 281, 282, 283, 288
Araliaceae, 94, 159
Araucaria araucana, 81, 82
Araucariaceae, 82
Arecaceae. See Palmae
Argentinean waterweed. See *Egeria densa*
Arisaema dracontium, 178
    griffithii, 178
    sikokianum var. serratum, 178
    triphyllum, 178
Arisarum proboscideum, 179
Aristolochiaceae, 180
Aronia arbutifolia, 95
    melanocarpa, 41, 95
    ×prunifolia, 95
Arnica, 195
arrow arum. See *Peltandra*
arrowhead. See *Sagittaria*
Artemisia lactiflora Guizhou Group, 179
Arum italicum 'Marmoratum', 180
    maculatum, 179
arum lily. See *Zantedeschia*
Arundinaria, 90
asarabaca. See *Asarum europaeum*
Asarum europaeum, 180
Asclepiadaceae, 180
Asclepias incarnata 'Alba', 181
    lanceolata, 181

purpurascens, 180
speciosa, 180
ash tree. See *Fraxinus*
Asphodelaceae, 230
Asplenium scolopendrium, 71, 72
Astelia chathamica, 181
    grandis, 181
Asteliaceae, 181
Aster ericoides, 47, 182
    novi-belgii, 181
    puniceus, 181
    trinervius, 182
Asteraceae. See Compositae
Astilbe 'Bronce Elegans', 182
    grandis, 182
    thunbergii, 182
Astilboides tabularis, 182
Athrotaxis, 86
Athyrium filix-femina, 78
    'Ghost', 78
    niponicum var. pictum, 78
Austrocedrus chilensis, 82
autumn crocus. See *Colchicum*
avens. See *Geum*
avocado. See *Persea americana*
Azolla filiculoides, 63

Baeckea, 136
balsam. See *Impatiens*
balsam poplar. See *Populus balsamifera*
Balsaminaceae, 226
bamboo, 95
Baptisia alba var. *macrophylla*, 210
bayberry. See *Myrica pensylvanica*
bayberry, Californian. See *Myrica californica*
bear garlic. See *Allium ursinum*
Beckmannia syzigachne, 215
beech. See *Fagus*
beech fern. See *Phegopteris connectilis*
beggar ticks. See *Bidens*
Bellis perennis, 195
Berberidaceae, 96–97, 133, 253, 275
Berberis canadensis, 97
    darwinii, 97
    julianae, 97
    ×stenophylla, 97
    thunbergii, 96
    wilsoniae, 96

berry fruit. See *Rubus*
Betula alleghaniensis, 16, 98
    ermanii, 98
    insignis, 98
    medwedewii, 98
    nigra, 98
    nigra 'Heritage', 98
    occidentalis, 98
    pendula, 16, 98
    utilis var. jacquemontii, 98
Betulaceae, 92, 98
Bidens aurea, 183
    cernua var. radiata, 183
    ferulifolia, 183
bilberry. See *Vaccinium*
bindweed. See *Calystegia*
birch. See *Betula*
bird of paradise. See *Strelitzia*
bistort, common. See *Persicaria bistorta*
Bistorta. See *Persicaria*
bittercress, 60, 186
black currant. See *Ribes nigrum*
blackthorn. See *Prunus spinosa*
bladder nut. See *Staphylea*
bladderwort. See *Utricularia*
Blechnaceae, 72
Blechnum chilense, 37, 48, 72–73
    minus, 72
    penna-marina, 48, 72
    spicant, 72
    wattsii, 72
bleeding heart. See *Dicentra*
bloodroot. See *Sanguinaria*
blue cohosh. See *Caulophyllum thalictroides*
blue flag, northern. See *Iris versicolor*
blue flag, southern . See *Iris virginica*
blue sow-thistle. See *Cicerbita*
bluebell. See *Hyacinthoides non-scripta*
bluebells. See *Mertensia*
blueberry, highbush. See *Vaccinium corymbosum*
bog-laurel. See *Kalmia polifolia*
bog-myrtle. See *Myrica*
bog-rosemary. See *Andromeda*
bog sunflower. See *Helianthus heterophyllus*

bogbean. See *Menyanthes trifoliata*
Boltonia, 195
Boraginaceae, 183–184, 190, 203, 241, 243, 245, 250, 256, 270, 272
Boston ivy. See *Parthenocissus tricuspidata*
bottlebrush. See *Callistemon*
Bowles' golden grass. See *Milium effusum* 'Aureum'
box; boxwood. See *Buxus*
Boykinia, 264
brake fern family. See Pteridaceae
bramble. See *Rubus*
Brassicaceae. See Cruciferae
Brewer's spruce. See *Picea breweriana*
Bromus ramosus, 215
brooklime. See *Veronica beccabunga*
Brunnera macrophylla, 14, 184
buckeye, Georgia. See *Aesculus sylvatica*
buckeye, Ohio. See *Aesculus glabra* var. *arguta*
buckeye, red. See *Aesculus pavia*
buckeye, sweet. See *Aesculus flava*
buckler-fern. See *Dryopteris*
buckthorn. See *Rhamnus*
buffalo currant. See *Ribes odoratum*
bugbane. See *Actaea*
bugle. See *Ajuga reptans*
bugloss. See *Echium*
bunchflower. See Melanthiaceae
bur-marigold. See *Bidens*
burnet. See *Sanguisorba*
Butomaceae, 282
Butomus umbellatus, 282
butterbur. See *Petasites*
button bush. See *Cephalanthus occidentalis*
Buxaceae, 99, 158
Buxus balearica, 99
hyrcana, 99
microphylla, 99
sempervirens, 19, 99

cabbage palm. See *Cordyline australis*
Cabomba caroliniana, 282
Cabombaceae, 282
Caesalpinioideae. See Leguminosae

Calamagrostis ×*acutiflora*, 184
arundinacea, 184
epigejos, 184
Calla palustris, 282
Callistemon acuminatus, 100
citrinus, 100
pallidus, 100
pinifolius, 100
rigidus, 100
salignus, 100
subulatus, 99–100
viminalis, 100
viridiflorus, 100
Callitrichaceae, 282
Callitriche autumnalis. See *C. hermaphroditica*
hermaphroditica, 282
Calluna vulgaris, 113
Calocedrus, 82
Caltha leptosepala, 185
natans, 185
palustris, 14, 184
palustris var. *alba*, 184
palustris 'Flore Pleno', 184
polypetala, 185
Calystegia sepium, 61
camas. See *Camassia*
Camassia cusickii, 56, 185
leichtlinii subsp. *suksdorfii* Caerulea Group, 56, 185
quamash, 185
Camellia granthamiana, 100
japonica 'Mrs. D. W. Davis', 100
oleifera, 100
pitardii, 100
reticulata, 100
sasanqua, 100
sinensis, 100
×*williamsii*, 46, 100
Campanulaceae, 236, 278
campion. See *Silene*
canary-grass. See *Phalaris*
Canna flaccida, 185
glauca, 185
indica, 185
'Phasion', 186
Cannaceae, 185–186
caper spurge. See *Euphorbia lathyris*
Caprifoliaceae, 129, 130, 157, 167
Cardamine enneaphylla, 187
pentaphylla, 187

pratensis, 14, 186
pratensis 'Flore Pleno', 187
trifolia, 186
Cardiocrinum cathayanum, 188
cordatum, 188
giganteum, 187
giganteum var. *yunnanense*, 187
Carex buchananii, 189
comans 'Frosted Curls', 49, 189
conica 'Snowline', 189
elata 'Aurea', 189
morrowii 'Variegata', 189
pendula, 189
riparia 'Variegata', 189
Carpinus betulus, 101
Carya aquatica, 102
cordiformis, 102
ovata, 102
Caryophyllaceae, 238, 265
Castanea sativa, 16
catchfly. See *Lychnis*
catkin yew. See *Amentotaxus*
cattail. See *Typha*
Caucasian alder. See *Alnus subcordata*
Caucasian pennycress. See *Pachyphragma*
Caulophyllum thalictroides, 97
Cautleya spicata 'Robusta', 219
cedar. See *Cedrus*
Cedrus, 84
Cedrus deodara, 81
celandine, greater. See *Chelidonium*
celandine, lesser. See *Ranunculus ficaria*
Celastraceae, 114
Celtis laevigata, 167
occidentalis, 167
Centaurea montana, 190
nigra, 57, 190
Cephalanthus occidentalis, 102
Cephalotaxaceae, 82
Cephalotaxus, 82
Ceratophyllaceae, 282
Ceratophyllum submersum, 283
Ceratopteris thalictroides, 283
Cercidiphyllaceae, 102
Cercidiphyllum japonicum, 103
magnificum, 103
Cerinthe major 'Kiwi Blue', 190–191

Chaerophyllum hirsutum 'Roseum', 191

chain fern. See *Woodwardia*

Chamaecyparis lawsoniana, 18, 83

Chelidonium majus, 191

Chelone obliqua, 192

cherry, bird. See *Prunus padus*

cherry, hill. See *Prunus jamasakura*

cherry, sweet. See *Prunus avium*

chervil. See *Anthriscus*, *Chaerophyllum*

Chilean guava. See *Ugni molinae*

Chilean lantern tree. See *Crinodendron*

Chinese fir. See *Cunninghamia*

Chinese ragwort. See *Sinacalia tangutica*

Chionochloa flavescens, 192

rubra, 192

Chionodoxa, 225

chives. See *Allium schoenoprasum*

chokeberry. See *Aronia*

chokecherry. See *Prunus virginiana*

Chrysalidocarpus lutescens, 140

Chrysanthemum parthenium. See *Tanacetum parthenium*

Chrysosplenium davidianum, 192

Chusquea culeou, 103–104

montana, 104

quila, 104

Cicerbita, 195

Cimicifuga. See *Actaea*

cinnamon fern. See *Osmunda cinnamomea*

cinquefoil. See *Potentilla*

Cirsium arvense, 61

Cladrastis kentukea, 42

lutea. See *C. kentukea*

cleavers. See *Galium aparine*, 60

Clematis armandii, 104

integrifolia, 104

montana, 104

Orientalis Group, 104

tangutica, 104

virginiana, 104

vitalba, 104

viticella, 104

Cleyera, 101

climbing fern family. See Schizaeaceae

cloudberry. See *Rubus chamaemorus*

clover. See *Trifolium*

cobra lily. See *Arisaema*

cocoyam. See *Colocasia*

Colchicaceae, 193

Colchicum autumnale 'Nancy Lindsay', 193

speciosum, 193

tenorei, 193

Colocasia esculenta 'Fontanesii', 194

columbine. See *Aquilegia*

comfrey. See *Symphytum*

common fleabane. See *Pulicaria dysenterica*

Compositae, 138, 139, 171, 179, 181, 183, 190, 194–196, 205, 207, 219, 228, 233, 235, 256, 261, 265, 266, 268, 271

coneflower. See *Rudbeckia*

Convallaria majalis, 48

majalis 'Fortin's Giant', 196

Convallariaceae, 196, 201–202

copper iris. See *Iris fulva*

coral-bells. See *Heuchera*

coralberry. See *Symphoricarpos orbiculatus*

Cordyline australis, 104–105

australis 'Albertii', 105

australis 'Torbay Dazzler', 37, 105

banksii, 105

indivisa, 104

Cornaceae, 105, 109, 137

Cornus alba, 19, 106

alba 'Elegantissima', 106

canadensis, 105, 106

controversa, 105

florida, 105

kousa 'Heart Throb', 106

mas, 105

nuttallii, 105

obliqua, 105

officinalis, 106

sanguinea, 17, 19, 105

stolonifera, 105

suecica, 105

Cortaderia, 57

richardii, 197

selloana 'Pumila', 196–197

Corylaceae, 101, 106, 138

Corylopsis, 119

Corylus avellana, 106

colurna, 107

ferox, 107

heterophylla, 107

maxima 'Purpurea', 106

tibetica, 107

Cotoneaster frigidus 'Cornubia', 108

horizontalis, 107

integrifolius, 107

cotton-grass. See *Eriophorum*

cottonwood. See *Populus deltoides*

cow parsley. See *Anthriscus sylvestris*

cowslip. See *Primula veris*

coyote willow. See *Salix exigua*

crabapple. See *Malus*

cranberry. See *Vaccinium macrocarpon*

cranesbill. See *Geranium*

Crassula helmsii, 63, 64

Crataegus douglasii, 109

laevigata, 108

monogyna, 108

orientalis, 109

persimilis 'Prunifolia', 109

tanacetifolia, 109

creeping buttercup. See *Ranunculus repens*

creeping-Jenny. See *Lysimachia nummularia*

creeping softgrass. See *Holcus mollis*

creeping thistle. See *Cirsium arvense*

crimson waterfall gladiolus. See *Gladiolus carinatus*

Crinodendron hookerianum, 109

patagua, 109

Crinum americanum, 197

bulbispermum, 197

moorei, 197

×*powellii*, 20, 197

×*powellii* 'Album', 197

Crocosmia ×*crocosmiiflora* 'George Davison', 198

×*crocosmiiflora* 'Solfatare', 198

Jenny Bloom (= 'Blacro'), 198

'Lucifer', 57, 198

masoniorum, 198

pottsii, 198

cross-leaved heath. See *Erica tetralix*

Cruciferae, 186, 247, 260

Cryptocoryne beckettii, 283

Cryptomeria japonica, 80, 86

Woodwardia areolata, 72
    fimbriata, 73
    radicans, 73
    unigemmata, 72
    virginica, 72
wormwood. See *Artemisia*
woundwort, hedge. See *Stachys
    sylvatica*
woundwort, marsh. See *Stachys
    palustris*

Xanthorhiza simplicissima, 169
Xanthosoma violaceum, 279

yellow archangel. See *Lamium
    galeobdolon*
yellow flag. See *Iris pseudacorus*
yellow rattle. See *Rhinanthus minor*
yellow waterlily. See *Nuphar lutea*
yellow wood. See *Cladrastis ken-
    tukea*
yellowcress. See *Rorippa*
yellowhead. See *Inula*
yellowroot. See *Xanthorhiza*
yew. See *Taxus*
Yorkshire-fog. See *Holcus lanatus*

Yucca flaccida, 170
    recurvifolia, 170

Zantedeschia aethiopica, 279
    elliottiana, 279
    rehmannii, 279
Zenobia pulverulenta, 170
zephyr lily. See *Zephyranthes*
Zephyranthes candida, 280
Zingiber, 219
Zingiberaceae, 218–219
Zizania aquatica, 216